Russian Regions and Regionalism

The emergence of large regions within Russia as centres of gravity for political and international power, and the changing relationship between these emerging regions and the centre are critically important factors currently at work within Russia. This book examines the whole question of Russian regions and regionalism, including demography, security, military themes and international relations, and looks at a wide range of particular regions and case studies. It discusses the extent to which regions have succeeded in establishing themselves as centres of power, and assesses the degree to which President Putin is succeeding in incorporating regions into a hierarchy of power in which the primacy of the centre is retained.

Graeme P. Herd is Professor of Civil–military Relations at the George C. Marshall Center for Security Studies, Garmisch-Partenkirchen, Germany. He was formerly Lecturer in International Relations and Deputy Director of the Scottish Centre for International Security (SCIS), University of Aberdeen. He has published extensively on post-Soviet security politics, and is a Research Associate of the Conflict Studies Research Centre.

Anne Aldis is Research Manager at the Conflict Studies Research Centre, where she has been an active analyst and facilitator of the processes of transformation taking place in the states of central and eastern Europe. For many years she has edited the Centre's publications, including *The Second Chechen War*.

Russian Regions and Regionalism

Strength through weakness

**Edited by Graeme P. Herd
and Anne Aldis**

RoutledgeCurzon
Taylor & Francis Group

LONDON AND NEW YORK

First published 2003
by RoutledgeCurzon
11 New Fetter Lane, London EC4P 4EE

Simultaneously published in the USA and Canada
by RoutledgeCurzon
29 West 35th Street, New York, NY 10001

RoutledgeCurzon is an imprint of the Taylor & Francis Group

Typeset in Times by Taylor & Francis Books Ltd
Printed and bound in Great Britain by Antony Rowe, Chippenham,
Wiltshire

British Library Cataloguing in Publication Data
A catalogue record for this book is available from the British Library

Library of Congress Cataloging in Publication Data
Russian regions and regionalism: strength through weakness/edited by
Graeme P. Herd and Anne Aldis.
Includes bibliographical references and index.
1. Central–local government relations–Russia (Federation)
2. Regionalism–Russia (Federation) 3. Russia (Federation)–Politics
and government–1991– I. Herd, Graeme P. II. Aldis, Anne.

JN6693.5.S8 R88   2002
320.8'0947'090511–dc21   2002028450

ISBN 0–7007–1735–8

Contents

Illustrations

Figures

Tables

Contributors

Anne Aldis is Research Manager at the Conflict Studies Research Centre, where she has been an active analyst and facilitator of the processes of transformation taking place in the states of central and eastern Europe. For many years she has edited the centre's publications, as well as the Strategic and Combat Studies Institute's *The Second Chechen War* (2000) and *Central and Eastern Europe: Problems and Prospects* (1998).

Oleg Alexandrov is a Doctoral Candidate and Lecturer in International Relations at Moscow State Institute of International Relations. His main interest is the role of regions in Russian foreign and security policy. His major publications include *The City of Moscow in Russia's Foreign and Security Policy: Role, Aims and Motivations* (ETH Centre for Security Studies and Conflict Research, 2001) and *On the Way to the Global World: Administrative and Networking Strategies of Russia's Regions* (co-author with Andrey Makarychev, ETH Centre for Security Studies and Conflict Research, 2001).

Dr Mikhail A. Alexseev is Assistant Professor of Political Science at the San Diego State University. He is the author of *Without Warning: Threat Assessment, Intelligence, and Global Struggle* (St Martin's Press and Macmillan, 1997) and the editor of *A Federation Imperiled: Center–Periphery Conflict in Post-Soviet Russia* (St Martin's Press and Macmillan, 1999).

Dr Derek L. Averre is a Research Fellow at the Centre for Russian and East European Studies, European Research Institute, University of Birmingham. His principal research interests are in Russian security and foreign policy issues, arms control and non-proliferation policy, on which he has published several articles and book chapters. He is co-editor of *New Security Challenges in Postcommunist Europe: Securing Europe's East* (Manchester University Press, 2002) and is currently writing a book on new security thinking in Russia.

Dr Pavel K. Baev is a Senior Researcher and the leader of the Foreign and Security Policies programme at the International Peace Research

Institute, Oslo (PRIO). In 1979–88 he worked in a research institute of the USSR Ministry of Defence, and in 1995–2001 he was the editor of *Security Dialogue*. Baev is currently researching Russian military reform, Russia's conflict management in the Caucasus and Central Asia, Russia's relations with NATO and the role of the energy complex in Russia's European policy. His recent publications include 'The Russian Armed Forces: Failed Reform Attempts and Creeping Regionalisation', *Journal of Communist Studies and Transition Politics* 17(1), 2001: 23–43; 'Russia's Policies in the Southern Caucasus and the Caspian Area', *European Security* 10(2), 2001: 95–110 and 'The Russian Army and Chechnya: Victory Instead of Reform?', in Stephen J. Cimbala (ed.), *The Russian Military into the Twenty-First Century* (Frank Cass, 2001).

Professor Michael Bradshaw is Professor of Human Geography at the University of Leicester. He is also an Honorary Senior Research Fellow in the Centre for Russian and East European Studies at Birmingham, and an Associate Fellow of the Russia and Eurasia Programme at the Royal Institute of International Affairs in London. Publications include: *Russia's Regions: A Business Analysis* (Economist Intelligence Unit, 1995)*, Regional Economic Change in Russia* (co-author with Philip Hanson, Edgar Elgar, 2000) and *The Russian Far East and Pacific Asia: Unfulfilled Potential* (editor, Curzon Press, 2001).

Professor Graeme P. Herd is Professor of Civil–military Relations at the George C. Marshall Centre for Security Studies, Garmisch-Partenkirchen, Germany. Whilst Lecturer in International Relations and Deputy Director of the Scottish Centre for International Security (SCIS), University of Aberdeen he helped co-ordinate two large EU PHARE/TACIS international projects on democratic security building in the Baltic and Black Sea regions. He has published extensively on post-Soviet security politics, and is a Research Associate of the Conflict Studies Research Centre.

Dr Steven J. Main currently works as a Senior Lecturer at the Conflict Studies Research Centre. His main research and publication areas are Russo-Baltic and Russo-Belarussian relations; Russian military reform and Moscow's relationship with the regions. He has also published a number of articles on various aspects of the history of the Red Army in the inter-war period (1918–41).

Dr Andrey S. Makarychev teaches comparative politics and international relations at Nizhniy Novgorod Linguistic University. In 1999–2001 he was a fellow at the Centre for Security and Conflict Research in Zurich. He is also Deputy Director of the Centre for Socio-Economic Expertise. His major international projects include 'Political and Administrative Aspects of Corruption in the Volga Federal District', 'Russian Regions as International Actors', 'Hard and Soft Security Challenges in the Volga Federal District'.

Martin Nicholson is an Associate Fellow of the Russia and Eurasia Programme at the Royal Institute of International Affairs. He retired from the British Diplomatic Service in 1997 after several postings in Moscow and a period as Adviser on Soviet and Russian affairs at the Cabinet Office, London. He is the author of *Towards a Russia of the Regions* (International Institute for Strategic Studies, Adelphi Paper 330, 1999) and has contributed to the journals of the Royal Institute of International Affairs, *The World Today* and *International Affairs*.

Dr Christer Pursiainen is Senior Researcher at Nordregio, Nordic Centre for Spatial Development, Stockholm. He has worked as Director of the Aleksanteri Institute – the Finnish Centre for Russian and East European Studies at the University of Helsinki – and as Senior Researcher at the Finnish Institute of International Affairs. His publications include *Russian Foreign Policy and International Relations Theory* (Ashgate, 2000).

Dr Alexander Sergounin is Head of the Department of International Relations and Political Science at Nizhniy Novgorod Linguistic University in Russia. His research interests include international relations, history and theory, political science, international security and Russian foreign policy-making. He has published numerous articles and books, including *Political Science: A Textbook* (Volga Industrial-Pedagogical Institute Press, 2000), *Russian Arms Transfers to East Asia* (Oxford University Press, 1999) and *Contemporary Western Political Thought: A Post-Positivist Revolution* (Nizhniy Novgorod Linguistic University, 1999). His most recent book was co-authored with Lyndelle Fairlie, *Are Borders Barriers? EU Enlargement and the Russian Region of Kaliningrad* (Finnish Institute of International Affairs, 2001).

Dr Mark A. Smith is a Senior Lecturer at the Conflict Studies Research Centre, specialising in Russian internal politics and foreign policy. He previously directed the Russian Programme at the Royal United Services Institute for Defence Studies. He has studied at St Antony's College, Oxford, the School of Slavonic and East European Studies, University of London, and Reading University.

Dr Stanislav L. Tkachenko is an Associate Professor of the Department of European Studies at the School of International Relations, St Petersburg State University. He is also a Vice-Dean of the School, responsible for research, PhD programmes and publications. He is the author of two books and about thirty articles on Russian foreign security and economic policy, and on the monetary history of the twentieth century.

Preface

Most scholars have argued that the Russian Federation, having survived the turbulence of 1992–3, has slowly developed a durable and sustainable *modus operandi*. However, throughout the 1990s the constituent parts of the federation gradually secured constitutional and political legitimacy, even to the extent of regionalising some federal military structures. They entered into economic alliances with newly privatised companies, created independent communication and information networks, and, to a more limited extent, developed foreign economic policies. Although this drift towards growing regional autonomy was kept more or less in check by the centre's ability to contain the wilder excesses of regional governors, the 1998 'Autumn Meltdown' disrupted the balance between centripetal and centrifugal forces within the federation by dramatically weakening the centre's power. This opened the possibility that Russia would become either a very weak federation dominated by large regional blocs, or a confederation.

With the election of Vladimir Putin as president, these trends appear to have been reversed. Two key tenets are constant: the centre (or vertical axis) was to be strengthened through the creation of seven federal districts; regional powers were to be restricted. Governors were removed from the Federation Council, thus also removing their immunity from criminal prosecution and providing a federal sanction against too much independence. The raft of reforms which Putin has proposed since his inauguration and rammed through the Duma and Federation Council have highlighted key questions that have yet to receive definitive answers eight years after the adoption of a Federal Treaty. Would Russia 'backslide from democracy to totalitarianism'? Would the federal district representatives usurp powers and interfere in the activities of regional governors? Would the weakening of the regions necessarily make the centre stronger? Does such fundamental reform, particularly of the Federation Council, necessitate constitutional change?

Or will the reform process stagnate, falling prey to overlapping competing jurisdictions and so serve as a crude mechanism for checks and balances between competing institutions? Will the concentration of federal functions into seven centres lead to the emergence of de facto 'inter-regional capital cities', the inequitable distribution of federal resources, the division of regional leaders into first and second class? Will this in turn lead, ultimately, to the disintegration of the Russian Federation through the creation of powerful, economically and politically integrated inter-regional associations ('quasi-states' or 'quasi-republics'), and so result in the formation of a confederation? Or will, in fact, the change prove more rhetorical than real, Potemkin-like and cosmetic in nature, providing a cloak for Putin's efforts to broaden his personal power base and so secure his regime?

The Russian political landscape of the new century bears only a superficial resemblance to that of even ten years ago. The regional power bases that burgeoned during the presidency of Boris Yeltsin are being reined in, and President Putin's raft of structural reforms may impose uniformity, if not unanimity, on the mechanisms and institutions of government. This much is clear. But the diversity of the Russian Federation's constituent parts is nowadays more open to foreign observation and analysis than it has been for the last century.

It would be impossible in a single volume to do justice to this diversity of interpretation and change. Nor do we intend to try to be comprehensive. Instead, we have attempted here to gather together some perceptions of where in the international political landscape the predominantly Slav regions of Russia find themselves now that the whirlwind of their recent history has become a steady breeze. While the regions included in these surveys stretch from Sakhalin to Kaliningrad, the non-Slav constituent parts, particularly those in the North Caucasus, have a plethora of ethnic, economic and social problems over and above those highlighted here. Although the non-Slav entities undoubtedly deserve much greater attention than they currently receive both from Moscow and from abroad, this book has a different aim. We are seeking to identify whether there is a common experience in Russia's regions, whether it is possible to discern certain trends in their relationships with central government, with each other and with the world at large.

First-rate, first-hand analysis from Russia's regions has not been widely published in English, and offers a unique perspective on the processes underway in Russia today. Our book therefore includes both thematic chapters and case studies, several written by people who live and work in the regions we discuss. The regions in our studies range from rich to poor, from cosmopolitan to remote; each has its own particular problems. What unites them is less easily categorised: how their people and politics have adapted to life without an ideological straitjacket; their changing relationship with the federal government; the need to make their way in an increasingly globalised economy.

Our book tries to bridge the chasm between theory and experience in Russian regional politics, although events are fast moving. We offer our insights as landmarks for today by which to chart tomorrow's course.

Acknowledgements

It is only possible to research and produce studies such as these with the help and understanding of the institutions for which the contributors work. In many cases they supply not just salaries and research infrastructure, but also the network of contacts and the opportunities to meet and collaborate with others in what must necessarily be a dispersed discipline. In particular, our thanks are due to the Scottish Centre for International Security at Aberdeen University and to the Conflict Studies Research Centre at Sandhurst, England, which have brought the contributors to the current volume together. A great deal was also contributed by the Centre for Security Studies and Conflict Research, ETH Zurich. In particular, Jeronim Perovic and Andreas Wenger organised a conference on 'Regionalisation of Russian Foreign and Security Policy' in July 2001, which provided the opportunity to invite Martin Nicholson, Mikhail Alexseev and Oleg Alexandrov to contribute chapters to this book.

Figure 8.3, Sakhalin island, is reproduced by permission of the Pacific Russia Information Group.

Contributors also acknowledge support from (in alphabetical order):

- Appalachian State University
- Centre for Security Studies and Conflict Research, ETH Zurich
- Copenhagen Peace Research Institute
- International Research and Exchanges Board (IREX)
- International Institute for Strategic Studies
- John D. and Catherine T. MacArthur Foundation
- Kennan Institute for Advanced Russian Studies
- National Council for Eurasian and East European Research
- Norwegian Defence Ministry
- Royal Institute of International Affairs
- San Diego State University
- United Kingdom Ministry of Defence
- United States Institute of Peace and the Pacific Basin Research Center at the John F. Kennedy School of Government, Harvard University

The views contained in each chapter are those of the chapter's author. They do not represent the views of all contributors, not those of any government or government department.

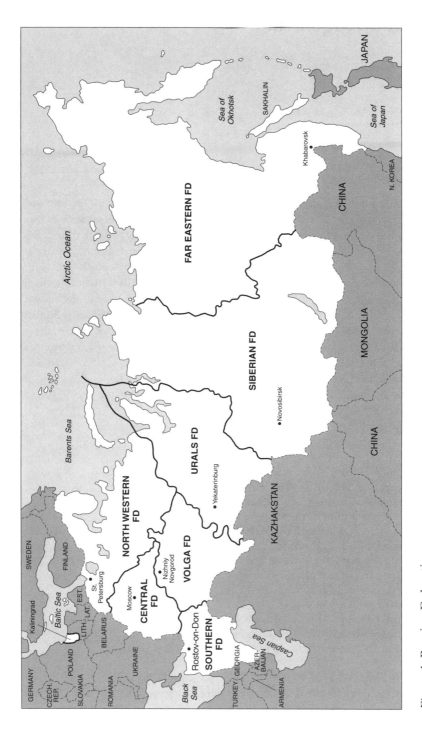

Figure 1 Russian Federation
Note: FD = Federal District

Part I

Introduction

1   Characterising centre–periphery relations in the Yeltsin era

Martin Nicholson

Introduction

Boris Yeltsin's term as the first president of independent Russia neatly encompassed the last decade of the twentieth century. Throughout this decade, Western eyes were fixed on two aspects of Russia's transformation from its Soviet past: the development of a multi-party system in place of the Communist Party's monopoly of power; and the creation of a market in place of the planned economy. In both cases, generally agreed criteria and models could be found in the developed world against which to measure Russia's progress. Less attention (other than by specialists) was paid to the attempt to create a federal system in Russia. There was anyway less certainty about what the aim should be – state systems, including federations, differ widely in the developed world. Only when conflict over the Federation went to extremes, in particular the separatist war in Chechnya, did the issue capture the headlines. Chechnya was a crucial issue in the Yeltsin era and remains so under the presidency of Vladimir Putin. But it was not the determining factor in centre–periphery relations. It is hard to pinpoint what was – centre–periphery relations evolved as one of the many conflicts and solutions that marked the emergence of the new Russia. For this reason, as good an approach as any to characterising centre–periphery relations in the Yeltsin era is to tell the story and pick up the common threads at the end.

The Soviet legacy

For centuries Moscow – imperial, Soviet and post-Soviet – has attempted to impose a top-down administration on a territory whose size and diversity constantly frustrate the effort. President Vladimir Putin made another attempt just a week after his inauguration in May 2000. It was undertaken because Putin and his advisers believed the Yeltsin leadership, or lack of it, had allowed the country to fragment dangerously. A basic problem was, and remains, that there was no received wisdom about where the balance of forces should lie in relations between the centre and the regions. That problem derived from the distorted federal structure of the Soviet Union, so it is with the Soviet Union that we must begin.

The Union of Soviet Socialist Republics (USSR) was an ideological construct, one of the few states in the world whose name gave no clue as to where it could be found on the map. This was deliberate: Vladimir Lenin and his Commissar for Nationalities, Iosif Stalin, wanted to build a state in which the liberated peoples of the former Russian Empire – Ukrainians, Georgians and others – voluntarily came together again in new, proletarian republics. Successive constitutions of the USSR provided for both the secession of the existing republics and the accession of new ones. In reality the secession clause was mere decoration. The Soviet leaders were convinced that the rule of the Communist Party, whose organisation was strictly centralised, would provide the cement to hold the republics together.

After seventy years, however, the cement proved faulty. The bankruptcy of the Communist Party's ideology allowed latent nationalism to rise to the surface in the republics. The structure of the USSR was undermined by the concessions its president, Mikhail Gorbachev, had to make in the first half of 1991 in order at least to hold on to the semblance of a Union. The coup mounted against him on 19 August 1991 was intended to claw back these concessions, but its failure fatally weakened the whole Soviet edifice and opened the way for the dominance of its largest constituent republic, the Russian Soviet Federative Socialist Republic (RSFSR). On 6 September 1991 the USSR was forced to recognise the independence of the three Baltic States. On 8 December three Union Republics, the RSFSR, Ukraine and Belarus, formally dissociated themselves from the USSR. On 25 December 1991 Gorbachev handed over his office in the Kremlin to Boris Yeltsin, who in May had been elected president of the RSFSR. On the same day the Supreme Soviet (parliament) of the RSFSR formally changed the republic's name to the Russian Federation (Russia), which became an independent state at the turn of the year.

The RSFSR was peculiar in that it was itself nominally a federation within the larger federation of the USSR. Like the nationality-based federal structure of the USSR, the structure of the RSFSR was intended as a showpiece of the Bolshevik nationality policy. Alongside ordinary, territorially based regions (*kray* and *oblast*), a number of the more significant national minorities, though far from all, were allocated their own territories as Autonomous Soviet Socialist Republics (ASSR) or Autonomous Regions (*avtonomnaya oblast*) and Districts (*avtonomnyy okrug*).

The Autonomous Republics of the RSFSR enjoyed a higher status than the more numerous territorially based regions – they had their own constitutions and state structures. But their status was lower than that of the Union Republics of the USSR. Whereas the Union Republics were deemed to have come together of their own volition (hence the secession clause in the USSR Constitution), the Autonomous Republics of the RSFSR were granted their status by central government. Their right to secede was never contemplated, still less written into any of the RSFSR constitutions.

As with the Union Republics, the creation of Autonomous Republics in the RSFSR initially played a part in promoting the culture and identities of national minorities.[1] But it was also inaccurate and divisive. For example, the Buryats were divided into three non-contiguous units, evidently to ensure that they were not strong enough to unite with their ethnic kin in neighbouring Mongolia. Bashkirs were outnumbered by Tatars in their own Bashkir republic, while in the North Caucasus ethnically distinct Turkic and Circassian peoples were deliberately lumped together in the Kabardino-Balkar Autonomous Republic and the Karachayevo-Cherkess Autonomous District.

Nor did the special status of the ethnic republics protect them from the depredations of the Stalin era. On the contrary, some of them were singled out for particularly harsh treatment. The Volga German Autonomous Republic (inhabited by Germans who had been in Russia since the eighteenth century) was abolished at the start of the war with Hitler's Germany, while towards the end of the war the Chechens and other North Caucasian peoples, whom Stalin suspected of collaboration under German occupation, were arbitrarily deported and their Autonomous Republics abolished. Nor did the Autonomous Republics in reality enjoy any special advantages over the territorially based regions in the RSFSR. The Communist Party acted as a levelling agent: it was represented at the same level of *obkom* (regional party committee) in the Autonomies as in ordinary regions. In the RSFSR, as in the USSR as a whole, the collapse of Communist Party rule laid bare an underlying legacy of bitterness among its variegated components. A desire to seize and exploit rights that had been enjoyed only on paper fed into the current of national reassertion that accompanied the last years of the Soviet Union and came to dominate centre–periphery relations in the early years of independent Russia under Yeltsin.[2]

The sequence of events that came to be known as the 'parade of sovereignties' began in 1990. One by one the Union Republics began unilaterally to upgrade their status with declarations of 'sovereignty'. This loosely applied term did not mean that they claimed to be states independent of the USSR, but they did assert ownership of the natural resources on their territories and maintained that their laws took primacy over the laws of the Soviet Union. The RSFSR declared its sovereignty on 12 June 1990. The declaration, which was supported for different reasons across the political spectrum, was intended to be – and was – a blow against the power and authority of the Soviet leader Mikhail Gorbachev. Boris Yeltsin, who had just been elected chairman of the RSFSR Supreme Soviet, was now able to use the whole of the huge republic as the platform for his barely concealed ambition – to displace the Soviet leader. Yeltsin's desire to exact revenge over Gorbachev for the humiliation of being thrown out of the Communist Party's Politburo in 1987 should not be underestimated.[3]

Yeltsin's scheme was to replace the vertical ties that bound the Union Republics to the Soviet centre with horizontal ties between the republics, bypassing the centre. His mantra was that power should flow from the bottom to the top, not the other way round. He encouraged the regions of the RSFSR, and particularly the Autonomous Republics, to follow suit. During a tour of Russia in August 1990, in the Tatar and Bashkir ASSRs, he made a statement that has since been much quoted: 'Take as much sovereignty as you can swallow'.[4] Taking him literally, a number of the ethnically based Autonomous Republics and even some of the smallest Autonomous Districts declared their own sovereignty, asserted the primacy of their laws over those of the RSFSR and renamed themselves simply 'republics'.

There was a real basis for the action of some of the Autonomies: the Tatar ASSR, for example, had long begrudged having lower status than the smaller Union Republics (e.g. Estonia), which it outclassed in size, population and industrial capacity. So when the Tatar ASSR declared its sovereignty (and renamed itself Tatarstan) in August 1990 it was acting not against the RSFSR, but against the institutions of Soviet rule.[5]

A worthy reason for Yeltsin to tolerate, even encourage, the rise of nationalism within the RSFSR was the influence of his advisers, including Galina Starovoytova, an expert on the struggle of the Armenian inhabitants of the Nagornyy Karabakh region of Azerbaijan. They counselled that attempts to suppress nationalism only added to its fervour. There can be little doubt, however, that uppermost in Yeltsin's mind was the advantage his 'bottom-up' approach gave him in the power struggle with Gorbachev. Subsequently, for much of his term in office as president of independent Russia, Yeltsin was trying to claw back the ground lost by this approach, and his successor is still doing so.

Gorbachev was also able to exploit Yeltsin's approach to his own advantage, if only temporarily. In July 1991 he embarked on a round of talks with leaders of the Union Republics at the Novo-Ogarevo government *dacha* outside Moscow in search of a new Union Treaty to replace the Treaty of 1922, under which the USSR had been formed. By this time the stronger Autonomous Republics, with Tatarstan in the lead, were claiming equal status with the Union Republics and a seat at the table. Gorbachev acquiesced, calculating that their presence would dilute Yeltsin's influence. The new Union Treaty was never signed: two days before the signature date a coup was mounted against Gorbachev in the name of preserving the Soviet Union as it had been. The coup, which failed, set in motion the process that ended in December with the collapse of the Soviet Union itself. But the aborted Union Treaty left a legacy that has bedevilled centre–periphery relations in independent Russia ever since.

The Autonomous Republics had been poised to sign the Union Treaty in two capacities: as components of the RSFSR, but also as components of the USSR, alongside and on the same level as the RSFSR. Thus Tatarstan and, to a lesser extent, Bashkortostan (as the Bashkir ASSR renamed itself) in their own view emerged from the wreckage of the Soviet Union as states with the same degree of independence as the former Union Republics. Accordingly, when Tatarstan later adopted its own constitution in November 1992, it maintained the position that the republic was merely associated with Russia.[6]

Creating the new Russian Federation

Thus when the Russian Federation became a genuinely sovereign state at the beginning of 1992 it was already fragmented. The former Autonomous Republics of the RSFSR were not prepared to give up the gains they had made in the negotiation of the aborted Union Treaty. Moreover, one of the former Autonomies, Chechnya, was already in open revolt. So one of Yeltsin's most pressing tasks was to obtain agreement on the basic principles that were to underlie centre–periphery relations in the new Russia. He managed this on 31 March 1992 by inducing all but two of Russia's republics and regions to sign a Treaty of Federation. This was in fact three treaties, one for each of the three types of administrative unit inherited from Soviet Russia:

- twenty nationality-based republics (increasing to twenty-one in June 1992, when Ingushetia, part of the Chechen-Ingush Autonomous Republic, became a republic in its own right);
- fifty-five territorially based regions (forty-nine *oblasts* and six larger *krays*) and two major cities (Moscow and St Petersburg) that were given the status of regions;
- ten autonomous districts (*okrugs*), homelands of a number of indigenous peoples, and one autonomous region, the Jewish Autonomous *oblast*.

The Federation Treaty was an essential holding operation: it bound the signatories to accept the existence of the new Russian state. The price of acceptance was the entrenchment in the first constitutional documents adopted by the new Russian Federation of the Soviet hierarchical, ethnoterritorial structure of state. In Soviet times the pervasive influence of the Communist Party had, as noted earlier, made the hierarchical structure little more than a showcase; without it, the differences in status between the nationality-based republics and the territorially based regions fuelled a growing mutual resentment.

The most separatist-minded republics objected to the Federation Treaty as too unifying. A number appended qualifications or had to be given special inducements to sign, while two – Chechnya and Tatarstan – refused to sign altogether. For Chechnya this was a stage on the road to a total rejection of the Russian Federation. Chechnya's rejection had far-reaching consequences, but it was to a large extent the product of its own historical experience and current political turmoil and did not directly affect the overall pattern of centre–periphery relations. For Tatarstan, non-signature of the Federation Treaty was a stage in a controlled power struggle between central and regional elites. It was an extreme example of a widespread phenomenon. The 'Tatarstan model' became the benchmark for the aspirations of the other republics and regions.

If the Federation Treaty was too unitary for the republics, it left the 'ordinary', territorially based regions dissatisfied because it appeared to give the republics a more secure title to assets on their territory and a greater degree of financial autonomy. The strongest of these regions, under the added pressure of inflation and shortages resulting from the liberalisation of most retail prices at the beginning of 1992, declared themselves to be republics and laid claim to the benefits corresponding to their new status. Yeltsin's home region of Sverdlovsk declared itself the 'Urals Republic' in October 1993, a much publicised but short-lived move, for which the head of the regional executive, Eduard Rossel, was dismissed.

The dangers of perpetuating the Soviet-era asymmetrical federation had long been recognised by Russia's constitutional experts. One of the draft constitutions under consideration in the early part of the decade would have refashioned the Federation into some fifty territorial units on the pattern of the German *Länder*. But the political current was against such a radical solution. Rational proposals fell victim to the developing political struggle between Yeltsin and the Russian Supreme Soviet. Both sides offered favours to, and sought support from, the provinces' leaderships, with Yeltsin paying particular attention to the republics and to the executive branch of regional administrations, while his parliamentary opponents leaned towards the ordinary regions and supported the regional Soviets (legislatures). This generated at regional level a replication of the political struggle at the centre that was to colour centre–periphery relations up to at least the presidential elections of 1996.

Yeltsin's victory over the rebellious parliament in October 1993 allowed him to push a hastily drafted constitution through a referendum. It came into force on 12 December 1993 and remains the basic document defining the relations between the centre and the regions. The Constitution refined rather than reformed the asymmetrical federal system. It narrowed the gap between the republics and regions, but did not eliminate it entirely. It continued to give the republics attributes of statehood (Article 5.2) and to list them above the regions in the old Soviet hierarchical order (Article 65.1), but at the same time it maintained that all components of the Federation were equal with each other in their relations with the federal centre (Article 5.4).

The Constitution also restored a degree of centralisation to the political system. It re-established the Russian Federation as a three-tier, top-down state. At the top come the federal bodies (president, government, parliament). At the next level come the eighty-nine components of the Federation, commonly known as 'the regions' (the Russian term is *subyekt*, a neutral word chosen to encompass all the component units, with their differing status). The third level is local government, i.e. municipalities and below. The Constitution's key centralising provisions are:

- the maintenance of a single economic space and a commitment to the free movement of goods, services and financial resources (Article 8.1), the right to issue money being reserved exclusively to the Central Bank (Article 75.1);
- the primacy of federal legislation (Article 4.2), and federal control over the judicial system (Article 71);
- federal control over foreign and security policies and institutions (Article 71).

But the Constitution is vague over how government is to be exercised in the regions. Such vital questions as the ownership of natural resources and state property, as well as the principles of taxation, were left in the sphere of joint competence between the Federation and its component parts (Article 72). Detailed provisions were to be made by federal laws, scarcely any of which were adopted in Yeltsin's time. Significantly, provision was made for further centre/region treaties to clarify the division of powers (Article 11.3).

The Constitution provides for the regions to be represented in the federal legislature through the Federation Council, the upper house of the Federal Assembly (parliament). The Federation Council has significant powers – it sanctions the despatch of Russian troops abroad, it approves the appointments of senior judicial figures (or turns them down, as it did frequently in the Yeltsin era) and it has the final voice in the impeachment of the president. But in the haste in which the Constitution was drafted and adopted, important questions of how the Council should be composed and function were left only half-solved. All the eighty-nine components of the Federation were given the right to two seats and two votes, one from the regional executive, one from the legislature. The Council therefore consists of 178 individuals (in practice 176, as Chechnya does not occupy its seats), who adopt decisions by simple majority vote (or two-thirds in specific cases) of the total membership. But the Constitution left undecided whether the two representatives from each component should be elected or occupy their seats *ex officio*. The issue was debated in the transitional period between December 1993 and December 1995, when both houses were initially directly elected. The eventual solution was to fill the upper house with heads of regional executives and legislatures *ex officio*, but on condition that they were first elected.

This compromise had two unintended consequences. First, for the leaders of the regional executives to have a seat on the central legislature violated the constitutional principle of the separation of powers. Second, and politically more important, once elected rather than appointed, elected regional leaders were safe from presidential interference (and they enjoyed parliamentary immunity to boot). And yet in the Federation Council they had the instrument through which they could remove the president from office. Yeltsin himself, who relied on his own political gifts to keep the majority of regional leaders on side, was not worried by this anomalous situation, but his advisers were. Their concerns finally found expression in Putin's federal initiative of May 2000, when he adduced the imbalance between the regional leaders' powers over the president through the Federation Council and the president's lack of power over the regional leaders as one of the reasons for removing them from that body.[7]

In the context of centre–periphery relations, the 1993 Constitution was another successful holding operation. But the compromises it involved perpetuated rivalry between the republics and the regions and left important aspects of centre–periphery relations to be negotiated later. In the meantime, as noted earlier, Tatarstan had adopted its own constitution, in which it arrogated to itself more rights than the new federal constitution allowed. A number of other republics and regions had followed its example. The only solution for the centre was to use the loophole provided by Article 11.3 of the Constitution. This article, as already noted, allowed power sharing between the centre and the regions to be established by separate treaties as well as by the Constitution itself. After hard negotiations, on 15 February 1994 Presidents Yeltsin and Shaymiyev signed a treaty between the Russian Federation and the Republic of Tatarstan that acknowledged the validity of both the federal and the Tatar constitutions, incompatible though they were on the issue of sovereignty. The treaty served as the umbrella for a series of agreements on the division of executive power, the most significant of which covered financial relations. Tatarstan retained the right it had claimed in 1991–2 to run its own fiscal affairs, remitting an agreed portion of its tax revenue to Moscow. This significant concession (and deviation from the constitutional norm of Russia as a single economic space) was not rectified until March 2001, well into the Putin presidency, when the federal Ministry of Finance was able to open a branch office in Kazan, capital city of Tatarstan.

The power-sharing treaty with Tatarstan, and a slightly less permissive one with Bashkortostan in August 1994, set off a competitive process of bargaining with the centre. Five more treaties were signed with republics in 1995, which increased the pressure on Yeltsin from the 'ordinary' regions – led again by Sverdlovsk – to be allowed into the arena. Yeltsin responded generously, as he was by then on the campaign trail for re-election as president. The result was a concentration of treaties with the regions in the first six months of 1996.

Not all regions negotiated power-sharing agreements, and some influential regional leaders opposed them in principle, but by the end of the Yeltsin era forty-two had been signed by forty-six components of the Federation (four of the Autonomous *okrugs* signed jointly with their 'parent' region). Equally important, hundreds of bilateral agreements with the regions had been signed at lower levels, most of which were kept secret in order to stop the competition for favours from getting out of hand. The political significance of the treaties lay in the practice they established of individual bargains, often with Yeltsin himself, as the main vehicle for the conduct of regional relations with the centre.

The claims to sovereignty of Tatarstan and other components of the Federation had implications for Russia's foreign policy under Yeltsin. Under the Constitution, all the major elements of Russia's foreign and security policies are a federal responsibility. Article 71 specifies these as: foreign policy, international relations and international treaties; questions of war and peace; foreign economic relations; and defence and security, including the production, sale and purchase of weapons. Article 72, however, with the ambiguity characteristic of the Constitution, lays down that co-ordination of the regions' international contacts, and also the implementation of the Federation's international treaties, is a joint federal/regional responsibility. A law that came into force at the beginning of 1999 clarified the issue.[8] It allowed regions to maintain foreign relations at levels below that of government and to sign agreements at this level provided these did not contradict federal legislation, impinge on other regions or purport to be international treaties. Regions could set up missions abroad so long as they did not claim to have the functions or status of diplomatic missions.

Chechnya aside, these restrictions on the regions' international activities were generally adhered to – most of the regions were more interested in attracting foreign investment and finance than in international status. Their most dangerous activity under Yeltsin was to take out loans that they could not repay, a practice that ceased after the financial debacle of August 1998. The regional leaders nonetheless retained significant influence over foreign investment in their bailiwicks through manipulation of those taxes over which they had control and by creating a more or less friendly environment. Novgorod *oblast*, though lacking resources, established itself by these methods as an attractive place in which to do business.

Russia's border regions also acquired an unexpected importance in Russia's foreign relations. The administrative boundaries of twenty-seven of Russia's regions, particularly with the former Soviet republics to the south, but also with Ukraine and the Baltic States, became international borders overnight when the Soviet Union ceased to exist. The task for the federal centre in this context was to encourage the regions' freedom of manoeuvre rather than restrict it, since the centre was in no position to provide the controls that mark an international border. Moscow was in any case focusing on maintaining a 'hard' border on the periphery of the former Soviet Union, which the Central Asian states themselves were unable to do. Left to their own devices, the regions by and large coped with the situation in a pragmatic way, justifying Yeltsin's laissez-faire approach. A more serious problem arose when individual regions, especially on the borders, claimed, and were granted all too easily, the status and privileges of special economic zones, which in the prevailing economic semi-anarchy meant that they became centres of smuggling and tax evasion. The town of Nakhodka, on Russia's far eastern seaboard, and Kaliningrad *oblast*, on the western, together with the republics of Kalmykia and Ingushetia, were prime examples.

Yeltsin and the regional leaders: conflict and compromise

The Constitution of 1993 was the prelude to a test of wills between the centre and the regions, in which Yeltsin, for a number of reasons – principally his instinctive confidence in the regional leaders (he had been one in Soviet times) and his electoral strategy in 1996 – constantly gave ground. A key issue was the election of 'governors', as the heads of the regional executives came to be called. With the demise of the Communist Party in 1991, leadership in the regions devolved for a time on the chairman of the executive committee of the regional Soviet, the largely powerless legislature of the Soviet era. Once Yeltsin had won his 1993 battle with the Supreme Soviet – the central legislature – he dissolved the regional Soviets, as redolent of the communist era, and appointed heads of administration to run the territorially based regions. It was not part of Yeltsin's strategy to have these governors popularly elected. He had initially endorsed the principle early in 1991 in order to circumvent the regional Soviets, but reversed his decision later that year when it became clear that many of the directly elected governors might oppose him. His resolve was strengthened by the events of 1993, when a number of governors took the side of his parliamentary opponents. In a decree of October 1994 Yeltsin reasserted his right to nominate and dismiss governors.[9] This was not against the Constitution, which, although it endorses the principle of elections as the expression of the power of the people (Article 3), does not provide in its terms for the election of the heads of regional executives. On the contrary, the Constitution endorses the 'unity of the system of state power' (Article 5.3) and states that the 'federal bodies of executive power and bodies of executive power of the components of the Russian Federation comprise a single system of executive power in the Russian Federation' (Article 77.2). These articles were often cited by officials in Yeltsin's administration and later used by Yevgeniy Primakov as prime minister to argue for a top-down structure of government and against the popular election of governors.

A number of considerations forced Yeltsin little by little to concede the principle of popularly elected regional leaders. The decisive one was the issue of the Federation Council, discussed above. Yeltsin had wanted the regions to be represented in the Federation Council by their executive and legislative leaders *ex officio*. He was concerned that an elected upper house might leave him faced by hostile majorities in both houses. The Duma (as the lower house was now called, replacing the Supreme Soviet) opposed an *ex officio* upper house on the grounds that almost half the members would be Yeltsin's appointees (as the heads of regional administrations were at that time). In a last-minute compromise it was agreed that the Federation

Council should be composed of the heads of the two branches of regional power *ex officio*, but that the leader of the regional executive should first have been elected locally (the leader of the regional legislature already was). By establishing the principle of electing the executive in the regions, this compromise had far-reaching consequences for the devolution of power. All the heads of regional administrations are now elected, and Putin's federal initiative of May 2000 left the innovation in place.

The regional electoral campaigns of 1996–7 initially replicated the ideological confrontation between Yeltsin and his defeated communist rival, Gennadiy Zyuganov, in the presidential election of May–June 1996. But the ideological content of the regional elections soon took second place to the practical: which candidate appeared best placed to further the welfare of his region, and in particular to lobby in Moscow for special regional programmes and off-budget funds. Despite their devotion to the democratic process where it promised to strengthen their hand in Moscow, the newly elected governors tended to interpret their popular mandate as giving them an exclusive hold on power in their region. This was not surprising, given their mainly Soviet background and the 'zero-sum' nature of post-Soviet Russian politics. They set out to create their own formal or informal 'parties of power' through which to control the regional legislature, while they gradually gained control of the regional media, usually by indirect means.

Local government was one of the victims of the increasing power of regional governors.[10] Under the Constitution (Article 12), local government is not part of the system of state power. In August 1995 a law on local self-government deprived the regional executive of the power to appoint officials at the local level. At most levels of local government traditional subservience and the lack of resources to implement their responsibilities rendered the law ineffective. But over the decade large municipalities gained increasing clout. In most of Russia's regions the principal town is the region's industrial base and main source of revenue. In Soviet times the regional boss nonetheless held the whip hand because he controlled the countryside that fed the town. But with large cities able to shop around for their supplies they were no longer ready to bow to the whim of the regional authorities. Mayors became increasingly serious rivals to regional governors. In his later years Yeltsin encouraged this trend, but only as a means of curtailing the power of the governors. Putin's top-down reform of the Federation has put local government back at the bottom of the heap: as a compensation for re-imposing the president's right to dismiss governors he had enacted amendments to the law of local self-government, giving regional leaders analogous powers over heads of local executives.

The increasing freedom of action enjoyed by regional leaders did not – or should not have – altered the fact that the Russian Federation remained a single economic and judicial space with a considerable federal presence in the regions. Federal offices included the regional departments of the security agencies, the Ministry of Finance, the Central Bank, the tax and customs agencies and the judicial organs – between thirty and fifty agencies in each region. In April 1999 the then prime minister, Primakov, acknowledged that there were 330,000 federal officials in the regions, not counting the Ministry of Internal Affairs or Tax Police – more than in the Soviet era.[11] A crucial factor, however, was that these offices were staffed by local employees. The stronger governors were able to ensure that officials trusted by them held all the crucial appointments. Eduard Rossel, who had returned to power as the elected governor of Sverdlovsk *oblast*, went as far as having this practice written into the region's bilateral treaty with Moscow. Nor was the judiciary free from local interference. The failure of the federal authorities to fulfil their responsibility to finance local courts made the latter materially dependent on the regional authorities and hence unable to escape from the pressure exerted by regional leaders or the business – and sometimes outright criminal – interests behind them.

One of Yeltsin's answers to the regionalisation of power was to appoint a presidential representative in each region (though not, initially, in the republics, in deference to their special status). They were first established in August 1991, ostensibly to check regional against federal legislation, but in reality to act as the president's eyes and ears in the regions, where the prevailing political climate was much less favourable to Yeltsin than in the centre. Once Yeltsin had appointed loyal governors, however, his representatives became little more than the political adjunct of the regional administration. The potential importance of the president's representatives increased again once Yeltsin lost his direct leverage over the governors following their popular election. In 1997 he gave his representatives a new role – that of co-ordinating federal institutions in their regions – but they did not shine at this. The fact was that, like other federal institutions at regional level, they depended on the regional authorities for their amenities, such as housing and office space. Lacking consistent support from a weakening centre towards the end of Yeltsin's presidency, they were ill placed to assert presidential authority. One of Putin's first measures as president, on 13 May 2000, was to abolish the existing system of presidential representatives in the regions. But it is instructive that he did not abandon the concept. He created seven new representatives overseeing a group of regions, who in turn appointed chief inspectors for each region in their federal district.

Once the regional leaders had achieved an unprecedented and unexpected level of power, by the middle of the decade, the question arose: to what purpose? Some of the rhetoric of the stronger republics and regions suggested that full independence was their aim. In practice – Chechnya again excepted – that was far from the case. History, geography and culture all militated against such extreme solutions. Their purpose was, first, to use their bargaining power to extract from the federal centre the best possible economic deal for their respective regions and, then, to ensure that the lion's share of it remained with them – the regional leaders – and their political and business associates.

In pursuit of the first objective they fought to gain control of as much tax revenue as they could. Their ability to bargain with the centre over this issue stemmed both from the indeterminate nature of the articles of the Constitution relating to centre–periphery relations and from the lack of a federal tax code. The working pattern of tax and budget relations was based on a presidential decree of January 1994 but was subject to constant change. Federal taxes (levied on enterprises, not on regions as such) were raised by the centre and shared with the regions in proportions that were decided annually in the budget. The regions were permitted to raise a large number of local taxes, for example on property and land. The regions had many justifiable reasons for unhappiness with the system – for example, the centre allocated to itself the steady, indirect taxes, such as VAT and excise, that were easy to collect, while leaving the regions to collect profit and income tax, which were both cyclical and easier to evade.

The system also led to antagonisms between the regions themselves, as well as between the regions and the centre. A proportion of the revenue accruing to the centre was set aside to support regions disadvantaged by geography and lack of resources. The arrangement relied on a complex system of weighting to establish which regions should be in the two categories of 'recipients' ('needy' and 'very needy') and which in the category of 'donor', where the net flow of revenue was from the region to the centre. It encouraged underperformance (or at least underreporting) among those regions that wished to remain 'needy' and rely on subsidies and a corresponding resentment on the part of the 'donor' regions, which felt they were being asked to subsidise inefficiency.

The regional leaders' second objective – securing the lion's share of such economic benefits as were going – involved profiting from the generally lax legal regime surrounding the privatisation of state assets. The first stage of privatisation, from 1992, played into their hands. It was administered by the Federal State Property Committee (GKI) through its regional branches, which functioned as departments of the regional administrations. This meant that the regional administration was responsible for managing, and in effect owned, property that was in transition between the state and a new corporate owner, who frequently turned out to be the same Soviet-era director. The regional elites consolidated their control of local economies by creating regionally based holding companies, where a number of enterprises were loosely amalgamated under a board of management in which the regional authorities were strongly represented.

The links and networks maintained and newly established in this period formed the nervous system of centre/region economic relations in the Yeltsin era. They were cemented in an economically irrational way by the non-payments crisis of the middle of the decade. In the economic conditions of the time, with enterprises failing to generate profits and the federal centre unable to pay its workers in the regions, cash disappeared from the regions, and local economies began to work to a system of barter, promissory notes and tax offsets. Complex mutually supportive, and also antagonistic, relationships were formed in the discounts, shady deals and gang wars that formed part of this system.[12]

The federal authorities had reluctantly sanctioned the entanglement in this 'virtual economy'[13] of the quasi-state natural monopolies – Gazprom, which controlled the production, transportation and distribution of all of Russia's natural gas, the electricity provider United Energy Systems (UES) and the railway system, which had a monopoly on tariff setting. A strict insistence on cash payment would have brought the economy to a halt. One of the declared aims of the short-lived ascendancy of 'young reformers' in government from early 1997 to mid-1998 was to rationalise the natural monopolies and, with that, to bring regional protectionism to heel. But corporate and regional interests, the flagging of political will, the obvious pain that such a course would have caused and, finally, the economic crisis of August 1998 proved too much.

The reaction of regional leaders to the financial crisis was strongly protectionist and 'go-it-alone'. A number of regions imposed price controls and banned the 'export' of foodstuffs from their territory. Others claimed that they were halting the remittance of tax revenues to Moscow. This was not only illegal but also difficult for all but a few to implement in practice. Much of the initial demonstration of regional strength and independence had been more declaratory than real. At the same time, the crisis prompted the regions to look for more substantial measures to secure their economic and financial self-sufficiency. Six regions created their own gold and foreign currency reserves, which, with limitations, they were legally entitled to do. Regionally based banks emerged relatively stronger than the regional branches of Moscow-based banks. Having little cash to start off with, they had had less exposure to the boom and bust of the market in state securities and had not borrowed heavily abroad.

The financial and consequent political crises of August 1998 revealed both the weakness of the centre in relation to the regions and the inability of the regions to 'go it alone' even if they wanted to. The advent of a more conservatively inclined government under Yevgeniy Primakov prompted a rethink of centre–periphery relations that was eventually to find expression under the presidency of Vladimir Putin. In the first instance, it added urgency to the drive to agree a new Tax Code, in order to regularise fiscal relations between the centre and the regions. In the second place, it reinforced the view in Moscow that mechanisms needed to be found to reassert the political weight of the centre over that of the regions.

Conclusions

If one is to look for a single word to characterise centre–periphery relations in the Yeltsin era, that word might be 'resentment'.[14] Yeltsin resented his treatment at the hands of Gorbachev and avenged himself by launching a

Kremlin power struggle in which the prize was the Kremlin itself. To win it, Yeltsin exploited the resentment of the Union Republics against the Soviet centre and encouraged the resentment of the Autonomous Republics of the RSFSR against the Union Republics. The enhanced status won by the Autonomous Republics during the agony of the Soviet Union and carried through to their relations with the centre in independent Russia was resented by Russia's ordinary regions, leading them to compete for similar status. The imperfect constitutional settlement and fiscal arrangements that were put in place after 1993 unleashed a new round of resentments – of poorly endowed regions against regions rich in natural resources, and of rich 'donor' regions against poor regions, whom they had indirectly to subsidise. All were resentful of the city of Moscow, into which foreign investment flowed, while Moscow was resentful of the federal government for parasitically feeding off its riches. The post-1993 Duma was resentful of Yeltsin's presidential powers and sought to curtail his influence in the Federation Council by insisting that its members be elected. The centre was resentful of the powers it had unwittingly conceded to the governors by allowing them to be elected, and sought to hem them in.

It need hardly be said that resentment is a characteristic of regional policy in most countries. It is difficult for any government to take account of the needs of particular regions while remaining fair to all. The lack of any regional history in the Russian Federation to use as a starting point, however, meant that there was no generally accepted framework within which these resentments could be contained. A sense of measure was missing. The lack of political culture nurtured a climate of absolutism, in which each level of the hierarchy demanded total freedom from control from above but, irrationally, was not prepared to devolve power downwards. Finally, the apparent lack of boundaries to political or material ambition, known as *bespredel*, bred a culture of reckless acquisitiveness, in which the regional elites were every bit as culpable as the better known 'oligarchs' based at the centre.

In these circumstances tactical considerations were usually uppermost in the minds of most of the players. Action was dictated by the constant political and economic crises in which the centre–periphery relations developed. Blueprints for the rational development of federal relations in the new Russia, of which there were many, took second place. In the end this may turn out to have been no bad thing. One of the benefits of Yeltsin's approach was its elasticity. By sensing and generally accommodating the political demands of the regions he may have avoided the crises that would have emanated from a stricter policy, especially in relation to the former Autonomous Republics. Many regions were able to test the boundaries of regional independence and come to the realisation that interdependence – among themselves and with the centre – was the common basis for their future development.

Notes

1 See Suny 1993: 98–126.
2 For detailed accounts of the emergence of today's Russian Federation, see Lapidus (1995: 79–113), Teague (1994: 21–57), Debardeleben (1997: 35–56) and Kahn (2001: 374–84).
3 Yeltsin's resentment of Gorbachev pervades the first, and most ingenuous, of Yeltsin's three autobiographies (Yeltsin 1990).
4 Aron 2000: 392–4.
5 Moukhariamov 1997: 216.
6 Article 61 of the Tatarstan Constitution reads: 'The Republic of Tatarstan is a sovereign state, a subject of international law, associated with the Russian Federation and Russia on the basis of an Agreement on the reciprocal delegating of plenary powers and subjects of authority.'
7 Vladimir Putin, *Address to the Citizens of Russia*, 17 May 2000, at http://www.president.kremlin.ru/events/34.html (in Russian).
8 'On Co-ordination of International and External Economic Relations of the Constituent Entities of the Russian Federation', adopted by the State Duma on 2 December 1998, signed into law by President Yeltsin on 4 January 1999.
9 Hahn 1997: 252–3.
10 Young 1997: 81–102.
11 Radio Russia, 24 April 1999, in *BBC Summary of World Broadcasts, Former Soviet Union*, 3518 B/9, 26 April 1999.
12 Two novels by Yulia Latynina, *Stalnoy Korol* (Moscow: Russkiy Proyekt, 2000) and *Okhota na Izyubrya* (Moscow: Russkiy Proyekt, 1999), provide a lurid, fictionalised, but accurate account of the interplay of economic, political and criminal forces at work in the steel industry in Siberia.
13 Gaddy and Ickes 1998: 53–67.
14 This is the best way I can render the very expressive Russian word *obida* in this context.

2 Putin

An end to centrifugalism?

Dr Mark A. Smith

Within the Russian Federation the break-up of the command-administrative system and the control of the Communist Party of the Soviet Union (CPSU) over the political system at the beginning of the 1990s saw a significant haemorrhaging of power from the central political authorities in both the Soviet Union and the Russian Federation. This process began before the collapse of the Union of Soviet Socialist Republics (USSR) in 1991. In August 1990, when in Tatarstan, Boris Yeltsin, who was then chairman of the presidium of the Supreme Soviet of the Russian Soviet Federative Socialist Republic (RSFSR), told the local authorities to 'take as much independence as you can'. In Bashkortostan he uttered his now famous statement to take as much sovereignty 'as you can swallow'.[1]

Both republics and other subjects of the Russian Federation took Yeltsin at his word, and the 1990s saw the development of centrifugalism in the Russian Federation as power flowed from the centre to the subjects (regions) of the Russian Federation.[2] In many cases this made it extremely difficult for the centre to assert its authority over the regions and ensure the supremacy of Russian federal law over laws passed locally. The federal authorities were unable to exercise full control over the constituent units of the federation, and it was impossible for them to achieve an agreed and stable demarcation of power and responsibilities with the regions of the federation. In addition, the disparities in rights between the republics and other regions of the federation meant that the federation was at best asymmetric. At certain periods of the Yeltsin presidency concern was raised as to whether the Russian Federation would emulate the fate of the USSR and fall apart. This concern was particularly acute following the financial crisis of August 1998.[3]

The flowing of power from the centre to the regions was part of a broader disintegration of the Russian state. The break-up of the communist system in the Soviet Union had seriously undermined the capacity of the state machine to perform its basic functions. The Yeltsin presidency did little, if anything, to remedy this state of affairs. Although the 1993 Constitution gave the president enormous power, Yeltsin did not use this power to create a state that would integrate social, institutional and political institutions within a framework based on the rule of law. Instead an undisciplined pluralism emerged in which regional and financial elites were able to ignore the attempts of the centre to enforce law. Yeltsin's toleration of corruption exacerbated the situation, and many of these elites were able to 'privatise' the state – that is, buy off parts of it – so it would be beholden to their will rather than that of the central government. The state was thus unable to 'tax resources, conscript manpower, and innovate and execute policy'.[4]

This was the legacy that faced Vladimir Putin when he became acting president on 31 December 1999. His essay *Russia on the Threshold of the Millennium*, released at the end of December 1999, devoted virtually no attention to the problem of centre–regional relations in the Russian Federation, other than to call for improving federative relations. It did, however, call for a strong efficient state that would improve its capacity to govern and enforce the existing constitution, warning that the toleration of unconstitutional laws would undermine the capabilities of the federal centre.[5] The rebuilding of the Russian state has been a central feature of Putin's leadership, and his reforms of centre–regional relations should be seen in that context. The rebuilding and hence strengthening of the state has raised the issue of whether this will hinder the prospects for Russia's further democratisation, or even possibly create the preconditions for a return to a more authoritarian political system. Putin's central task is to 'create a central government that is strong enough to keep the country whole, yet limited enough to prevent a return to tyranny'.[6]

The underlying theme of Putin's first state of the nation address in July 2000 was the need to create an efficient state machine. In this address he warned that Russia was a decentralised rather than a federal state. He noted:

> One must admit that in Russia federal relations are incompletely built and undeveloped. Regional independence is frequently treated as a sanction for the disorganisation of the state. We keep talking of the federation and its strengthening. We have been talking of this for years. However, we have to admit that we do not yet have a full-blown federal state. I want to stress this. We possess, we have created, a decentralised state.[7]

Putin said very little about centre–regional relations during the presidential election campaign in early 2000. Indeed he said relatively little about any major policy issue. However, there were indications in early 2000 that he was thinking about the need to assert the power of the federal centre over the regions.[8] In early February 2000 the Federation Council and State Duma held a joint closed session at which, it was believed, Putin's desire to strengthen the control of the centre over the regions was discussed. There were claims that Putin intended to establish a 'dictatorship of law' over the regions in order to establish the demarcation of power between the centre and the regions outlined in the 1993 Constitution. There was speculation that Putin might abolish elections for regional governors and return to the previous practice of appointing them. He stated that he opposed such a move, although he said that governors should not show so much independence.[9] In the opening months of 2000 there was much debate about the future of the relationship between the federal centre and the regions. In March 2000 Sergey Pravosudov outlined six means of restricting the powers of governors, in an article in *Nezavisimaya Gazeta*.[10] He advocated the following:

- Introducing a law to define precisely the powers of regional leaders. This law would also give the president the right to dismiss regional leaders who abuse their powers and to introduce federal rule.
- Enhancing the powers of local government as a counterweight to regional leaders. Local government leaders should be given greater powers to distribute federal funds as a means of reducing the power of regional leaders as distributors of largesse.
- Bringing the power structures in the regions under greater federal control. This would mean ending the rights of regional leaders to have any input in the appointment of the heads of the regional FSB (Federal Security Service) and MVD (Interior Ministry) administrations. The funding of these regional administrations should also come directly from the centre.
- A party of power should be strictly controlled from the federal centre, so that regional governors who are members of this party would be beholden to the centre and act as 'party commissars' in their regions.
- The Federation Council should be reformed so that governors are removed from it. It violates the distribution of powers to have executors of the law acting also as legislators.
- The federal centre should offer additional funding to regions in exchange for compliance with the centre.

In early May 2000 Yuriy Danilov, of the Higher Economics School in Moscow, proposed the creation of the institution of governor-general in the Russian Federation.[11] The governor-general would be appointed by the president and be a representative of the federal authorities. He would monitor the implementation of federal laws by regional leaderships; monitor the use of state investments and other parts of the federal budget in the regions; monitor the activities of the regional branch of the federal treasury; monitor the gathering of federal taxes; implement transfers of the federal budget; implement presidential rule in subjects where this is introduced; administer the legal system in his governor-generalship; manage federal property; monitor the buying and selling of land; co-ordinate the activities of federal ministries and agencies in his governor-generalship.

Danilov proposed that a governor-generalship should comprise between two and fifteen subjects of the federation and that the number of governor-generalships should number anything between eight and sixteen.

Given the clear debate that was going on in the first half of 2000, it was little surprise that once he had obtained a mandate from the electorate Putin moved to limit the power of regional leaders. This implied achieving a greater system of central control over regional leaders, along with reform of the Federation Council, the upper house of the Federal Assembly in which regional leaders and the chairmen of regional legislatures sat.

Strengthening the power vertical

From May to September 2000 Putin introduced the main features of the reform of centre–regional relations.[12] This was often referred to as strengthening the power vertical – that is, the vertical structure of administration to ensure the supremacy of the federal centre at the top of that vertical. Many of Putin's measures embodied the proposals of Pravosudov and Danilov. These were:

- The creation of seven federal districts in which the eighty-nine subjects of the federation were incorporated. Each district was headed by a presidential representative, whose task was to ensure that regional administrations conformed to federal law.
- The reform of the Federation Council, changing the nature of its composition. Regional executive leaders and the chairmen of regional legislatures would no longer be able to sit in the upper chamber.
- The president would acquire the right to dismiss regional leaders who enacted measures that contravened federal law.
- Changes to the law on local government which would allow regional leaders to dismiss local government leaders who enacted measures that violated federal and regional law.
- A State Council would be created in which all regional leaders would be represented.
- A process of legal harmonisation that aimed at bringing regional laws and constitutions into line with federal law and constitution.
- Enhancing the power of the federal authorities over federal spending in the regions.

The creation of federal districts

On 13 May 2000 Putin issued a decree confirming the creation of seven federal districts (see Appendix for details of what each district comprises).[13] According to this decree the presidential representatives are the representatives of the president in their respective districts and are appointed by and accountable to him. They are part of the presidential administration, and the operational leadership of the presidential representatives is carried out by the head of the presidential administration. In

January 2001 some of the functions of the Main Territorial Directorate of the presidential administration were transferred to the federal districts.

The main tasks of the presidential representatives were to ensure the realisation in their federal districts of the main direction of the domestic and foreign policy of the state, as defined by the president. They were to monitor the execution of federal policy in their district and ensure the implementation of the president's personnel policy. They were to provide the president with reports on the maintenance of national security in their district and on the political, economic and social situation. Their most important functions were defined as follows:

- to work out with the inter-regional economic associations the economic interaction of the subjects of the federation and socio-economic programmes for their subjects;
- to co-ordinate candidates for appointment to federal posts in their districts and other posts if these appointments were to be made either by the federal president, the federal government or other federal bodies;
- to verify the execution of federal laws and decrees and other normative acts of the federal president and federal government, and also the implementation of federal programmes;
- to co-ordinate draft decisions of federal organs concerning the interests of their federal district or of subjects within their district;
- to take part in the work of organs of state power of subjects in their federal district, including organs of local government;
- to organise, by the authorisation of the president, conciliation procedures to resolve disputes between federal organs of government and regional organs;
- to make proposals to the president about halting the implementation of acts of regional executive authorities if these acts contradict the federal constitution, federal laws, the international obligations of the Russian Federation or human rights;
- to interact with the Main Control Administration of the federal president and procuracy organs to organise checks on the execution of federal laws, decrees and normative acts of the president and of the federal government.

In short, they would ensure that federal law and federal personnel policy were enforced in their respective federal districts. This would ensure that appointments to federal positions in the regions would be made by the federal centre and not by regional leaders, as had often been the case. Their co-ordinating function would also help the Kremlin to identify and avoid divergences of policy both at the centre and in the federal subjects.

This decree was intended to counteract the flow of power from the centre to the regions that had taken place in the 1990s and ensure that the central authorities would be able to exercise the power over the regions accorded to

them in the 1993 Constitution. Yeltsin had appointed presidential representatives to each of the eighty-nine subjects during his presidency to perform
essentially the same role, but many of these representatives had 'gone native'
and became little more than spokesmen for regional leaders *vis-à-vis* the
central authorities rather than instruments of presidential control over the
regions.[14] This was largely because the regional governments provided
federal agencies in the regions with office space, housing, transport and
other necessities. Under the decree of May 2000, the presidential administration and regional governments are to work together to provide these needs,
which will be paid for by the presidential administration. This will enable the
federal government to control its own employees better and ensure that they
enforce the will of the federal government rather than become the instrument of regional leaderships. As the vast majority of federal civil servants
are located in the regions (of 381,000 federal civil servants, only 29,000 are
located in Moscow),[15] there is an obvious need to ensure that they are
beholden to the federal authorities and not to regional ones.

All but two of the presidential representatives (Kiriyenko and
Drachevskiy) are from the power structures. The obvious enhancement of
the role of these structures in Russian political life should therefore give the
centre more levers to use in its attempts to control the regions. The boundaries of the federal districts also coincide with the boundaries of Interior
Ministry districts for the Russian Federation and this may facilitate the
ability of the Interior Ministry to operate in the federal districts.

The idea of creating presidential representatives to oversee a group of
regions did not arise out of thin air. It was a revival of an idea that had been
expressed in a decree issued by Yeltsin back in July 1997.[16] Yeltsin had then
considered replacing the system of presidential representatives, which he had
set up in 1991 in all eighty-nine subjects of the federation, with a smaller
number of representatives who would oversee groupings of regions. This
would reduce the likelihood of a representative being unduly influenced by
an individual governor.

The appointment of the presidential representatives – who became
members of the Russian Federation Security Council, thus achieving representation at the apex of the political system – was a significant step in
ensuring that federal policy prevailed over the regions. In addition, they can
attend cabinet meetings. In August 2000 the prime minister, Mikhail
Kasyanov, signed a decree permitting the presidential representatives to
participate in government meetings and cast a consultative vote. The
creation of the presidential representatives was intended to ensure that
central control could be maintained without abolishing gubernatorial elections. Such a step would have been deeply damaging for Putin, as it would
have undermined his claims to support democracy. This would have affected
both his legitimacy within the Russian Federation and his image abroad.

After the establishment of the seven federal districts, the most significant
moves were the reform of the Federation Council and the granting to the

president of the right to dismiss regional governors. Both these moves were directed at further reducing the powers of the regional leaders in the political system. Putin outlined his views on these matters in a television address on 17 May 2000.[17] In this address he called for the following:

- Reform of the Federation Council. Regional leaders and the chairmen of regional legislatures would no longer have the right to sit on the Federation Council. They would be replaced by representatives of the regional executive and legislative bodies. In Putin's view this would improve the efficiency of law-making as the representatives could sit permanently on the Federation Council, leaving regional leaders and parliamentary chairmen to concentrate on their domestic tasks. It would also remove regional leaders from direct representation in the federal political system, which Putin saw as a violation of the division of power. Their removal from the Federation Council would also strip them of the legal immunity they enjoyed as members of the Federal Assembly. This would enable the federal authorities to prosecute them if they opposed federal law in their regions.
- The president to have the right to dismiss regional leaders and parliamentary chairmen who enforced legislation that contradicted federal legislation.
- Regional leaders to have similar rights to dismiss local leaders who undertook acts that violated federal or regional laws.

Reform of the Federation Council

The Federation Council is the upper house of the Russian legislature.[18] It includes two representatives from each subject of the Russian Federation: one from the legislative and one from the executive body of state authority. Unlike the State Duma, it cannot be dismissed by the president.

The Constitution gives it exclusive rights to approve internal border changes; presidential decrees declaring martial law and states of emergency; the use of Russian armed forces outside the Russian Federation; the dates of presidential elections; impeachment of the president; the appointment of judges of the Constitutional Court, Supreme Court and Higher Arbitration Court; the appointment or dismissal of the procurator-general, and of the deputy chairman and half the auditors of the Accounting Chamber.

Like the upper houses in most bicameral parliaments, it acts as a revising and amending chamber. All federal draft laws passed by the State Duma have to be sent to the Federation Council within five days. If more than half the members of the Federation Council vote for a draft law passed by the State Duma, then that draft law is considered approved by the Federation Council and passed to the president for signing. If the Federation Council does not consider a law sent to it by the State Duma within fourteen days, then the draft law is considered approved. If the Federation Council rejects a

law, then both the Federation Council and State Duma may create a conciliation commission to overcome the differences. Once this has been achieved
the State Duma is to recognise the draft law. If the State Duma disagrees
with the Federation Council, then a federal law shall be considered adopted
if during the second vote at least two-thirds of the State Duma vote for it.

The reform of the Federation Council proved controversial. This was
only to be expected: the draft law had to pass through both the State Duma
and the unreformed Federation Council before it could become law.
Unsurprisingly, many members of the Federation Council were reluctant to
pass measures that would deny them the right to sit on the Federation
Council. The law passed through the State Duma quickly, but in June 2000
the Federation Council vetoed it. A State Duma–Federation Council conciliation commission was set up to suggest amendments to the law. Some
changes were made and the law was adopted by the State Duma and then
approved by the Federation Council at the end of July 2000. It was signed
into law by Putin on 5 August 2000.

This law confirmed that members of the Federation Council were no
longer to be regional leaders and regional parliamentary chairmen. Each
region would instead have two representatives on the Federation Council,
one from the region's executive structures and one from the legislative structures. The representative from the executive structures is to be appointed by
the governor/president of the subject for the period of his term in office.
This appointment is to be confirmed by the legislative assembly of the
subject. If more than two-thirds of deputies vote against the governor/presi-
dent's nomination then the appointment is vetoed.

The representative from the legislative structures is to be chosen by the
members of the subject's legislative assembly for the term of that assembly.
The chairman of the parliament then nominates the successful candidate as
the Federation Council representative. If other candidates receive the
support of more than one-third of deputies, then they too can be considered
as candidates. Existing Federation Council members (i.e. governors/presi-
dents and chairman of legislative assemblies) were allowed to remain as
members until their term expired or until no later than 1 January 2002,
whichever came earlier.

This reform of the Federation Council, along with the passing, on 29 July
2000, of the law allowing the president to impeach governors, significantly
strengthened the power of the federal centre *vis-à-vis* the regional leaders
without the need for the abolition of elected governors. It should be noted
that, although the president now has the legal power to remove governors,
he cannot do so automatically.[19] If a governor issues decrees or other
normative acts that violate federal law a court can find the decree unconstitutional. The governor must then annul the law within two months or face a
warning decree from the federal president. The president can also annul the
regional decree by decree. The governor must then comply with the decree
within two months or appeal to a court or face a warning. If the warning is

ignored, then the federal president can remove the governor from office. The decree removing the governor has a ten-day waiting period before it is implemented. During that time the governor can appeal to the Supreme Court. The president can also remove a governor on the recommendation of the procurator-general if there is evidence that he has committed serious crimes and an indictment is planned.

These measures were a significant triumph for Putin as they strengthened Russian statehood in a way that contained no overt threat to the principle of elected governors. Putin's measures represented the first major move by the federal government to reverse almost a decade of centrifugalism in the Russian Federation.

Legal harmonisation

As part of the process of intensifying central control, Putin began forcing regional leaderships to bring their legislation into line with federal legislation. In May 2000 he issued decrees ordering Bashkortostan to align its constitution with that of the federation, and suspending Ingush legislation which contradicted federal legislation. In June 2000 he took similar measures in relation to Adygeya.

In June 2000 the prosecutor-general, Vladimir Ustinov, identified departures from the federal constitution found in the constitutions and charters of some of the constituent parts of the Russian Federation which he considered threatened state security.[20] He listed Dagestan, Ingushetia and North Osetia as republics whose constitutions proclaimed national sovereignty. Bashkortostan, the Republic of Komi, Kabardino-Balkaria, Tatarstan, Tyva and Sakha-Yakutia had proclaimed the superiority of their legislation over the federal constitution. Adygeya, Buryatiya, Ingushetia and Kalmykia had appropriated the right to introduce a state of emergency. The Republic of Altay, North Osetia, Krasnodar *kray* and Rostov Region had introduced their own labour legislation. Bashkortostan and the Republic of Komi had proclaimed the superiority of the main local ethnic group. Ustinov said there were major violations of major rights and freedoms of citizens, and that most republics of the North Caucasus, along with Bashkortostan and Tatarstan, violated the federal electoral legislation by introducing language requirements for candidates standing at local elections. He also said that Ingushetia, Kabardino-Balkaria, Karachay-Cherkessia, North Osetia, Stavropol *kray*, Volgograd Region, Moscow Region and Moscow violated the citizen's right to travel freely.

In July 2000 Yury Chayka, the Russian minister of justice, reported that 20 per cent of the laws passed in the constituent parts of the Russian Federation ran counter to the federal constitution.[21] The Prosecutor-General's Office and the Ministry of Justice played a major role in forcing regional leaderships to alter their legislation (and where necessary their constitutions and charters) to conform with federal legislation and the federal constitution. In May 2001 Chayka claimed that only 5–6 per cent of regional laws were still incompatible with federal legislation.[22] The process of legal harmonisation thus appears to have had considerable success, and those regional leaderships most opposed to Putin's measures have been able to do little to oppose this process.

In June 2001 Putin decreed the creation of a commission to draft proposals on power sharing between federal, regional and local authorities.[23] This commission would presumably examine precisely how Article 72 of the Federal Constitution, which outlines the areas of joint competence between the federal and subject authorities, was to be applied. The commission was to review the power-sharing treaties signed by the federal centre and various regions in order to ensure that they complied with the federal constitution. Forty-two of these treaties were in existence. This process was to be completed no later than 30 July 2002. The commission was headed by Dmitry Kozak, deputy head of the presidential administration. In July 2001 four regional leaderships (Perm, Ulyanovsk, Nizhniy Novgorod *oblasts* and the Mari El Republic) annulled the treaties they had with the federal centre, which indicated a further reversal of centrifugalist trends.[24]

The formation of the State Council

In July 2000 the Kremlin began to talk about the desirability of creating a State Council where regional leaders would be represented. This followed suggestions made earlier by some governors to set up such a body[25] as a substitute for the Federation Council, from which regional leaders would be removed. In September 2000 Putin issued a decree announcing the formation of the State Council.[26] All regional leaders were to be represented on this body, and the federal president would be the chairman. The council has a seven-member presidium whose membership rotates every six months. The presidium members comprise leaders from one of the seven federal districts. The council's task is to monitor the implementation of federal law. The president can also recommend that it consider draft laws and decrees. The State Council is also to discuss the federal budget and its implementation. It is to meet at least once every three months. Its agenda is decided by the president, although he probably consults the presidium on this matter. The State Council has a secretary from the presidential administration.

Between November 2000 and March 2001 the State Council met four times. It has discussed such matters as constitutional reform and set up a commission headed by Yuriy Luzhkov to discuss this issue. It also discussed the restoration of the old Soviet national anthem, federal relations and local self-government. The State Council asked the Tatarstan president, Mintimir Shaymiyev, to prepare a report on the demarcation of power between the centre and the subjects of the Russian Federation. However, its proposals were so at variance with the wishes of the Putin leadership that it was shelved by the presidium of the State Council at the request of the Kremlin.

The State Council is a consultative body. It cannot pass legislation. The most it can do is ask the president to submit a bill to the State Duma. It does, however, provide a voice for governors at the federal level, and it also acts as an alternative source of information for the president. It is supposed to reach decisions by consensus. Putin's decree makes no mention of voting as a means of making decisions. There have been calls for the State Council to be given the powers of the Federation Council, but it is highly unlikely that Putin will agree to such requests.[27]

The impact of the reforms

Some have argued that the presidential representatives have achieved relatively little, other than creating an extra level of bureaucracy in the country. The State Duma deputy, Vladimir Ryzhkov, argues that Putin's decree creating the presidential representatives is vague in defining their powers.[28] He says that the decree simply states that they are to ensure the exercise of the powers of the head of state within their federal districts and ensure the implementation of the guidelines of internal and foreign policy laid down by the president. Ryzhkov considers that the vagueness of this decree has resulted in each presidential representative deciding his own activities: Viktor Kazantsev therefore decided to devote himself to Chechnya; Sergey Kiriyenko concentrated on harmonising the constitutions of the republics in his district and creating a talent pool; Konstantin Pulikovskiy engaged in a power struggle with Governor Yevgeniy Nazdratenko of Primorskiy *kray*; Petr Latyshev was in conflict with the Governor of Sverdlovsk Region, Eduard Rossel, over personnel, economic and political issues.

The process of legal harmonisation was performed mainly by the Prosecutor-General's Office and the Ministry of Justice rather than by the presidential representatives, who often complicated the task, as Rakhimov's comments below make clear (see p. 31). The role of the presidential representatives in co-ordinating the activity of federal structures in the districts could indeed cause conflict with federal ministries, as it undermines the vertical chain of command in these ministries. Furthermore, the demand of the presidential representatives to have some say in the allocation of the federal budget in their districts also brings them into conflict with the Russian government. Their objective of monitoring the implementation of federal policy in their respective districts often results in them usurping the functions of the regional governments, which causes conflicts. The vagueness of their remit resulted in December 2000 in their seeking an expansion of their powers, which Putin has so far rejected.

Legal harmonisation may be seen as the main success of Putin's reforms, although it would be premature to speak of a unified legal space in the Russian Federation. The parliamentary elections in Adygeya in March 2001 were based on an electoral law that violated federal law and had been declared unacceptable by the Supreme Court, yet the federal centre did nothing to enforce the law. The Tatarstan and Bashkortostan constitutions still contain clauses on state sovereignty that have been declared to be in violation of federal law. It is an exaggeration to claim that the federal centre has completely established the dictatorship of law over the regions. Putin did not use the law enabling him to dismiss governors to remove Yevgeniy Nazdratenko from Primorskiy *kray*. Instead, he bought him off by offering him a position as head of the State Fisheries Committee and securing from him a promise not to participate in the new gubernatorial elections.

There is a natural desire on the part of presidential representatives to expand their power. The presidential representative of the Far Eastern Federal district, Konstantin Pulikovskiy, has called for presidential representatives to be granted controls over budget flows in their districts so they can exert greater influence on socio-economic processes.[29] He also wishes to create a council for the district in which the heads of all subjects of the district and representatives of all legislative assemblies would meet to take decisions on socio-economic programmes. Decisions adopted by this council would be binding on all subjects in their region. If realised, this would effectively make the federal district a quasi-government. In March 2001 the presidential representative of the Southern Federal District, Viktor Kazantsev, presented to Putin a five-year plan for the economic development of this district.[30] This was an ambitious plan costing around R150 billion, 10 per cent of which was to be funded by the federal government. It envisaged 600 different projects, and Kazantsev proposed that an executive committee to administer the plan be set up in Rostov-on-Don, headed by the Ministry of Economic Development. If this plan is implemented, it is difficult to see how it will not usurp some of the powers of regional leaders.

Their plans would appear to be in harmony with Putin's decree of 13 May 2000, which authorises representatives to 'work out with the inter-regional economic associations the economic interaction of the subjects of the federation and socio-economic programmes for their subjects ... and ... to take part in the work of organs of state power of subjects in their federal district, including also organs of local government'. It would appear, however, that parts of this decree may mean that the presidential representatives are intruding upon the work of regional governments.

Both Kazantsev's and Pulikovskiy's plans would appear to give their federal districts quasi-governmental powers. If this trend is repeated elsewhere, then the federal districts will effectively replace the subjects of the federation as the basic federal units. Such a measure would require changes to the Constitution.

Opposition to the reforms

Most regional leaderships have gone along with Putin's reforms. There was little opposition to the creation of the seven federal districts. There was more opposition to the plans to remove governors and regional parliamentary chairmen from the Federation Council, but this was eventually accepted. The most articulate opponent of the process has been Nikolay Fedorov, president of Chuvashia. Fedorov has always been one of the most outspoken regional leaders. In 1995 he was extremely critical of the Yeltsin leadership's decision to use force against Chechnya. In 2000 he asked the Constitutional Court to rule on the constitutionality of Putin's decision to create the seven federal districts and reform the Federation Council. He wrote on this issue in *Nezavisimaya Gazeta* in October 2000, where he criticised these measures as unconstitutional.[31] He also said the reforms were creating unaccountable organs of power that would only strengthen the power of the Kremlin bureaucracy. He feared that this would heighten the danger of dictatorship and could provoke separatism rather than weaken it. The Constitutional Court has yet to issue a ruling. However, the very existence of these districts may contradict Article 5 of the 1993 Constitution, which states that 'the Russian Federation shall consist of republics, territories, regions, federal cities, an autonomous region and autonomous areas which are equal subjects of the Russian Federation'. There is no mention of federal districts in this article and Putin's decree of 13 May 2000 may therefore be unconstitutional.

Another notable critic of Putin's measures has been the president of Bashkortostan, Murtaza Rakhimov. He has criticised Putin for inadequate attention to nationalities policy and is deeply critical of the creation of the seven federal districts. He sees them as bringing no benefit.[32] He has commented somewhat dismissively on the work of Sergey Kiriyenko, the presidential representative in the Volga-Urals district. Rakhimov argues that the federal districts are superfluous and that all tasks should be resolved by the president and government. He noted that when Bashkortostan amended its constitution to bring it into line with the federal constitution this was done by direct contact between the federal and Bashkortostan leaderships, and a special conciliation commission was set up to carry out this work in accordance with Article 85 of the federal constitution. The commission's work was approved by the presidential administration and then the presidential representative's team interfered in the process, creating extra unnecessary work.

Tatarstan's president, Mintimir Shaymiyev, was also critical, and it was therefore no surprise that his report for the State Council on demarcation of powers was unacceptable to the centre, although he was less outspoken than Rakhimov. He argued that the institution of presidential representatives was not the only means of ensuring effective central control.[33] He advocated instead the creation of a special structure attached to the federal president, which would consist of officials from regional governments, parliaments and industry, to perform the functions that are currently performed by the presidential representatives. Each structure would be in charge of two or three subjects. He argued that it would always be difficult for presidential representatives to perform their functions, as federal ministries would be reluctant to concede any of their own functions to them.

The position of the governors

Although the removal of governors from the Federation Council deprives them of legal immunity and means that they can no longer directly partici- pate in law-making at the federal level, it is not clear how damaging the reform is to them. As governors can appoint a representative from the regional executive to sit on the Federation Council it may be argued that the reforms will make little difference. Nevertheless, a major plus for Putin must be noted: the absence of major regional leaders from the Federation Council deprives anti-Putin leaders (and possible contenders for the presidency) of a presence in the national legislature, and hence of an important national plat- form. Their replacement by relative nonentities may make the Federation Council more manageable. Many of the new members are Moscow-based individuals who have stronger ties to the Kremlin than to the regions they represent. Putin is thus creating a more submissive upper chamber.

A pro-Putin group, *Federatsiya*, has been formed in the Federation Council, consisting of more than 100 members (out of a total of 188), and this gives the president an important pillar of support in the upper house.[34] As the Federation Council has the final decision in any attempt to impeach the president, the loyalty of this body to the president is important. The Federation Council may become a more efficient legislative body, in that its new representatives can meet more frequently. Under the old system gover- nors/presidents and parliamentary chairmen obviously had to spend most of the time in their respective subjects fulfilling their functions there. Under the new system Federation Council members will be able to spend more time in Moscow and devote more time to considering federal legislation. Putin will thus have an upper chamber that is both more efficient (in that it can meet more frequently) and more obedient. While this obviously benefits Putin, it is hardly conducive to the development of a healthy system of checks and balances.

The impression has been created that centrifugalism will be tolerated less than it was previously. This is true, and the federal government has scored another significant success by ensuring that it has greater control over the federal budget. In the 2001 federal budget 55 per cent of all tax revenue collected in Russia was assigned to the federal government, leaving 45 per cent to the regions. The 2002 budget will consist of the same proportions.[35] Prior to Putin's reforms regions controlled over 50 per cent of the tax revenue. Putin, like Yeltsin before him, is forced to enter into a constant bargaining relationship with regional leaders. However, the access of gover- nors to the president is now reduced, and presumably attempts to lobby the centre are now likely to proceed more through the presidential representa- tives than directly to the federal centre. This may make it easier for the centre to ensure adherence to federal laws and policy.

Thirty-five gubernatorial elections took place in late 2000 and early 2001, in which twenty governors were re-elected.[36] In another two regions the named successors of retiring governors were elected. In a further nine regions governors who had been elected in 1996 held pre-term elections and were re-elected. In thirty-one cases out of thirty-five, therefore, the party of power secured re-election. This has been seen as an indication of the Kremlin's lack of success in using these elections to install pro-Putin governors. It has been speculated that the dismissal of Sergey Samoylov, the former head of the presidential administration's territorial department, was because of his failure to secure more victories for pro-Putin candidates in the regions.[37]

Governors are still often the masters of their house in their own regions, and those who have formed alliances with local business interests are usually extremely powerful and difficult to dislodge from power. The only alternative for Putin would be to abolish elected governors and have them appointed by the president. A bill proposing this was presented by the Yedinstvo deputy, Viktor Lednik, in the State Duma in February 2001, but was defeated on its first reading.[38] Mikhail Prusak, the governor of Novgorod *oblast*, made the same proposal in May 2001.[39] It is highly unlikely that Putin would perform a volte-face and introduce such a measure, as it would be extremely damaging to his own image if he were seen to be attempting to abolish democracy at the regional level. Depriving regional electors of the right to choose their own governors would risk creating serious dissatisfaction, thus in fact weakening the centre's authority. The Kremlin may secure a victory if the draft law forbidding regional governors from running for more than two terms is eventually accepted by the Federation Council, as this would obviously limit the ability of an individual governor to stand up to the federal leadership.[40]

Conclusions

Putin has made the curbing of centrifugalist tendencies in centre–regional relations a major objective of his presidency. The measures introduced since May 2000 have set about enhancing the power of the federal centre over the regions in order to ensure the primacy of federal law over the laws of republics and regions. This aims at the creation of a single legal space within the Russian Federation. The federal leadership feels that effective economic reform can only be implemented if such a legal space is created.

The measures implemented by Putin have downgraded the powers of the regional leaders. The creation of the seven federal districts and the appointment of presidential representatives accountable only to the federal president were meant to ensure that federal policy would be carried out in the regions and that regional leaders would not hinder its implementation. The reforms of the Federation Council and the passing of a law empowering the president to dismiss governors further enhanced the power of the federal centre.

However, it is not clear that these reforms have succeeded in creating a single legal space throughout the Russian Federation. It is debatable whether regional leaders are any more submissive towards the centre than they were before May 2000. It is difficult to imagine a regional leader with strong local support, such as Mintimir Shaymiyev in Tatarstan or Murtaza Rakhimov in Bashkortostan, ever submitting to the federal centre on issues they considered vital for their republics.

The regional elections of 2000–1 appear to signify a strengthening of gubernatorial regimes, and Putin will have to deal with governors by the usual process of bargaining that existed under his predecessor. It is unlikely that there will be any change to the status quo. The only way to ensure more submissive governors would be to appoint governors instead of having them elected, or for the Kremlin to engage in more blatant attempts to influence the outcome of gubernatorial elections. Both would be highly controversial and damaging to Putin's image. Such moves would therefore be more trouble than they were worth.

The removal of governors from the Federation Council is a major plus for Putin, in that it deprives them of representation at the federal level and so deprives them of a platform. This will make it more difficult for governors to develop a national profile, and thus it will be more difficult for any governor with ambitions to run in a federal presidential election and challenge Putin. It may be to Putin's advantage to have a lower-profile and possibly more pliable Federation Council, but it undermines the development of the Federal Assembly as an effective check on the executive. It has been suggested that the Federation Council should have directly elected members like the US Senate.[41] This should in theory ensure a democratically elected upper chamber with regional representatives. Putin is likely to oppose this for the reason that he obviously desires a low-profile lower chamber that is unlikely to be a forum for opposition. An elected chamber would not be low profile, and elected members with a popular mandate would be able to use the Federation Council as a platform for self-promotion. Such an upper chamber would be less submissive to the president. Some members would probably use their position on the Federation Council to run for the presidency. It is true that Putin does have to contend with a directly elected State Duma, and this chamber enables opposition politicians to develop a national profile. Previous presidential contenders Gennadiy Zyuganov, Grigoriy Yavlinskiy and Vladimir Zhirinovskiy are all Duma deputies. Yeltsin often had a stormy relationship with the State Duma, which was then dominated by opposition forces. It would probably be politically impossible for Putin to introduce constitutional reform that would create a non-elected State Duma.[42] It would seem he has no choice other than to live with a directly elected State Duma, and with the possibility that deputies could emerge with the stature to challenge him for the presidency. As the State Duma elected in December 1999 contains a substantial number of pro-Kremlin deputies, this is so far only a theoretical problem for Putin.

The problems of developing a more harmonious centre–regional relationship where a single legal space can be created and exist in fact as well as in theory may be partly due to the fact that the Russian Federation has so many subjects within its federation. Eighty-nine is an extremely large number of federal units. The USA, which has a bigger population than the Russian Federation, comprises only fifty states. Canada, whose population is admittedly much smaller (31.28 million) but whose area is almost two-thirds that of the Russian Federation, has only thirteen federal units (ten provinces and three territories). Brazil, with a population of almost 173 million and an area just under half that of the Russian Federation, has twenty-six states and one federal district. It would therefore make sense to reduce the number of subjects. The Kemerovo governor, Aman Tuleyev, has proposed that the number be reduced to thirty-five, and the leader of the Narodnyy Deputat faction in the State Duma, Gennadiy Raykov, to twelve or fifteen.[43]

There are eleven officially designated economic regions in the Russian Federation, and logically one could perhaps use either these regions or the seven federal districts created in May 2000 as the constituent units of a federal system.[44] While this may be logical in theory it would require the merging of various subjects of the Russian Federation, and hence require democratically elected politicians to give up their power voluntarily. It is thus difficult to see such a change happening, and the most likely prognosis is for the continuation of the status quo in centre–regional relations, with the president engaged in a constant bargaining game with regional leaderships, even though this bargaining process is now mediated through the presidential representatives.

Notes

1 For Yeltsin's statements in Tatarstan and Bashkortostan, see the references in Aron (2000: 393).
2 A subject (*subyekt*) is the generic term for the eighty-nine federal units of the Russian Federation. It therefore covers the terms republic, *oblast*, *kray*, federal city, autonomous *oblast* and autonomous *okrug*. Note that the chief executives of republics tend to be presidents, and the chief executives of other subjects tend to be governors. At the subject level, therefore, the terms president and governor are synonymous. For the purposes of analytical convenience, the terms subject and region are synonymous in this chapter.
3 See Herd (1999: 259–69). See also the reply to Herd by Alexseev (2001: 101–6) and Herd's response (*ibid.*: 107–12).
4 Huntington (1969: 1; cited in Huskey 2001b: 95).
5 'Russia on the Threshold of the Millennium', in Putin (2000: 215–6).
6 Solnick (2000a: 137; cited in Huskey 2001b: 96). For a disussion of Putin's attempts to rebuild Russian statehood, see also the policy memoranda by Gelman (2000a) (no. 146) and Stephen Hanson (2000) (no. 148) from the Harvard University Program on New Approaches to Russian Security (PONARS) website, at http://www.fas.harvard.edu/ponars/memos.html.
7 *BBC Summary of World Broadcasts*, SU/3888, 10 July 2000.
8 Yekaterina Grigoryeva and Olga Tropkina, 'They Want to Take Back Sovereignty, Which Was Yeltsin's Gift to the Regions', *Nezavisimaya Gazeta*, 4

February 2000; and Kirill Travin, '"Dictatorship of Law" for the regions', *Nezavisimaya Gazeta*, 11 February 2000.

9 *BBC Summary of World Broadcasts*, SU/3777, 1 March 2000; and SU/3790, 16 March 2000.

10 Sergey Pravosudov, 'Six Means to Limit the Power of Governors', *Nezavisimaya Gazeta*, 18 March 2000.

11 Yuriy Danilov, 'It Is Necessary in the Final Analysis, to Think of the Interests of Russia', *Nezavisimaya Gazeta*, 4 May 2000.

12 For a comprehensive coverage of Putin's reforms of centre–regional relations, see Hyde (2001: 719–43). (See also Huskey 2001a; Evangelista 2000; Petrov 2000; and Solnick 2000b.)

13 For the text of the decree, see *Rossiyskaya Gazeta*, 16 May 2000.

14 Huskey 1999: 192.

15 Marina Kalashnikova, 'The Centre Prepares to Tame the Regions', *Nezavisimaya Gazeta*, 12 April 2000.

16 See the text of Yeltsin's decree of 9 July 1999 in *Rossiyskaya Gazeta*, 16 July 1997, and the discussion in Huskey (1999: 194–5). Nikolai Petrov argues that the measures taken by Putin in 2000 to reform centre–regional relations had long been discussed during the Yeltsin presidency (see Nikolai Petrov, 'Consolidating the Centralized State, Weakening Democracy and the Federal System', in *Russian Regional Report*, vol. 6, no. 23, 19 June 2001).

17 *BBC Summary of World Broadcasts*, SU/3844, 19 May 2000.

18 See Chapter Five of the 1993 Russian Constitution.

19 See the text of the law in *Rossiyskaya Gazeta*, 1 August 2000, and the discussion in Solnick (2000b).

20 *BBC Summary of World Broadcasts*, SU/3856, 2 June 2000.

21 *BBC Summary of World Broadcasts*, SU/3888, 10 July 2000.

22 *BBC Summary of World Broadcasts*, SU/41781, 1 June 2001.

23 *BBC Summary of World Broadcasts*, SU/4197, 27 June 2001.

24 Olga Tropkina, 'The Useless Initiative of the Volga Governors', *Nezavisimaya Gazeta*, 10 July 2001.

25 See the following articles by Lyudmila Romanova: 'Governors Call for a Meeting with the Kremlin', *Nezavisimaya Gazeta*, 24 May 2000; 'Do the Governors Want to Change the Basic Law?', *Nezavisimaya Gazeta*, 31 May 2000; and 'The Kremlin Concedes a State Council to the Governors', *Nezavisimaya Gazeta*, 12 July 2000; and by Aman Tuleyev: 'Less Ambitions – More Benefits', *Nezavisimaya Gazeta*, 3 June 2000.

26 See text of the decree in *Rossiyskaya Gazeta*, 5 September 2000. See also Andrei Zakharov and Alexander Kapishin, 'The State Council in the Russian Power System', *Russia on Russia*, issue 5, June 2001, pp. 10–15.

27 The governor of Saratov *oblast*, Dmitry Ayatskov, has put forward such an argument (see *BBC Summary of World Broadcasts*, SU/4001, 18 November 2000).

28 Vladimir Ryzhkov, 'Presidential Representatives in the Federal Districts', *Russia on Russia*, issue 5, June 2001, pp. 24–30.

29 Lidiya Andrusenko, 'Career Suicide or a Precise Plan?', *Nezavisimaya Gazeta*, 29 June 2001.

30 Marina Kalashnikova, 'Kazantsev Presents His "Five Year Plan" to the President', *Nezavisimaya Gazeta*, 30 March 2001.

31 Nikolay Fedorov, 'About Dictatorship and the Law', *Nezavisimaya Gazeta*, 25 October 2000.

32 See the interview with Rakhimov, 'The President and the Government Should Resolve All Questions in Russia', *Nezavisimaya Gazeta*, 25 April 2001.

33 *Nezavisimaya Gazeta*, 1 December 2000.

34 For a discussion of the Federation Council under Putin, see Vladimir Lysenko, 'The Federation Council Fails to Become a House of Lords', *Russia on Russia*, issue 5 , June 2001, pp. 16–23.

35 *Russian Regional Report*, vol. 6, no. 20, 30 May 2001.

36 Rostislav Turovskiy, 'Strong Centre – Strong Regions?' *Nezavisimaya Gazeta Stsenarii*, no. 3, 14 March 2001.

37 Robert W. Orrtung, 'How Effective Are Putin's Federal Reforms?', *Russian Regional Report*, vol. 6, no. 11, 21 March 2001.

38 *BBC Summary of World Broadcasts*, SU/4073, 17 February 2001.

39 RIA news agency, 18 May 2001, at http://news.monitor.bbc.co.uk.

40 *BBC Summary of World Broadcasts*, SU/4121, 21 July 2001. On 14 November 2001 the Duma failed by fourteen votes to overturn the Federation Council's veto.

41 Boris Vishnevskiy, 'Should Governors be Federal Politicians?', *Nezavisimaya Gazeta*, 1 February 2000.

42 The State Duma currently consists of 450 deputies, half of whom are elected on a party list system and half of whom represent constituencies, being elected on a first past the post system.

43 Aman Tuleyev, 'The Country Is at a Turning Point', *Nezavisimaya Gazeta*, 17 March 2000; Gennadiy Raykov, '89 Subjects – Too Many', *Segodnya*, 10 August 2000.

44 See Morozova (2000: 230) for a list of the eleven economic regions.

Part II

Thematic aspects of Russian regionalism

3 Russia's demographic crisis and federal instability

Professor Graeme P. Herd

'A threat to the survival of the nation'

Russia is undergoing a demographic crisis that is unprecedented in peacetime: the population of Russia declined at comparable rates only when experiencing world wars, repression or the famine of the 1930s.[1] The dynamics of Russian demography, their causes and the consequences of changing settlement and migration patterns will have both domestic policy-making and international security implications for the Federation well into the future. Indeed, in the Russian State Duma elections of December 1999 the newly created Unity Party, which supported the prime minister, Vladimir Putin, stated: 'Unity's main goal is to extricate Russia "from the fatal logic of the development of events"'. The Unity Party elaborated a proposed blueprint for resolving the 'problem of the year 2003', when a peak in foreign debt payments will be accompanied by the 'obsolescence of fixed productive capital and demographic decline'.[2] Once elected president in 2000, Putin again raised this issue in his first address to Federal Assembly:

> Before talking about priorities and setting tasks, let me list for you the most acute problems facing our country. Population decline threatens the survival of the nation. We have come to regard Russia as a system of bodies of authority or as an economic mechanism. But Russia is first and foremost people. People who look on it as their home. Their welfare and a worthy life for them are the main tasks facing the powers that be – whoever these may be. But the fact is that our home today is far from being a comfortable one. For very many people it is still difficult to bring up children, to ensure a fitting old age for their parents – life is difficult. As each year goes by there are fewer and fewer of us citizens of Russia. For several years past the population of the country has been diminishing on average by 750,000 a year. And if we are to believe the forecasts – which are based on realistic work by people who are experts in such matters, who have devoted their entire lives to this – then in fifteen years from now there may be 22 million fewer Russians. I ask you to ponder this figure – one seventh of the country's population. If the present tendency continues there will be a threat to the survival of the

nation. We are under a real threat of becoming a drifting nation. Our demographic situation today is an alarming one.[3]

The government duly responded and in September 2000 set up a special working commission for solving the '2003 problem'. The Fatherland–All Russia faction leader Yevgeniy Primakov reported that '[t]his commission will address the strategic problems that could threaten Russia's existence as a state' and focus on the problems of demography and the erosion of basic funds in Russia.[4] Moreover, in February 2001 the prime minister, Mikhail Kasyanov, called for the creation of a concept for Russia's demographic policy in the period up to 2015 and for proposals that concentrate on combating infant deaths and accidents at work.[5] He also resolved to give assistance to Russian-speaking citizens outside Russia to return to Russia, particularly those qualified workers and experts from member-states of the Commonwealth of Independent States (CIS), and expressed the need to create a new migration policy.

However, these government initiatives and remedies are likely to have a limited impact on the implosion of the Russian population. Immigration into Russia is drying up. The State Statistics Committee (Goskomstat) reported that Russia's population decreased by 458,400, or 0.3 per cent, in the first half of 2001, to 144.4m. In the first six months of 2000 the country's population shrank by 425,400. Immigration provided only limited relief: 'The increase of the population due to migration for the first half of 2001 compensated for only 5.5 per cent of the natural decrease.' This represented the 'lowest indicator for the entire period of population decrease from 1992 to 2000. Despite the reduction of the natural decrease', the ratio

Table 3.1   International migration (per 1,000 population)

	1999	2000	2001
Arrived in the Russian Federation, total including from:	*367,105*	*350,874*	*187,413*
CIS and Baltic region	366,655	350,288	186,226
Other regions[a]	450	586	1,187
Emigrated from the Russian Federation, total including to:	*214,963*	*161,178*	*137,573*
CIS and Baltic region	129,704	83,438	62,545
Other regions[a]	85,259	77,740	75,028
Migration increase, decrease (−), total including the result of migration exchange with the countries of:	152,142	189,696	49,840
CIS and Baltic region	236,951	266,850	123,681
Other regions	−84,809	−77,154	−73,841

Note:

a   Data of the Ministry of Internal Affairs of the Russian Federation

Source: *Goskomstat Handbook*, 'Russia 2001' and 'Russia 2002'.

is 'the result of a considerable reduction (from the first half of 2000) in the migration increase' (see Table 3.1).[6]

Thus, short of an economic catastrophe in Belarus or civil wars in Ukraine or Kazakhstan and consequent mass immigration to Russia, it appears that the demographic decline will progressively worsen, by some estimates through to 2050 and 2075. The raft of security issues that such decline raises is very real. Specialists within Goskomstat have analysed the link between power and population size and argued that 'the problem is not what place the Russian Federation will be in population-wise, but what place it holds in terms of general demographic dynamics, its strategic conse-quences'.[7]

Demographic data and forecasts

Accurate demographic data are particularly poorly served by the failure by the Russian state to hold a census in 1999 – ten years after the last Soviet census. The previous census had provided a composition of the Russian population 'by age, sex, nationality, place of birth, length of residency, branch of the economy, level of education and settlement size'.[8] Although the data represented a benchmark in assessing subsequent changes in popu-lation composition, Goskomstat territorial agencies and appropriate departments in 2001 only took the first preparatory steps towards carrying out the all-Russia population census in October 2002.[9] Goskomstat is working with the Justice Ministry to come up with 'an acceptable legal formulation enabling it to submit a draft census law to the Duma, stipu-lating that it is permissible to gather information on individuals for abstract, or statistical, rather than personal purposes'.[10]

Despite these limitations, demographers have reported an observable tendency towards population decrease in Russia since 1992 (see Table 3.2). During 1992 the country's population decreased by 219,700 according to Goskomstat. Other figures show that since the collapse of the Soviet Union the population of the Russian Federation has declined as follows: from 148.3m 1992 to 145.8m in 1998; and from 144.5m in May 2001 to 144.8m in April 2002. On the basis of the trajectory established between 1992 and 2002, demographers generally agree that over the next fifteen years Russia's population profile will fall thus: to 142m by 2005; to 138m by 2010; and to 132–4m by 2015/16. Goskomstat forecasts, for example, that by the year

Table 3.2   Russia's population (as of 1 January; millions)

	2000	2001	2002
Total resident population	145.6	144.8	144.0
	106.1	105.6	105.0
	39.5	39.2	39.0

Source: *Goskomstat Handbook*, 'Russia 2001' and 'Russia 2002'

2016 the population in Russia will have fallen by 10.4m people against the beginning of 2001, and is expected to total 134.4m.[11]

According to the UN forecast the number of people in Russia in 2050 will be little more than 121m, moving Russia from seventh to fourteenth among the world's most populated countries.[12] Some assessments are even more pessimistic. Murray Feshbach, a leading US demographer, calculates that as socio-economic conditions in Russia will continue to decline, the Russian population will be 100m by 2050. Unless demographic trends improve, leading expert Nataliya Rimashevskaya, director of the Institute of Socio-economic Problems of the Population at the Russian Academy of Sciences, has argued, Russia's population could shrink by approximately 60 per cent over the next half-century: to 87m in 2025 and 55m in 2050.[13]

What is certain is that by 2015 the decline in numbers will take the Russian population into the mid-130 millions based on the known current population size of childbearing age and the fertility rate, which can be calculated against the current death rate. However, the longer-term forecasts for 2050 and especially 2075 are too distant in time to make an accurate prediction. These forecasts are based on a number of factors, not least the assumption that the current dynamics of decline will be sustained, and this is open to question over the long term. The long-range forecasts also fail to take into account the impact of any future state policy or initiative that might encourage stabilisation of or even growth in population.

Accounting for the decline: Soviet legacy v. post-Soviet transition

A number of reasons are given for the startlingly dramatic decline of Russia's population in the post-Soviet period. Many of the explanations are located in the experience of the Soviet era. President Putin, for example, in an address to the nation on the 60th anniversary of Germany's invasion of the Union of Soviet Socialist Republics (USSR), noted that: 'Even Russia's current demographic problems are largely a consequence of the war'.[14] Some academic analysts also locate the explanation in the Soviet period, arguing that Russian population growth and ageing have both been affected by the Great Patriotic War, the Civil War and the famine, producing a marked imbalance in the age–sex structure of the population.[15]

Thus an understanding of the Soviet modernisation paradigm, particularly when related to the family and society, provides a context within which contemporary demographic decline can be placed.[16] Here, a financial incentive structure within hospitals, based in part on the number of occupied beds, promoted a state-led 'abortion culture'.[17] After the Second World War, it is argued, the Soviet emphasis on economic modernisation reduced the birth rate as more women entered the workforce. Moreover, Soviet economic development stressed the importance of heavy industrialisation over consumer goods 'that helped families in other nations to manage the demands of work and home'.[18] Thus, in sparsely populated Siberia, the Far East and the north life expectancy is lower and infant mortality higher – reflecting the problems the Russian healthcare system faces in these remote areas, while they are better in the Caucasus, Volga and Black Earth regions. Working-age mortality among males in the north and northwest is higher, reflecting the prevalence of 'civilisational ills' such as cardiovascular diseases.

However, although some of the population decline can be attributed to the changing age structure of the population, falling age-specific birth rates suggest that Russia's post-Soviet economic and social difficulties are the primary causes. The end of the Cold War and post-war structural reform, systemic change and the breakdown of functional security and geopolitical space is 'reflected in the pauperisation, demoralisation of the population, accompanied by the deterioration of health and demographic indices that this entails'.[19] The mortality increase in particular has been attributed to a host of factors associated with the political and economic changes following the Soviet collapse.[20] Economic and social distress, the deterioration of the healthcare system (the free healthcare guaranteed by Article 41 of the Constitution has effectively disappeared), and growing homicide and indus-trial accident rates account for mortality increases. Moreover, as the retired population grows, the state lacks the necessary financial resources to meet their needs.

There is thus a relationship between economic reform and health status, particularly when the economic reform takes the form of shock therapy through price liberalisation, privatisation and rapid political transformation. The Institute for Social and Economic Problems of the Russian Population calculates, for example, that approximately one-third of the Russian popula-tion (50 million people) live below the poverty line. Nataliya Rimashevskaya reported that more than half of Russia's children were growing up in poor families, and as a consequence beggars, tramps and homeless children make up about 10 per cent of the population in Russian cities. The number of Russians who considered themselves poor was 1.5 times (50 per cent) higher than official indices showed, indicating that up to 60 per cent of Russian citizens had incomes lower than their idea of what was decent.[21]

These dramatic socio-economic changes occurred ahead of the develop-ment of a sustainable social protection network and have led to increased social polarisation within Russia.[22] Social capital – 'the stock of networks that are used to produce goods and services in society of which health is one example' – has also dwindled in the post-Soviet period, reinforcing a break-down in social cohesion and impacting negatively on health.[23] Urban regions in European Russia, in other words those that were most economi-cally developed, were most affected. The prerequisites for stress-related mortality were in evidence: 'high rates of labour turnover, large increases in reported crime, and more unequal distribution of household income'.[24] There is also a correlation between environmental degradation – 40 per cent of Russians live in 'environmentally dangerous conditions' – and the population decline. Mikko Vieonen, a World Health Organisation (WHO) representative in Moscow, has also drawn the link between Russia's tax regime and population decline:

> As long as a bottle of vodka costs the same as a kilo of apples, milk is more expensive than beer, and a packet of cigarettes is cheaper than chewing gum, you ought not to worry about a demographic crisis. Under such circumstances, any country would have a demographic crisis.[25]

Identifying population dynamics

Demography consists in the study of *population composition* and *population dynamics*. That is, it examines both the characteristics of a given population (size, gender/ethnic/age balance, geographical distribution, etc.) and the changes through time in the population composition, caused by fertility, mortality and immigration/emigration.[26] Population size and density have traditionally been used as one of the factors within the 'bucket of capabilities' that determines potential state power and influence in the international system.[27] Recent scholarship has stressed the dynamic, rather than static, impact of population on potential state power.[28] This 'dynamic' paradigm argues that it is not merely population size, but rather 'the interactions between population pressures and environmental degradation, mass migrations, resource depletion, forced refugee flows, ethnic conflict, hypernationalism, and urbanisation' that better determine state power and stability.[29] Let us analyse current population dynamics within the Federation (see Table 3.3).

In the Southern Federal District, Chechnya, unsurprisingly, has suffered the worst decline in population. Goskomstat released figures showing that the population of Chechnya declined by almost 50 per cent, or 505,000, in the period 1994–1999. Its population declined by 211,000, or over 25 per cent, in 1999 – the year in which the Second Chechen Campaign began and

Table 3.3   Vital statistics (per 1,000 population)

	1999	*2000*
Births	8.4	8.7
Deaths	14.7	15.3
Natural increase, decrease (–)	–6.3	–6.6
Infant mortality (infant deaths under 1 year per 1,000 births)	16.5	15.3
Marriages	6.3	6.2
Divorces	3.7	4.3

Source: Goskomstat

in which the republic's population decline was the greatest.[30] Chechnya, though, is exceptional and its population decline is clearly linked to warfare and the exodus of refugees into Ingushetia, Dagestan and Georgia. A better guide to explaining the prevalence of population decline is to analyse the three major positive and negative factors that influence population size and growth: births and deaths, immigration and emigration, acquisition and loss of territory and its peoples.[31]

According to the prime minister, Mikhail Kasyanov, to maintain the population at its present levels every family in Russia needs to have 2.3 children.[32] In 1987 Russian maternity clinics registered 2.5m newborn, by 1999 1.2m, and by 2010 it is calculated there will be as few as 600,000.[33] The number of children under 16 has decreased by 3 million, or 10 per cent, and the number of children under 6 years old has decreased by 4 million, or 35 per cent. There are 33 million children in Russia, according to the press service of the Russian Children's Foundation; 600,000 of these youngsters are disabled, and of these 30,000 are orphans and so are being raised in orphanages. Other statistics note that nearly 700,000 children are brought up in boarding schools and children's care centres, and at least one-tenth of them have no parents.[34] The Institute of Gynaecology, Perinatology and Maternity reports that 2.3m abortions are registered in Russia every year and 10 per cent of women are left infertile by abortion. There are only twelve specialist centres in the Russian Federation where female fertility can be treated, and as *in vitro* fertilisation can cost up to US$5,000 this option is open to only a few.[35]

In twenty-seven regions of Russia death rates exceed birth rates by two to three times, although a slight increase in birth rates from 8.3 to 8.7 per 100,000 people was reported in 2000 against the 1999 birth statistics. The overall death rate grew steadily from 1991, peaking in 1994 then gradually abating. This reflects the well-publicised increase in male (and, less markedly, female) mortality during the first half of the 1990s. In a health statistics report released by Academician Oleg Shenin at a meeting of the board of the Russian Health Ministry in August 2001, it was noted that particularly high death rates have been registered among the economically active population. A pressing demographic problem is thus the high premature death rate – in 1999 27 per cent (500,000) of all deaths consisted of able-bodied Russians of working age.[36] Renowned Russian haematologist Andrey Vorobyev, Fellow of the Medical Science Academy, argues that widespread alcoholism and smoking have led to a rise in cancer and heart disease.[37] The survival rates of the 400,000 Russians who contract cancer each year, for example, is 30–40 per cent (compared to 60 per cent in the US), mainly due to late diagnosis.[38]

This has resulted in a negative natural increase. In 2000 1.23m babies were born – but to maintain normal reproduction of the population Russia needs another 750,000 babies over and above that every year. The combination of the two preceding developments has produced annual natural decreases in Russia's population. In 2000 the population grew in only fifteen regions (mainly through internal migration). Russia has the lowest life expectancy among males for a developed country in peacetime, and the largest gap between male and female life expectancy in the world.[39] Life expectancy is currently 65 years: 72.4 years for women and 58.9 years for men.[40] As women live on average 12.5 years more than men (in developed countries the average gap is within the 6–8 years range) a gender imbalance is becoming more marked.[41] Moreover, according to Goskomstat, in 2000 the inward migration surplus only offset 6.3 per cent of the natural decrease in the population.[42]

Regional variations and population decline

Broadly speaking, in rural regions the number of old people is greater than the number of young and the population decline registered in European Russia (territories west of the Urals) is smaller, relative to the population of the northern and eastern territories of the Russian Federation. Between 1992 and 1999 demographic decline was highest in the regions of the Russian Far East – an area that covers 36 per cent of Russia's territory but holds only 5 per cent of its population – which suffered a 10.9 per cent decline in population. It is calculated that by 2016 the population of the Russian Far East, which currently stands at 7.168m, will continue its fall, to 6.284m, representing a 12 per cent drop.[43] Relative to the eastern territories, the decline of Russia's northern population between 1989–1998 was less, at approximately 7 per cent and this progressive decline is set to continue.[44] According to the first deputy minister of Labour and Social Development, Galina Karelova, the population of the northern territories is also expected to fall, by 12 per cent by 2016.[45] Of the sixteen federal constituent parts that comprise the Russian North, eleven are ethnic homelands of indigenous peoples, although the non-indigenous population comprises the majority.

This depopulation during a turbulent post-Soviet transition reverses the historical (Tsarist and Soviet) trend of migrants relocating from the European core to the north and east as labour/production/transport costs have risen, incentives and subsidies have been reduced or abolished and living conditions have deteriorated.[46] Studies of migration patterns in Russia have also revealed that certain groups have a higher degree of 'migratability' – that is, 'the propensity to use migration as a strategy of adaptation' is higher in some groups than others. Educated ethnic Russian migrants of working age lead the net emigration towards the European core. Semi-sovietised indigenous people, pensioners, unskilled workers and invalids who cannot effectively exploit the natural resource potential of these territories are left behind to languish in a poverty trap. In the north, for example, between 1989 and 1998 72 per cent of emigrants were Russians, 77 per cent were Slavs, while most indigenous peoples remained.[47] This promotes the effective de-Russification of the north and east.

In the European core the majority of illegal migrants (who are not resident in the Russian Far East) and intra-Russia migrants are to be found in large urban centres, such as Rostov-on-Don, Volgograd, St Petersburg and, especially, Moscow. The Moscow regional external economic affairs minister, Mikhail Amirbegishvili, quoting the Moscow Region statistics committee's data at a Moscow Regional Duma session in June 2001, argued that half of the migrants in Russia settle in Moscow and Moscow Region.[48] The capital appears to be the only constituent part of the Federation in which the death rate is not much higher than the birth rate.[49]

Mortality and fertility rates in Russia can also be differentiated according to ethnicity and religion. This ethno-religious dimension is most striking in the differing fertility rates between ethnic Slav Orthodox and Islamic (ethnic Slav or otherwise) populations on Russian territory. It is notable that those areas with the highest concentrations of Islamic religious communities have crude birth rates (rates of birth per 1,000 population) about one-quarter higher than those of other areas of Russia.[50] Moreover, the mortality rates in the areas of highest Islamic community concentrations in Russia are lower than elsewhere within the Federation.[51]

Socially significant infectious diseases such as AIDS, tuberculosis and hepatitis A, B and C have increased significantly since the mid-1990s; they are spreading rapidly and are developing a regionally specific impact. HIV prevalence levels can be used to project the number of future illnesses, deaths and orphans – the figure for deaths due to AIDS follows the HIV infection curve by several years – and it is therefore critical to assess accurately the rise of HIV in Russia. In the first half of 2000 the number of people infected with HIV in Russia rose by over 50 per cent against the previous year, and according to Nikolay Mashkilleyson, AIDS co-ordinator with the WHO, 'the HIV epidemic is developing progressively' in Russia. According to various sources, the number of people infected with HIV in Russia is between 250,000 and 700,000. By 31 August 2001, Vadim Pokrovskiy, head of the Russian Federal AIDS Prevention Centre, reported, 144,233 people infected with HIV were registered in Russia. 'If officially there are almost 150,000 people infected with HIV, their actual number, according to the calculations that are generally accepted in the world, is ten times more, and maybe even twenty times more', he said. If the current infection rate persisted, and Pokrovskiy stated that it would, 1 million Russians would be infected with HIV by the end of 2001.[52] As a result Russia has become an 'AIDS epicentre', in which Ministry of Health officials predict that 10 per cent of the Russian population could have HIV by 2005.[53]

The majority of new cases of HIV (90–5 per cent) continue to be among drug users; people with HIV reside in cities where drug use is highest. Thus Moscow, Moscow Region and Irkutsk Region account for 70 per cent of all new cases, and the Ministry of Health expects an upsurge in cities such as Samara, Ulyanovsk and Orenburg, which straddle the main Tajikistan–Kazakhstan–Russia drug route through to Western Europe.[54]

The interior minister, Boris Gryzlov, has stated that '[d]espite all the efforts on Russia's southern borders, just 5 per cent of the drugs pushed into our country are seized'.[55] The majority of those infected with HIV were registered in Moscow Region (15,595) and Moscow (12,995), then Sverdlovsk Region (10,500), Samara Region, Irkutsk Region and St Petersburg (over 8,000).[56] Boris Gryzlov addressed a conference of law-enforcement agencies in Maritime Territory in July 2001, warning:

> While just 451,000 addicts are officially registered, the actual number must be six to seven times that. What is important is that most addicts are young people aged 15 to 25. This implies that every fifth young man in Russia is an addict.[57]

Security implications of demographic decline

It has been argued that demographic change 'can cause conflict in two major ways: by directly causing increased tensions between states in a region, or by altering the domestic politics of a given state so that it becomes a security problem for its neighbours'.[58] Adopting a broader or extended concept of security to embrace economic, political and societal security issues as well as the military sector, it is clear that demographic change can also cause conflict in a third way, by exacerbating latent stresses and generating new tensions within a state. Multinational federations, such as Brazil, Nigeria, India, Indonesia, China and the Russian Federation, are particularly prone, it has been argued, to these non-traditional sources of insecurity. It has also been noted that 'demographic shifts can affect domestic politics in four ways: the creation of revolutionary states, the creation of failed states, the outbreak of ethnic warfare, and the ecological marginalisation of poorer socio-economic groups'.[59] However, within multinational federal entities, such as the Russian Federation, demographic dynamics have the ability to create all four scenarios simultaneously within one state.

Political

Although Vladimir Kontorovich has noted that 'the political implications of uneven population distribution are not well understood', it can be argued that there is a correlation between voting behaviour and the socio-economic and demographic indices of different regions.[60] As the process of economic transformation in Russia has proved highly uneven, rich and poor citizens within the Federation are geographically spread through richer and poorer regions. Some studies have analysed the spatial voting patterns of different elections by reference to underlying socio-economic traits apparent in the eighty-nine constituent parts of the Russian Federation and uncovered important spatial variations in the regional distribution of the electorate.

Clem and Craumer, for example, have argued that 'certain characteristics of the electorate in the different regions have a very consistent statistical relationship with voting preference'.[61] Their study of the March 2000 presidential election indicates that agricultural workers and pensioners, who have suffered most from shock-therapy privatisation and transition to the market economy, tend to vote for parties of the left, nationalist and anti-reform parties. Younger, white-collar and urbanised citizens more generally tend to vote for change and reform parties.

As well over 50 per cent of the registered voters that comprise the total electorate reside in twenty of the most populous regions, the political security implications of demographic change are not as important as one might at first suppose. Elections tend to be won or lost according to the voter preference in the ten most populous regions, and therefore the voting preference of the sparsely inhabited regions of the east and north are marginal to the result. The ten largest regional electorates in 1996 and 2000 were as follows: Moscow City, Moscow Region, Krasnodar *kray*, St Petersburg, Sverdlovsk and Rostov *oblast*, Bashkortostan, Nizhniy Novgorod *oblast*, Tatarstan and Chelyabinsk.[62] Moreover, a general pattern emerges in which there is higher turnout in the west and south, lower in the north and east, so compounding this differential in regional voting power. Thus, continued population decline in the north and east will not be a determining factor in Russian elections, particularly as the internal migrants will gravitate towards urban centres in the European core.

However, demographic decline, while not impacting radically on election results, does increase the politico-military security importance of sparsely populated border regions to the centre. In November 2000 the Security Council held a key conference on the defence of Russia's national interest on the state border and within border regions. The role and significance of the state border increases in significance in the overall system of ensuring Russia's security, the conference argued, as global stocks of raw hydrocarbons, drinking water and agricultural land diminish and the world's population grows.[63] Implicit within the discussion was the realisation that as Russia suffers from population decline it is clear that it faces security problems of a different order, magnitude and dynamic to other states.

Furthermore, demographic decline could lead to the gradual process of re-centralisation of state power – 'the politics of Putinism' – becoming associated with Russian ethnocentrism. Russia is a multi-ethnic state, where 128 'nationalities' (ethnic groups) constitute 18 per cent of the total population, ethnic Russians (*russkiy*) the other 82 per cent. All are citizens of Russia (*Rossiyanin*). However, the advent of the Second Chechen Campaign, the perceived threat of 'Islamic terrorism', the reduction in the sovereignty of Russia's ethnic republics have all helped re-centralise state power. Moreover, the creation of the Federal District structure, the association of state and Orthodox Church and Putin's calls for a national idea based on the 'traditional values' of Russians – patriotism, *gosudarstvennichestvo* and social solidarity – allow Putinism to become associated with Russian ethnocentrism.[64]

Indeed, in August 2001 Alexander Blokhin argued that no ethnic group that does not form a majority in a compact territory should have territorial autonomy; rather, these groups should enjoy extraterritorial cultural autonomy. Under this proposed system, they 'would be candidates for dissolution and inclusion in larger, non-ethnically based federal units'.[65] This would mean that only six of the twenty-two ethnically based federal units would survive the cull, and this would increase tension between Russian and non-Russian constituent parts of the Federation. If this phenomenon emerges, then the variable geometry of demographic decline (migration from ethnic republics on the periphery to the European core, and differential Slav/non-Slav birth and death rates) will exacerbate such initiatives. This in turn will further promote political tensions, grievances and insecurity.

This risk is particularly relevant in view of Russia's Muslim minority, an extremely controversial topic of debate in Russia. In the late Soviet period Muslims constituted 40 per cent of the total population of the USSR and were projected to cross the 50 per cent threshold by 2005. A more accurate figure for the number of Russian Muslims will be revealed by the 2002 census, but it is currently estimated that their number is between 20 million and 30 million, approximately 15–20 per cent of the Federation's total population. Dmitri Glinski-Vassiliev has argued that the state imposition of Orthodoxy and political uniformity from above and an increasing assertiveness in Islamic society from below will exacerbate the current political asymmetry between the size of Russia's Muslim minority and its representation in the national elite. This in turn could encourage 'radicalism and the use of undemocratic means in political struggle on the part of Russia's Muslims'.[66] In the current context of a war against Chechnya and Russia's part in an international coalition against terrorism, this would have international repercussions.[67]

Military

The Russian military has been contracting since the early 1990s. The number of men aged 17–19 will reduce from 3.46m in 2000 to 1.99m in 2016. By 2001 Russia was unable to conscript 350,000 18-year-old men for military service, around 30 per cent of the available pool; approximately one-third had their service deferred for health reasons (ill health/body-weight deficiency), one-third were alcoholics or drug addicts, 15 per cent had criminal records and 50 per cent had failed to complete secondary education. By 2016 annual conscription requirements will be reduced to around 300,000, representing nearly half the available 18-year-old men. Given socio-economic and health indicators, it is likely that Russia will struggle to conscript 15 per cent of this number.[68]

To take an example from a single region: Anatoliy Baturin, Sverdlovsk Region's military commissar, is forecasting a sharp fall in the number of conscripts healthy enough to serve in the army, and expected the region to supply almost 1,000 conscripts fewer than in autumn 2000, due to demographic and health factors. Because of the poor health of the youth, the Sverdlovsk authorities have suggested that the Defence Ministry change the call-up age from 18 to 19. This will not alter the demographics, however. Whereas in the late 1980s 90 per cent were deemed fit, the figure is now around 60 per cent, with military enlistment offices reporting a sharp increase (90 per cent) in the number of drug users. Thus, whereas in the early 1990s the Sverdlovsk Region could supply up to 20,000 conscripts, in 2001 the figure was slightly above 10,000.[69]

Thus demographic factors will largely shape the nature, pace and direction of military reform in the conventional forces. Demographic change will force the Russian military to accept a radical downsizing. Marshal Igor Sergeyev stated that 'the demographic slump will probably meet its peak in 2015', implying that Russia would effectively end mass conscription and move by default to the creation of a professional army.[70] That the Russian population is declining is not in itself a direct cause of concern for Russian military planners, in that the force structure and composition can be adapted to meet the new demographic dynamics, even if this adaptation occurs through default rather than design. Indeed, the 'Revolution in Military Affairs' embraces low-number, high-capital-expenditure armies: 'The enormous investments required to equip and train first-class units will make it very difficult for even populous states to maintain large force structures.'[71] However, as the projected 'dependency ratio' between the able-bodied and the ageing population increases after 2006–10 there are clear resource and finance implications for future levels of gross domestic product (GDP) and affordable military spending for the Russian Federation. In short, the greater the state resources directed towards Russian pensioners, the less the state revenue available for military expenditure.

Moreover, the downsizing of Russia's armed forces has the unintended consequence of reinforcing internal migration patterns. For many communities the presence of large armed formations acts as a magnet for other networks and industries. The reduction in military forces, a feature of the 1990s and early 2000s, has been particularly acute, for example, in the Far Eastern Military District and has contributed to the reduction in the population as employment opportunities related to the military have diminished. Between 1989 and 1997 ground forces shrank from 24 to 10 armoured and motorised divisions, 120 submarines to 43, and 77 surface ships to 45.[72]

On the basis of this example, it could be hypothesised that military reductions might in turn reduce populations in peripheral regions below recoverable levels. As the armed forces reduce their size the likelihood that populations in peripheral communities will migrate to European Russia increases. This in turn increases the necessity for the state to deploy troops to defend these peripheral and further depopulated regions, but at the same time renders this task more difficult. One analyst, aware of the population differentials on the Russo-Chinese border (1:15–20) has even suggested that:

> Perceptions of low Russian population densities in the Russian Far East could lead to low-level Chinese probes and low intensity conflict in the next 10–20 years, but the continued existence of a substantial Russian nuclear arsenal will probably prevent the Chinese from seriously considering the option of launching a conventional military campaign to seize large parts of Russian territory as a result of demographic factors.[73]

Economic

The economic consequences of population decline are critical to Russia's ability to modernise through the twenty-first century. That the population is declining is predicted and to an extent can be factored into long-term economic planning, but the nature of the decline – who dies and when – is more unpredictable and non-linear, and this has economic costs. Demographic decline impacts on 'capacity deepening' among the labour force (building on existing skills in order to increase productivity), and the reduction in savings and thus rates of investment reinforces the decline in economic growth.

Russia faces the problem of widespread elderly poverty, as the social safety net does not receive the financial resources to keep it viable, despite the fact that some men relieve the state of the necessity of paying pensions, with life expectancy at 58 years old on average. Government plans to launch a fifty-year pension reform were announced by the prime minister, Mikhail Kasyanov. He noted that planned reform should take account of the country's current and expected future demographic situation and also its economic situation.[74] Kasyanov was responding to the inadequacy of a Russian pension system 'designed for an age structure of a population of a nation that no longer exists, where population pressures would not have been great, but whose pension mandates cannot now be easily changed.'[75]

As the population of Russia will decrease by an average 1.5m annually in the period between 2002 and 2004 (to 142.2m), this will impact on Russia's economic growth (see Table 3.4). The first deputy economic development and trade minister, Ivan Materov, has argued that the demographic situation is 'an important component of the forecast' of Russia's socio-economic development in the period between 2002 and 2004. He stated that, although the average annual able-bodied population will increase from 87.9m in 2002 to 89.3m in 2004 (i.e. by 1.4m), '[t]he anticipated rates of economic growth in 2002–2004 will not cause an adequate increase of the people employed in the [Russian] economy'.[76] Thus, in the short term (2002–4) the workforce supply will continue to exceed the demand for it, and the dependency ratio – the ratio of persons not of working age ('dependants') to those of working age – will actually decrease from 42 per cent to 36 per cent of the popula-

Table 3.4 Economically active population (thousands)

	1999	*2000*	*2001*
Economically active population[a]	72,431	71,732	70,968
Males	37,649	37,159	36,846
Females	34,782	34,572	34,122
Including:			
Employed in the economy[b]	63,337	64,732	64,664
Males	32,848	33,379	33,435
Females	30,490	31,354	31,229
Unemployed, total	9,094	6,999	6,303
Males	4,801	3,781	3,411
Females	4,293	3,219	2,983
Unemployed officially registered by state employment services[c]	1,263	1,037	1,123
Males	383	322	360
Females	880	715	763
Including those receiving unemployment benefits, total	1,090	909	1,007
Males	334	285	328
Females	756	624	679

Notes:

a   In accordance with sample employment surveys at the end of November 2000.
b   Including employed at private household plots producing goods for sale.
c   In accordance with the data of the Ministry of Labour and Social Development of the Russian Federation; end of year.

Source: Goskomstat, www.gks.ru/eng

tion. This creates a small window of opportunity for the Russian government to reform the pensions system.

However, the dependency ratio will swing in the other direction by 2006–10, resulting in the diversion of greater state finance towards the elderly and less to the economy or military. According to Anatoliy Sudoplatov of the demographics faculty at Moscow State University, '[t]hese demographic trends block any attempts to raise the standard of living in Russia, because the government has to allocate such large sums of money to look after the ageing and sick population'.[77] In other words:

> Russia may face particularly acute problems in supporting its elderly when the large number of persons born in the 1950s leaves the workforce and is replaced by a much smaller number of persons born in the 1990s. Such problems may be overcome by increasing capital, and thereby productivity per worker, but contraction of the Russian economy may prevent this option.[78]

Moreover, as well as facing a shortfall in the labour reserves, Russia faces an economic security dilemma in some parts of the Federation. If moderate economic growth is recorded in the Russian Far East, for example, it is calculated that this will increase the mobility of the population and allow the current deferred migrants to leave for European Russia. It is economic stagnation that keeps emigration at current levels, and only a massive economic resurgence would return incentives, subsidies and benefits to workers in these peripheral regions, so increasing immigration.

Societal

A further security dilemma for the Russian Federation emerges. In order to maintain a constant total population over the next fifty years Russia would have to admit over 500,000 migrants every year until 2050. As a result, approximately 25 per cent 'of the Russian population would comprise migrants of the first half of the twenty-first century or their descendants'.[79] Olga Semionova, chief for demographic policy at Goskomstat has stated that Russia is interested in 'desirable migrants' who share Russian education and mentality, strongly expressing an implicit preference for migrants from the former Soviet republics.[80] However, as noted above, immigration from former Soviet Union states will only provide a partial solution to Russia's economic insecurities, namely the projected shortfall in labour reserves and thus an inability to rejuvenate economically, because it is calculated that potential immigrants from the former USSR will not be able to compensate for a more than 40 per cent manpower shortage.[81]

Thus Russia is reliant on immigration from China, Korea, Vietnam and Central Asian states. By 2050 the proportion of immigrants in the labour reserves will rise to at least 20 per cent, while 10–20 million Chinese will live in the Russian Federation. According to sociologists' forecasts, the bulk of the population in border regions in the Far East will be Chinese illegal immigrants. Zhanna Zayonchkovskaya, head of the population migration laboratory at the Russian Science Academy's Institute of Economic Forecasting, believes that by 2050 the Chinese in Russia may become the second largest ethnic group within the Federation, after ethnic Russians. They will constitute an inalienable component of the Russian workforce, capable of reviving the national sector of services, construction, municipal transport and agriculture.[82]

However, this economic dependency on primarily Chinese immigrants raises the issue of societal security within the Russian Federation, although it can be argued that Chinese immigration will be vital for Russian economic revival and security – just as were the Turks in Germany or Arabs in France in the 1950s. Immigrants from Asia (Chinese, Koreans, Vietnamese) and from the CIS, particularly Central Asia (Tajiks, Kazakhs, Kyrgyz and Uzbeks), grew up in societies which were completely different in ethnic and cultural terms. Indeed, as Alexseev has noted:

> On the one hand, cross-border exchanges improved the supply of food and consumer goods, provided jobs, increased local tax revenues, and

generated investment. On the other hand, the cross-border flow of Chinese migrants and business people gave rise to concerns about national identity and sovereignty amongst local Russians.[83]

Thus the following questions arise: will the arrival of large numbers of immigrants cause societal insecurity within the Federation and why might this occur?

A societal security dilemma can occur in independence when political and economic disenfranchisement of new minorities takes place.[84] This may be accompanied by an upsurge of nationalism among the majority society and the passing of legislation which legitimises the downgrading of minorities' political and economic rights. Within the hypothetical context of mass Chinese migration to the Russian Far East, the majority Slav and indigenous societies might perceive a potential threat to their identity through the domination of the political community by 'colonial' minorities and so adopt extreme legislation. The reinforcement of the majority society's identity would be perceived as weakening the minority Chinese society's identity, and this would generate inter-ethnic and interstate (Russo-Chinese) tension, resulting in a spiral of instability within the Russian Federation.

Thus, although migration could offer a solution, Anatoliy Vishnevskiy, the director of Moscow's Centre for Demography and Human Ecology, has argued that Russia 'is not ready for that, either economically or even psychologically'.[85] Migration as a Russian state policy to rectify population decline runs a high risk of exacerbating the problem it attempts to resolve. Societal security dilemmas and societal conflict could easily emerge, as the preconditions for frustrations are present: Russia has a constricted housing market, negative growth, a decaying infrastructure and inter-societal tensions. Migrants will become associated with high crime rates, unemployment, housing shortages and epidemics. Russia's border regions will receive a disproportionate share of the migrants despite having higher than average unemployment and lower than average wages and housing availability. This increases the importance of the societal security sector.

Moreover, given that the ethnic Russian Slav populations are declining within the Federation but that some minority peoples and nationalities – particularly in the Southern Federal District – are increasing, there is also scope for growing ethnic cleavages within the Federation arising from causes other than immigration. Paradoxically, such conflict may even arise over different strategies for population revival adopted by separate nationalities and ethnic groups within the Federation. The Council of Muftis of Russia supports the right to polygamy. They argue that compulsory monogamy, as an institution of external pressure, cannot lead to love or harmony in a marriage, but simply facilitates unofficial polygamy, allowing many social ills to flourish and women's rights to be unprotected. The chairman of the Council of Muftis of Russia, Ravil Gaynutdin, suggested that polygamy could resolve Russia's demographic problems and observed:

Russia's Muslims are citizens of a secular state. They obey secular laws but in their daily lives, their lives on Earth, they also obey the laws of the Almighty and the teachings of the religion sacred to them and that religion allows Muslims to take a second wife with the consent of the first and a third with the consent of the first and second. I think that some areas of the Russian Federation, given their specific features and the tradition and religion of the people, could combine Shari'ah law and secular legislation as was the case, for example, at the beginning of Soviet power when Muslims and the peoples of the North Caucasus were permitted to live according to Shari'ah law in combination with the authorities' secular laws. This did the state system and the country's legislation no harm whatsoever.[86]

This proposal has received limited analysis in Russia, but, within the context of a re-centralising state, President Putin has declared his intention to secure a unified legal space and standardise juridical, constitutional and political differences between the centre and periphery.[87] It is therefore extremely unlikely that it will be countenanced.

It is also argued that societal identity within Russia is increasingly coming to be defined by economic wealth. At a session of the special scientific council of the Russian Security Council Nataliya Rimashevskaya delivered a report entitled 'Analysis of Threats to the Security of Standards of Living and Provision of Social Guarantees for Russian Citizens'. She depicted the implementation of the social aspect of the economic programme of the economic development and trade minister, German Gref, as a direct threat to the state's main resource – its human potential. A recent report on obstetrical care, for example, indicated that the cost of a pregnant woman's stay in a high-comfort ward would be US$10,000 for the whole observation period, including midwifery, whereas in an ordinary ward the cost would be US$2,000–3,000. She argued that the measures envisioned by the programme would escalate the polarisation and impoverishment of a major part of the population; the nation's genetic pool would be weakened; social tensions would increase. The country would be thrown back into the past to the period of the Civil War:

> For a long time now we have not had one country for all. There is Russia of the rich and Russia of the poor, which differ greatly not only in terms of their income levels (the incomes differ by a factor of 100 or more), but also in terms of their behaviour, values and preferences. Often they know very little about each other, just as the person who never uses the subway does not know what is happening underground: what the routes, stations and passengers look like. One gets the impression the authors of the social aspect of the programme belong to the elite minority and simply do not know the country about which they write their works. Otherwise it would be hard to interpret the fact that

the main object of the future reform is some kind of average statistical citizen. This category does not exist in nature; society is layered. ... The programme does not say a word about any specific measures regarding any particular sections of society, although those kinds of measures should have been developed long ago; the only exception is the group of people with above-average incomes which, in the opinion of the authors of the programme, should be offered an infrastructure meeting its demands (casinos, restaurants, holiday centres and the like). Analysis of the socioeconomic situation demonstrates that shock therapy is absolutely unacceptable to Russia for many reasons, including the population's mentality; absolutely different measures are required.[88]

Scientists from this Institute suggested that the following measures might effectively combat the greater degree of social polarisation and impoverishment: a reduction in the difference between employees' compensation levels; a rise in the minimum wage based on subsistence level indicators; reform of the social sphere, particularly improvement of children's and young people's health; protection of the state's intellectual potential.[89] They argued that such a programme could only be financed through economic growth, which could only be achieved through mass immigration. If it is to reduce intra-societal polarisation within Russia – particularly European Russia – the state risks an increase in inter-societal tensions and stresses at the periphery – that is, the Russian Far East and Siberia.

Demography as destiny?

Russia's demographic decline both reflects and reinforces other structural, systemic and functional transformations that occurred at the end of the Cold War. For this reason, analysts of Russian regional development should be encouraged to study the implications of Russia's demographic transformation. It represents a threat that cuts across each of the security sectors and the hard/soft security divide, and it demands a coherent, consistently applied strategic plan to contain then reverse its trajectory. If population size has traditionally been used as one of the determinants of state power, then the protection and sustainability of the population is a litmus test for the effectiveness of a state. The larger a population, the larger the territory, the stronger the economy and the more effective its military power. Russia's demographic decline indicates that Russia will have to adjust its 'Great Power' foreign and security policy ambitions and refocus on domestic policy and the attendant consequences of population implosion – not least healthcare reform, pensions, internal migration and the expected ethnic, religious and societal security dilemmas.

Russia's demographic challenges can also be said to demonstrate the exercise and effectiveness of power in contemporary Russia. They have promoted responses from the centre in terms of policy initiatives designed to reverse or manage the current demographic decline and distribution of the population. The emergent demographic concept and migration policy, once formulated and implemented, will reveal the strengths, weaknesses and limitations of federal power under Putin. It will be particularly interesting to analyse the role of the Federal Districts in this respect – do they continue to be merely administrative structures or do they take on socio-economic functions as they implement these policies?

In the face of this demographic crisis, the nature of initiatives from the centre and the types of responses from the regions will shed light on the nature of state power in the new century. Will Russian demographic decline elicit more rhetorical than practical responses from the state? It is possible that policies might only emerge in a piecemeal fashion, be applied in an ad hoc manner and be driven by default rather than design. Russia's ability to manage this crisis will shape stability within the Federation in a profound manner. Demographic decline challenges existing federal and sub-federal institutional structures, the coherence of Russian political culture, and exacerbates latent social stresses and cleavages.

Notes

1 *Moskovskiy Komsomolets*, Moscow, 29 November 2000. All references to Russian media sources are taken from the BBC Monitoring Global Newsline (FSU Political and FSU Economic) online service.
2 *Segodnya*, Moscow, 7 September 2000.
3 Russia TV, Moscow, 8 July 2000.
4 Interfax news agency, Moscow, 13 September 2000.
5 Centre TV, Moscow, 15 February 2001.
6 Interfax news agency, Moscow, 20 August 2001.
7 Interfax news agency, Moscow, 5 January 2001.
8 Heleniak 1999: 159.
9 ITAR–TASS news agency, Moscow, 3 January 2001.
10 DaVanzo & Grammich 2001: 3.
11 ITAR–TASS news agency, Moscow, 7 August 2001. See also the World Bank Group, at http://devdata.worldbank.org/hnpstats/DPselection.asp.
12 Interfax news agency, Moscow, 2 January 2001.
13 Interfax news agency, Moscow, 29 May 2001.
14 Russia TV, Moscow, 22 June 2001.
15 Vassin 1996.
16 Vishnevsky 1996.
17 Rozenfeld 1996.
18 DaVanzo & Grammich 2001: 21.
19 Field 1995: 1,469; Shlapentokh 1995.
20 Rozenfeld 1996.
21 ITAR–TASS news agency, Moscow, 17 October 2000.
22 Liu *et al.* 1998.
23 Rose 2000: 1,422.
24 DaVanzo & Grammich 2001: 43.
25 Gentleman 2000: 19.
26 Nichiporuk 2000: 3.
27 Morgenthau 1967; Waltz 1979.
28 Tuchman Matthews 1989; Homer-Dixon 1991.

29 Nichiporuk 2000: 6.
30 NTV, Moscow, 2 July 2000.
31 Field 1995: 1,471.
32 Russia TV, Moscow, 9 July, 2000.
33 *Moskovskiy Komsomolets*, Moscow, 29 November 2000.
34 Interfax news agency, Moscow, 21 May 2001.
35 ITAR–TASS news agency, Moscow, 29 October 2000.
36 ITAR–TASS news agency, Moscow, 7 August 2001.
37 RIA news agency, Moscow, 24 October 2000.
38 RIA news agency, Moscow, 21 November 2000.
39 Shkolnikov & Mesle 1996.
40 ITAR–TASS news agency, Moscow, 6 June 2001.
41 Interfax news agency, Moscow, 7 March 2001. See also USW Census Bureau Population Pyramid Summary for Russia, at http://www.census.gov/cgi-bin/ipc/idbpyrs.pl?cty=RS&out=s&ymax=250.
42 Interfax news agency, Moscow, 22 June 2001.
43 Interfax news agency, Moscow, 2 January 2001.
44 Heleniak 1999: 195.
45 ITAR–TASS news agency, Moscow, 16 March 2001.
46 Kontorovich 2000: 370–1.
47 Heleniak 1999: 190.
48 RIA news agency, Moscow, 20 June 2001.
49 Russia Centre TV, Moscow, 20 October 2000.
50 DaVanzo & Grammich 2001: 43.
51 Pashintseva *et al.* 1998.
52 Interfax news agency, Moscow, 9 July 2001. Indeed, this prediction was fulfilled, as there were over 250,000 registered HIV-positive people in Russia by 2002 (Interfax news agency, Moscow, 11 April 2002). Thus, the 1 million HIV-infection barrier was breached in 2001.
53 *Segodnya*, Moscow, 22 November 2000.
54 ITAR–TASS news agency, Moscow, 27 November 2000.
55 Interfax news agency, Moscow, 17 October 2001.
56 Interfax news agency, Moscow, 1 September 2001.
57 Interfax news agency, Moscow, 28 July 2001.
58 Nichiporuk 2000: 29.
59 *Ibid.*: 39.
60 Kontorovich 2000: 380.
61 Clem and Craumer 2000: 478.
62 *Ibid.*: 469.
63 *Nezavisimaya Gazeta*, Moscow, 30 November 2000.
64 Simonsen 2000: 378.
65 Goble 2001b.
66 Glinski-Vassiliev 2001.
67 M. Smith 2001.
68 NATO 2000.
69 Russian Public TV (ORT), Moscow, 2 April 2001.
70 Russia TV, Moscow, 22 February 2001.
71 Nichiporuk 2000: 32.
72 Kontorovich 2000: 368.
73 Nichiporuk 2000: 34.
74 Interfax news agency, Moscow, 19 March 2001.
75 DaVanzo & Grammich 2001: 67.
76 Interfax news agency, Moscow, 19 April 2001.
77 Gentleman 2000: 19.

78 DaVanzo & Grammich 2001: 67.
79 *Ibid.*: 82.
80 ITAR–TASS news agency, Moscow, 20 October 2000.
81 *Izvestiya*, Moscow, 23 June 2001. As Kontorovich (2000: 375) has observed, '[i]mmigrants from ex-republics will constitute, at best, a marginal addition to the population of the Russian Far East, too small to compensate [for] intra-Russian out-migration and the natural decline'.
82 *Izvestiya*, Moscow, 23 June 2001.
83 Alexseev 2001: 2.
84 Posen 1993; Roe 1999.
85 Goble 2001a.
86 Ekho Moskvy radio, Moscow, 25 May 2001; Antonov 2000.
87 Alexseev 2001; Herd 2001.
88 *Nezavisimaya Gazeta*, Moscow, 5 August 2000.
89 *Ibid.*

4   Transborder security and regionalism

Dr Derek L. Averre

Introduction

The rapid transformation of Russia's security environment since 1991 has been driven both by internal political and economic turmoil and by external processes which the Russian government has struggled to manage. Indeed, the concept of security itself has undergone a radical re-evaluation: the Soviet state was largely able to maintain order at home and therefore saw security essentially as, first, the ability to withstand strong and hostile powers at its borders and, second, the external projection of political-military power and influence. This has been succeeded by a Russian Federation in which internal challenges to order – even the survival of the state – are, despite concerns about certain geopolitical developments, seen as crucial. Regionalism has complicated Moscow's response to these challenges.

Key developments since the early 1990s – the fragmentation of the former Soviet space and the creation of new external political borders in place of former internal administrative borders to the west and south, the enlargement of a unified economic, legal and political space in the form of the European Union (EU) to the country's northwestern borders, the emergence of multiple ethnic conflicts, leading to territorial divisions and widespread instability in the south, and the economic and demographic problems of the Russian Far East in the face of China's growing economic power – make security in Russia's border regions[1] a rich area of investigation. Too rich, indeed, to be adequately covered in such a short piece of work, particularly given the diversity of conditions across these regions. This chapter therefore aims to reflect the main trends in transborder security arrangements, the impact on the regions involved and the main problems facing the Russian government in this sphere. How do we conceptualise contemporary security challenges faced by Russia in its borderlands? How will transborder security relations develop? What is the impact of regionalism on Russia's security relations with countries and regions on its periphery?

The first section briefly considers the changing nature of the concept of security and the altered state of Russia's security environment in the context of regionalism. Following this we examine the situation in specific border regions and highlight the problems which the government of the Russian Federation faces in formulating a national security policy to deal with the diverse range of challenges in the borderlands. In the penultimate section the focus shifts to the changing nature of Russia's borders and how policy might address transborder security issues. The conclusions section addresses the subtitle of this book: is regionalism a source of weakness or strength in terms of building effective and durable transborder relations in the changing international situation?

Security challenges in the new Russia: ten years on

The ongoing changes in the security environment, shaped by major geopolitical shifts following the end of the Cold War and accelerating processes of globalisation – the attenuation of external military threats to states and the move away from confrontation to seek co-operative security arrangements in many areas of the world; the broadening of the security agenda beyond traditional, 'hard' political-military issues to include a range of non-traditional 'soft' threats and challenges; and the shift away from a state-centric emphasis on 'national security' to consider security at the individual, societal, regional or transnational level – have begun both to transform our understanding and to produce an impact at the policy level.[2] In Russia's case fundamental changes in political, economic and social life, the weakening of state capacity and evolution into a federation with a strong element of regionalism have together added to the challenge posed by the new security environment. The impact of transnational challenges – economic dislocation, environmental degradation, organised crime, mass migration, the spread of communicable diseases – has as a result been felt much more keenly. Moreover, the lack of internal cohesion has combined with a fluid and, in some subregions, unstable and conflict-ridden situation across Russian Federation national borders to feed 'traditional' security concerns over the territorial integrity and sovereignty of the state.

The Union of Soviet Socialist Republics (USSR) virtually formed, apart from limited contact with 'fraternal' socialist countries, a country apart in terms of political, economic, social and cultural exchange with the outside world. External borders were highly militarised and difficult to penetrate for most citizens; internal cohesion was maintained through rigid administrative and police controls. The Russian Federation which emerged from this could hardly have been more different. Shorn of territories on its periphery, some of which 'did not only *belong* to Russia ... they were an *integral part of it*', and where 'historically, there was no border, only the outer limit of Russia's advance',[3] it was faced with demarcating former administrative borders as national borders; these new borders became much more porous in terms of movement of people and trade. Regions in the west and south which were formerly 'internal' Soviet administrative-territorial units became new borderlands overnight, all of them without exception facing new and diverse security-related challenges, involving a range of political-military, political, economic and socio-cultural factors.

Beyond the transformed political geography of the former Soviet space, however, were fundamental changes in the international and national identity of Russia which had begun some years before the break-up of the USSR. Moscow's position *vis-à-vis* post-Cold War security arrangements was no longer founded on ideological differences and was much less inspired by purely geostrategic and territorial considerations and the projection of political-military influence. Changes in Russia's internal governance have been even more crucial. Devolution of political and economic authority to the regions – an uneven process, but one which is likely to be irreversible – has transformed the nature of the polity.

The process of self-determination has proved a painful experience, however. The cumulative impact of the changes described above – positively viewed in the West in terms both of improvements in its own security situation and of allowing Russia to open up to and benefit from globalising influences – has been widely perceived in Russia to have weakened the state and reduced its ability to manage both traditional and non-traditional security challenges. Many regions – border regions among them – are weak in terms of economic development, political resources and social cohesion. Establishing a stable periphery has so far proved impossible, while the relative openness of the country has left it vulnerable to terrorist violence, trafficking in drugs, weapons and people, and illegal migration, both as a target and a transit country.

The government has found defining its national interests a difficult task. The Russian Federation National Security Conception provides little guidance in terms of priorities and the choice of policy instruments open to it, since it represents a collegiate assessment of the full panoply of threats, risks, challenges and opportunities deriving from the state's changed security environment. The latest version of the Conception reflects Moscow's sense of insecurity; although priority appears to be given to internal challenges and threats to the state's territorial integrity from the disintegration of centralised state structures, it also emphasises threats to the state's sovereignty stemming from political-military pressure from powerful or emerging states or coalitions.[4] The potential negative consequences of such developments on Russia's status, influence and position in the world continue to drive a perception among sections of the policy elite that, as one perceptive analyst argues, '[t]he Russian Federation cannot exit from the "old empire" without risking its territorial integrity, and not just in the borderlands'.[5] While there has been substantial change in the way Russia views the world over the last generation, these concerns have occasionally surfaced and had an inhibiting effect on its foreign relations.

State-level attempts to put in place a political-military security regime in the Commonwealth of Independent States (CIS) have been fitful. Integration with Russia at the centre, originally envisaged by the 1992

Tashkent Treaty on Collective Security, which initially attracted only six out of the twelve states, has provided only a weak 'core' of attraction in security terms.[6] Cooperation under the Tashkent Treaty has been accompanied by bilateral treaties between Russia and other member states, and by multilateral arrangements involving outside countries (the Shanghai Co-operation Organisation involving Russia, Kazakhstan, Kyrgyzstan, Uzbekistan, Tajikistan and China). This rather patchy security map is explained by the outward political and economic orientation of many of the states and a reluctance to submit to Russian influence, and by the very different security issues each faces.

Security arrangements have included Russia's residual military involvement in countries of the Commonwealth of Independent States (CIS). Initially Moscow was prepared to take on responsibility for security along external CIS borders; however, only a few of the newly independent states (Belarus, Armenia, Kazakhstan, Kyrgyzstan, Tajikistan and, for a period, Georgia and Turkmenistan)[7] concluded bilateral agreements to allow deployment of Russian troops on their borders. As a result a variety of arrangements developed on CIS external borders. With the withdrawal of Russian troops from Moldova and Georgia, Russian Federation border troops are now only engaged in policing Armenian and Tajik borders and are being scaled back. Efforts are still going on to find an acceptable system of ensuring secure border controls throughout the CIS while leaving Russia with the resources to guard its own new external frontiers. Progress has been made on border co-operation with the Baltic states, Ukraine and Belarus as part of broader subregional agreements involving other European countries, but co-operation to the more unstable south is likely to continue to be limited and patchy, and it is important for Russia to secure its own borders with these countries.

Russia's border regions: security or insecurity in diversity?

The first post-Soviet decade was characterised by a highly volatile security environment, with very different sets of circumstances determining transborder relations at the various European and Asian points of Russia's periphery. In the northwest, EU enlargement means that Poland and the Baltic states are likely to join Finland within the next few years as part of the integrated European 'core'. There will be a long common border between Russia and the EU, with the Kaliningrad *oblast* becoming an exclave wholly surrounded by EU – and, in the event of Lithuania being invited to join the Alliance, NATO – territory. In the west the authoritarian and economically retrograde Belarus, currently Russia's only political ally, may in the longer term prove only slightly less of a concern than the political instability and social and economic crises afflicting Ukraine. In contrast to the relative stability of borders to the northwest and west, the troubled borderlands of the North Caucasus need little introduction. The long land border with Kazakhstan is currently stable, but some commentators see potential problems in the future; despite Russia's formal acceptance of borders with the other USSR successor states, codified in the documents which established the CIS in December 1991 and in the 1993 Russian Law On the Border, the presence of large ethnic Russian minorities might complicate transborder relations if the process of their assimilation stalls for any reason. Finally, the longer-term developmental and demographic problems of the Russian Far East, and the growing economic power of China, have led to perceptions of an altered but very real threat to the eastern borderlands.

The Russian government has put in place various political and administrative arrangements to co-ordinate policy across its forty-five border regions. A department of the Ministry of Foreign Affairs was set up in 1994 to co-ordinate federal and regional policy on foreign relations,[8] and since then offices of the Ministry of Foreign Affairs have been established in a number of border regions. Other federal agencies which also operate in the regions provide a powerful tool of federal control,[9] including some with responsibility for aspects of border security, for example the Border Troops and Customs Service. Co-ordination at the federal level of transborder links is in the hands of the Russian Federation Interdepartmental Commission for the Development of Border Co-operation. Border regions have a special legislative status at the federal level for developing overseas contacts via transborder co-operation agreements signed between Russia and several neighbouring countries.[10] In November 1998 Russia signed the 1980 European Framework Convention on border co-operation between territorial communities and authorities[11] and the Ministry of Foreign Affairs has submitted the convention for ratification in the State Duma so that it becomes part of Russian Federation legislation.[12] Finally, in February 2001 the government of the Russian Federation confirmed the Border Co-operation Agreement, which agrees to observe the European Framework Convention, lays out the division between federal and regional authority on border issues and discusses border co-operation measures.[13]

Below we discuss the current security situation in the five subregions discussed above – Russia's northwest, the European borders with Ukraine and Belarus, the North Caucasus, Kazakhstan and the Far East, each of which contains different sets of specific issues.

Russia's northwestern borders[14]

Although there have been disputes over the status of territory in Russian Karelia and the Arctic Ocean, and over demarcation of borders with Estonia and Latvia, this subregion has been substantially demilitarised since the end of the Soviet period[15] and there is little prospect of serious conflict. However, it has been the focus of political concern: the enlargement of the EU and especially NATO, and perceptions of the dividing line potentially represented by these institutions' new borders with Russia, goes to the heart of Russia's evolving relationship with mainstream Europe.

A number of initiatives put into effect since the early 1990s – in particular the Council of the Baltic Sea States (CBSS), the Council of the Barents Euro-Arctic Region (BEAR), the Arctic Council, the EU's Northern Dimension initiative and a number of Euroregions – have provided fora in which countries in northern Europe, including Russia, have come together to discuss and implement security arrangements. These subregional initiatives have largely avoided 'hard' security and instead concentrated on 'soft' security issues. Moscow has generally welcomed the opportunity for transborder co-operation; more importantly, Russia's northern and northwestern regions have played an active role in these various programmes. Some commentators have argued that a discursive framework for a kind of subregional foreign policy at the EU's external borders, a kind of loose transnational system of governance involving subnational as well as national authorities, is emerging and that this sits well with a 'Europe of regionalities' in which decision-making in the area of security governance is devolved to subregions.[16]

However, initiatives aimed at attenuating subregional territorial boundaries in the Baltic Sea subregion have tended to be overshadowed by security arrangements inspired largely by traditional state-level security concerns and centring on NATO[17] and the EU. The Common Strategy of the European Union on Russia[18] – essentially the first tentative steps towards a common European foreign and security policy for Russia – and Russia's Medium-Term (2000–10) Strategy for the Development of the Russian Federation with the European Union[19] voice a general commitment to security co-operation. These documents pledge co-operation to deal with the common 'soft' security challenges which both parties face in Europe and to lay the foundations for a closer political and security dialogue as part of an overarching framework of political, economic and social exchange. However, they are short on identifying the two sides' strategic interests and on the modalities of the political-military relationship, apart from opening up the possibility of Russia's participation in conflict-management operations. With the EU enlarging to include Poland and the Baltic states, Moscow's fear is that the line which formerly divided Western Europe and the Warsaw Pact will simply shift eastwards. Also, in the first post-Cold War decade the demands of state building and the search for national identity combined to reinforce political borders between Russia and other states in the subregion, particularly the Baltic states. Thus 'soft' initiatives in the subregion are not excluding practical decisions about enlarging security institutions and establishing 'hard' border arrangements.

A recent study by the present writer focusing on security perceptions among elites in Russia's northwestern regions[20] suggests that the threat of Russia's exclusion from Europe is not simply a geopolitical phenomenon, but also involves economic, social and cultural exchanges and the development of institutions and civil society. Indeed, concern in Russia's northwestern regions over borders appears to be linked more to subregional relations – much more important than NATO and EU enlargement is the cross-border movement of people threatened by the imposition of the Schengen *acquis*. Borders are perceived as 'contact zones' rather than boundary lines, often presenting different security challenges to those dominating the national security agenda.[21]

The impact of strategies ameliorating subregional security relations is uneven. Relations with their Baltic, Finnish and Polish neighbours are positive, but elites have little sense of inclusion in any wider project and feel that regional needs must be heeded more by both Moscow and Brussels. The economic dimension of subregional security – the regions' capacity to develop and find a niche within the larger subregional economic system – is also vital; Russia's northwestern regions share many of the challenges faced by neighbouring territories on the periphery of a prosperous 'core' Europe.

European borders: Ukraine and Belarus

Ukraine and Belarus – despite the establishment of the Russia–Belarus Union – are probably emerging as permanent sovereign states between an enlarging 'core' Europe and Russia, a 'new Eastern Europe'.[22] While these are relatively stable political borders with no major security alerts, several factors – the strategic importance of these countries to Russia in terms of a buffer separating it from NATO and of energy and transport routes, the relationship of each with European neighbours and institutions, the relatively free movement of people who for a long period of history formed part of one state, and the strong ethnic Russian representation in eastern Ukraine and Crimea – make them important and create certain new challenges for Russia to the west. This is particularly the case, as one experienced analyst argues, since 'the main threat to Ukraine's stability stems not from Russia but from its critical internal situation'.[23] Russian companies' growing business interests in the two states are also a factor likely to cause some controversy.

The Russian–Belarusian border is being de-demarcated and restored as an administrative border.[24] Since 1997 there has been a joint Russian Federation–Belarus border committee and Moscow has agreed to help equip Belarus' border with Latvia and Lithuania. However, lack of resources has meant that this has proceeded slowly, leaving loopholes for illicit trade and migration. The Treaty on Co-operation and Partnership signed by Russia and Ukraine in May 1997 and subsequently ratified by Russia in 1999 finally recognised the border and the territorial integrity of each, although, unlike Belarus, Ukraine has not agreed to integrate border controls with Russia.

Whereas Belarus is at present primarily developing a close relationship with Russia, and is alienating itself from mainstream Europe due to the political and economic orientation of the Lukashenko regime, Ukraine has its own Partnership and Co-operation Agreement with the EU and agreement with NATO, and is seeking a closer relationship with these two institutions. However, its continuing inability to make progress in political, economic and social modernisation means that relations are likely to remain transitional for some time and, like Belarus, Ukraine will remain outside the emerging European 'core'.

The troubled south

The situation on both sides of Russia's southern borders differs, in terms of immediate security challenges, from that on Russia's European borders. Weak and in some cases fragmented states in a subregion with no effective security regime in operation, ethnic divisions (there are more than thirty large ethnic 'nations' as well as a large number of smaller peoples),[25] and the influence of Islamic groups have resulted in armed conflicts and severe economic disruption. Moscow's fears of the involvement in these conflicts of major powers to the south, mainly Turkey and Iran, have hitherto not been realised, although relations between states in the subregion have sometimes been tense. However, leaky and unstable borders have made acute the 'soft' security problems of illicit movement of goods, weapons and people, and conflicts have fed a cycle of criminalisation of the economy and breakdown of governance and social order.

The lack of a cohesive strategy on the part of Russia has meant that any settlements of disputes are likely to be temporary. The subregion remains unstable and in parts ungovernable. Measures to address the challenges are being discussed at summits of the 'Caucasus Four' – Russia, Georgia, Armenia and Azerbaijan. Putin, speaking at a seminar devoted to 'peace and development in the Caucasus', has expressed hopes that this grouping will 'grow into an effective mechanism of strengthening regional coopera-tion'.[26] Politics in the Russian North Caucasus is restricted mainly to transactions between Moscow and the regions, with insufficient develop-ment at the supra- and subregional levels.

Chechnya presents Russia with its main immediate crisis, where all of the abovementioned problems coalesce and have wider repercussions for Russia's national security and, indeed, its international security role. Russia has waged its only war there to prevent the secession of part of its territory, thereby signalling its intent to defend, by force of arms and direct central control if necessary, the principle of sovereignty and territorial inviolability – a clear signal to other regions of Russia which might harbour separatist ambitions. The conflict has had a knock-on effect on relations with its newly independent neighbours to the south, with Russian attempts to seal borders with Georgia via a new visa regime. The manner of waging war and the perceived reluctance of Moscow to seek a political solution have drawn criti-cism from international institutions and called into question Russia's commitment to established international norms. For its part Moscow has identified an Islamic fundamentalist 'terrorist *internationale*' and the poten-tial geopolitical threat of an Islamic-dominated stretch of hostile territory along its southern borders.

Kazakhstan

Kazakhstan is important to Russia both by virtue of its own position – a long common border, which is still being demarcated, and an industrialised country with a large ethnic Russian minority – and as a bridge to the USSR successor states in Central Asia. Moscow does not have the resources to equip their common border fully, and so is concerned over external borders to Kazakhstan's south and east. The stability of the Central Asian states and their ability to modernise is in the longer term uncertain; if, with the exception of Tajikistan, the situation there is not immediately as critical as in the Caucasus, it presents many of the same problems to Russia in terms of both 'hard' and 'soft' security. The Russian security establishment perceives that, even though there are no common borders with the Central Asian republics, any serious deterioration there could destabilise the subregion, threaten Russia's military-strategic bases and result in a flood of refugees into the Russian south.[27] Co-operative security arrangements within the CIS Collective Security Treaty, the Shanghai Co-operation Organisation and the Conference on Co-operation and Confidence-Building Measures in Asia[28] have, despite regional rivalries and problems with establishing a far-reaching collective security regime, provided institutional channels to combat common security threats in the subregion.

Some commentators also foresee problems if the Kazakh leadership is unable to create an integrated state incorporating Kazakhs and ethnic Russians – the latter heavily represented in the north of the country and prominent in the Soviet years in important industrial centres. There is little prospect of Kazakhstan presenting an external military threat to Russia; of more concern are the prospect of internal instability there and the presence of yet another weak state vulnerable to outside influence and a source of 'soft' security threats. The prospect of international competition for oil reserves in the Caspian Sea subregion complicates the security picture in the subregion.

China and the Russian Far East

The much-improved relationship between Russia and China, which culminated in the signing of a Treaty of Good-Neighbourliness, Friendship and Co-operation in July 2001,[29] compared to that of the later Soviet period has provided a breathing space as far as security along the Far Eastern border is concerned. China's own drive towards economic and military-technical modernisation and problems with separatist movements, notably the Uighurs in Xinjiang province bordering Kazakhstan, Kyrgyzstan and Tajikistan, as well as concern over international developments – Washington's plans for national missile defence, the US strategic presence in Asia, NATO intervention in Kosovo – have demanded a co-ordinated approach with Russia on many security-related questions. These amicable relations, as most commentators agree, are not far-reaching enough to constitute the basis for a political-military alliance, however; nor are the prospects for economic co-operation on a level which would rival Russia's current trade with the EU and China's with the US and other developed countries. As one commentator concludes, '[t]he indispensable force of international capital and technology means that multilateralism focused on economic cooperation, not bilateralism centred on strategic partnership, is the logical path to regional development'.[30] The challenge facing both countries is how to balance national interests and economic interdependence with the West in order to secure advantage in the global system.

Much has been written in recent years about the long-term threat to Russia's geopolitical interests – and potentially even to its territorial integrity and sovereignty – posed by the growing military and economic power of China. This threat might still be considered valid in a part of the world where relations between states remain 'modern'; it has certainly been used by elites in the Russian Far East for their own political ends.[31] However, the main problems facing Russia there stem from internal structural factors, namely the poor economic performance of its Far East, which has been heavily oriented towards heavy and defence industry, the population decrease as people move into the European part of Russia – in many respects a microcosm of Russia's national decline – and Moscow's inability to provide solutions. A recent article argues that 'the civilisational, economic, and political nature of Russia as a Eurasian power' has been downplayed in comparison with the European element, but that

> Russia's niche in the world today and, even more important, in the future world of high technologies, economic globalisation and regionalisation can be identified in the Eurasian context ... the social-economic conception of Russia's development as a federation should take into account the Asia-Pacific factor of its economic growth.[32]

The long-term challenge of the Russian Far East is complex and difficult. Reconciling the national security policy of a weak (in terms of its ability to integrate) and remote Russian federal government with the growing demands of regional interests, as well as problems arising from demographic pressures on border regions from the numerically superior, economically more vibrant and culturally different Chinese population, present real security problems. The need for labour in the Russian Far East and closer geographical ties with Asia inevitably point to an eastern orientation; although borders have largely been demarcated, the problem of how, and how far, population and trade flows should be regulated remains. With tight border controls virtually impossible to achieve in the modern era, economic modernisation is probably the only means of averting large-scale security problems in the shape of illicit trafficking in goods and people, and possibly drugs and weapons. Development, and particularly the prospects for outside investment, however, may be threatened by subregional tensions and by the desire of Russian economic agents to retain control over regional resources.[33]

What kind of transborder security?

The complex mix of political-military, economic and socio-cultural issues, the interplay of external and internal factors involved and the very different sets of circumstances across the border regions make a systemic analysis of Russia's transborder security challenges problematic. This section attempts to conceptualise the main trends and pose some key questions.

To Russia's northwest the key dynamic is provided by the enlargement of the 'post-sovereign' pluralist European political system in the shape of the EU. Through its Northern Dimension initiative it has aimed to downplay traditional political-military factors and concentrate on integrating member states' policy on non-traditional challenges and economic and social development. This has had a positive impact on subregional security relations, and Russia's northwestern regions have been attracted by this dynamic process.[34] Schengen borders which leave Russia 'outside' are likely to be established but many elites in neighbouring countries to Russia's west are beginning to realise that, in order to be more genuinely secure, as well as opening their western borders they need to keep their eastern borders open.

It is likely that, though sections of the national elite perceive the border primarily as a marker of territorial integrity to be defended against traditional military threats and may still seek a drum to beat over NATO enlargement, Russia's western borders will become points of greater rather than lesser co-operation and subregional integration. Despite the administrative reforms designed to strengthen the link between regions and Moscow, the latter is unlikely to be able to solve problems of development and governance on its own. As the Russian economy opens up, the attraction of northwestern regions to Europe does not have to lead to their decoupling from Russia, as is often feared; a number of internal Russian regions are developing even stronger economic ties with Europe. Border relations with Ukraine and Belarus will also increasingly be shaped by this dynamic. Given their weak political and economic state these two states face many of the same problems as Karelia or Kaliningrad and are likely to remain outside the European 'core'.

Integration into 'core' European structures offers the prospect of political, economic and social stability and would help to address many contemporary security challenges, but it also raises fundamental questions. A key one is: to what extent are national elites prepared to abandon part of their national sovereignty if there are pressures from Russia's regions for integration into this 'post-sovereign' European system? Such limitations are often presented as a threat to statehood; the question is whether this threat is stronger than that posed by their inability to establish a strong political, economic and legal base.

In Russia's present stage of political development there is a clear tension between preserving and strengthening the sovereignty and integrity of the state and seeking closer integration into a broader European political community. The degree to which the regions have autonomy in matters of transborder security governance will have a great impact on how Russia's relations with Europe develop. One commentator argues that present co-operation through subregional fora focuses only on low-key issues and that in larger issues of governance 'too much is at stake for the Russian foreign policy elite to enable it to make any concessions'.[35] If there is a longer-term trend towards a foreign policy firmly based on participating in the economic, infrastructure and information networks which are transforming Europe and creating 'fragmented sovereignties, overlapping authorities, virtual networks, vanishing borders, and new regional entities',[36] rethinking security in terms of an altered conception of state sovereignty and redefining national interests accordingly will take some time.

The nature of Russian regionalism reflects this. The Russian Federation Constitution reserves matters of 'hard' security for the federal authorities, with joint jurisdiction of federal and regional authorities over many 'soft' security matters.[37] However, there is still uncertainty regarding the division of authority between the federal and regional governments in this sphere. Putin's creation of seven federal *okrugs* headed by governors reporting directly to the Kremlin, with extensive powers to oversee the regions' compliance with federal laws and presidential decrees and monitor national security interests in the regions, is aimed at ensuring greater state co-ordination of regional policy.[38] This state-centric conception of regionalism is driven by political considerations; it contrasts with the conception of region-alism prevalent in mainstream Europe, which is shaped by forces from within and outside the state and follows a political logic dominated by economics, leading to the creation of multi-layered institutional power in new subregional structures. Russian regionalism has lacked both co-ordination and a strong integrative drive at a supranational level.[39]

The picture to Russia's south is rather different. Whereas the northwestern borderlands have the prospect of integration through shared governance, the southern borderlands are threatened with disintegration through an absence of governance. While some Moscow elites are still preoccupied with a poten-tial 'modern' rivalry between major states in the subregion for influence and even territorial gain,[40] the more pressing reality is that of 'pre-modern' frag-mentation.[41] With no strong core of attraction capable of establishing rules of governance and providing substantial economic support, it is left to a combination of armed force,[42] conflict prevention/management, hard polit-ical bargaining by states in the subregion and limited outside involvement by European institutions to try to mitigate the worst effects. Russia's frag-mented southern border regions have become remote outposts acting as shock absorbers for 'soft' security threats; their prospects for modernisation are poor. Political imperatives demand that these southern borders have to be guarded against 'soft' security threats – in a sense mirroring the EU's dilemma between 'openness' and 'security' in its Schengen border policy.[43]

One experienced commentator recommends the establishment of region-wide bodies, such as a North Caucasus parliamentary assembly, which would decide wider subregional issues, including socio-economic matters – in effect a multi-level approach to governance – along with greater involvement of European institutions, especially the EU and the Organisation for Security and Co-operation in Europe (OSCE).[44] In response to appeals from leaders in the South Caucasus a Western-based team has produced a more comprehensive and ambitious framework of multi-level governance, economic, demilitarisation and peacekeeping measures which is currently under discussion. This involves trilateral EU/Russian/US sponsorship of a 'Southern Dimension' initiative paralleling the Northern Dimension, a subregional security agreement under the OSCE, a South Caucasian Community 'with long-term perspectives of integration into the EU' and a subregional trade and energy co-operation programme.[45] However, an authoritative analyst has argued that Moscow still lacks a strategy for the subregion and voiced doubts over whether it has sufficient interest in and resources for a stability pact.[46]

The Far East might appear to represent the 'hardest' borders – between two major geopolitical powers which, despite the reduction of tension, are sensitive to potential threats to their sovereignty and territorial integrity. Again, however, the nature of borders and the security issues involved have changed: 'The Russian–Chinese border can be compared to a thin membrane between two areas of very different "demographic pressure". This promises more rather than less tension between the two countries in the medium- and especially longer-term.'[47] Here traditional and non-traditional security challenges merge, and may present the most difficult problem for Russia in the next generation or two. It may be a propitious time to de-securitise the issue; the fact that there are few real security concerns with other major states in the region (the dispute with Japan over the Kurile islands is not proving problematic) may provide opportunities for regional co-operation. A raft of diplomatic and legal measures to ease the pressure of Chinese immigration, assimilate economic migrants and give both countries a stake in development could be a first step. However, rather than simply assimilating Chinese and other Far Eastern nationals into Russian economic life, and to forestall the incorporation of parts of the Russian Far East into a Chinese sphere of influence, the long-term aim should be integration of their borderlands within a wider regional system – initially economic and subsequently political.[48]

Though much weaker than the EU, there is a developing 'core' here in the Asia-Pacific Economic Council (APEC). The Baykal Economic Forum has been established to ensure closer contacts between Russia's Far Eastern regions and APEC and similar Pacific bodies, involving government, political, business and civic organisations and dealing with questions of inter-regional and international co-operation. Its agenda is essentially developmental: energy, infrastructure, environmental and socio-economic policy.[49] In essence, it provides a formative 'Eastern Dimension', again paralleling the EU's Northern Dimension:

> [Russia] should become an organic part of Asia-Pacific economic integration and an active intellectual, economic and political participant in the multilateral quest for mutually acceptable, globally most efficient ways and mechanisms for adapting the national economies of the Asian countries and the regional economy of the [Asia-Pacific Region] as a whole to the tendencies of economic and political globalisation.[50]

Strategies in the area of fuel and energy and transport are already under discussion between countries in the region. Close economic relations are developing between southern regions in the Russian Far East and Chinese regions.[51] However, it will doubtless take a carefully considered programme of co-operation to reconcile the various regional economic interests.

'Soft' security challenges – which predominate at Russia's borders at the current time, and which exacerbate the situation in those regions beset by armed conflict threatening Russian territory – require political and economic co-operation and a commitment to stable governance rather than military means, though the latter still have a role to play. The balance between political-economic-legal and military instruments depends on an assessment of the scale of these challenges at specific points along Russia's borders: the uncontrolled flow of weapons and the movement of armed bands which have destabilised the entire North Caucasus are qualitatively different from the crime and relatively modest flow of illegal migrants across the Karelian border with Finland. Similarly, different causes of migration – for example, ethnic conflicts in Russia's south and economic needs in the Russian Far East – have different impacts and require different solutions. In any case, the involvement of regional elites as part of wider subregional co-operation to tackle these challenges is crucial.

The present security situation at Russia's southern and eastern borders raises more fundamental questions which are beyond the scope of this chapter to consider. In the globalising world can civilisational or cultural divides be overcome or at least attenuated, so that socio-economic and socio-cultural systems can be assimilated – or even integrated – into a subregional and ultimately a global system? Do economic interdependence and high rates of development automatically lead to a reduction of military force as an instrument of policy and the extension of the 'zone of democratic peace'?

Conclusions

In the first post-Soviet decade new security challenges emerged, many of them stemming from the redrawing of the political map of the former Soviet space and the process of self-determination of states and nations at the new Russia's borders. Internal Russian development was also crucial, with the transition from unitary state to a federation in which many of its *subyekts* have found a strong regional identity. These processes have not developed in isolation: in many respects there has been a distinct subregional, transborder element. These general processes continue, with different specifics in each subregion, and in many cases reflect long-term developments which will transform Russia and its relations with neighbours on its periphery.

As we enter the second decade it is clear that fundamental common challenges are emerging despite the different agenda of security problems at borders in each subregion and the different choice of policy instruments to deal with them. Of increasing importance will be, first, the establishment of effective transborder multi-level governance in which both central and regional actors play a part and, second, the addressing of economic and developmental challenges in these mostly peripheral subregions, engaging all sections of civil society. As one commentator argues:

> The challenge for Moscow is to understand these processes in terms of a "new geopolitical thinking", where economic interdependence and an international division of labor play a more significant role than tight control over the territory or national borders ... in the case of the above-mentioned border regions, geopolitics turns into something different, namely geoeconomics, global economy, and global governance.[52]

In Russia's northwest in particular there is a disjunction between 'geopolitical' national security concepts and the key security challenges facing the regions. Several years of participation in co-operative initiatives have concentrated attention on economic development, trading links, social and demographic problems, and have allowed regional elites to internalise the norms and values of governance, so that not only do they accept the legitimacy of rule deriving from political institutions and mutual economic interests, but they also establish trust based on shared experience. The government of the Russian Federation has started – including through exploratory talks with the EU – to respond to the regional needs of northwestern Russia and to consider the economic imperative in the future development of the Baltic Sea subregion. It remains to be seen how far subregional integration will develop, however.

Important challenges lie ahead for European institutions as well. Enlargement to incorporate the Baltic states into the 'zone of stability' provided by 'core' Europe implies that East–West cultural and political boundaries remain, even if prospects for renewed political-military confrontation are remote. This makes further subregional co-operation difficult. The EU faces a delicate balance between keeping borders open enough to allow economic and social flows to facilitate increasing integration, and ensuring control over cross-border trade and the illegal movement of people. There are fears that EU policy on borders, following the Treaty of Amsterdam[53] and involving Schengen-inspired visa regimes, will affect subregional actors' co-operation on a range of 'soft' security issues.[54]

Policy-related studies have argued that an enlarged EU will need to nurture existing economic and cultural links between its new member states and their eastern neighbours and ensure the adoption of more flexible visa regimes as part of a comprehensive immigration policy: a 'fortress Europe' approach undermines the broader foreign policy role of the EU and may not work in practice. Engagement with neighbouring regions in states which remain outside an enlarged EU in support of their economic development, administrative reform and political stability is imperative.[55] The alternative to wide-ranging economic co-operation and an inclusive and cohesive system of governance across the subregion may be institutional gaps where informal regimes and networks of power emerge to hinder attempts to meet new non-traditional security challenges – what one academic has termed 'the new security dilemma'.[56]

Russia's relationship with the EU, from its strategic foreign-policy and trade aspects down to subregional and transborder governance, will also be important in building positive relations with Ukraine and Belarus – promoting economic projects and pursuing joint initiatives on border regimes, minorities and the 'soft' security challenges of crime, migration and the environment. Though the south presents many of the same challenges, these have had a more substantial impact on the political, economic and social fabric of the subregion. Russia's task there is more difficult; though the help of Europe and states in the subregion may be enlisted, Moscow will have to take the lead in establishing stability and preventing further fragmentation, and may well then have to contribute heavily to subregional economic programmes. This would involve a considerable drain on political, administrative and economic resources – which some doubt that Russia possesses[57] – but may bring gain in terms of longer-term influence and a measure of genuine security. The Shanghai Co-operation Organisation may be a positive step as far as establishing stability in Central Asia is concerned.

To the east lies what some commentators consider Russia's greatest security challenge: developing the remote Far Eastern borderlands and opening them up to co-operation with China while managing demographic challenges and contributing to the development of a regional political and economic system capable of providing absolute gains for all, thereby obviating concerns with relative gains. As in the south, time and judicious use of resources will be needed to accomplish even part of the task which lies ahead.

While still occupied with its internal 'political construction site' – one academic's metaphor for the state-building process[58] – Russia, a weak federation where the influence of a range of actors has grown significantly since the early 1990s and 'spells the end of the unitary state structure',[59] is being increasingly drawn to confront the security implications of dynamic developments to its west, south and east, and to devise a flexible and long-term transborder policy. The federal government still has a strong role to play; Russia's regions still depend on the institutional support and regulatory functions of the centre, and Russia's financial resources are dominated by Moscow. However, it is becoming clear that inclusive subregional solutions – in which both Moscow and the regions play a co-ordinated role within a true federative structure – are the only viable way ahead.

Notes

1 In this chapter 'region' refers to the administrative-territorial subdivisions of the Russian Federation or, in a few cases, to a large area of the world such as the Asia-Pacific region; 'subregion' is used to denote smaller areas such as the Baltic Sea or Caucasus.

2 For an accessible account of these changes, see Croft and Terriff 2000; see also D. Averre and A. Cottey, 'Introduction: Thinking About Security in Postcommunist Europe', in Cottey and Averre 2002.

3 Trenin 2001: 23 (italics in the original), 196–7.

4 *Nezavisimoye Voyennoye Obozreniye*, no. 1, 2000: 1, 6–7. In Section III of the text, entitled 'Threats to National Security', internal threats – the state of the economy, imperfections in the system of state power and civil society, social and political polarisation, crime, terrorism – which bring with them the danger of separatism are given prominence before threats stemming from the international situation.

5 Trenin 2001: 24.

6 Recent reports have, however, assessed positively plans to assume strict military commitments, including establishing a rapid deployment force and measures to combat terrorism in Central Asia; see *Current Digest of the Post-Soviet Press*, vol. 53, no. 34, 2001: 4, and vol. 53, no. 21, 2001: 14. Russia, Armenia, Kazakhstan, Kyrgyzstan, Tajikistan and Uzbekistan were original signatories to the treaty; Azerbaijan, Belarus and Georgia subsequently joined. Azerbaijan, Georgia and Uzbekistan withdrew in 1999.

7 Trenin 2001: 119; Pain 2000.

8 Nicholson 1999: 64.

9 *Ibid.*: 41–2.

10 Makarychev 2000b: 19; Orlov 2000a: 86.

11 Orlov 2000a: 88–9, 91.

12 Avdeev 2000a: 168.

13 Text at www.ln.mid.ru/website/ns-osndoc.nsf/; see also *Diplomaticheskiy Vestnik*, no. 6, 2001: 66. The federal authorities are responsible for concluding international agreements, regulating foreign economic activity in border territories, determining customs procedures and representing Russian border interests in international organisations; there is joint federal–regional responsibility for co-ordinating international and foreign economic links of the regions and determining procedures for foreign economic activity, as well as carrying out federal programmes on border co-operation; the regions are authorised to negotiate with regions of neighbouring countries and, with the permission of the federal government, with their government bodies on border issues, as well as making proposals for foreign economic activity procedures in border regions.

14 This and later parts of the chapter draw on Averre 2001.

15 Sergounin 2001: 24–5.

16 See Joenniemi 2000; Moeller 2000; Joenniemi and Sergounin 2000; Cronberg 2000.

17 For example, NATO's Partnership for Peace (PfP) and Euro-Atlantic Partnership Council (EAPC), the NATO–Russia Permanent Joint Council and the new Nato–Russia Council; and the 1997 NATO–Ukraine agreement. Andrew Cottey

(2000: 41) notes that some subregional co-operation has been developing within the PfP and EAPC.

18 Document 1999/414/CFSP, 4 June 1999.
19 Text in *Diplomaticheskiy Vestnik*, no. 11, 1999: 20–8.
20 Averre 2001.
21 See Berg 2000.
22 Trenin 2001: 107.
23 Moshes 2001: 10.
24 See Trenin 2001: 120, 161.
25 Pain 2000: 371.
26 See *Diplomaticheskiy Vestnik*, no. 6, 2001: 126.
27 Pain 2000: 379.
28 For details of the June 2001 Shanghai Summit and the text of the joint declaration of the six states, see *Diplomaticheskiy Vestnik*, no. 7, 2001: 22–30. The organisation's members have signed a convention on combating terrorism and separatism and are discussing common responses to 'soft' security measures; see Vorobyev 2001.
29 Text and accompanying speeches in *Diplomaticheskiy Vestnik*, no. 8, 2001: 20–30.
30 Rozman 2000: 199.
31 Pavlyatenko 2000: 176.
32 Titarenko and Mikheyev 2001: 56–7.
33 For an overview, see Garnett 2000; Trenin 2001: 208–20; Titarenko and Mikheyev 2001; Pavlyatenko 2000: 157–96.
34 See the 'Vision and Strategy Around the Baltic Sea 2010' concept, in Reut 2000: 25.
35 Morozov 2001: 16.
36 Thanks to Andreas Wenger for sharing his thoughts on this.
37 See Orlov 2000a: 81.
38 Presidential decree no. 849 of 13 May 2000; *Sobraniye Zakonodatelstva*, no. 20, 2000: 4,318–24. See also *Current Digest of the Post-Soviet Press*, vol. 52, no. 20, 2000: 4.
39 Makarychev 2000b: 12.

> If, within the EU, regional policy ... [is] one of the priorities of EU activity, in the Russian Federation with its 89 subjects, so diverse in natural resource, industrial, scientific and cultural potential and in level of development, and finally in terms of geopolitical position, there has hitherto been no proper clearly formulated regional policy.
>
> (Deryabin 2000: 56)

40 Pain 2000: 369.
41 Trenin 2001: 19.
42 As military operations give way to the search for a political solution, one influential newspaper sees Chechnya being governed for the foreseeable future by a combination of federal military and local civilian authorities (I. Maskakov, 'Chechen War Demands a New Political Understanding', *Nezavisimoye Voyennoye Obozreniye*, no. 30, 2001: 1–2).
43 See Monar 2000.
44 See Tishkov 2001.
45 *A Stability Pact for the Caucasus*, Centre for European Policy Studies, Working Document No. 145, May 2000. See accompanying documents at www.ceps.be/Research/Caucasus/index.htm.
46 Baev 2001a.
47 Trenin 2001: 220.

48

> The globalized economy and politics are a challenge that prompts another stage of Asian collective security: 'security through dynamic cooperation' ... the demands of globalization have brought the [Asia-Pacific region] governments face to face with the need to submit part of national sovereignty to the regional interests, to delegate part of national authority and power to future regional institutes [*sic* – presumably institutions]. Today, few of the countries are prepared to accept these demands. It is probably unwise to force them to accept this requirement ... the situation has to ripen all by itself.
>
> (Titarenko and Mikheyev 2001: 61)

49 Titarenko and Mikheyev 2001: 66–7. The Foreign Ministry has recently organised meetings and seminars with the APEC Business Consultative Committee; see *Diplomaticheskiy Vestnik*, no. 6, 2001: 124–6.
50 Titarenko and Mikheyev 2001: 68.
51 Sergounin 2001: 31.
52 *Ibid.*: 21.
53 See Joenniemi *et al.* 2000: 20.
54 See Grabbe 2000; Bort 2000.
55 See Amato and Batt 1999; Grabbe 2000; Monar 2000.
56 See Cerny 2000.
57 Pain 2000: 396.
58 Kolsto 2000.
59 Trenin 2001: 310.

5 'Regionology' and Russian foreign policy

Identifying the theoretical alternatives

Dr Christer Pursiainen

Regionalism, or the role and development of the eighty-nine constituent parts of the Russian Federation,[1] has been one of the major themes in contemporary Russian studies. Indeed, 'regionology has emerged as a new research branch here'.[2] While a trend towards more hierarchical relations can be identified with President Putin in power, they still remain a variable to be considered both in empirical and theoretical studies and in normative debates about the ideal political system of the Russian Federation.[3]

Federalism and regional development belong to the mainstream themes of social sciences, and, consequently, theoretical and methodological debates are well developed. By contrast, it seems to be much less clear how to take the relative autonomy of the regions into account in the study of Russia's external relations. The traditional foreign policy analysis models, as well as more contemporary theories of international relations, are not usually applied explicitly when discussing Russian regions from this point of view. Consequently, in most cases the underlying theoretical and methodological assumptions remain rather implicit.

This chapter discusses three puzzles in particular. First, even when the regions are at the centre of our attention we may have several alternatives as to the basic unit and level of analysis, just as we have several alternative units and levels of analysis when discussing interstate relations and state foreign policies. Second, we face a methodological choice when discussing the action principle of the chosen actors, i.e. whether we rely on the methodological assumption of a rational actor facing external restrictions and strategic choice situations, or whether we emphasise the limits of rationality and place more emphasis on cognitive factors. Third, on the basis of the two first questions, we must ask a more empirical question, namely: what are the mechanisms, channels and factors through which the regions are supposed to affect Russian foreign policy, and do they make any difference in the first place?

Regions as instruments of a rational state

To begin with, we might understand the Russian state as a traditional 'black box' making rational foreign policy decisions and acting accordingly, at least from a methodological point of view. This would be to contend that Russian regions may or may not be important in the domestic political processes, but theoretically we would not have to go 'inside the state' in order to explain Russian foreign policy decision-making or action.

Should we want to consider empirically the role of regions in this scheme, we might understand them simply as state policy instruments in a state's rational decision-making process and foreign policy activity. At the input side of the black box of foreign policy decision-making, the regions, or their representatives, might be used by the state apparatus as a source of information in making state-level decisions. In this practical and instrumental capacity, the knowledge of regions may be most important for the centre in fulfilling the basic requirements of a state's rational decision-making, namely to define a problem or an objective on the basis of sufficient information, assess all alternative ways to realise this objective, and, finally, choose the one that seems to correspond to the objective in the best possible way. For example, in 1994 'the Ministry of Foreign Affairs set up a consultative council of constituent parts of the Russian Federation for international and economic ties'.[4] This active consultation, in order to make balanced and well-informed decisions in the field of Russian foreign policy or Russia's international economic relations, might well be interpreted in terms of the rational decision-making process described above.

Also, at the 'output' side of the state decision-making apparatus, regions may be used in one way or another as instruments in implementing the state policy. For example, a Russian region may or may not be allowed to conclude external economic and political agreements autonomously, and the Russian Federation thereby signals its foreign policy line in the question of how the nature of international relations should be institutionalised in practice.

This was the case, for example, in 1996, when Kaliningrad was transformed from a 'free economic zone' into a 'special economic zone' by the federal law. Federal oversight was thereby emphasised, which 'left little room for independent foreign relations' for Kaliningrad.[5]

Fundamentally, though, it does not matter whether the state policy is more liberal or more restrictive in relation to the regions' rights; both approaches can be regarded as indications of Russian foreign policy. The regions may be involved in the foreign policy process, but in theoretical terms the actor is the state, which uses regions as instruments or channels to fulfil its general foreign policy goals. As Russia's foreign minister, Igor Ivanov, put it:

> We wait for concrete results from cooperation between [cross-border] regions and see in it an effective channel of Russia's participation in processes of European integration and Federation components getting direct experience in building a new Europe with no dividing lines.[6]

Should we accept such a role for regions as described above, from a theoretical perspective the regions would not alter the principle of 'state as an actor', although they may be appreciated by the Russian leadership as new instruments in their foreign policy toolbox, especially in implementing Russia's declared policy towards pan-European integration with Russia as an active member of a common economic space.

Regions as interest groups

Should we give more credit to the regions as political subjects, it is quite possible to understand them as domestic interest groups. This turns our attention to Russia's political system and presupposes that the nature of a country's political system is somehow reflected in its foreign policy. It contends that we should open the black box and take a closer look at the Russian political process, and then find out how the regional interest groups can produce outcomes at the level of Russian foreign policy formation. In some analyses, the different ways in which regions attempt to affect Russia's foreign policy through the state are referred to as 'indirect methods' (as opposed to 'direct methods' more or less bypassing the state level).[7]

The claim that Russia's political system is characterised by the existence of interest groups which in turn affect (foreign) policy-making, is in itself nothing new. Until the early 1960s the only way to interpret the Soviet political system was a so-called totalitarian model, presupposing a fairly monolithic state apparatus. From the early 1960s onwards the totalitarian model was criticised for misinterpreting the whole picture of the Soviet political system. The totalitarian model was challenged by different bureaucratic models emphasising the organisational and corporative character of the Soviet system, and in the late 1960s, somewhat surprisingly, pluralistic models emerged that paid attention to the diffusion of power between different interest groups in the Soviet Union.[8]

Fairly soon, as might be expected, the conclusion was reached that Soviet interest groupings could and did exercise influence and share political power in the Soviet policy process. It was thought that during the Khrushchev period and afterwards certain specialised elite interest groups were able to express their views in a vigorous debate on public policy, as well as to exert some influence on the decisions in areas such as education, military strategy, industrial management, legal reform, science, art and literature.

Today the interest groups model has been resurrected in Russian studies, again emphasising the importance of different regional, economic, political, social and corporative elites, and other elitist interest groups. As to the question of how exactly these interest groups are supposed to affect foreign policy-making, we must not necessarily presuppose any participatory role for the regional interest groups; what is required is that the interests of the regions are somehow represented in decision-making. In their attempts to gain representation on the decision-making organs and bring their particular interests into the agenda of the state apparatus, the regions have to compete with each other and with other interest groups.

This was the case in the 1990s, when 'lobbying of the regional leaders in the central power institutions', especially on issues connected to foreign economic relations, was in many cases 'accompanied by or had to compete with lobbying activities of other interest groups'.[9] Thus the regions are seen as very traditional interest groups in foreign policy processes. In this role the regions function basically in the same way as did the military-industrial complex or other interest groups during the Soviet period in their efforts to influence foreign policy decision-making for their own benefit.

The Kaliningrad case mentioned above serves as a concrete example of this kind of pattern. As was reported in early 2001, even the status of a 'special economic zone' came under serious threat, but the local authorities were successful in defending their interests:

> [I]n January of 2001 the State Customs Committee cancelled these privileges despite the Federal Law and provoked real economic crisis in Kaliningrad when dozens of companies were soon near bankruptcy, prices increased dramatically and the population began to make dangerous declarations that Kaliningrad could be proclaimed independent. Happily, the new recently elected authorities of Kaliningrad were wise enough to appeal to the court and fight judicially for cancellation of the decree of the State Customs Committee and normalise the situation.[10]

Regions as bureaucratic institutions

Should we consider foreign policy decision-making in more participatory terms, regions could also be understood in terms of regional bureaucracies participating in the decision-making of the state apparatus and not just lobbying from outside. The upper chamber of the Parliament, the Federation Council, is composed of representatives of the legislative and executive authority of each region, and regions participate in foreign and national security policy in accordance with their constitutional rights.

Although one might claim that regional elites also played a role during the Soviet period, in some analyses it is claimed that more institutionalised regional influence on foreign policy in particular is a new phenomenon, and actually a result of post-Soviet developments:

> The political decentralisation of the Russian Federation has significantly complicated the foreign policy making process. In the Soviet system the constituent republics and regions had no part to play in the policy making process and regional leaders were unlikely to question Moscow's policy direction. Now policy makers in Moscow must be sensitive to the interests of the regions, particularly those regions that

form Russia's borders with the outside world. Increasingly foreign policy formulation involves consultation with regional authorities. Governors are now invited to joint diplomatic visits as official members of the Russian delegation. ... Regional representatives are also gaining access to discussions between the Federal Government and international organisations.[11]

Therefore we may conclude that the regions', or at least regional leaders', power and possibilities to influence national policy, presumably foreign policy included, have grown. Indeed, in one survey the newspaper *Nezavisimaya Gazeta*'s regular monthly ranking of the 100 most important political figures in Russia was considered from this point of view. It was concluded that, while in 1993, when the first ranking lists were published, regional leaders accounted for 12 per cent of the list, by 1998 it was 25 per cent.[12]

However, if we understand foreign policy-making more narrowly, we may note that the central foreign and security policy organ, the Security Council, involves members that can also be viewed as representatives of Russia's regional interests. The regions are literally represented by the chairman of the Federation Council. In principle, the presidential envoys to the seven 'super-regions' or districts, all members of the Security Council, can also be seen as representatives of their respective regional interests, even if at the same time they represent the centre in their districts. Interestingly enough, it has been claimed that Yeltsin's representatives in the regions often 'went native' and exhibited greater loyalty to the provincial leaders than to the president of Russia, being sometimes even transformed from the president's watchdogs into the governor's emissaries to Moscow.[13] While the new presidential envoys are much more independent of the governors than the Yeltsin era presidential envoys, they are at the same time much more powerful, and might become loyal to the regional interests if not to the regional leaders.

The bureaucratic politics model offers a basic mechanism of how the interests of the regions are transferred to policy in this scheme. From the viewpoint of this model, even in the system of decision-making dominated by one person – the president, as is the case in Russia – decisions are not made by that person alone, but collectively, with other surrounding high-level actors, aides and consultants. The president is to a considerable extent dependent on the behaviour of other state bodies in terms of the different kind of resources they represent, be that material resources, information, political resources and so on.

The objectives and interests of a bureaucratic actor that might have an impact on a policy or on decision-making can pertain to the national interest, organisational (in our case regional) interests or personal interests. While the general factors pertaining to the national interest can be largely accepted and shared, a dispute often arises over how one or another detail or decision influences the national interest. Accordingly, regional interests can be understood by maintaining that representatives of a region, like representatives of any bureaucratic organisation or administrative unit, are inclined to believe that it is especially their organisation's well-being that is crucial from the point of view of the national interest. The well-being of a region, in turn, is to a large extent dependent on the preservation or enhancement of its own influence and securing of necessary resources. These interests and resources, of course, are in many cases connected to a region's relations across Russia's external borders. Personal interests of a representative of a region in the field of foreign (economic) policy may in turn often make a considerable difference to how the individual interprets national or regional interests.

It is notable that if we deal with regions as bureaucracies within the system of Russian foreign policy-making, we at the same time challenge the assumption of rationality and the methodological individualism applied to a state actor in rational models. In the bureaucratic politics model the preferences of internal actors of a state compete with each other, and the materialised outcome is not rational in any traditional sense. The outcome results from the campaign of representatives of various institutions with different interests and different degrees of formal and informal power; of their compromises, bargaining, conflicts, mutual confusion, bewilderment and so on.

In this scheme the task of a researcher is, therefore, to study a state's decision-making, the rival views and interests, and lobbying processes around an issue or decision much more carefully than would be the case should one rely on the assumption of a state as a unitary rational actor. To date, however, such detailed studies on Russia's regions' foreign policy-related activities are hard to find.

Regions as individual foreign policy players

Regions can also be considered as foreign policy players in their own right, in terms of having, at least in some issues, their own policies towards the outside world. Perhaps the main impetus for scholars who have chosen Russian regions and foreign policy as their research subject in the first place is that it is relatively easy to find empirical examples of this kind of activity, the most extreme version naturally being a constituent part of the Russian Federation which openly proclaims separatism and looks for international recognition for this purpose, as Chechnya has done on several occasions.

Although the current trend appears to have turned towards a more clear-cut hierarchical relationship between the centre and the regions, some scholars tended earlier to treat regions as independent actors in the same way as states. As it was articulated in a 1999 analysis:

> After the 1995–97 wave of gubernatorial elections, the federal influence in regional politics became even more insignificant. Therefore, it seems useful in analysis of regional political regimes in Russia to treat regional entities as if they were nation-states. Within this framework, federal

authorities (as well as other actors outside a particular region) may be regarded as 'external' actors. That is, one may consider their impact on regional politics as if one were analysing the impact of international influence on national politics.[14]

However, as is the case with states in international politics, regions, even if regarded as individual foreign policy players, are also under external limitations – often parametrical or given in practical terms. This means that if the actor is to be one of Russia's constituent parts its action alternatives in the field of a foreign policy issue are constrained by many factors.

The institutional and normative structure of the Russian Federation defines the basic framework or limits of a region's foreign policy activity. As the status of Russia's constituent parts varies from region to region, this is true also in foreign policy terms.[15] There are nevertheless some restrictions common to all constituent parts – such as the absence of their own armies (perhaps with the exception of the rebellious Chechnya between the two recent wars) – that seriously limit the independent foreign policy activity of the regions.

As stated above, the centre's hold over the regions weakened sharply throughout the 1990s, and consequently the differences between regions have grown. In many cases regional constitutions placed local laws on an equal footing with federal legislation. This tendency allowed the local leaderships to ignore federal programmes. In order to establish a more hierarchical power relationship between the centre and the regions, in May 2000 the president introduced a new level of administrative policy, seven new districts (*okrugs*) headed by presidential envoys or 'general governors', who are also members of the Security Council and are supposed to represent its policy at the regional level. The situation in one of the districts, the Volga Federal District, headed by the former prime minister Sergey Kiriyenko, was described as follows before the centralising efforts were fully implemented:

> Regional laws which are not in accordance with the federal legislation were divided by Sergey Kiriyenko into several groups. The first one consists of those documents which are recognised by the regions as unconstitutional. The second group form those legal acts whose correspondence to the federal legislation is still being debated. The third group contains regional legal documents that are of better quality than their federal counterparts (for example, the Law of Tatarstan on Emergency Situations). In the fourth group Kiriyenko placed regional legislation with no analogies on the federal level.[16]

This system of seven new federal districts with their respective presidential envoys was established to ensure that the regions adhere to federal laws, while still maintaining the principle of locally elected governors. Under pressure from these envoys, the regions have already made amendments to their local laws to match the Russian Constitution and federal legislation. In another reversal of recent trends, the regions have also vowed to transfer a larger share of tax revenues to Moscow. Moreover, President Putin has succeeded in abandoning the automatic right of regional governors and presidents to a seat in Russia's upper house of the Parliament, the Federation Council, which means, among other things, that they will be deprived of legal immunity, which will thus make them more vulnerable to legal pressures from the federal centre.

In foreign policy-related literature on the subject, there are two basic tendencies as to how the regions' own foreign policy activity is to be understood or interpreted: one emphasising the self-declared freedom of the regions in their external relations and another, closer to the Russian official line, which stresses the constitutional rights and limits of the regions in evaluating their foreign policy activity.

In terms of the former, the activity of the regions is sometimes labelled as 'paradiplomatic contacts with foreign partners', including basically all kinds of transborder co-operation between neighbouring areas where a region borders a foreign state.[17] Also, those foreign policy statements and actions of regional leaders that clearly go against Russia's official foreign policy line, as well as regional leaders' own campaigns in questions related to state policy issues, have usually been interpreted as expressions of a region's relative independence in foreign policy.

Among the examples that are frequently referred to in this trend of literature are Boris Nemtsov's attack (when still a governor of Nizhniy Novgorod) against the union with Belarus; Moscow mayor Yuriy Luzhkov's active policy and diplomacy on the Crimean issue, representing a clearly more assertive line than the official Russian one, as well as his similar activity on the issue of Russian minorities in the Baltic States; and the refusal of Primorskiy *kray* governor Yevgeniy Nazdratenko to recognise the agreement on delineation of the common Russian–Chinese border.[18] Should one look at the results of these campaigns on the official Russian line, however, it is easy to conclude that they are limited.

In the literature reflecting the Russian official line, in turn, it is usually noted that the Russian Constitution of 1993 is based on a division of labour. Thus, even the regions' own foreign policy activity is not framed as an example of independent action. This division of labour is further confirmed and detailed with the 1999 federal law on co-ordination of international and foreign economic relations of the subjects of the Russian Federation. This law can be summarised as follows:

1   The Federation directs Russian foreign policy.
2   The Federation together with the subjects (regions) co-ordinates the subjects' external relations.
3   The subjects implement and preserve the external relations.

On the federal side the co-ordination is conducted by the Foreign Ministry, who, for example, between 1998 and 1999 organised 130 co-ordinative meetings with the governors and other representatives of the regions. Moreover, in about half of the regions the ministry has a local representative.[19] Also, the seven presidential envoys fulfil a co-ordinating role in their efforts to push the federal line, including that of the Security Council, through more effectively at the regional level.[20]

All in all, in practical or empirical terms the trend seems to be towards less independent regional activity in foreign policy-related issues. According to official statistics, while in 1997 there were over a hundred cases where the regions had not followed federal rules in their external relations, in 1999 there were only eleven registered cases. Also all kinds of cross-border co-operation are tightly controlled by the Federation, at least in principle.[21] The basic ideological goal here, proclaimed by the federal authorities, is an optimal balance between federal and regional interests, or the 'strong centre, strong regions' formula.[22]

Apart from the institutional constraints, the regions are also conditioned by their resources and general ranking within the Russian Federation. While some regions have large resources – whether related to financial resources, production, trade or raw materials – others have none, and consequently are much more dependent on the federal power.[23] However, when examining the statistics one notices that there is no automatic positive correlation between a region's foreign economic activity and other indicators of its socio-economic situation such as the quality of life, production and financial situation. Although in most cases there is a positive correlation, one can also find examples of the opposite.[24]

This implies that there are many factors in combination affecting the level of a region's external trade relations, and presumably also political relations. Furthermore, the degree of foreign economic *activity*, in terms of either import or export, does not reveal much about the independent foreign *policy* role of a region.

There are also geopolitical sources of behaviour affecting and conditioning a region's potential independent foreign policy role. The term 'geopolitics' usually refers to the idea that the size and location of a state influences the formation of foreign policy, particularly the opportunities available and the limitations imposed. If we accept that Russian regions do have an independent foreign policy, then these geopolitical conditions should also apply to Russian regions.

Against this background, it has been noted that Russia's regions' 'openness to the outside world' depends particularly on their geopolitical location vis-à-vis foreign countries, i.e. they are either 'inland regions', regions bordering the near-abroad former USSR countries, or they border on the 'far-abroad' countries.[25] Some researchers go beyond the mere territorial definitions by differentiating between exclusive and inclusive border regimes,[26] whereas others are even more detailed and distinguish between alienating, half-transparent, uniting and integration borders.[27]

Regions can also be considered as independent players not only under external restrictions, but also as players in a strategic choice situation. From a region's point of view this means that it is an actor in its own right, but it must assess the possible actions of others, most notably those of the centre, on the one hand, and foreign actors, on the other hand, which may call for an estimation of how others assess the actions of the actor itself. In this strategic interaction, actions are chosen both for their immediate effect and for the effect they have on the other player's choice.

Methodologically, this starting point would offer a so far unused possibility to apply sophisticated game theory or decision models to describe the strategic choice situations regions may face in the interesting triangle between them, the centre and foreign powers, and thereby make an effort to explain the choices they make.

Regions as collective identities

Identity refers to a collective set of beliefs held by a certain group of people usually sharing the same language, culture, religion, history and traditions. How is a region's identity supposed to affect Russian foreign policy?

In those texts where identities are dealt with, the basic, often implicit assumption is simple: the more the identity of a region differs from that of Russia as a whole, the more independent foreign policy the region is supposed to follow. This is the case when cultural and ethnic identity is regarded as one of the factors 'which might underpin the wish of regions to achieve more autonomy or even independence'. Focusing on northwest Russia in particular, the analysis goes further by concluding, however, that 'all the Western border regions are solidly Russian as for language, religion and culture', and, while they have some specific features, they 'rather complement the common Russian identity'.[28]

Perhaps a somewhat opposite case is found with the 'strong Muslim identification' of some southern regions of Russia, and illustrated, for instance, by the fact that in the mid-1990s Tatarstan, Bashkortostan and Kabardino-Balkariya signed bilateral agreements with Abkhazia, a rebellious region of Georgia, thereby violating the Russian Federation's international commitments.[29]

Whether this development of regional identities would be strong enough to promote Russia's disintegration into independent states or separatist movements, as in the case of Chechnya, was and to some extent remains one of the main questions of Russian studies. The non-Russian nations in particular have been the focus of attention:

> Language has been the cornerstone of Russian culture for centuries, but the re-emergence of ethnicity within Russia poses a serious challenge to

the notion of Russian identity in the future. For example, in Tatarstan Russian is still the official language and is spoken by all citizens. However, the Tatar language has gained more prominence in schools, business, and local government. Tatars have begun to identify them-selves by ethnicity first, rather than nationality. Most Tatars do not feel that they are being disloyal to the Russian state, but rather that they are returning to their culture and heritage after decades of oppression.[30]

However, apart from the clearly non-Russian republics such as the North Caucasian regions and republics, Tatarstan or Bashkortostan, Russia's disin-tegration seems to have become more questionable and unlikely on ethnic or identity-related grounds. Rather, it is emphasised that Russia is by its very nature a multi-ethnic state. As one analyst put it in 2001:

> Disintegration along the boundaries of the Russian regions, of course, is a scenario, not an option. ... The notion of a '(ethnic) Russian republic within the Russian federation', which was debated in the late 1980s and early 1990s, made the map of Russia appear like Swiss cheese. In terms of culture as well as territory, there is no such thing as an ethnically purified Russia.[31]

Another way of treating regions as collective entities with specific iden-tity-related characteristics which in their turn would condition or direct their foreign policy behaviour is to look at their political system. Some approaches to international relations theory contend that democracies are supposed to behave differently from authoritarian countries (democratic peace theory and the debates around it), and democracy is thus perceived to be a precondition for integrative developments with other democratic coun-tries (integration theories). In the same way, Russian regions also could be imagined to behave differently according to the specific characteristics of their political system.

This possibility becomes obvious if we accept the claim that the regions differ very much from each other in their political systems. The transition from an authoritarian rule towards 'something else' has taken different routes, and the goal at the regional level may be, as some scholars remind us, not necessarily democracy at all but something open-ended:

> In the late 1990s the variety of political regimes in Russia includes some features of pluralist democracy in St Petersburg, authoritarianism in Kalmykia, and even 'warlordism' in Primorskiy *kray*, as well as some hybrid regimes in some regions.[32]

One might easily think that in this situation those regions with a clear 'Russia as a part of Europe' identity, being closer to pluralist democracy in terms of their political system and at the same time situated closer to

Russian borders with western or northern Europe, might be more inclined to pro-integration foreign policy independently and as a part of the Russian Federation. St Petersburg and other northwest Russian regions in particular might have a special impetus to see themselves as a part of northern European or European culture, thus being particularly enthusiastic about Russia's closer integration with the European Union.

Thus, we may find some studies relying on or utilising more or less identity or related factors, and these factors may give rise to further speculation, hypotheses and investigations. Nevertheless, this genre in 'regionology' would also benefit from a more theoretical treatment of identity, relying on theories of identity formation as well as on those theories that try to provide a causal link between collective identities and state/regional interests.

Opening the regional 'black boxes'

The regions are discussed above as either sub-national units that may have some role in state foreign policy making or as more independent actors with their own particular identities in the arena of international politics; however, they are treated as unitary actors in both cases. In fact, most studies of the role of regions in Russian foreign policy stop here. With the exception of some studies that delve a little bit deeper, or that propose the agenda to do that,[33] there is usually no effort to differentiate between the actors within a region itself.

However, we might as well open the 'black box' of regions as we did with the state. In those cases where actors other than governors or the heads of the republics, as synonymous with their respective regions, are discussed at all in foreign policy terms, they are usually political parties, businesses and sometimes non-governmental organisations (NGOs). However, it is difficult to find a systematic treatment of regional power struggles that have been linked to foreign policy issues. Consequently, the relationship to be analysed remains that between the regions and the centre, both entities representing a rather homogenous and/or illustrative picture of the respective administrative or political level.

This does not have to be the case. Empirically we know for sure that there are no 'regional interests' as such, but many, often contradictory, understandings of what would be in the best interest of a certain region. Bureaucratic struggles and interest-group competition are as real and severe on the intra-regional level as they have been in Russian national politics. To illustrate this with an extreme example: in the city of Vladivostok the internal rivalry, reflecting the regional elite's struggles with the regional governor's programme and person, went so far that one day two officials 'turned up at the mayor's office early in the morning, both claiming the mayoral chair'.[34] Both of them had a very different opinion of how to manage this Far Eastern city internally, but also in relation to Moscow and neighbouring countries.

This small example, of course, implies that a mere bureaucratic position does not explain everything. This theoretical move, in turn, challenges once again the assumption of rationality. While the bureaucratic politics model challenges the assumption of rationality of a state or a region, it is nevertheless consistent with the assumption that individuals are acting rationally on the basis of national, organisational, bureaucratic or individual interests and desires, or of some combination of these.

Should one instead start from the viewpoint based on values, beliefs and interpretations, this perspective seems to challenge the assumption of the rationality of an individual decision-maker. One way of resolving this puzzle would be to claim that there is no need to consider the interests and desires of an actor as given, but to accept that emotions, identities, values and beliefs greatly affect one's preferences. In principle, preferences rooted in emotions are perfectly acceptable, even from a game-theory point of view. The rationality of an individual could be identified, and after that one should move further on the basis of the assumption of rationality. One might continue to use the assumption of rationality as a measure, but before that one should tailor this measure to each particular actor.

The 'cognitive boundaries of rational decision-making' have often been studied with the help of such research methods as cognitive maps or operational codes, which are supposed to uncover the particular features of a decision-maker's behavioural and thinking pattern. So far, there are no studies that look at regions or their agency in foreign policy matters from this point of view – making a deep analysis of the regional leaders' operational code or belief system, for instance, and trying to find out how this affects their foreign policy aspirations and formulation. Thus, explanations of an individual's actions usually do not go beyond restating the governors' statements and their possible implications on the level of action.[35]

This state of affairs in 'regionology', which comes close to pure descriptive studies or journalism, and in the best case statistics, could be improved by either accepting the rational model and its methodologies or by going further in the direction of cognitive and psychological approaches, and focusing, for instance, on some particular decision-making situation.

Transnational regionalism

Above, our attention was limited to the role of Russian regions either within the Russian domestic system or as more or less autonomous actors in a state-centred international system. The question was whether we should appreciate and investigate the role they may play in Russia's foreign policy formulation as subordinated state entities, or whether we should also emphasise their independent roles as some kind of semi-states, having their own foreign policies and paradiplomatic activities different from Russia's. While some part of the literature discussed above tends to give more weight to one or another of these understandings of the foreign policy role of the Russian regions, there are many analyses that emphasise both perspectives: Russian regions work both independently and through the state apparatus, and thus produce foreign policy outcomes different from that of a unitary or state-centric Russia.[36]

Developing further the notion of the growing independent impact of regions in foreign relations, some regional studies nevertheless question the whole state-centred nature of contemporary international politics – some of them, in fact, carefully avoiding the term international. What is happening here is basically a theoretical shift similar to one that took place at the beginning of the 1970s, when some international relations scholars opposing the realist state-centred mainstream focused on international organisations, transgovernmental relations and transnational corporations.

The main advocates of these ideas defined transgovernmental relations as 'sets of direct interactions among sub-units of different governments that are not controlled or closely guided by the policies of the cabinets or chief executives of those governments'. They distinguished between two major types of transgovernmental behaviour: namely, lower-level policy co-ordination, in terms of smooth implementation or adjustment of policy in the absence of detailed higher policy directives; and transgovernmental coalition building, which takes place when 'sub-units build coalitions with like-minded agencies from other governments against elements of their own administrative structures'.[37]

Although this debate of the early 1970s did not focus on territorial and administrative regions, but rather on traditional lower-level state bureaucracies and agencies, the same argumentation could be applied to regions as well. While lower-level policy co-ordination is more or less comparable to the behaviour of many Russian regions, as described above, transgovernmental coalition building is the point where 'the unity of the state as a foreign policy actor breaks down'.[38] The issue here is that new units, and new levels, should replace the old state level of analysis, because that is what is perceived as taking place in reality.

Currently, regions – and not only in Russia – appear to be among the main challengers of the state, both in theory and practice. First, there is an identifiable assumption that in the post-Cold War world the weight of regional forces, which had operated beneath the surface of superpower confrontation, has increased: 'International politics thus is increasingly shaped by regional, as well as national and local, dynamics.'[39] Coming to the same conclusions through a somewhat different route, some argue that the collapse of bipolarity has removed the principal organising force at the global level, where regions will be left to sort out their own affairs.[40]

In practical or political terms, some have proposed that the traditional problems related to borders and territories, such as the 'Karelian question' between Finland and Russia, for example, have been or at least will be resolved by these new developments. Instead of changing statist borders and making territorial adjustments, we can identify 'a certain de-territorialisation of politics', which may lead to a 'downgrading of many of the previous concerns leaning on a traditional statist approach regarding borders and territorial issues'. While there will be a regulating or supportive role for the states in this picture, the decisive actors are the regions, with more emphasis on functional aspects of co-operation.[41] Developments, especially in the co-operation of northwest Russian regions' co-operation with their Finnish and other Nordic counterparts at the regional level, seem to fulfil the promise of these ideas.

The literature also suggests that in these new region-to-region relations the emphasis is on 'low politics', which 'assumes a far more cooperative nature' for border relations than the traditional emphasis on 'high politics' between Russia and its neighbours.[42] This has been concretised by some researchers with regard to the Russian–Baltic States border as follows:

> While the Kremlin has been mired in geopolitical anguish over balancing NATO and EU enlargement with tighter Belarus–Russia union, the panoply of regional and local activism has been increasingly linking Russia's north-west with the budding Baltic–Central European trade area.[43]

When discussing regionalism in a wider sense, what becomes important is the question of what a region is in this context. Some analyses point out that they are not fixed territorial or administrative units, but 'polities-in-the-making', i.e. integration and fragmentation of space and regional practices. As to the Russian regions, this reshaping of space may include very concrete goals and forms:

> Accordingly, the building of 'horizontal' transport routes in Northwest Russia is aimed both at the regional independence from the centre and the integration with the adjacent areas (e.g. the Urals region) and Europe.[44]

Following the above path, we soon encounter other actors than official regional or local decision-makers. Some scholars have labelled these developments as 'transnational regionalism' bypassing the national borders:

> Yet patterns of regionalisation do not necessarily coincide with the borders of states. Migration, markets and social networks may lead to increased interaction and interconnectedness tying together parts of existing states and creating new cross-border regions. The core of such 'transnational regionalism' might be economic (as in the development of industrial corridors, or networks linking major industrial centres), or it can be built around high levels of human interaction.[45]

If we add to this the familiar concept of globalisation, or the internationalisation of domestic politics resulting from growing interdependence and integration, the sharp delineation between domestic and foreign policies could be abandoned.[46] Some researchers distinguish between 'globalisation from above' and 'globalisation from below'. The former refers to the leading states and main agents of capitalism, whereas the latter 'rests upon the strengthening over time of the institutional forms and activities associated with global civil society'.[47]

At the same time as this perspective widens our concept of international politics, it also reverses the direction of influence compared with traditional foreign policy approaches. This increasingly global context constrains or determines domestic political actions, or norms and rules within a society. While the sovereignty of states may not disappear, national borders become open, providing added space for transnational or global civil society activities. In other words, a movement of non-governmental organisations from the local to the global level can be identified, largely due to the globalisation of communication via the Internet, which makes it physically and financially feasible for civil society actors to establish and maintain transnational co-operation.[48]

Moreover, against this background Russian regions might be understood not in terms of administrative units, but rather as parts of or bases for transnational or global civil society development 'from below'. This type of transnationalism opens up many kinds of inter-relationship between Russia and the outside world at the regional level.[49] For instance, Russian civil society actors – and through them Russian society as a whole – may be affected by outside actors and tendencies; or Russian civil society actors may themselves be active in influencing the outside world; or Russian civil society actors may collaborate with their transnational non-governmental and/or governmental partners in efforts to deal with some common, global or regional questions beyond national borders.

We may find examples of all these relationships if we consider the practices of Russian civil society. However, it can be argued that usually the object in these transnational relations is not outside the country, but Russian society itself. In most cases Western NGOs operate with their Russian NGO counterparts independently but are financed by Western governments and organisations, and by that very fact this activity is restricted in its ideologies, strategies and tactics, and it cannot easily undercut the general ideas and values that are legitimised in Western political and social practices.

In this process, however, it is not only Russian civil society that becomes transnational, but the Western NGOs, and through them their societies are influenced as well. This activity may lead to a genuine multicultural dialogue overcoming traditional statist boundaries. Domestically, the transnational character of Russian civil society may not have a great immediate or direct impact on Russian official policy-making because of the lack of institution-alisation in domestic civil-society–state relations. Nevertheless, indirectly this kind of transnationalism certainly shapes the domestic structures, first of all, in Russia at local, regional and federal levels, but also in other countries, and helps to legitimise the activities of transnational civil society actors in general, which, in turn, may be reflected in Russian and Western official policies in the longer run. Meanwhile, it keeps Russia open to outside influence and enables communication at the grassroots level.

Should one also follow this logic in terms of regions' economic activity, it is the global or regional markets, rather than local markets, that provide the basic setting. Some scholars go as far as to suggest – perhaps unrealistically? – that Russia's 'regions now find their fortunes tied to the global system rather than their home economies. In such a context, it is no surprise that many of Russia's regions have sought to create an independent identity in the global political economy'.[50]

Conclusions

As has been illustrated, there are several alternative starting points from which to initiate a discussion on the role of Russia's regions in international relations. Levels of analysis can in principle range from that of an individual to the level of a global system. Also, methodologically we may choose between rational and non-rational models, or positivist and post-positivist approaches, as in any social scientific study. All these choices have then partially already decided the outcomes of any empirical research in advance, in terms of the causal or other mechanisms through which the regions are supposed to affect international relations.

It must be said that Russian foreign policy-related literature as a whole does not usually consider the role of regions in this context. At the same time, one should note that the existing literature on the theme of Russian regions and foreign policy hardly utilises the theoretical possibilities or develops any new theoretical constructions, and consequently the overwhelming majority of the literature remains fairly vague in its argumentation.

Perhaps the most original and potentially most fruitful approaches, however, are the ones which consider Russia's regions in the global context of change. In this context states may not disappear from the international arena, but their role is changed and the present order is increasingly challenged by spatial developments connected to transnational and regional developments 'from below'. Nevertheless, even here there is a great need for more theoretical and methodological rigour to really challenge the existing theoretical mainstream, which is still rooted firmly in the traditional nation-state world picture.

Notes

1 This refers to the eighty-nine territorial and administrative entities of power of the Russian Federation (republics, regions, etc.). Hereafter they are referred to as 'regions'.
2 Oldberg and Hedenskog 2000: 8.

3 See Zubov 2000; Mommen 2000; Warhola 1999: esp. 50, 51.
4 Makarychev 2000a: 124.
5 Hedenskog 2000: 66.
6 Tenth Conference of Russian Foreign Ministry 1999: 103, 104.
7 Sergounin 2000a: 29–36.
8 For a (critical) overview of these models, see Odom 1992.
9 Kobrinskaya 2000: 52.
10 As reported (and published on 2 February 2001) on http://www.websites.ru/news.html.
11 Makarychev and Bradshaw 2001.
12 Grezheyshchak 2000: 35.
13 Huskey 1999: 192.
14 Gelman 1999: 942.
15 Oldberg 2000: 12–15.
16 Makarychev et al. 2000.
17 Makarychev 2000a: 127.
18 Makarychev 2000a: 122, 123, 131; Kobrinskaya 2000: 50, 51; Sergounin 2000a: 33.
19 Orlov 2000b.
20 Makarychev et al. (2000) describe in some detail these efforts to co-ordinate foreign and security policy-related matters in the Volga Federal District.
21 Orlov 2000b.
22 Ibid.: 55; see also Kuzmin 1999.
23 See Bylov 1998.
24 Granberg 2000b: App. III.
25 Kobrinskaya 2000: 50.
26 Makarychev 2000a: 130.
27 Granberg 2000a.
28 Oldberg 2000: 20, 26.
29 Makarychev 2000a: 134.
30 Quoted from 'Russia in the International System', NIC Conference Report, 1 June 2001, which can be found at http://www.cia.gov/nic/pubs/conference_reports/Russia_conf.html#toc2, 'Roundtable: Impressions from Russia's Regions'.
31 Trenin 2001: 317.
32 Gelman 1999: 942.
33 Perovic 2000: 23.
34 Huskey 1999: 198.
35 An example of a study that does not apply any theoretical approach but goes deeper in interpreting a regional leader's statements and opinions is Berendsen et al. 1999.
36 This attitude is clearly expressed at least by Sergounin (2000a), when he distinguishes between 'direct' and 'indirect' influence; and by Perovic (2000), as well as Makarychev and Bradshaw (2001).
37 Keohane and Nye 1991: 232, 233.
38 Ibid.
39 Katzenstein 1996: 123.
40 Buzan et al. 1998: 9.
41 Joenniemi 1998: 200, 201.
42 Joenniemi 1998: 194.
43 Alexseev and Vagin 1999: 60.
44 Pynnöniemi 2000: 147, 148.
45 Makarychev and Bradshaw 2001.
46 See, among many others, Luard 1990; Goldmann 1989.

47 Falk 1993.
48 Willetts 1997.
49 Pursiainen 2000: 24–6.
50 Makarychev and Bradshaw 2001.

6 Russia's regionalisation

The interplay of domestic and international factors

Dr Alexander Sergounin

Introduction

In contrast with the de facto unitary system of government in the Soviet period, today's Russia is developing a federative model. Regionalisation has become an integral part of Russia's economic, social and political life. It should be noted that for some Russian and foreign analysts this process is synonymous with the further disintegration of the Russian Federation. Gloomy prognoses regarding the future of the country become popular from time to time, especially in periods of economic and political crisis: the early Yeltsin administration, the First Chechen War, the financial meltdown of August 1998 and so on. Few observers regard Russia's regionalisation in a positive way.

There are several simplistic explanations of Russia's regionalisation in Russian and Western literature. Some analysts view Russia's regionalisation as a natural continuation of the decentralisation and disintegration of the former Soviet Empire. But this can be only a partial explanation. Other experts believe that all federative states based on the national-territorial principle are doomed to failure in the age of globalisation. However, this is not confirmed by international experience. Some specialists tend to explain the above phenomenon mainly by the economic crisis of 1998, which, according to this point of view, led to Moscow's inability to control regions and thus encouraged the process of creeping autonomisation. However, the country's regionalisation started much earlier than 17 August 1998, when the crisis occurred. The crisis was a catalyst rather than a cause of regionalisation.

This study aims at examining two interconnected questions: first, what are the main factors of the regionalisation of Russia (both domestic and international); and, second, how do they interact? A number of fundamental factors that provoked the process of region-making in post-Communist Russia can be identified.

The sources of Russia's regionalisation

Domestic factors

The lack of a proper legal basis

It is well known that a federation can be created on the basis of either constitutional or contractual principles. In the former case a constitution defines the prerogatives of the federal centre and the members of a federation (the United States, Germany, etc.). In the latter case bilateral or multilateral treaties between the centre and regions are signed (the Soviet Union was created in this way). However, these two principles were mixed in the process of building the post-communist Russian federalism.

Initially, President Yeltsin favoured the contractual principle and along these lines a Federative Treaty was signed in 1992 (Chechnya and Tatarstan refused to sign it). Then the December 1993 Constitution of the Russian Federation made it clear that the constitutional principle was preferable. However, in 1994, under pressure from the local elites, Moscow resumed signing agreements with regions by concluding a set of bilateral treaties with seven republics (the first one was with Tatarstan). Forty-seven treaties had been signed by the end of 1998.

The treaties are relatively general documents describing the nature of the division of powers and shared powers. Each treaty differs slightly from the others, although they contain some common elements. They are accompanied by a series of agreements, which could be signed any time after the conclusion of the treaties. The agreements are far more detailed than the treaties and are, therefore, different for each region depending on its particular policy concerns and resource endowments. Yekaterinburg, for example, signed eighteen agreements, ranging from the region's investment policy, the use of natural resources, to health and cultural policies, in addition to its original treaty. In contrast, in the 1990s Kaliningrad signed only three agreements: one on education and science, another on cultural questions and the third on maintaining law and order in the region.[1]

Regions also may propose additional agreements. Many of the agreements were made for a set period of time (two to five years). Their terms allow for cancellation by either party prior to the expiry of the agreement. If no such notice is provided, the agreements are automatically renewed for an additional two to five years.

President Yeltsin tried to find a compromise between the constitutional and contractual principles by issuing his decree no. 370 (12 March 1996). The decree stipulated that the treaties and accompanying agreements are not to violate the Russian Constitution and must respect its supremacy. Nor can they change the status of a member of the Federation or add to or change what is enumerated in Articles 71 and 72 of the Constitution, which assign federal and joint authority, respectively.

However, a number of the treaties and agreements in fact either contradicted the Constitution or went beyond what was envisioned in it. Spheres that in the Constitution are ascribed to the federal centre exclusively (Article 71) appeared as areas of joint jurisdiction in many documents. For example, the treaties with Bashkortostan, Kabardino-Balkariya, North Osetia and Tatarstan granted these republics the right to defend state and territorial integrity. Yekaterinburg and Udmurtiya gained authority over the functioning of the defence industry. In some treaties members of the Federation had authority to establish relations and conduct agreements with foreign states. Areas identified in the federal law as spheres of joint authority appeared in some treaties as the exclusive jurisdiction of regions, including civil rights protection and control over local precious metals and stones.

The Russian Constitution itself is rather vague with regard to defining areas of joint authority. Rather than taking the lead in defining and limiting what regions have the right to do, Moscow has either taken a wait-and-see attitude or simply reacted to what regions demanded. For example, until 2002 no federal law on private ownership of farmland existed and some members of the Federation (the Saratov, Novgorod and other regions) passed legislation of their own. The 1994 treaty with Tatarstan and the accompanying agreements simply codified what was already in place in areas such as need-based social assistance programmes, foreign trade and external ties. In accordance with the 1996 Yekaterinburg treaty, the region has the right to establish its own civil service and internal legal regulation of spheres of joint regional and central jurisdiction, and even to suspend the normative acts of federal ministries and agencies.[2]

As a result of historical traditions and the confusion of the constitutional and contractual principles, members of the Russian Federation now have different powers and statuses. The Federation consists of eighty-nine federative units; namely, twenty-one national republics, six provinces (*kray*), forty-nine regions (*oblast*), one autonomous region (*avtonomnaya oblast*), ten autonomous districts (*okrug*) and two cities of federal subordination (Moscow and St Petersburg).

In sum, this led to so-called asymmetric federalism in Russia, with rather contradictory implications. On the one hand, it helped to appease local elites and prevent separatist tendencies (at least temporarily). On the other, asymmetric federalism could not be seen as a panacea; rather, it was only a partial solution to numerous problems faced by the Russian political leadership and regions themselves. Moreover, the growing dissimilarities between members of the Federation were a permanent source of inter-regional rivalry and political instability in the country, which made the above model fragile and vulnerable.

It should be noted, however, that asymmetric federalism created a rather favourable environment for the further regionalisation of Russia. Both the gradual devolution of power from the centre to the members of the Federation and inter-regional competition were conducive to region-making.

The regional elites used the lack of clarity in federal law to carve out their own policies and thus become more independent from Moscow.

However, with Putin's coming to power the situation radically changed. The president assigned his envoys in the newly created federal districts the task of bringing the local legislation in line with federal legislation. By the end of 2000 most of the regional normative acts that conflicted with the Russian Constitution had been either abolished or revised.

Historical legacies

A typical Russian region is not an incidental or mechanical combination of some proximate territorial units. It used to be an end-product of long-term economic, social and political developments. However, it should be noted that these processes were not necessarily organic and some regions were formed on a rather artificial, unnatural basis. The latter is particularly typical of the Soviet period, when some completely different ethnic and religious groups were lumped together merely because of administrative considerations. Nonetheless, the legacy of the Soviet command-administrative system (especially in the economic sphere) should be taken into account to understand both the sources of and current trends in Russia's regionalisation.

There were eleven economic zones in the Russian Socialist Federative Soviet Republic (RSFSR): Northwestern, Northern, Central, Central–Black Earth, Volgo-Vyatskiy, Volga, North Caucasian, Urals, West Siberian, East Siberian and Far Eastern zones.[3] Interestingly, the country's regionalisation followed a similar pattern. The economic inter-regional associations that emerged in the late Soviet and post-communist periods almost coincided with the above zones. An idea of enlarging Russian regions and forming approximately twelve mega-regions ('economic conglomerates', according to the former prime minister Yevgeniy Primakov) to replace the eighty-nine subjects of the Federation emerged in the context of the 1998 financial crisis.[4] Again, the spatial characteristics of the proposed mega-regions and the ex-Soviet economic zones had much in common. Putin's seven federal districts also resembled the configuration of the military and internal troops districts that also were inherited from the past.

Decentralisation as a result of democratisation

Not only the economy, but also the Soviet political and administrative systems were highly centralised. Along with the administrative structures (the Soviets), control over the regions was maintained through the Communist Party, Komsomol (the Young Communist League), labour unions and other public associations. With the disbanding of the command economy and the gradual rise of the market economy, devolution of power away from the federal centre took place as private interests continued to grow. The introduction of representative government and the election of governors in the subjects of the Federation also contributed to decentralisation. It became difficult for Moscow to remove or discipline the elected leaders and bodies in regions since they had a popular mandate and were accountable to their constituencies rather than to Moscow. For example, for several years Yeltsin failed to remove Yevgeniy Nazdratenko, a self-willed governor of Primorskiy *kray* who conducted rather independent policies in areas such as taxation, social assistance, energy supplies, foreign economic relations, Sino-Russian relations and so on.

The lack of a strong party system

Political parties have many important functions: articulation, aggregation and representation of different social interests; production of political ideologies; recruitment of elites and political leaders; organisation and servicing of the election system: execution of political control over the bureaucracy: provision of feedback within the political system; etc. In a stable federal state, parties oversee the equally important integrative function by serving as instruments of political representation for regions and control over local officials by central officials. In other words, parties are important ties that bind federal states together.

However, post-communist Russia lacks a strong party system at the regional level. Only the Communist Party, the Liberal Democratic Party (led by Vladimir Zhirinovskiy) and perhaps Yabloko (Apple) have more or less developed organisational structures in the provinces (mainly in the biggest cities, such as Moscow, St Petersburg, Nizhniy Novgorod, Yekaterinburg, Samara). Other parties have little institutional presence outside Moscow. Few regional leaders have clear party affiliation. Most of them prefer to be elected on a non-partisan basis and build their own political coalitions. All attempts by the Moscow-based political leaders to create either a pro-presidential or pro-governmental party in the regions (for example Chernomyrdin's *Our Home – Russia*, Luzhkov's *Fatherland*, Shoygu's *Unity*) seem not to have been very successful. Speaking generally, there is little evidence that the present Russian party system is capable of performing unifying functions, and it thus hinders the development of a well-integrated Russian state.

Under these circumstances interest groups try to replace parties, although they are incapable of taking over all party functions within the political system. Some political organisations that call themselves parties are in fact vehicles for group interests rather than real parties. The State Duma, the lower chamber of the Russian Parliament, is surrounded by a network of lobbyist structures. The Council of the Federation, the upper chamber of Parliament, is a sort of forum for representing regional lobbies, which compete with each other for federal subsidies.

It should be noted that interest groups play a rather contradictory role within a federal state. On the one hand, there are some groups (such as oil and gas lobbies, the so-called financial-industrial groups) that are interested in Russia being a strong federative state in order to keep their business. On the other hand, many pressure groups have only parochial, region-oriented interests, which are not conducive to the integration of the country.

The rise of regional elites

In Soviet times regional leaders were an important source for recruitment of the national elite. For instance, both Gorbachev and Yeltsin were brought to the Olympus of political power from the periphery (from Stavropol and Sverdlovsk/Yekaterinburg, respectively). However, in the Soviet Union regional elites never played an independent political role and were absolutely loyal to Moscow. In contrast with the Soviet practices, post-communist regional leaders tried to build political coalitions of their own and be independent from Moscow to the maximum possible. Along with the above factors, regional elites became a driving force of regionalisation, hoping to benefit from this process.

Given its shrinking resource base in the 1990s, the federal government became more dependent on regional elites. Remarkably, during the debates over Chernomyrdin's candidature in September 1998 Yeltsin appealed to the Council of the Federation, where regional leaders sat, rather than to the State Duma. It is also interesting that when there was a possibility of dissolving the Duma in case of the third rejection of Chernomyrdin's candidature the majority of Russian senators promised to support Yeltsin. Primakov also met governors regularly to persuade them that he needed their support and advice.

Moscow not only acknowledged the growing role of local leaders but also tried to co-operate with them and – in a typically Soviet way – to bring them to the capital in order to introduce fresh blood into the federal elite. For example, in spring 1997 Yeltsin invited a number of popular reformers from the regions (Boris Nemtsov, Sergey Kiriyenko, Oleg Sysuyev, etc.) to take up key ministerial positions in the Chernomyrdin cabinet. After Chernomyrdin's resignation in March 1998 Kiriyenko became prime minister. Primakov acted along the same lines. For example, he appointed Vadim Gustov, a former governor of the Leningrad Region, to be his deputy. Putin surrounded himself mostly with the representatives of the 'St Petersburg' group. By employing regional leaders for federal jobs Moscow tried both to capitalise on their political authority and to neutralise potential rivals in the periphery.

The crisis of the old model of federalism

Prior to the economic crisis of 1998 regionalism was mainly understood as Moscow's policy towards the members of the Russian Federation based on the redistribution of resources between regions via the federal budget and subsidies. However, this top-down model of state intervention in a region proved to be inefficient in light of the systemic crisis in Russia.

Since the federal government failed to collect taxes and help net receiving regions through the federal subsidies, many subjects of the Federation realised after the 1998 crisis that they had to rely on their own resources alone. Moscow was perceived by many regions as an unnecessary, redundant structure that consumed resources rather than provided them. The regions that were rich in natural resources and could potentially be donors were particularly discontented with the tax policy of the centre. Under Russian legislation, state and private companies which extract natural resources must pay taxes at the place of their registration rather than in the region where they operate. Since such companies are mainly registered in Moscow money never reached local budgets. From time to time the regions – via their lobbyists in the State Duma and the Council of the Federation – initiated bills aimed at changing tax legislation, but they have so far not succeeded.

In sum, by the end of the 1990s the old model of federalism had stopped working and this also served as a powerful incentive for Russia's further regionalisation.

International factors

The global dynamics

It has become a commonplace to assert that globalisation and regionalisation are two sides of the same coin, and different words (e.g. 'glocalisation', 'fragmegration') are used to denote this complex phenomenon. The entire world faces processes such as the erosion of the nation-state and national sovereignty, the shift of power from the national level towards supranational and regional institutions.

Russia is a part of this global dynamic and cannot ignore the rules dictated by it. Russia is particularly affected by regionalisation in Europe (EU enlargement, Baltic and Nordic subregional co-operation), Eurasia (the Commonwealth of Independent States, CIS), and the Asia-Pacific (Asia-Pacific Economic Council, APEC). Moscow also tries to adapt itself to the new realities: Russia concluded a partnership and co-operation agreement with the EU and welcomed the EU's Northern Dimension Initiative, which aims to integrate Russia's Northwest into the European economic space. Moscow participates in the activities of various subregional organisations such as the Council of the Baltic Sea States (CBSS), the Barents Euro-Arctic Council (BEAC), the Arctic Council and the Black Sea Economic Co-operation regime (BSEC). Moscow tries to exercise economic and political leadership in the CIS. Finally, Russia joined the Association of Southeast Asian Nations (ASEAN) Regional Forum (1996) and APEC (1998) as a fully fledged member.

It should be noted that many foreign countries and international organisations prefer to deal with Russian regions rather than with Moscow. They regard regionalisation as both a means of bypassing the Moscow bureaucracy and a good solution to many Russian problems. For example, the EU established a special INTERREG (EU Inter-regional Initiative) programme to promote co-operation between the border regions in Europe, including Russia. The TACIS (EU Technical Assistance to the CIS) programme, another EU initiative, is oriented to stimulating cross-border co-operation and local government in Russia as well. The EU's Northern Dimension has the same aims. The Euroregion concept is another opportunity for subregional co-operation. For example, Kaliningrad belongs to the Baltic Euroregion, which began in 1998. It was established as an international lobbying group of local governments from Poland, Sweden, Denmark, Lithuania, Latvia and Russia. The most important task for co-operation between communities from various countries was subregional economic planning and construction of transport routes.[5]

The Western foundations and organisations specialising in education and research support programmes also emphasised their regional priorities. For instance, in the late 1990s the Nordic Council of Ministers and the British Council launched special fellowship programmes for the Russian northwest. In 1998 the Soros Foundation started its Mega-project, aimed at supporting and developing Russian peripheral universities. Despite the territorial dispute with Russia and the lack of a peace treaty, Japan co-operates with Russian regions such as the Kurile Islands, Sakhalin and the Maritime Province.

Geopolitical factors

The geographic position of the region, access to land and sea communications, abundance or lack of natural resources, climatic conditions, etc. shape a region's economy, transport system, trade, foreign policy orientations, relationship with the centre and so forth. The Russian Far East, for example, cannot ignore the proximity of the two regional powers China and Japan, which have a serious interest in exploiting its natural resources, conquering its huge market and resolving some bilateral problems inherited from the past. The Russian south has to deal with the implications of the turbulent processes in the North Caucasian and adjacent South Caucasus regions. EU enlargement affects the development of the Russian Northwest and encourages various collaborative projects such as the EU's Northern Dimension, Baltic and Barents/Arctic co-operation.

Due to geopolitical factors some Russian border regions in the northwest (especially Kaliningrad) and in the Far East feel closer – in terms of their day-to-day life – to neighbouring countries than to the capital, and consider themselves as a part of regional/subregional economic, trade, infrastructural and information systems rather than the national economy. This is normal in the age of globalisation and growing interdependency, although Moscow is concerned about a possible drift of these regions towards foreign powers.

Military-strategic factors

Determinants such as military alliances, deployment and configuration of foreign armed forces, and military conflicts in the country's vicinity also affect the formation and development of the Russian border regions. In the Cold War period several Russian regions were highly militarised and oriented towards defence/industrial functions – Kaliningrad, the Kola Peninsula, the Russian Far East, the Urals and so on. A 'garrison-town' psychology affected the local thinking for a long time – even during the *pere-stroyka* and post-communist periods, and to some extent this still exists in these regions. For example, areas dependent on the military-industrial complex and depressed for this reason are usually unable to develop international co-operation and attract investment. They rely on federal subsidies rather than on their local resources. There is even a sort of nostalgia for the Cold War era in these regions because in the past they were economically prosperous and strategically important to the centre. Some of these backward-looking groupings try to capitalise on external threats – real or hypothetical – such as NATO enlargement, Chinese expansion and Japanese territorial claims in order to restore the former military-strategic significance of their regions.

Fortunately, the conservatives are unable to dominate the regional or national foreign policy thinking. Despite pressure from the military-industrial lobby, many former militarised and closed areas are rather dynamic in terms of economic reforms and international co-operation (Kaliningrad, Velikiy Novgorod, Murmansk, Archangel).

Although the significance of military-strategic factors decreased in the 1990s, some of them still affect the nature of Russia's regionalisation. For example, the Southern Federal District was designed to cope with armed conflicts in Chechnya, Dagestan, South and North Osetia, Abkhazia, etc. As mentioned above, the seven federal districts created in May 2000 are similar to the military and interior troops districts in terms of their size and borders.

Foreign economic relations

Russia's regionalisation is accelerated by the economic influence of neighbouring countries. Given the current economic decline and disruption of inter-regional co-operation, for many border regions collaboration with foreign partners offers better prospects than collaboration with other Russian regions. These regions view economic co-operation with foreign countries as the best way of overcoming the depression and building a viable economy. They look to foreign countries as a possible source of investment, advanced technology and training assistance, and promising trade markets.

A number of Russian regions have developed very close economic relations with neighbouring countries, to the extent that they have formed interdependent and complementary economic organisms (Kaliningrad–Poland–Lithuania, Karelia–Finland, Murmansk–northern Norway, the Russian Maritime Province and the Chinese Dongbei, Orenburg–Kazakhstan, Belgorod–Kharkiv). Of course, the creation of single transregional economic complexes with Russia's participation still remains a distant prospect, but the abovementioned regions already have such potential.

It should be noted that the configuration of the new administrative system under Putin also takes into account the existing structures of cross- and transborder co-operation. For example, the Northwest Federal District includes Russian regions that are subjects of international co-operation under the auspices of the EU's Northern Dimension, and the Far East Federal District is involved in close co-operation with the APEC area.

In sum, the above factors facilitate the country's regionalisation. It should be noted that they are of a long-term rather than short-term character and, for this reason, will likely affect the Russian regional dynamics in the foreseeable future. Along with the factors that cause regionalisation, some tendencies which serve as catalysts to the decentralisation process can be identified. The crisis of 1998 was one of them. As Herd put it, some peculiarities of Russian political life such as the type of presidency, the character of the president, the way he exercises power and the stress of election campaigns also affect centre–periphery relations and thus contribute to the devolution of power from the federal government to regions.[6]

Regionalisation is a rather contradictory process, which both poses challenges to and provides for the federative state. Will Russia be able to cope with the challenges and seize the opportunities or not? The discussion below addresses this fundamental question.

The challenges of regionalisation

Economic disintegration

The decentralisation process may lead to the disintegration of a single economic and financial space and disrupt a traditional system of division of labour between and within regions. For example, in the post-Soviet period the Cherepovets Metallurgical Combine, which traditionally provided central Russia with steel and rolled iron, decided to reorient its ties to the west-north direction (including the Nordic countries) because the new partners had turned out to be much more reliable and profitable than the old ones. This created a range of problems for traditional customers. For instance, Vladimir Pugin, ex-director-general of the Nizhniy Novgorod Automobile Plant, had to make a special trip to Cherepovets in February 1999 to persuade the local managers to provide his enterprise with the necessary products and secure good relations for the future. In economic terms, the Kaliningrad, Leningrad and Murmansk regions and Karelia are more integrated with the Baltic and Nordic economic space than with Moscow or, let us say, the Urals. The Russian Far East is also more dependent on trade with China, Japan and South Korea than on ties with other parts of Russia.

The 1998 crisis intensified the process of fragmentation of the Russian economic and financial space. Many Russian regions established quotas on export/import of some products and erected customs checkpoints on the borders. For example, in September 1998 the Volgograd regional government issued decree no. 469, which prohibited the export of foodstuffs from the region. This led to conflict with local farmers who tried to sell their products in the neighbouring Voronezh Region where prices were better.[7] Some governors in fact established monopolies on the local vodka markets by prohibiting the import of vodka from other regions or by introducing a complex certification procedure for rivals. Interestingly, they undertook such measures under the pretext of fighting fake vodka and organised crime. Some regions, being short of cash, had to issue quasi-money (coupons, local securities, etc.) to pay salaries and keep the local financial system afloat. Some members of the Russian Federation even started to form gold reserves of their own to secure themselves from federal instability.

Regionalisation of the economic space and autarkic tendencies made the Federation more fragile and less cohesive. In turn, this led to disparities between regions and encouraged an unhealthy competition between them.

Degradation of the party system

With regionalisation of the country, the social base for national parties can be further fragmented. Hence a strong national party system, which could be a pillar for an efficient federation, can never be created. Instead, the rise of regional parties and increasing pressure of interest groups on the federal bodies can easily be predicted. As the 1999 elections in St Petersburg demonstrated, regional parties and coalitions can be more successful than the national-level organisations. For instance, the Boldyrev regional bloc (Boldyrev was one of the founding fathers of the Yabloko party) easily beat the Yabloko candidates in the St Petersburg legislative assembly.

It should be noted that the ability of regional parties and lobbies to organise local politics to represent regional interests in the national capital and to serve as a sort of liaison mechanism between the centre and the periphery is unquestionable. However, as mentioned above, their integrative capabilities are much weaker than those of national political parties. Moreover, regional blocs and lobbies are much more susceptible to corruption and 'pork-barrel' politics and less accountable to the broad public than national parties.

Regionalisation of the armed forces and security services

In the Yeltsin period the growing dependence of the so-called 'power structures' on the local authorities was one of the negative and rather dangerous
implications of regionalisation. Given the lack of funds and shortage of
food, energy and accommodation, many military commanders had to apply
for assistance from local governments. For example, by the end of October
1998 the Baltic Fleet owed R75.5 million (US$5 million) to the Kaliningrad
Region for food supplies. As a result of this the Kaliningrad bakeries (whose
'share' in the fleet's debt was R5 million) refused to provide the navy with
bread on a credit basis.[8] In 1997–8 the local energy companies several times
cut off electricity supplies to the Pacific Fleet's land facilities (even early-
warning systems and hospitals). To help the military and secure social
stability in their region, some local governments provided federal troops
with basic provisions from regional budgets. For example, the then governor
of Primorskiy *kray*, Nazdratenko, paid wage arrears to the Pacific Fleet
from regional budgets in return for ensuring that only those officers born in
the region served in the Fleet. In July 1998 the Krasnoyarsk governor,
Aleksandr Lebed, reached an agreement with the leadership of the Siberian
Military District on supplying federal military units with basic provisions
from local funds.[9]

Some recent trends in force structure and deployment facilitate the army's
regionalisation. According to the Russian concept of military reform,
commanders of military districts should co-operate with regional leaders.
Local politicians even have some say in decision-making in areas such as
mobilisation capacities, supplying the federal troops with basic provisions
and defining where the conscripts must serve. One of the documents of the
Defence Ministry suggested that regional collegiate bodies made up of the
heads of local government, the command of military districts and other
troops, military formations and agencies should be created. These collective
bodies would enable civilian officials and heads of non-army services to
participate in operational command both in the centre and in the regions.[10]

New types of relationships between the local military commanders and
politicians emerged in post-communist Russia. Some of them are based on
dependency; others look like alliances. Nonetheless, these processes break
traditional loyalty within the federal security structures and make them
more fragmented and less manageable. As the post-Soviet developments in
the Caucasus region demonstrated, in case of political instability, civil or
ethnic war regional military commanders can easily be transformed into
local warlords who supply the warring parties with arms and implement the
famous imperialist principle 'divide and rule'. Moreover, the question of the
reliability of centralised control over nuclear weapons scattered around
Russia inevitably arises.

As far as other security structures (the Ministry of Interior forces, the
Federal Security Service (FSB), tax police, local police, etc.) are concerned,
they are even more susceptible to regionalisation than the armed forces: on

the one hand, they always were more dependent on local authorities in terms of basic provision than the military; on the other hand, regional elites traditionally regarded them as a valuable asset in building a power base and, for this reason, were interested in co-operation with local organs of the militia or the KGB/FSB. In fact many security services have been well integrated into the regional power structures since the late Soviet period. However, it took some time to replace the old party *nomenklatura* with the new regional elites. For example, on his way to power in the Nizhniy Novgorod Region, Boris Nemtsov portrayed himself as a person persecuted by the KGB and the police. However, when he assumed office as head of the regional administration after the August 1991 aborted coup he set aside his conflicts with the security services and, moreover, used them extensively against his local political rivals, such as Andrey Klimentyev, a famous Nizhniy Novgorod businessman and politician (albeit a man with an alleged criminal 'flavour').

It should be noted that the union of security services and the local elites used to be rather detrimental to democracy in a region. The local politicians used the power structures to consolidate their positions rather than fight organised crime or secure democratic reforms. For example, Murtaza Rakhimov, the president of Bashkortostan, urged the local FSB station to gather sensitive information and discredit his rivals during the presidential election of June 1998. The same 'election technology' was then exported to Udmurtiya. The Dagestani leadership repeatedly used police forces to put down ethnic and religious risings in the republic. The neglect of peaceful methods of conflict resolution on the part of Makhachkala brought Dagestan to the brink of civil war.

Some regional leaders use security services not only against their domestic enemies but also to confront other regions. For example, both Ingushetia and North Osetia used police units to fight each other during border conflicts. The local security services were also involved in kidnapping, terrorist operations and smuggling. In the Yeltsin era Moscow was unable to stop the regionalisation of the security services. Moreover, the federal centre allowed the local elites to control the power structures in return for their loyalty to Moscow. For instance, in February 1999 Moscow signed an agreement with Ingushetia which subordinated the local police to the president, Ruslan Aushev, and enabled the republic to form a militia 'in accordance with local traditions and norms'.

However, with Putin's administrative reform Moscow tried to reverse this dangerous process and bring the power structures back under its control. This was one of the most important tasks of the presidential envoys in the federal districts. Each power ministry (ministries of defence, justice, interior and emergency situations, and the FSB) established representative offices in the federal districts to monitor the activities of their local subordinates.

Separatism

The most unpleasant implication of regionalisation for Moscow is the separatist tendencies in various parts of Russia. Not only Chechnya but also some other national republics have demonstrated their secessionist sentiments from time to time. In the early 1990s Bashkortostan and Tatarstan were suspected of being separatist minded. There was even the idea of creating an independent Idel-Ural republic consisting of the Muslim peoples of the Volga region. For instance, the History Dean of Kazan University (Tatarstan), Indus Tagirov, argued in October 1993 that 'the idea of the Idel-Ural has become a necessity now'. Fanil Fajzullin, Dean of Humanities at Ufa State Aviation and Technical University (Bashkortostan), admitted that 'if the dictatorship of Moscow persists with its demands for a unitary state, centrifugal forces may triumph and a new federation may be formed in the region of Idel-Ural and in the North Caucasus'. The Head of the Bashkir Cultural Society, Robert Sultanov, was also willing to agree in October 1993 that 'if the Russian Federation disintegrated', Bashkortostan and Tatarstan 'would become the subjects of a new confederation, while retaining their independence'.[11]

The Russian Far East, another troubled region, repeatedly discussed plans for independent development. For example, in 1994 Viktor Ishayev, head of the administration of the Khabarovsk Province, claimed that the Russian government 'has done all it could to sever the Far East from Russia'. The workers of the Khrustalnyy tin-extracting company, who were not paid for several months, wrote in their declaration:

> The government and the president don't pay any attention to our troubles. We have concluded that they have given up on us. Therefore we must also give them up and form our own republic with an independent government. There is no other way to survive.[12]

Secessionist movements can be found in Karelia, Kaliningrad and the North Caucasian republics as well. However, to date Chechnya is the only breakaway republic. Other potential candidates for secession are not pressing for independence immediately.

The promises of regionalism

Many analysts focus only on the detrimental effects of the process of Russia's regionalisation. However, along with negative implications, which have been analysed above, regionalisation brings about a number of positive changes.

First and foremost, regionalisation encourages further democratisation of the Russian administrative system. Now a director of an enterprise does not need Moscow's approval for changing an assortment of products and a university professor need not ask the ministry's permission to publish a textbook or monograph, as was the case in the past. The introduction of representative government, a multi-party system, independent mass media and free elections in the regions have drawn millions of people into political life and made the democratic reforms irreversible.

Second, regionalisation provides an opening to other models of federalism in Russia. Contrary to the old 'top-down' model, a new interpretation of regionalism as a basic characteristic of civil society is gradually taking root in the country. Interestingly, with the 'help' of the crisis of 1998 many Russians have discovered that civil society really exists in the country (albeit in embryonic form) and that it is much more reliable than the state, which failed to fulfil its commitments and deceived its citizens once again. The crisis stimulated individuals, groups and organisations to form a system of non-vertical, non-hierarchical, horizontal networks and connections which is a basis for civil society. Subregional, inter-regional and transregional co-operation can be considered part of this endeavour.

Third, the division of labour within a region and co-operation with other Russian and foreign regions helped many members of the federation to survive in the period of transition. This is particularly important for the remote and border regions. In 1992–4, the Russian Far East managed to cope with the shortage of foodstuffs and some other consumer goods thanks to the barter trade with China.[13] In the autumn of 1998 Poland and Lithuania provided Kaliningrad with humanitarian assistance. Japan launched a similar programme for the Kuriles.[14]

Fourth, devolution of power in Russia boosted foreign relations of the subjects of the Russian Federation and made them real international actors. For example, in the period 1991–5, the Russian regions signed more than 300 agreements on trade, economic and humanitarian co-operation with foreign countries.[15] This helped to undermine Moscow's monopoly in foreign relations and turned diplomacy away from 'grand policy' issues to the pressing needs of the Russian periphery. Moscow can no longer take decisions concerning international status for the regions without at least consulting them. For example, with the assistance of the Russian Foreign Ministry the local governments of Kaliningrad, Karelia and St Petersburg actively participated in negotiating and concluding a number of agreements on cross-border and transregional co-operation with EU member states and some Baltic and Nordic countries. In turn, these developments resulted in fundamental institutional changes: the Foreign Ministry had to establish a special unit on inter-regional affairs. In addition to the national republics, which traditionally had their own foreign offices, the Russian Foreign Ministry has established its offices in regions engaged in intensive international economic and cultural co-operation.

Fifth, regionalisation can serve as an instrument for problem-solving in Russia's relations with neighbouring countries. For example, Kaliningrad's close co-operation with Lithuania, Poland and Germany prevented the rise of territorial claims on their part and reduced their concerns about excessive militarisation in the region. Co-operation between Finland and Karelia also eased Finnish–Russian tensions on the Karelia issue. Cross-border co-operation between the Kuriles, Sakhalin and Japan gave way to a quiet Russia–Japan dialogue on disputable questions.

Last but not least, regionalisation is helpful in opening up Russia to international co-operation as well as in the country joining a worldwide process of intensive transregional co-operation. In this regard, regionalisation has a very important civilisatory function: it prevents Russia's marginalisation or international isolation and helps to build bridges between different civilisations.

The institutional dimension

Operationally, there are three main levels of regional co-operation in Russia. The first level is bilateral co-operation between members of the Federation, ranging from economic, social and environmental to cultural and even security issues. Such co-operation is developed both by adjacent regions (for example, Karelia and the Murmansk Region) and by regions which have no common borders but share common interests (for instance the Nizhniy Novgorod and Krasnodar Regions, the Komi Republic and Karelia). Bilateral co-operation used to be institutionalised in the form of agreements between local governments and/or individual companies, enterprises, universities, non-governmental organisations, etc. This level is a basic unit for other forms of regionalism.

The second level of regionalism in Russia is co-operation in the framework of either economic or administrative mega-regions. There are a number of subregional associations in Russia, such as the Northwest Association, the Greater Volga Association, the Chernozem (Black Soil) Association, the Ural Association, the Siberian Accords Association, etc., which mainly deal with economic and social issues. The members of these associations meet several times each year to discuss issues of common interest which need co-ordination, such as transport, communication, foodstuff and fuel supplies, and joint projects. Regional blocs are seen by some analysts as tools in the struggle for regional domination.[16] For example, the Northwest Association is considered to be the 'sphere of influence' of St Petersburg, while the Urals Association is dominated by Yekaterinburg. However, on the other hand the members of regional blocs understand that these organisations are rather useful in managing regions which have many common economic, social, environmental and cultural problems. It is not surprising that after the crisis of 1998 many regional blocs intensified their activities.[17]

The seven federal districts are another institutional framework for subregional co-operation. Some of them are close to economic associations in terms of their territorial configuration (e.g. Northwestern and Siberian); others are different. The federal districts are sometimes rather artificial structures and lack internal coherence. Many Russian regions have complained that the new administrative system does not take into account their economic, cultural and historical identities. For example, the Perm Region and Bashkortostan argued that in economic terms they are closer to the Urals District, though they were attached to the Volga Federal District. The Astrakhan and Volgograd Regions also pointed out that they are traditionally oriented to the Volga area rather than to the North Caucasus. However, given the powers that the presidential envoys were granted by the president, the federal districts quite soon became new centres of gravitation. The federal districts are gradually establishing themselves as new poles of regionalisation, and traditional actors (including the economic associations) have to tailor their activities in accordance with the new administrative system.

The third level of regionalism is international co-operation, which in turn includes cross-border co-operation (co-operative projects between neighbouring regions) and transregional co-operation (collaboration with and within multilateral organisations). For example, a number of Russian and Chinese regions have developed very close economic relations. In fact, the southern part of the Russian Far East and China's Dongbei Province formed an interdependent and complementary economic organism.[18]

The Russian northwest regions also pay great attention to co-operation with the Nordic countries. For instance, Finland and Karelia traditionally co-operate in areas such as economy, transport, communication, tourism, ecology, culture and so on. For example, 56 per cent of joint ventures in Karelia were established with Finnish participation. It was decided that Kostomuksha free economic zone would receive international status in the framework of a special agreement between Russia and Finland. The unique geographical location of the republic on the border of Russia and the EU and the historical specialisation of the Karelian economy made it one of the leading exporters among members of the Russian Federation: its share of exports exceeds 40 per cent of the total volume of output.[19] In fact the Finnish and Karelian economies are complementary, and an embryo of the mechanism of interdependence has been created.

Along with bilateral channels, some multilateral institutions (CBSS, BEAC, APEC, etc.) make co-operation possible. For example, at the May 1996 Visby summit the CBSS adopted an ambitious programme aimed at regional co-operation in areas such as the economy, trade, finance, transport, communications, conversion, ecology, border and customs control, and fighting organised crime.[20]

The EU is also an important player in the sphere of cross-border and transregional co-operation, establishing several programmes with Russia. Since the 1997 Finnish initiative the EU has been developing the Northern Dimension of the EU's Common Foreign and Security Policy.[21] According to Brussels, the Northern Dimension project should pool all other collaborative programmes and increase their interoperability.[22]

Conclusions

This study shows that many domestic and international factors are long-term rather than short-term developments – the birth of a new Russian model of federalism, political realignments both at the local and national levels, geopolitical shifts, the rise of international regions, transborder economic co-operation, military-strategic determinants, ethno-territorial and religious conflicts, and cultural diversity. They will certainly serve as powerful incentives for the country's further regionalisation.

While the domestic environment should be taken into account, the nature and directions of Russia's regionalisation depend greatly on the international environment as well. Hence it is very important to provide Russia with positive external inputs, such as friendly and balanced policies in neighbouring countries, Russia's active participation in various forms of transregional and transborder co-operation, and its engagement in intensive dialogue on regional issues with foreign policy-makers and academics.

However, despite the significant role of the external determinants, they were not a crucial factor in Russia's regionalisation. Domestic determinants have prevailed. And yet the interplay of internal and external factors will remain an important determinant shaping Russia's regional structure.

Regionalisation may have both positive and negative implications. The problem for the Russian political leadership (both federal and regional) is how to harness the above dynamic processes so as to make them work towards democracy, not against it.

The above analysis demonstrates that regionalism does not just offer opportunities; it has already borne some fruit and received institutional support. Moreover, regionalisation has become both an instrument of Russia's search for a new national identity and the environment where this search is conducted. As this study shows, regionalism is set to play an important role in defining Russia's future. Depending on political wisdom and the degree of democratic culture of Russian political actors, regionalism can serve as a catalyst either to successful reforms or to the disintegration of the country.

Notes

1 Stoner-Weiss 1998: 22.
2 Sergounin and Rykhtik 2000.
3 Lappo 1983.
4 *Rossiyskaya Gazeta*, 31 October 1998: 3; Herd 1998: 16.
5 Fairlie 2000: 97.
6 Herd 1998: 3.
7 *Rossiyskaya Gazeta*, 3 October 1998: 3.
8 *Rossiyskaya Gazeta*, 31 October 1998: 3.
9 ITAR–TASS news agency, Moscow, 28 July 1998.
10 *Argumenty i Fakty*, December 1997, no. 48.
11 Petersen 1996: 137.

12 Matveyeva, Y., 'Russia's Far East: Tired, Cold and Ready for Independence', *Moscow News*, 30 September–6 October 1994: 13.
13 Portyakov 1996: 80.
14 *Rossiyskaya Gazeta*, 30 October 1998: 2.
15 Matviyenko 1996: 91–2.
16 Goerter-Groenvik 1998: 96.
17 *Rossiyskaya Gazeta*, 29 October 1998: 1.
18 Kerr 1996: 934–9.
19 Ministry of Foreign Relations of the Republic of Karelia 1998: 4.
20 *Diplomaticheskiy Vestnik*, 1996, no. 8: 9–11.
21 Heininen and Kakonen 1998: 33–4, 37–8.
22 See the Action Plan for the Northern Dimension, at http:/europa.eu.int/comm/ external-relations/north-dim/ndap/06_00_en.pdf.

7 Military aspects of regionalism

Dr Pavel K. Baev

Introduction

In the turbulent development of regional processes in Russia during the first decade of its post-Soviet existence it was mostly the interplay between political intrigues and economic interests that appeared to be the main driving force. There were, however, other forces at work as well, with significant impacts on the dynamics and directions of these processes; the transformation of military structures in particular deserves attention in this regard. The immediately obvious feature is the opposite direction of the two trajectories: while regionalism, with all its zigzags and interruptions, was generally on the rise,[1] the armed forces went into prolonged decline, which combined 'natural' deterioration caused by sustained under-financing and damage inflicted by combat operations, first of all in Chechnya. It appears to be possible to make an analytical connection between these dynamics: rapid dismantling of the Soviet military machine opened the way for the development of regional processes, and the growth of regionalism reduced the share of resources available for the centre and thus caused further shrinking of the military structures. By the end of the 1990s that interplay had reached a level at which the army was no longer able to survive as a centralised institution and had to turn to regional sources of supply and support, so that 'healthy' units were found mainly in rich regions. By and large, however, the armed forces were able to preserve their integrity against centrifugal forces; this chapter will examine this resilience, taking a chronological approach to the course of events.

With the end of Boris Yeltsin's era, the character of regional processes has significantly changed, while a new attempt at arresting the decay of the armed forces has also been undertaken. President Vladimir Putin has executed a series of measures aimed at restoring the efficiency of central control, seeking to advance his design of a vertically integrated state. He relies heavily on the power instruments for implementing this project, and in fact started the Second Chechen War as a means of launching it. The ability of the armed forces to respond to the new impulses cannot be explained only by the fact that they have received much presidential attention and enjoyed priority financing. It is possible to assume that progressive weakening of the centralised state generates a reaction in the military aimed at preserving their institutional integrity; Putin is able to tap into that 'survival instinct' and achieve strong internal mobilisation. Whether these changes amount to clear breaks in both the trajectories of rising regionalism and declining military power or merely temporary setbacks is unclear as yet; this chapter will attempt to produce a preliminary answer, seeking also to look into possible interplays between the two processes in the near future.

The pains at the start

The collapse of the Soviet Union produced such a powerful and destructive resonance that the newborn states were all challenged to prove their survivability. President Yeltsin, as one of the initiators of the break-up, which was very unpopular in his own country, had to move quickly and resolutely to build the foundation of a new Russian state. He prioritised economic reforms, expecting them to consolidate his support after a short period of 'shock therapy' (which proved to be a bad miscalculation). He also gave priority attention to relations with regional leaders, pushing for the approval of a new Federal Treaty as early as late March 1992.[2] Military matters, in contrast, were left largely unattended for several crucial months. While that was arguably the best possible moment to launch a far-reaching reform project against which the military leadership – demoralised by the fiasco of the August coup and stunned by the spontaneous disappearance of the Union of Soviet Socialist Republics (USSR) – would hardly be able to muster much resistance, Yeltsin decided to let the opportunity slip away.[3]

There was perhaps more to that neglect than mere lack of administrative resources and a short attention span. Yeltsin, with his keen political instinct, might have sensed the brutality of forthcoming political battles, both *vis-à-vis* the regions and in the centre, and have seen the need to win the loyalty of the army; enforcing inevitably painful reforms was definitely not the way to achieve that. Leaving the military until May 1992 to comprehend the increasingly obvious impossibility of preserving any quasi-Soviet integrity,[4] he then embraced the Ministry of Defence and the General Staff (commonly abbreviated as *Genshtab*) as the High Command of the Russian state, thus not only assuming responsibility for sustaining the military structures, but also subscribing to the particular military-bureaucratic culture embodied in these two institutions.

The armed forces had by mid-1992 found themselves facing risks of loss of control over poorly connected units in faraway provinces and further disintegration – but not due to the spectacular growth of regionalism in the Russian Federation. The High Command saw its combat units taking sides with separatists in Transnistria, its garrisons besieged in Azerbaijan and Georgia, its troops threatened by mutinous crowds in Tajikistan and harassed in the Baltic states. While for republican presidents and *oblast* governors in Russia the notion of regionalism had begun to mean high status and tangible fruits of real power, for the top brass it was associated with violence and wars. The only way to preserve the unity of the Russian army was to take a resolute course in those 'hot spots' where it found itself engaged, and indeed Moscow started to issue combat orders, starting with Transnistria.[5]

This proactive course was not aimed at implementing some 'neo-imperialist' design, if only for the obvious reason that the policy-makers in the Kremlin were at that time plainly unable to present to the military any 'positively patriotic' ideology and were absolutely uninterested in any expansionist schemes.[6] In fact the series of risky but overall remarkably successful engagements in violent conflicts in the former USSR contributed to the emergence of a new post-Soviet institutional identity for the armed forces, which was quite narrow in scope and focused on the figure of the commander-in-chief. The military gradually reinvented itself as a 'presidential institution' which – reviving the old monarchical tradition – acted only on orders from the man in the Kremlin and expected his special care, rejecting all attempts to establish parliamentary or democratic control.

This 'presidential' identity was supplemented by the evolution of the military culture in which the old Soviet bureaucratic patterns were increasingly blended with new war-fighting habits and 'warrior' style. This cultural trend was implicitly reinforced by the general reorientation of the armed forces from the west more towards the south, which occurred in the course of massive withdrawals from Germany and the Baltic states. Conducted under strong political pressure, these redeployments resulted in irreparable damage to many elite units, and the loss of combat capabilities aggravated the loss of self-confidence, creating a new inferiority complex, against which the 'small wars' in the southern periphery were the best possible medicine.

President Yeltsin was carefully cultivating these shifts in identity and culture, indeed showing his 'special care' (at least in terms of financing in 1992/3) and sheltering the army from the political squabbles and clashes that were steadily escalating from early 1993.[7] Yeltsin was fully aware that his prolonged confrontation with the Supreme Soviet eroded his ability to control regional elites, who were eager to swallow more and more sovereignty, and he was firmly set on resolving the crisis through a total victory that would bring the power back to the Kremlin.[8] He also knew that such a victory could be achieved only by violent means, but was certain that the army would deliver; hence his 'surprise' that the High Command was so hesitant to give the battle order on the critical night of 4 October.[9] But the tanks did arrive at the White House and their guns indeed secured for Yeltsin the victory he had been craving, destroying not only the Parliament but – by deafening resonance – the regional opposition as well.

Many analysts were inclined to see in that forceful entry of the military into the political arena a permanent arrival that would secure for the top brass a position of power in the state hierarchy and the ability to exert heavy influence on state policies.[10] In fact the opposite proved to be true. The tank salvos did not just confirm the army's 'presidential institution' identity but turned it into a trap, since there was no other way for the military to justify its actions. The armed forces, accepting the role of the final arbiter, established themselves as an anti-parliamentary and, by extension, also an anti-regional institution. The president, however, saw the military as an instrument whose political usefulness had expired but whose loyalty could now be taken for granted.[11] The first manifestation of that attitude was the deep cuts in the 1994 military budget, which took the top brass by surprise. There was more to come, and the worst came by the end of the year, when the 'management' of the conflict in Chechnya by means of special operations conducted by the Federal Counterintelligence Service (FSK) had degenerated into a complete mess and the army was ordered to move in and sort it out.

The pains of war

The First Chechen War was a multi-dimensional disaster that served no rational political purpose and inflicted much damage on every component of Russia's national interests. The analyses of decision-making in the Kremlin leading to that war (inconclusive as they are) show the astonishing impact of petty intrigues and tremendous miscalculations.[12] But there was a certain logic to this blunder, since the 'imperial presidency' established by the 'victory' of 4 October 1993 was invariably set towards resolving political dilemmas by force – and Chechnya was indeed a 'natural' target.

It has been established beyond reasonable doubt that the High Command tried to argue against the invasion but – being marginalised in the Kremlin corridors – was unable to muster sufficiently strong resistance.[13] It is also clear that the armed forces, despite their general reorientation towards 'small wars' in the south, went into Chechnya unprepared and, despite the *Genshtab* tradition of meticulous planning, had scant idea about what they were doing. Their unpreparedness can be explained by the lack of time and resources to build a real 'frontline' military district in the North Caucasus;[14] that they did not know what they were doing can be logically connected with the experience of previous 'peace operations', which were generally low-cost enterprises with heavy emphasis on conventional deterrence.[15] Both, however, could also result from deficiencies in the new military culture, where bureaucratic and 'warrior' codes overlapped and worked at cross-purposes.

What is less clear is how that war affected the emerging regional networks of the armed forces. We can safely assume that the impact was complex and involved not only physical structures and resources but also identity and culture. For that matter, the very fact that the army had little choice but to follow the order of the commander-in-chief to go to war (notwithstanding the unclear character of that order and the resignations of many officers, from battalion commanders to deputy defence ministers)[16] further reinforced its 'presidential' identity. While the war caused splits in the establishment and conflicts in the political elite,[17] the military – as it was in the middle of the battle – had to stick to the president's side, since again that was the only way to justify their actions, some of which can only be qualified as atrocities.[18]

The scale and intensity of the war greatly strengthened the war-fighting traits of the military culture, including the high value of battlefield camaraderie and the low value of human life. At the same time it created a new, deep split between the army and society, which by and large turned against the war. That created a painful feeling of betrayal among the military, who saw no appreciation of their sacrifices. The military culture, being essentially rejected by society, became increasingly self-defensive and introvert.

The war, for which the armed forces were so ill prepared,[19] necessitated the mobilisation of all reserves and the deployment of composite units assembled from troops arriving from various military districts. Sustained overwork, while debilitating for the integrity of the military structures in the medium term, generated a strong centralisation impulse in 1995, which lasted perhaps until mid-1996. Rotating the combat units relatively quickly (sometimes after just three months), the armed forces across the whole country (except for the Strategic Rocket Forces and the navy, which sent only its marine battalions) felt united by the war.

That unifying effect stood in stark contrast to the general impact of the war on Russia's unity. While the propaganda attempts to justify the invasion through the 'falling domino'-type challenges to Russia's territorial integrity never held much water,[20] the war itself weakened the authority and the efficiency of the federal centre *vis-à-vis* the regions.[21] The problem was not that many republican leaders declared their opposition and made symbolic anti-war gestures, but that the levers of administrative control available to Moscow were progressively diminishing as the regional elites were consolidating. The Kremlin was forced to make new concessions to the regions, first trying to secure the vote for the pro-government party 'Our Home – Russia' in the December 1995 parliamentary elections (with only limited success), and then desperately campaigning for Yeltsin's re-election in spring 1996.[22] Yeltsin's electoral victory did not reverse the gains for the regions, since soon afterwards most governors and republican presidents were able to consolidate their own support bases in regional elections.[23]

Overall, up until autumn 1996 the armed forces, while shrinking in size and degenerating, isolated and alienated from society, remained essentially untouched by the accelerating regional processes and retained their centralised character and 'presidential' identity. That picture changed when the fiasco in Chechnya became official.

The pains of defeat

The Khasavyurt Accords of August 1996, for which Aleksandr Lebed took the credit, and later the blame, were accepted with great relief by a society that was by then eager to make peace at almost any price – and with much disgruntlement by an army that felt betrayed again.[24] The peace did little to bridge the gap between the army and society, as the army, completing the retreat, discovered that society had lost all interest in military matters and had no intention of making up for the losses suffered in combat operations. In principle, the defeat – in much the same way as the Crimean War in 1856 and the Russo-Japanese War in 1905 – created the necessary conditions for deep military reforms, but those required strong political leadership and sustained public support, neither of which was forthcoming. When in mid-1997 the efforts of General Rokhlin turned the neglect of the army into a political problem, President Yeltsin quickly reacted by issuing a package of decrees, but those prescribed mostly palliative measures, effective only for defusing the political bomb.[25]

The armed forces were left mostly to their own devices and it is precisely through that neglect that the effects of regionalism started to penetrate. The key agent was certainly the shortage of resources. Many observers started to notice that under-financing had multiple impacts (like forcing many units to rely on the local draft and abandoning the system of rotation of officers, pushing for developing ties with local suppliers and tempting officers to take second jobs), all of which encouraged the military to participate in the growth of regional networks.[26] However, unpaid salaries, accumulating utility bills and crumbling logistics were not the only incentives for the military to go 'native': besides failing in its resource-distribution function, the 'centre' (which for the military has always had an omnipotent and almost mystical meaning) failed to perform its command-and-control role and its quintessential purpose-providing role as well. Military identity as a 'presidential institution' became almost meaningless as the president lost interest in the armed forces and neglected to show any 'special care'. Besides, there were quite a few other 'presidential power structures', from the Federal Security Service to the Ministry of Emergencies, which were much more successful at proving their value and at getting the desired attention (which mostly meant resources).

This identity crisis was aggravated by the crisis in the professional culture, since the defeat in Chechnya deeply undermined the war-fighting ethos and 'warrior' style. Yeltsin's choice of a new defence minister confirmed this cultural trend, since Marshal Sergeyev had made his career in the Strategic Rocket Forces, where diligence, efficiency and dedication were cultivated as the core values.[27] Nuclear weapons, while heavily loaded with symbolism, were never perceived as war-fighting instruments, and that encouraged the development of a professional culture in this service on bureaucratic lines. Sergeyev therefore personified this trait in military culture and indeed had little sympathy towards 'Chechen warriors', placing loyal subordinates in the key positions in the Ministry of Defence. Sergeyev's 'rocket cabal' was able to set a clear priority in resource allocation towards the Strategic Forces (making the intercontinental ballistic missile (ICBM) *Topol-M* the single best-funded project),[28] but this 'favouritism' seriously alienated the battered Ground Forces, which were directly subordinated to the General Staff.

The combination of starvation, identity crisis and internal cultural conflict was strongly pushing the military towards the regions, where dynamic economic processes went hand in hand with political sovereignisation and identity building.[29] The main questions at that time were how fast the army would become enmeshed in regional political processes and how violent these would become as a result.[30] The main limitations here were in fact set by the scale of interests of regional elites. While often tempted to make grand gestures (Aleksandr Lebed's suggestion that he assume responsibility for strategic assets on the territory of Krasnoyarsk *kray* made most headlines abroad, but Yuriy Luzhkov's generosity in financing the construction of a new strategic submarine and housing projects in Sevastopol was of the same order), in practical terms the regional leaders were not that interested in 'privatising' expensive but not very usable military units. Their interests were much more focused on 'domesticating' the Interior Ministry and other law-enforcement structures in their respective domains: the most attractive were the OMON (Special Purpose Militia Unit) and SOBR (Special Rapid Reaction Unit) forces.[31]

The landmark event that reduced the ability of regional leaders to sustain their own 'armies' and forced them to scale down their sovereignty ambitions was the August 1998 financial meltdown. While the instant reaction in the regions to that catastrophe was self-protective (like erecting extra trade barriers or introducing their own ersatz money), in a matter of a few weeks they all flocked back to Moscow, looking for a co-ordinated strategy of recovery and granting support to the new prime minister, Yevgeniy Primakov, who in fact cherished a couple of centralist ideas (like doing away with regional elections altogether).[32] While the bankrupt regions had few possibilities to support the military structures, the armed forces were also badly hit by the August 1998 crisis, and their deterioration towards disintegration continued unchecked and unnoticed.

Putin's harmony

This disheartening picture of material degradation, identity crisis and cultural marginalisation changed miraculously during the second half of 1999, and the miracle had a name: Vladimir Putin. It was hard to take this little man seriously when Yeltsin appointed him as yet another prime minister and proclaimed him as his true successor. However, within one month this unspectacular character with no experience in leadership turned Moscow's political arena upside down, using the military as the Archimedean lever. Instead of handling the wounded armed forces with gentle care and examining their many weaknesses with due attention, Putin ordered them into a new war, first on a limited scale (Dagestan, September

1999),[33] and when it proved to be not only successful but also quite popular – back into Chechnya.

The analysis of the electoral instrumentalisation of the Second Chechen War goes beyond the scope of this chapter,[34] but its complex impact on the Russian armed forces must be examined. The impact has spread much further than the urge of the 'hawks', like General Troshev or General Shamanov, to take revenge or their hopes of reviving the 'combat spirit' of the army; it has been more profound than the aspirations, cherished by the *Genshtab*, of diverting more resources into military structures and raising the prestige of the armed forces. The war initially appeared to restore the integrity of the army, to convince society to embrace it once again, to forge for it a new meaningful identity, to secure coherence in its professional culture – but could this harmony be real and lasting?

This author instinctively leans towards a negative answer, while fully aware that this view might stem from a combination of professional scepticism and Russian pessimism ('that harmony is too good to be true'), anti-Putin bias ('that man is up to no good') and anti-war sentiment ('nothing good could come from that war'). In order to test this answer, three different perspectives are taken; each has a regional angle inserted into a mixture of tangible parameters and unquantifiable assessments.

Resources and reconfiguration

Launching a new Chechen campaign, Putin – then a fresh prime minister – made sure that this effort was properly financed. Broad societal support for the war made it not only possible but even necessary to channel extra resources there, since the public wanted to see Russian soldiers battle worthy.[35] However, Putin's ambitions stretched much further than simply sustaining the war effort; as early as September 1999 he proclaimed his intention of rebuilding the strength of the armed forces through complex modernisation that would reconnect the military-industrial complex and make the army a major customer on the weapons market.[36] That vision stretched beyond the dreams of the *Genshtab*, but Putin insisted that he was serious. The 2000 military budget was R143 billion, compared with R109 billion in 1999 (a jump from 17.2 to 21 per cent of budget spending),[37] including military costs for the Chechen War that were estimated at about R25 billion.[38] In 2001 the military budget was further increased to R219 billion (18.8 per cent of budget spending), with inflation expected to reach 20 per cent and the military costs of Chechnya going down to about R10 billion. In the draft 2002 budget, R282 billion were allocated to the military (only 15.1 per cent of budget spending, which is roughly the same as is spent on state debt servicing), but expenditure on Chechnya and other anti-terrorist operations cannot be estimated even approximately.[39]

In practical terms, these increases in funding have not advanced the modernisation programmes very far: there was – and still is – an urgent need to cover debts and arrears, to raise salaries and to pay for all sorts of emergencies. The bill for the *Kursk* was certainly the heaviest in the latter category, but the number of explosions, fires and other military accidents has been extraordinary.[40] Leaving the 'human factor' aside, we can safely assert that under-investment in military infrastructure during the 1990s was such that sustained support and not firefighting were necessary before the risks could be reduced to an acceptable level. This demand significantly narrows the scope of any weapon-modernisation programmes. Besides, and most fundamentally, the very possibility of financing the war and of allocating extra funds to the armed forces is created by high oil prices, which generate a healthy budget surplus. Putin's government cannot count on this 'good weather' lasting through 2002,[41] particularly if one takes into consideration the impact on the global economy of the devastating terrorist attacks in the US on 11 September 2001.

The much-improved resource situation in 2000/1 significantly reduced the pressure on military units to search for local supply sources and 'sponsorship'. In the other part of the equation, regional leaders also saw their financial reserves much reduced, as the centre claimed a greater share in the distribution of tax revenues, abruptly cutting the bargaining known as 'budget federalism'.[42] Putin has been so successful in this financial recentralisation that he has so far discovered no need to channel the resources through the seven macro-districts created with a big fanfare in mid-2000 to kickstart federal reform.[43] The grand design was to create a solid new level in the territorial organisation of Russia's space, but the functional efficiency of that design still remains questionable.[44]

Much was made by politologists of the fact that the boundaries of Putin's districts mostly coincided with those of Military Districts (in fact much closer correspondence exists with Interior Forces districts).[45] But in reality the integration of 'power structures' in this seven-unit framework has not advanced far, since purely administrative measures without control over resources have not had much of an impact.[46] The proposal to merge the logistic structures of the armed forces and other 'armies' (first of all, the Ministry of Interior forces) has met stiff resistance from the latter (who are generally much better off in terms of supplies than the military) and now appears stillborn.[47] Even the adjustment of the boundaries of various 'power structures' districts has proceeded with much procrastination,[48] and the armed forces, for their part, carried on with the implementation of the long-planned merger of the Volga and Urals Military Districts, which finally happened on 1 September 2001. While the merger makes clear operational sense, focusing the larger Volga–Urals Military District on interventions in potential conflicts in Central Asia and further south,[49] it certainly defies the logic of building a coherent heptagonal framework. In fact, the only one of the newly created 'presidential districts' that makes practical sense from the military point of view is the Southern, led by General Kazantsev, who has been much involved in co-ordinating regional responses to the 'complex emergency' of Chechnya. While dominating the regions politically and economically, Putin has not built any reliable institutional fortifications against a possible new rise of regionalism.

Identity and image

The Second Chechen War instantly and radically altered both the self-perception of the military and societal attitudes towards the armed forces. Putin's confident leadership had restored a meaningful 'presidential identity' to the army even before he was actually elected to the post. What was more, Putin offered the military an opportunity to broaden their identity through participation in his 'Great Russia' project. Subscribing to that project, the army has been able to present its (increasingly inglorious) role in the war as patriotic service, despite its deliberately low-key nomenclature as an 'anti-terrorist operation'. That ability, of course, was a function of high societal support for the war and acceptance of its brutality across the whole country.

Explanations for the sharp contrast in popular support with the First Chechen War bring together the Kremlin's firmer control over and more skilled manipulation of the media, genuine fear and anger in the streets about terrorism,[50] and frustration that had been building from the pains of economic decline and particularly of the August 1998 meltdown.[51] What is particularly remarkable about that support is that it dissipated much more slowly than had been expected by most experts as the war arrived at the familiar deadlock; but by mid-2001 the level of approval had slipped below the 50 per cent level, and by mid-March 2002 the level had declined further, albeit still slowly, so the writing has indeed appeared on the proverbial wall.[52]

Two qualifications should be added before jumping to any conclusion about a forthcoming new identity crisis in the military. One is that support for the war was not directly translated into support for the army; while Putin claimed that 'the army has regained trust in itself and society believes in and trusts its army',[53] a more precise indicator was the negative societal attitude towards the draft – and that did not change much.[54] Indeed, the atmosphere in the barracks has remained bad beyond description, and desertion has become not only more violent but also massive in scale.[55] The second reservation is that the broad support in society for the presidential 'Great Russia' project has never had a real mobilisational drive. It has noticeably weakened fledgling regional identities,[56] and the public has generally been positive towards the statist discourse but has shown no readiness to make sacrifices for the sake of restoring Russia's power and prestige.[57] More specifically, that means that the allocation of extra resources to military programmes has been possible only insofar as it has not hurt important economic interests, including regional ones.

With these qualifications added, the conclusion about widening cracks both in the public perceptions of the armed forces as the embodiment of Russia's power and in the self-perception of the military as a proud and respected 'presidential institution' appears better proven. The deadlock in Chechnya opens these cracks still wider every day, but also makes the military worried, if not paranoid, about every mention of a 'political solution'. Whatever Putin's own personal nightmares about the outcome of this 'presidential war', the top brass are certain that any compromise would be as devastating to their identity and integrity as it was in 1996, opening the way for regional forces to pull the army apart. The High Command is therefore firmly set on delivering a clear victory, which in fact is achievable, if deadly force is applied consistently and systematically.[58] While the rebel attack on Gudermes in mid-September 2001 proved yet again that the deadlock would be unsustainable, a 'military solution' involving thorough destruction of southern Chechnya may have become more feasible in the context of the US-led war against terrorism, which Putin was so quick to join.

Culture and cadre

That the war has brought back with a vengeance the war-fighting elements in military culture is self-evident; what is less so is that the bureaucratic elements have shown great resilience. The conflict between these two cultural traits was personified in the headlong collision in July 2000 between the defence minister, Sergeyev, and the chief of the General Staff, Kvashnin, which received much media attention.[59] Most specialists expected hard-driven Kvashnin, who from day one was in charge of operations in Chechnya, to score an easy victory, particularly since he had been promoted to full membership of the Security Council.[60] The president, however, took a very cautious approach towards that embarrassing scandal, obviously seeing more to it than just a personal animosity.[61] He removed Sergeyev, who was resigned to his failure to integrate all strategic assets under one command, but replaced him with the civilian Sergey Ivanov, his most trusted 'lieutenant', so Kvashnin could by no means claim victory. In fact, the profile of the General Staff (as well as that of Security Council) is visibly in decline, and that may open the way to eliminating the traditional overlap in functions and responsibilities in the High Command, but it could as easily lead to disorganisation of the rigid control system cultivated by the *Genshtab*.[62]

Himself a product of a bureaucratic culture (it would be fundamentally incorrect to interpret his background as a 'spymaster'),[63] Putin has much better insight into the workings of the monstrous military bureaucracy in Moscow than he has understanding of, or trust in, the war-fighting culture emanating from Chechnya. Starting the first round of cadre reshuffling in the Defence Ministry and the General Staff, Putin and Ivanov were very careful not to promote any of the 'Chechen heroes', relying more on 'paper generals'.[64] Several suitable opportunities to remove the 'warriors' from the ranks were found in regional politics (General Shamanov was elected governor of Ulyanovsk *oblast*, General Pulikovskiy was appointed the president's representative in the Far Eastern District, and General Kazantsev in the Southern District). But, typically, in moving several generals to the Moscow political arena, Putin has not selected a single Chechen veteran, perhaps seeking to avoid a mistake similar to that with the maverick General Rokhlin.[65] Overall there is hardly any evidence that would support the early assessments of many experts about the growing influence of the military on the course of Putin's recentralisation/remilitarisation of the country.[66]

This cadre policy, carefully planned as it is, creates the potential for a new cultural conflict in the armed forces. Transferring the main responsibility for Chechnya to the Federal Security Service (FSB) did not change the fact that most of the fighting there, as well as most of the tasks in other local conflicts (the list of potential 'counter-terrorist' emergencies remains long), has to be undertaken by the army. These conflicts remain manpower intensive, hence the failure to reduce the grouping in Chechnya or, indeed, to execute significant cuts in the total strength of the army.[67] There is an objective need to cultivate the 'war-fighting' culture, and painful experiences with the 'warriors' – who rarely make easy-to-handle political puppets (until his death Aleksandr Lebed continued to be a sharp reminder of that)[68] – do not diminish this need. Keeping the 'Chechen generals' out of Moscow, smart as that may seem to the Kremlin political technologists, might add a regional dimension to this cultural conflict, so that distrust and irritation against the High Command could come together with growing involvement in local affairs and create a powerful centrifugal force.

Conclusion: reforms and regions

It was one of the main achievements of the first two years of Putin's presidency that the spontaneous growth of regional processes in Russia was held firmly in check and recentralisation became the dominant trend. It is much more doubtful whether Putin has succeeded in arresting the rot of the military structures. The war in Chechnya initially produced a positive impact on the integrity and prestige of the armed forces,[69] but this was only of a temporary nature and in fact provided the High Command with the opportunity to postpone serious reforms even further.[70] It was only in mid-2001 that the drive towards implementing a new reform project gained some momentum, but the sheer amount of accumulated problems will make it much more difficult to compensate for the lost time.

With all his hands-on management style, Putin is yet to commit himself to a meaningful reform project that would bring together consistently the resource base available for the army, the threats it is expected to meet, its present posture and its desired shape. The choices that were facing him at the start of his term are still there,[71] but the amount of pain associated with each has seriously grown – and Putin's readiness to accept responsibility for this pain is increasingly in doubt. Bureaucratic streamlining (Ivanov's main task) and modest downsizing with generous resourcing (Putin's declared priorities) are not even beginning to address the combined crisis of integrity, identity, control and culture into which the armed forces are sinking. One major step in arresting this muddle-down could be a shift to the professional army and abolishment of the draft, which is arguably the main source of the anti-military attitude in the public. So far there is no indication that Putin and Ivanov are contemplating such a step: their attempts to bridge the gap between the army and society involve mainly manipulative 'political technologies'. Even if the political will is generated, the war is certain to undermine many of the reform efforts; resource drain is the immediate problem, but the impact of Chechnya on the professional culture and morale of the army is certain to be profound and lasting.

While in the late 1990s it was the growth of regionalism that affected the integrity of the armed forces,[72] by 2005 it could be the aggravation of the multiple crises in the military that spill over into the regions and cause deformations in the regional processes. The area which appears most worrisome in this respect is the North Caucasus. Paradoxically, it is the current successes that may contain seeds of future troubles: indeed, it is in the Southern 'presidential' district that the boundaries of various 'power structures' are most coherent; it is also there that the integration of their activities is proceeding most smoothly. Behind these achievements, however, are the interests of the 'core Russian' regions in the area – first of all Stavropol *kray* and Krasnodar *kray*, backed by Rostov, Astrakhan and Volgograd *oblasts*, which see direct practical sense in uniting their efforts to counter the security threats emanating from the south. While Dagestan and Ingushetia find themselves within the Chechen war theatre, internal divisions permanently plague Kabardino-Balkaria and Karachay-Cherkessia. All these instabilities could escalate if the course towards achieving a military victory in Chechnya is indeed implemented; the spillover from a 'Stalinist solution' may be much stronger than from the war itself, primarily due to the deep radicalisation of ethnic conflicts. In this situation of sharp dividing lines being drawn by violent conflicts, the Southern District could evolve into an alliance of five 'Russian' regions (with North Osetia becoming its bridgehead in the Caucasus). This alliance might effectively privatise the combat units of the North Caucasus Military District and perform power-projection in a proactive foreign policy in the Caucasus region, with or without Moscow's consent. While it is admittedly a far-fetched scenario,[73] this points up the risks of militarised regionalism discernible through the fog of the Chechen War.

Notes

1 Nikolai Petrov, one of the most insightful analysts of Russian regional processes, has argued that 'the balance of forces between the federal centre and regional leaders has been changing like the swings of a pendulum', describing the ups and downs of that 'centralization–decentralization pendulum' in the period 1990–7 (see his chapter on 'Centre–Periphery Relations' in Petrov 1999b). In my under-

standing, however, the trajectory of regionalism has resembled more an ascending spiral.

2 Valery Tishkov, while describing the negotiations leading to the Treaty as an 'elitist enterprise', also asserted that it played a useful role as a 'provisional compromise' (1997: 61–2).

3 I have looked into the intrigues surrounding that non-decision elsewhere (Baev 1996: ch. 3).

4 William Odom (1998) has thoroughly analysed the military dimension of the break-up of the USSR (see particularly the last chapter, 'The Illusion of the CIS Armed Forces').

5 For a balanced analysis, see the chapters by Edward Ozhiganov and Brian Taylor in Arbatov *et al.* 1997.

6 I have examined the gap between military actions and political guidelines elsewhere (Baev 1994: 531–3).

7 See Stephen Foye, 'Russia's Fragmented Army Drawn into the Political Fray', *RFE/RL Research Report*, 9 April 1993: 1–7.

8 Reddaway and Glinski (2001: 632), who consider the October coup as a 'key turning point in modern Russian history' also argue that '[t]he Yeltsin regime's persistent attempts to strengthen its grip without addressing the legitimacy problem produced a vicious circle of escalating autocratic centralization of executive powers within a government whose administrative capacity was progressively declining' (*ibid.*: 371).

9 In his memoir, Yeltsin reflects upon 'silence, a terrible, inexplicable silence' (1994: 384–6) that was the reaction of the High Command to his urge to move troops into Moscow. Liliya Shevtsova, one of the most insightful analysts of Yeltsin's court, noted that 'Yeltsin was forced to humble himself, going personally to the generals to beg for help'. She also insists that 'the president's advisors underestimated how the military and Defence Minister Grachev would resist taking part in the action and overestimated their readiness to support the president' (2000: 86–7).

10 Thus Yuriy Afanasyev (1994) wrote: 'The real winner in the October 1993 showdown … was the military-industrial complex acting in unison with the bureaucracy'. (A good example of Western expert analysis is in Desch 1993.)

11 See Stephen Foye, 'Civilian and Military Leaders in Russia's New Political Arena', *RFE/RL Research Report*, 15 April 1994: 1–6.

12 Anatol Lieven, whose epic book *Chechnya: Tombstone of Russian Power* stands apart in the bibliography of that war, asserted that 'the Russian administration stumbled from one bungled approach to another, finding itself progressively drawn in deeper and deeper'. However, he also reminded the reader that 'there is nothing especially mysterious, or indeed Russian about it' (1998: 90).

13 Thus Roy Allison argued that '[t]he decision to intervene with force overrode not only the prudence of the military leadership but also specialist advice on the North Caucasus' (see his chapter on 'The Chechenia Conflict: Military and Security Policy Implications' in Allison and Bluth 1998: 243).

14 See Stephen Foye, 'Huge Military District in the North Caucasus Planned', *RFE/RL News Brief*, 30 June 1994.

15 For an excellent analysis of the strategy on the early phase of the war, where the official rhetoric regarding the 'disarming of illegal formations' was mixed with military misperceptions about the nature of the operation, see Thomas 1995b.

16 See Allison and Bluth 1998: 245–6.

17 It is typical in this respect that the State Duma came the closest to impeaching President Yeltsin in May 1999 on charges of violating the law by unleashing the Chechen War.

18 See Lieven 1998: 130–5.

19 Thus, on the very eve of the invasion (10 December 1994) eleven generals from the High Command of the Ground Forces, led by the commander-in-chief Colonel-General Vladimir Semenov, appealed to the Parliament against launching the war, rejecting the defence minister, Grachev's, claim that the army was ready (see *Komsomolskaya Pravda*, 11 December 1994; for a detailed assessment by Russian experts, see Novichkov *et al.* 1995).

20 Tishkov asserts that 'No fatal threat to the territorial unity of Russia existed, except that which it allowed itself' (1997: 227). Leonid Smirnyagin also argues that 'the threat of disintegration in the 1980s and 1990s was due not to the aggrandizement of power by the regions, but to the weakening of central authority. However, the momentum of centrism was sufficient enough to avoid this danger by 1994' (see Azrael and Pain 1998: 3).

21 Thus Richard Sakwa argued that '[r]ather than enhancing the unity of the Russian Federation, the Chechen war probably contributed in the long-run to centrifugal pressures' (1996: 209).

22 See Petrov 1999b: 59; Reddaway and Glinski, estimating that the real cost of Yeltsin's electoral campaign 'probably surpassed $100 million by a wide margin', pointed out that

> [He] opened wide the coffers of the state budget for an aggressive clearance sale of government favors and services. ... Most of Yeltsin's campaign trips to the provinces were marked by granting of government credits and tax breaks, and by outright giveaways of money.
>
> (Reddaway and Glinski 2001: 514)

23 Examining these developments, Gail Lapidus warns: 'While a healthy dose of decentralization was initially viewed as an important element of political democratisation, given a long tradition of hyper-centralization of state power, Russia now faces an uncontrolled and seemingly uncontrollable unravelling of central power' (2001: 350).

24 For an accurate juxtaposition of political 'pacifism' and military complaints about the 'stolen victory', see Vitaly Shlykov, 'Chechnya and the Posture of the Russian Army', *Voyennyy Vestnik* no. 6, Moscow: MFIT, October 1999.

25 Several proposals for reforming the military were developed at that time; a good overview can be found in Arbatov (1998). However, when the Council on Foreign and Defence Policy made an effort to launch public debate (with the report 'Military Reform of Russia', *Nezavisimoye Voyennoye Obozreniye*, no. 25, June 1997) it fell perfectly flat.

26 Thus Martin Nicholson (1999) pointed out that 'the penury of the armed forces has made local commanders increasingly dependent on regional elites for pay, food and housing'. For an earlier diagnosis, see Thomas (1995a).

27 For a sympathetic portrait that emphasised Sergeyev's reformist credentials, see Aleksandr Golts, 'The Technocrat's Last Chance', *Itogi* no. 30, 28 June 2000.

28 For a sharp analysis of this prioritisation, see Galeotti 1998.

29 On identity building, see the chapters by Yuri Perfilyev (on regional symbolism) and Nikolai Petrov (on vodka brands) in Petrov (2001a).

30 Alexei Arbatov (1998) looked into the possible consequences of deliberate as well as spontaneous regionalisation of the armed forces in his excellent article. My speculations along these lines can be found elsewhere (Baev 1999/2000).

31 For a typical example we can take Yulia Latynina's novel *Hunt for the Elk* (1998), where a Siberian oligarch routinely brings the regional SOBR unit to Moscow for protection against criminal rackets. While certainly a work of fiction, it can perhaps be accepted as evidence, since the author is a well-known economic correspondent for several respected Moscow periodicals.

32 For a balanced and thought-provoking analysis, see Herd (1999), and the follow-up debate in the January 2001 issue of the same journal.

33 Media reports from the theatre showed a familiar picture of incompetent planning and poor co-operation (see, for instance, Vadim Solovyev, 'New Invasion Revealed Flaws in Russia's Military Posture', *Nezavisimoye Voyennoye Obozreniye* no. 35, 10–16 September 1999). General Troshev, in his recent memoir, presents a much more professional performance (see Gennady Troshev, 'Prelude to the Second Chechen War', *Nezavisimoye Voyennoye Obozreniye*, 24 August 2001).

34 See Sergei Kovalev, 'Putin's War', *New York Review of Books*, 10 February 2000.

35 Characteristically, while according to one VTsIOM poll from mid-March 2000 66 per cent of respondents expressed support for the war, another poll from the same time showed that only 12 per cent supported allocation of funds from the state budget for rebuilding Chechnya (see *Johnson's Russia List* no. 4273, 13 April 2000; no. 4211, 30 March 2000; the whole collection of National Public Opinion Research Centre (VTsIOM) polls can be found at www.polit.ru/vciom).

36 The goal of increasing production for the armed forces was set by Putin when he chaired the meeting of the Military-Industrial Commission in Severodvinsk (see Igor Korotchenko, 'Turning Towards Defence Industry', *Nezavisimoye Voyennoye Obozreniye*, 24–30 September 1999). Putin elaborated on this goal in a 21 March 2000 speech in Nizhniy Novgorod (for sharp criticism, see Vitaly Shlykov, 'Inescapable Complex', *Itogi* no. 19, 12 May 2000).

37 For official figures, see the website of the Finance Ministry (www.minfin.ru).

38 For estimates of the costs of the Chechen War, see Vladimir Georgiyev, '330 Million Dollars for the Fight with Chechen Fighters', *Nezavisimaya Gazeta*, 17 July 2001.

39 For sharply critical but competent comments on this draft budget, see Mikhail Delyagin, 'A Liberal Demagoguery Budget', *Versty*, 25 August 2001.

40 My short list for June–July 2001 includes the crashes of transport planes (Il-76, near Moscow, July 2001) and modern fighters (Su-33, outside Pskov, June 2001), explosions of air-to-air missiles (three batteries of much-advertised S-300, Moscow *oblast*, June 2001) and artillery depots (Nerchinsk, June 2001; Buryatiya, July 2001), and fires at a satellite control centre (Kaluga *oblast*, June 2001); for an update, see www.grani.ru/incidents.

41 The budget for the year 2002 is constructed with a surplus of 1.2 per cent of gross domestic product (GDP), assuming prices for Russian oil averaging US$17 per barrel. For expert criticism of that assumption, see Konstantin Smirnov, 'Budget with Redundancies', *Kommersant-Dengi*, 29 August 2001.

42 Yulia Latynina offered a more precise term in the title of her article: 'Budget Feudalism', *Expert* no. 1, 12 January 1998. On the military burden for the regions, see I. Ivanyuk, 'Can the Governors Feed the Army?', *Krasnaya Zvezda*, 19 April 2000.

43 Putin himself defined their role as 'consolidating and cementing Russia's state-hood' (see Marina Volkova, 'The Kremlin Wants to Transform the State', *Nezavisimaya Gazeta*, 19 May 2000).

44 Experts argued that from the point of view of management theory seven units in the middle level is too few for eighty-nine units on the third, while the relative size of the seven units is disproportional (the Central and Volga Districts have together nearly half of Russia's population) (see Zubarevich *et al.* 2001: 175).

45 See, for instance, Andrey Korbut, 'The Kremlin Unites the Powermen in the Regions', *Nezavisimoye Voyennoye Obozreniye* no. 17, 19 May 2000; Aleksandr Golts, 'Seven Jokers in One Pack', *Itogi* no. 21, 26 May 2000.

46 Experts now conclude that 'the real political resource of presidential representatives has turned out to be quite limited: they have been unable to resolve by themselves a single serious economic or political conflict'. Their estimates single

out Viktor Kazantsev for high involvement in redistribution of spheres of influence in his Southern District (see Dmitriy Yevstafyev, 'Russia's Seven Hamlets', *SMI.RU*, 14 May 2001).

47 For an argument in favour, see the interview with General Isakov, chief of the rear of the armed forces, 'Troops Are Strong Through Their Magazines', *Nezavisimoye Voyennoye Obozreniye*, 2 March 2001.

48 On the discrepancies and attempts to minimize them, see Petrov 2001b.

49 On the area of responsibility, see Vladimir Petrov, 'The Urals Has Come Closer to Pamir', *Grani.ru*, 27 August 2001.

50 A VTsIOM poll from August 2001 showed that the number of respondents who were 'very afraid' of becoming a victim of a terrorist attack had dropped from 42 per cent in September 1999 to 30 per cent (the low point in August 2000 was 27 per cent) (see www.polit.ru/documents/437282).

51 For a thoughtful analysis of these attitudes, see Pain 2001; Ulrich 2000.

52 One VTsIOM poll from July 2001 showed that only 33–6 per cent of respondents supported the continuation of combat operations and only 24 per cent thought that the war contributed to maintaining a 'combat spirit' in the army (www.polit.ru/documents/434213).

53 Putin, speaking at the ceremony in the Kremlin's Aleksandr Hall on 12 February 2000 (see Andrei Shukshin, 'Putin Praises Army, Promotes Generals', Reuters in *Johnson's Russia List* no. 4125, 21 February 2000).

54 According to a VTsIOM poll from February 2000, 45 per cent of respondents expressed a positive attitude towards the army (up from 19 per cent a year before) but only 30 per cent supported compulsory military service (see 'Russians Trust the Army but Do Not Want to Serve in It', *Polit.Ru*, 24 February 2000). Two respected analysts concluded that 'the Chechen war is a sentence passed on the conscript army' (see Aleksandr Golts and Dmitriy Pinsker, 'The Babylonian Vertical', *Itogi* no. 35, 15 August 2000).

55 The remarkable event that emphasised the scale of this problem was the desertion of a whole company of 589 Motor-Rifle Regiment based outside Samara on 22 August 2001. For an updated compilation of current cases, see www.ntv.ru/dosiex.html.

56 A symbolically important step was the Kremlin's firm line on cancelling the bilateral treaties with various regions and republics, which saw only weak resistance due to the fact that the regions, according to Ilya Gorfinkel, 'have found their ability to influence the federal processes reduced to the minimum' (see 'Parade Is Over', *Ekspert-Ural* no. 16, 27 August 2001).

57 Steve Hanson (2001) has argued that Putin attempts to combine the values of 'pragmatism' (in essence, self-interested instrumental rationality) and 'patriotism' (willingness to sacrifice for the fatherland), but the combination is weak in both parts.

58 I have elaborated on this option elsewhere (Baev 2000).

59 See, for instance, Vadim Solovyev, 'Generals' Fighting Bursts Open from under the Carpet', *Nezavisimaya Gazeta*, 14 July 2000.

60 That status rise, caused primarily by the Chechen War, was widely seen as creating the situation of 'two-power-centres' (*dvoyevlastiye*) in the armed forces (see, for instance, Aleksey Petrov, 'Nothing Is Worse Than Two Commanders in the Army', *Nezavisimaya Gazeta*, 27 July 2001).

61 Aleksandr Golts argued that 'the President and his team, considering the military vertical to be an ideal management mechanism, were absolutely unprepared for the conflict in the army leadership' (see *Itogi* no. 33, 15 August 2000).

62 For an argument on the overblown role of the *Genshtab*, see Vitaly Shlykov, 'Does Russia Need a General Staff?', *Voennyy Vestnik* no. 7, Moscow: MFIT, October 2000.

63 On Putin's bureaucratic patterns, see Herspring and Kipp 2001.
64 See Aleksey Tikhonov, 'Genshtab Subscribes to the Chuchhe Ideas', *Grani.ru*, 3 September 2001.
65 On the political careers in Moscow of the generals, see Andrey Korbut, 'Men in Uniform Turn into Bureaucrats', *Nezavisimaya Gazeta*, 31 August 2001.
66 See, for instance, Busza 1999.
67 On the numbers game with the military personnel, see Pavel Felgengauer, 'Military Cut Illusory', *The Moscow Times*, 30 August 2001.
68 A rich regional profile of the maverick general can be found in Petrov 1999a.
69 Speaking in Volgograd on 22 February 2000, Putin asserted that 'all that talk about our army falling apart and losing preparedness is all blatant lies' (see Irina Demchenko, 'Hawkish Putin Beats Drum on Russian Campaign Trail', Reuters in *Johnson's Russia List* no. 4127, 23 February 2000).
70 I have looked into that impact of Chechnya elsewhere (Baev 2001c).
71 I have elaborated the best case and the worst case options for military reforms during Putin's first presidential terms elsewhere (see Janes 2001).
72 For a sharp snapshot analysis, see Galeotti 1999.
73 I have indulged in speculations along these lines in my paper 'Russia: Super Power Turn Battle-Ground' presented at the workshop (Washington, 10 July 2001) of the Future Landpower Environment Project (FLEP), which forms part of the study *All Our Tomorrows*, conducted by the Defense Threat Reduction Agency, US Department of Defense.

Part III

Russia's regions under Putin

Case studies

8 Sakhalin *oblast*

Sectoral globalisation

Professor Michael Bradshaw

Introduction

In all sorts of ways Sakhalin *oblast* presents a microcosm of the problems facing the Russian Far East and Russia more generally.[1] It has a complex history, suffers from a narrow resource-dependent economy and is trying to come to terms with its increasing isolation and dislocation from the mainland of the Russian Far East and from the Russian economy generally. As we shall see, its traditional resource industries suffered during the 1990s, but it still has substantial resource potential. Nevertheless, after Moscow, Sakhalin has received more foreign direct investment than any other region in Russia. This is entirely due to the presence of oil and gas reserves off shore that have attracted the world's largest oil companies to the island. Consequently Sakhalin presents an interesting case study, as it highlights the processes involved when a Russian region becomes incorporated into the global energy economy. This chapter is divided into three major sections: the first provides details of the inherited structure of the economy of Sakhalin *oblast* and its performance during the 1990s; the second examines the various offshore oil and gas projects and their progress to date; the third considers the various scales of interaction and the numerous actors now involved in realising Sakhalin's potential as an oil and gas producer. The chapter concludes by considering the inter-relationship between Sakhalin's political and economic relations with the federal government in Moscow and with the global political economy.

Economic structure and performance

Sakhalin *oblast* includes Sakhalin Island and the Kuril island chain, both of which lie off the coast of Khabarovsk *kray* (see Figure 8.1). Possession of the Kuril islands has been a subject of dispute between Japan and Russia for more than three centuries. The region has a complex history. Japan held the southern Kuril islands from 1855 until the end of the Second World War in 1945. Japan also won control of the southern part of Sakhalin Island from 1905 until 1945. During that period the northern part of Sakhalin, which was under Soviet control, was part of Khabarovsk *kray*. Much of Sakhalin's

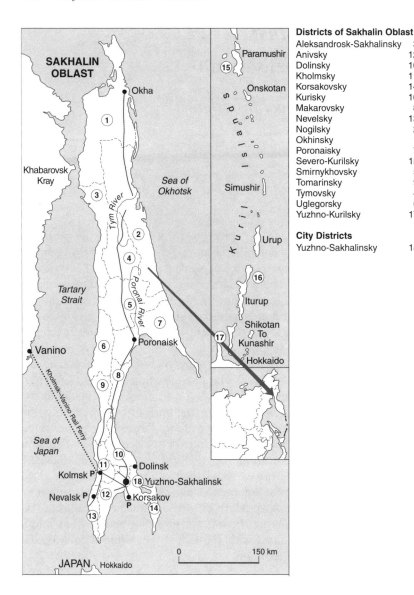

Districts of Sakhalin Oblast	
Aleksandrosk-Sakhalinsky	3
Anivsky	12
Dolinsky	10
Kholmsky	11
Korsakovsky	14
Kurisky	16
Makarovsky	8
Nevelsky	13
Nogilsky	2
Okhinsky	1
Poronaisky	7
Severo-Kurilsky	15
Smirnykhovsky	5
Tomarinsky	9
Tymovsky	4
Uglegorsky	6
Yuzhno-Kurilsky	17
City Districts	
Yuzhno-Sakhalinsky	18

Figure 8.1 The administrative districts of Sakhalin *oblast*

industrial base owes its origins to the period of Japanese control in the south and to the work of Japanese concessions in the north. In the post-1945 period Sakhalin became a closed garrison region, but its economy continued to develop within the sectors first developed by Japanese entrepreneurs: coal, oil, forestry and fishing. Today Sakhalin *oblast* occupies a territory of 87,100 square kilometres. The total population of the *oblast* at the beginning of 2000 was 598,000, a 15.8 per cent decline on the 1989 population of

710,000. The *oblast*'s capital is Yuzhno-Sakhalinsk, which is located in the south of Sakhalin Island. According to the 1989 census, 81.6 per cent of the population is ethnic Russian.

Figure 8.2 shows the trend in industrial decline in Russia, the Russian Far East and Sakhalin. On the face of it, Sakhalin seems to have fared better than the Russian Far East as a whole. Recession came early to Sakhalin, but recovery seems to have arrived early as well. According to official figures, the level of industrial production on Sakhalin at the end of 2000 was 60 per cent of that in 1990, compared with 56 per cent for Russia and 45 per cent for the Russian Far East as a whole. In 2000 three sectors accounted for 85.1 per cent of industrial production (in 1990 their share was 81.2 per cent, and in 1995 76.2 per cent): energy, 40.4 per cent, food (mainly fishing) 40.5 per cent and forestry 4.2 per cent (significantly down from 11.7 per cent in 1995).[2] All three sectors faced severe problems during the 1990s and, with the recent exception of oil production, their increasing dominance is down to the collapse of other sectors of industry rather than an increase in physical production (see Table 8.1 and Figure 8.2).

The fortunes of each resource sector tell a different story. Much of the *oblast*'s industrial base owes its origins to the period when the southern part of the island was part of Japan. During that time even the northern parts of the island, which were Russian and later Soviet territory, were developed by Japanese concessions. The island's coal, oil and pulp and paper industries were developed during that inter-war period. For example, in 1926 Japanese entrepreneurs founded the North Sakhalin Oil Company, a joint stock

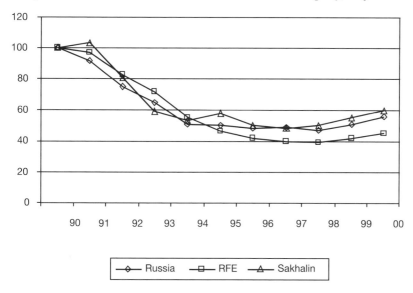

Figure 8.2 Industrial decline 1990–2000

Note: 1990 = 100: Russia, Russian Far East (RFE) and Sakhalin

Table 8.1 Production of important industrial products, 1990–2000

	1990	1991	1992	1993	1994	1995	1996	1997	1998	1999	2000
Electricity (billion kW hrs)	3.4	3.5	3.4	3.1	2.8	2.7	2.7	2.5	2.4	2.5	2.7
Oil (million tonnes)	1.9	1.8	1.7	1.6	1.6	1.7	1.7	1.7	1.7	1.8	3.4
Coal (million tonnes)	5.0	4.4	4.5	4.3	2.9	2.7	2.8	2.4	2.4	2.5	2.8
Sawn timber (thousand square metres)	2,669	2,395	2,242	1,581	1,124	1,088	818	560	560	733	766
Paper (thousand tonnes)	204	200	147	60.9	11.0	14.0	6.7	0.7	0.7	9.1	9.5
Fish and seafood (thousand tonnes)	927	856	576	491	378	414	357	442	442	452	420

Source: Goskomstat Rossii (2001) *Regiony Rossii, 2000 Vol. 1*, Moscow: Goskomstat: 595; and Sakhalin Obkomstat (2001) *Doklad o Sotsialno-ekonomicheskom Polozhenii Sakhalinskoy Oblasti*, Yuzhno-Sakhalinsk: Sakhalin Obkomstat: 18–22

company, to exploit some of the oil reserves of northern Sakhalin. Between 1926 and 1944 the Japanese extracted and exported to Japan more than 2 million tonnes of oil.[3] The Soviet government founded the Sakhalinneft Trust in 1928 to exploit the Soviet part of the oilfields and between 1928 and 1945 produced almost 6 million tonnes of oil.[4] Industrial production of coal began in southern Sakhalin in 1909 and total Japanese output up to 1945 was more than 48 million tonnes, of which 18 million tonnes was exported to Japan.[5] It is probably fair to say that for the Soviet Union Sakhalin's strategic position was more important than its economic output, most of which was oriented to local needs. Vysokov states: 'After 1945, as in the previous two centuries under Russia and Japan, Sakhalin continued to be little more than a "resource appendage to the centre" '. [6]

The island is isolated from the Far Eastern energy grid and has its own coal-based power-generation system, but the system is fragmented; there is no island-wide transmission system. The energy sector has suffered from a lack of investment, escalating costs and a non-payments crisis. This has resulted in persistent energy shortages on the island. The Sakhalin administration has restructured the island's coal industry, closing down the most inefficient mines and expanding opencast production. Production peaked at 5.8 million tonnes in 1979 and is now down to 2.7 million tonnes a year. However, the arrival of offshore natural gas and the subsequent gasification of the island's energy system will significantly reduce local demand for coal. The Sakhalin administration still has hopes of exporting significant amounts of coal to Japan and elsewhere in the Russian Far East.

Onshore oil production rose from 0.6 million tonnes in 1950 to 2.4 million tonnes in 1965 and then levelled off, rising to 2.6 million tonnes in 1986.[7] During the 1990s production slumped, averaging 1.7 million tonnes (see Table 8.1). The oil and gas industry in the north was badly damaged by the Neftegorsk earthquake in 1995. Onshore production has long since peaked, and substantial new investment is needed to enhance existing fields and develop new wells. Khabarovsk *kray* has traditionally been the major market, but non-payment problems added to the industry's difficulties. In 1999 Sakhalin oil production was significantly bolstered by the first offshore production (see Table 8.1). Production from Sakhalin-2's Molikpaq platform reached 1 million tonnes a year in 2000, and more than 70 per cent was exported, mainly to China, Japan and the US.[8] The future of the sector is tied to the development of offshore production rather than onshore. The distinction between the two is somewhat blurred as some of the offshore fields are being developed using onshore horizontal drilling, thus reducing the need for offshore platforms. Substantial future increases in oil and gas production will require significant investment in oil and gas pipelines and export terminals.

The forestry industry, and in particular the pulp and paper mills, owes its origins to Japanese industrialists and received relatively little investment during the Soviet period. The mills are now terribly antiquated and production has more or less ceased. Consequently the sector has retreated back into logging operations for export. Substantial capital investment is required to breathe life into the forestry sector and to develop more sustainable practices. Many forestry operations form the basis of single-enterprise towns in the interior of the island. The *oblast* administration has invested in new forestry equipment to improve the efficiency of the remaining enterprises, but the pulp and paper industry is beyond recovery. In addition, past forestry practices have wrought extensive environmental disruption, and more sustainable forestry management techniques are required to maintain production.

The situation in the island's fishing industry is somewhat different and very difficult to analyse. The sea off Sakhalin offers rich pickings, yet the island's fish-processing industry has fallen on hard times (see Table 8.1). The fish-processing industry has attracted foreign investment and there are a number of successful Russian–Japanese joint ventures; however, the problem for the formerly state-owned enterprises is that much of the catch is no longer landed on Sakhalin. Sakhalin's fishing industry now faces competition from mainland fishing fleets in home waters and overfishing has resulted in depleted stocks, so much so that the annual quotas are often not met. A case of too many boats chasing too few fish. This situation is the result of large-scale illegal fishing, both by Russian and foreign boats. Much of the fish caught by the Far East's fishing fleets is not landed in Russia. Instead fishermen sell their catch to foreign fish-processing ships out at sea or land it in Japan. Much of the revenue from these transactions remains off shore, or returns as cars and consumer goods for sale on the domestic market. Furthermore, most Russian fishing boats are now repaired and serviced in ports in Korea and China. Thus, revenue generated by fishing does not circulate through the island's economy, except in the booming trade in second-hand Japanese cars. The Russian Federal Security Service claims that Russia loses more than US$1 billion a year from the illegal sale of crab and salmon off shore. Japan's records of sea products imported from Russia show a volume three or four times higher than that shown by Russian records of exports to Japan. Nevertheless, fish and fish products are the *oblast*'s second most important export after oil.

This brief review of the Sakhalin resource economy shows the variety of problems that currently face the island. The *oblast* suffers from an acute energy shortage that will only be solved by offshore oil and gas development, but probably at the expense of the coal industry. The forestry sector has retreated into the export of reduced volumes of low value-added products such as logs and sawn timber. The fishing sector suffers from high levels of illegal exports that have starved the onshore economy of fish and funds, and that now threaten the viability of fish stocks. Thus, while it is clear that the island's economy has retreated into its traditional resource sectors, it also seems clear that these sectors cannot form the basis for sustainable economic recovery. Substantial new investment is required to modernise production and processing facilities, and new resolve is required to stop illegal fishing.

Politicians on the island and in Moscow lack the resolve to do what is necessary to stamp out corruption and deal with the current economic problems. In this context it is easy to understand why they see the offshore oil and gas projects as an easy solution to all Sakhalin's problems. Undoubtedly, in the long term the oil and gas projects will bolster the island's economy, but their progress has been slow, and the population of the island has so far seen little material benefit and remains concerned about possible environmental damage.[9] In fact, one could argue that the prospect of a future oil and gas Eldorado has resulted in neglect of the underlying structural problems that face the *oblast*'s economy. At present, Sakhalin Energy (Sakhalin-2) is paying money into the Sakhalin Development Funds (a total of $100 million over five years). Various other bonus payments have also been paid, and once Sakhalin-1 declares commercial development it will pay into the development fund. However, the sums involved (estimated as a total of almost $130 million between 1994 and 2000) are modest compared to the problems that confront the *oblast*.[10] Only the substantial income associated with large-scale oil and gas production can generate the kinds of sums needed to address the *oblast*'s economic and social problems.

Offshore oil and gas projects

The offshore oil and gas projects date back to the 1960s[11] but really came to fruition during the 1970s. The energy crisis of the early 1970s forced Japan to look for alternative sources of oil. At that time (as is still the case with Russia) the Soviet Union lacked the capital and technology to develop the resource potential of the then Soviet Far East. As a result of the perceived complementarity between resource-poor Japan and the resource-rich Soviet Far East, a number of large-scale, long-term compensation agreements were signed. Under these agreements the Japanese government advanced credits to be used by the Soviet partners to purchase equipment to develop the Far East's resource base. In turn, the export of future resources would generate funds to pay off the initial loan. Such projects were developed in the coal industry (the South Yakutian Coal Complex), the forestry industry (the so-called KS agreements) and the oil industry, the Sakhalin project. In the case of the Sakhalin project credits were used to purchase equipment to explore the offshore potential of the Sakhalin continental shelf. The theory was that revenue from offshore developments would then pay off the loan. To cut a long story short, the Sakhalin project did not move much beyond the initial exploration phase. Operating conditions were difficult and the Soviet side had limited experience of offshore exploration; nevertheless, oil and gas fields were delimited. The project then fell foul of US sanctions to protest the Soviet invasion of Afghanistan, and then falling oil prices and the poor shape of the Soviet economy made the projects less attractive. Nonetheless, throughout the 1980s the local oil and gas enterprise, Sakhalinmorneftegaz, continued exploration activities. In the early 1990s the projects were rejuvenated and two projects were tendered based on the fields discovered during the 1970s and 1980s. These projects have become known as Sakhalin-1 and Sakhalin-2. In 1995, after a long and highly contentious tendering process, the two projects became the first to be developed in Russia under production-sharing agreements (PSAs).

In the winter of 2000 the energy crisis in the Russian Far East and the subsequent resignation of Primorskiy *kray*'s governor, Nazdratenko, captured the headlines in the national and international press. However, such energy problems have become an annual event, as the region's power-generation, transmission and heating systems are gradually falling apart.[12] The region's problems are exacerbated by the fact that it is isolated from the national power grid and dependent on expensive local coal for the majority of its electricity generation – dependence that is a major cause of air pollution – but the coal industry is also an important employer. This system was sustainable when it was part of the Soviet Union; however, the marketisation of the Russian economy has revealed the high cost of the region's fuel–energy system. Prices for power generation and transport have increased dramatically, and the profitability of local enterprises and the income levels of the population have declined; the result is that consumers cannot pay their energy bills. The utilities respond to this reduced cash flow by putting their prices up. The net result is a constant non-payments crisis and power shortages. The federal government acknowledges the problem and has a plan to deal with it, the Gasification Programme for the Russian Far East; however, it has yet to set aside the necessary money for the programme and, at present at least, it does not have the natural gas to fuel the programme.

This is where Sakhalin enters the picture. Sakhalin is a microcosm of the Far East's problems. It has modest onshore oil and gas production in the north of the island, but no island-wide pipeline system or electricity grid. Instead, most of the oil and gas is exported off-island to Khabarovsk *kray* via oil and gas pipelines or by oil tanker to export markets. In 2000 Sakhalin's total exports were worth $964.8 million; crude oil constituted 61.9 per cent of export earnings.[13] Burning local coal generates over 70 per cent of Sakhalin's electricity. Most power stations only supply a local market with electricity and heating. They also pollute the surrounding area. Every winter Sakhalin experiences power shortages as coal supplies dwindle and consumers fail to pay their bills. The construction of a gas-fired power station at Nogliki has provided a limited local solution for that part of the island, but the capital region in the south is still dependent on coal-fired generation. Offshore of Sakhalin sit substantial oil and gas deposits. The Sakhalin projects are the beneficiaries of two of the three functioning PSAs signed in Russia (in 1996), with a third PSA on the way.[14] As a result of these agreements, over $1.7 billion has been spent on oil and gas exploration by two projects. As has already been noted, this investment has placed Sakhalin second after Moscow city in terms of accumulated foreign direct investment.

Despite the obvious domestic need for Sakhalin's oil and gas and the huge export potential, these projects have been plagued by conflict and delay. This has usually been because of the imperfect nature of Russia's PSA legislation, conflict between ministries in Moscow, conflict between Moscow and Sakhalin, and most recently between Khabarovsk and Sakhalin. The oil companies, both foreign and domestic, have found themselves caught in the middle. The first phase of the Sakhalin-2 project, which produced oil in 1999, required over 2,000 licences.[15] The operators faced numerous problems with Russian Customs and were illegally charged VAT on imports. Meanwhile, people in the Russian Far East freeze to death and the region's economy continues to struggle. In September 2000 President Putin attended the PSA-2000 Conference on Sakhalin and announced that 'PSAs are for Russia'. He then charged German Gref and his Ministry of Economic Development and Trade with overseeing the PSA process. However, the regulations necessary to achieve this were not signed in Moscow until February 2001.[16]

The current status of the Sakhalin projects signifies Russia's confusion and ambivalence towards foreign investment. As was noted above, the projects have a history that dates back to the early 1970s; for thirty years foreign companies (initially Japanese) have been trying to develop the fields. The offshore operating conditions are extremely challenging and the technology and marketing skills needed to bring oil and gas to market are beyond Russia's oil and gas companies. They also lack the $25–45 billion in capital investment that may be required. In short, these are not projects that Russia can develop by itself. They should be flagship projects that illustrate the benefits of international co-operation and foreign investment. Instead, they illustrate the huge problems that remain when trying to invest in multi-billion-dollar projects. Furthermore, it is not the local politicians who are making life difficult; they are in favour of development. Rather, Sakhalin is held hostage by political debate in Moscow about the costs and benefits of foreign investment. As the first two Sakhalin projects progress beyond the first phase of early oil (and Sakhalin-1 is still not there yet), big decisions will have to be made about multi-billion-dollar investments. In 2002 Shell, the operator for Sakhalin-2, decided whether or not to proceed with an US$8–10 billion investment in Phase Two of the project in cooperation with Gazprom. This investment will secure the construction of oil and gas pipelines from the offshore fields on shore and then south to a yet to be constructed liquefied natural gas (LNG) plant outside the town of Korsakov. Already feasibility studies are underway and Sakhalin-2 is marketing gas to potential buyers. If the project goes ahead it will be a major boost to Sakhalin, the Russian Far East and Russia; if the investors decide that the time is not right, then it will be an equally big blow. The project operators are upbeat and positive. ExxonMobil, the operators of Sakhalin-1, are further behind, remain cautiously optimistic, but are not at all convinced by the current status of the PSA legislation.

The Sakhalin projects: who's who

At present there are seven distinct offshore oil and gas projects, all at different stages of development: two were awarded PSAs in the mid-1990s, two won tenders and are still trying to secure PSAs, and three have yet to be tendered (see Figure 8.3 and Table 8.2).

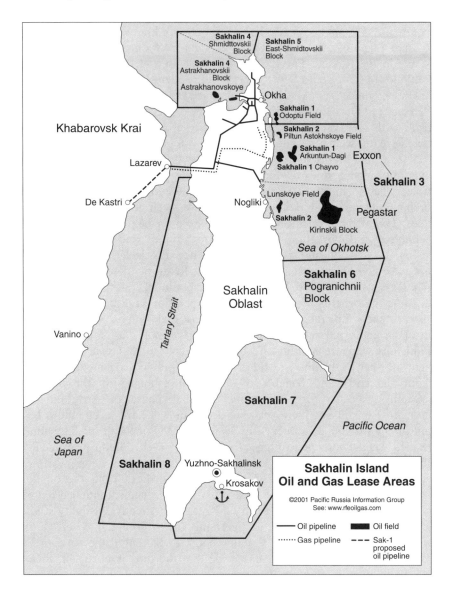

Figure 8.3 The Sakhalin Oil and Gas Project, as of late 2001

Source: Sakhalin–Alaska Consulting Group (reproduced with permission)

Table 8.2   Sakhalin oil and gas projects and participants (as of late 2001)

Project	Participants
Sakhalin-1	
(PSA)	
Expected investment	ExxonMobil (US) [30%]
US$12 billion	Sodeco (Japan) [30%]
Estimated reserves million tonnes equivalent	Rosneft and SMNG (Russia) [20%]
fuel: 1,000	ONGC (India) [20%]
Sakhalin-2	
(PSA)	
Expected investment	Shell (UK/Netherlands) [55%]
US$10 billion	Mitsui (Japan) [25%]
Estimated reserves million tonnes equivalent	Mitsubishi (Japan)[20%]
fuel: 850	
Sakhalin-3	
Krinskiy block	
(Negotiating PSA)	ExxonMobil (US) [33%]
Expected investment	ChevronTexaco (US) [33%]
US$15 billion	Rosneft and SMNG [33%]
Estimated reserves million tonnes equivalent	
fuel: 1,500	
Ayyash and East Odoptu blocks	
(Negotiating PSA)	ExxonMobil
Expected investment	Rosneft
US$13.5 billion	SMNG
Sakhalin-4	
(Drilling licence, no PSA)	BP (UK)
Estimated reserves million tonnes equivalent	Rosneft
fuel: 700	SMNG
Sakhalin-5	
(Yet to be tendered)	BP (UK)
Estimated reserves million tonnes equivalent	ROSNEFT
fuel: 600	SMNG

Sakhalin-2

So far it is the Sakhalin-2 project that has made the most progress. The project has pursued a first phase of oil production, and first oil was produced in the summer of 1999. In 2000 the project saw a full season of production, and in the summer of 2001 Sakhalin-2 planned to produce 1 million tonnes of oil. Oil is being produced from the Vityaz complex, which includes the Molikpaq drilling platform and a storage tanker, the *Okha*, from which oil is transferred to oil tankers for delivery to ports in Japan, China and South Korea. Until recently the Sakhalin Energy Investment Company (SEIC), which runs the Sakhalin project, involved Marathon Oil (US), Shell (UK/Netherlands), Mitsui (Japan) and

Mitsubishi (Japan). In 2000 Marathon left the project and Shell took over its stake. Subsequently some of Shell's shares were sold to Mitsubishi, so that Shell now holds 55 per cent, Mitsui 25 per cent and Mitsubishi 20 per cent. There is no Russian involvement in the project, even though Rosneft and Rosneft–Sakhalinmoreneftegaz (the local subsidiary of Rosneft) would like to be involved. The Sakhalin-2 PSA does require 70 per cent Russian content on contracts over the lifetime of the project, so Russian industry should benefit. The PSA also binds Sakhalin-2 to achieving 70 per cent Russian content, and this is proving to be a difficult task – not from any lack of desire on the part of Sakhalin Energy, but rather because of a shortage of viable Russian partners. Moscow politicians seem ready to criticise the foreign operators for failing to give contracts to Russian companies, but they fail to accept the sorry state of industry in the Russian Far East and on Sakhalin in particular.

Following the drilling programme in 2000, the estimated reserves of the Lunskoye field have been increased by 40 per cent, from 14 to 18 trillion cubic feet of gas. Therefore Sakhalin-2 has sufficient proven reserves to proceed with the next phase. Shell, the project's operator, is currently planning phase two of the project, involving expansion of offshore oil production and the start of gas production. Sakhalin-2's budget for 2002 is approximately US$500 million. Phase Two involves the construction of substantial onshore infrastructure, including oil and gas pipelines to the south of the island, and the construction of an LNG plant and oil export terminal. Feasibility studies have been conducted and SEIC will shortly present a blueprint strategy for Phase Two. By the completion of Phase One SEIC had spent $1.25 billion, and the estimated cost of Phase Two is $7–8 billion. However, commitment to Phase Two will not be made until long-term contracts have been signed with customers for the delivery of LNG.[17] Shell has made it clear that to proceed with Phase Two it wants a more streamlined approvals process for the PSA, as well as satisfactory completion of current amendments to the PSA and the associated 'enabling laws' that ensure that the PSA is compatible with other Russian laws. In other words, although Shell is telling potential customers that the PSA provides a stable legislative basis for this multi-billion-dollar investment, the company remains unhappy with the current legal situation surrounding the PSA. The date of possible first delivery is set as 2005–6. Thus, by the end of 2001 or early 2002 Sakhalin-2 must find the necessary customers and commit to the infrastructure investment. The moment of reckoning is fast approaching.

Sakhalin-1

The Sakhalin-1 project is of similar vintage to Sakhalin-2 but is now some way behind the other project. Difficult reservoir conditions impeded progress, and licensing problems caused additional delays. However, in the summer of 2000 Sakhalin-1 had a very successful drilling season and project managers are convinced that an early-oil strategy is viable. Like Sakhalin-2, recently there have been changes in the project's participants. For a long time the Sakhalin-1 project involved three partners: Exxon, Sodeco and Rosneft (through Rosneft–Astra) and Sakhalinmorneftegaz (SMNG). Exxon's acquisition of Mobil means that ExxonMobil is the operator now (this is significant because of Mobil's involvement elsewhere on Sakhalin). Sodeco is actually a consortium of Japanese companies and is a reorganised version of the company of the same name that was involved in the initial Soviet–Japanese project. Today Sodeco is 42.9 per cent owned by the Japan National Oil Company and the remaining majority share is held by a further thirteen companies. Sodeco is generally a passive partner in the project. Late in 1999 there were rumours that Rosneft and Rosneft–SMNG were looking to sell half of their 40 per cent share in the project. Neither ExxonMobil nor Sodeco wished to increase their ownership in the project, nor did ChevronTexaco (a partner with ExxonMobil in Sakhalin-3) wish to invest. A number of companies, including British Petroleum (BP), allegedly expressed interest. In the spring of 2000 it was announced that a 20 per cent interest in the project was to be sold to India's Oil and Natural Gas Corporation (ONGC Videsh Limited). It was reported that ONGC paid $315 million, which included $90 million to cover Rosneft and Rosneft–SMNG's investment so far and $225 million as a premium. In addition, ONGC will carry the Russian companies through the exploration phase until the project becomes cash positive. In all, it is expected that ONGC will invest $1.5–2 billion. Questions are now being asked in India as to why ONGC has paid so much to get into a project that has not yet been declared commercially viable. Indian government officials say that the investment makes sense in economic terms and that it has not been guided by strategic considerations. As a result of ONGC's involvement the current ownership structure of Sakhalin-1 is as follows: ExxonMobil (30 per cent), Sodeco (30 per cent), Rosneft (8.5 per cent), Rosneft–SMNG (11.5 per cent) and ONGC (20 per cent). Until late 2000 the project was making slow progress. In 2001 the participants intended to spend a modest $154 million to purchase equipment and elaborate a feasibility study for developing the Sakhalin-1 reserves. However, on 29 October 2001 they announced the commerciality of the first phase of the project. Total investment to the beginning of 2001 is said to have been $475 million. It is now expected that the total cost of the first phase will be in the region of $4 billion. The earliest that first oil can be expected from the Chaivo field is late 2005.

Sakhalin-1 has upset the Sakhalin administration by pursuing an early-oil strategy that involves horizontal drilling from on shore (reducing the initial need for offshore platforms) and then moving the oil by pipeline to the mainland to be exported from a terminal at De Kastri in Khabarovsk *kray* (see Figure 8.3). This involves existing pipelines, again reducing the cost.

Rosneft–SMNG has a loan from the European Bank for Reconstruction and Development (EBRD) to modernise the existing infrastructure. The governor of Sakhalin is unhappy because he wants Sakhalin-1 and Sakhalin-2 to share the substantial infrastructure investment required to build oil and gas pipelines down the island to the proposed LNG plant and oil export terminal in the south. The governor has his own plans to build an oil refinery in the south. The gas phase of the Sakhalin-1 project seems unlikely until the end of the decade, thus shared infrastructure is difficult as the two projects are on different time lines. It is also complicated by the fact that Sakhalin-1 favours a pipeline strategy over LNG. Nevertheless, sooner rather than later the infrastructure on shore will be built, but the governor, for understandable reasons, wants to maximise investment and employment opportunities now.

Sakhalin-3

The next group of projects has been tendered, but is awaiting the approval of PSAs. Unlike the first two Sakhalin projects, which were based on acreage that had already been subject to drilling programmes, these blocks have only had preliminary seismic work. Therefore they are essentially exploration projects, which have to face the geological risk that no commercial reserves of oil and gas will be discovered. The tenders were awarded in 1993 and since then the companies involved have been trying to get their PSAs approved. The two projects are both known as Sakhalin-3. The Sakhalin-3 Kirinskiy block originally involved Mobil, Texaco, Rosneft and Rosneft–SMNG. Following various mergers, the project now involves ExxonMobil (33 per cent), ChevronTexaco (following Chevron's acquisition of Texaco; 33 per cent) and Rosneft and Rosneft–SMNG (33 per cent). The project has suffered one delay after another, usually in Moscow. Now it is being held up by the transfer of the responsibility for PSAs from the Energy Ministry to the Economic Development and Trade Ministry. The decree transferring responsibility to Gref's ministry was not signed until February 2001, and so far limited progress has been made. Furthermore, many of the ministries and officials previously involved in the PSA process now feel sidelined and are not inclined to co-operate. For Sakhalin, the shift has broken well-established lines of communication; similarly, the foreign oil companies are unsure whom to talk to in Moscow. In an attempt to resolve things, President Putin has actually made matters worse by reshuffling key government personnel. The earliest exploration can start is the summer of 2003. ExxonMobil, Rosneft and Rosneft–SMNG hold the other part of Sakhalin-3, the Ayyash and East Odoptu blocks. These companies also are awaiting the approval of their PSA. However, because of their partners' involvement in Sakhalin-1 and the Kirinskiy block of Sakhalin-3 they are unlikely to make much progress in the near future.

Sakhalin-4

The exploration rights to the Sakhalin-4 block, the Astrakhanovskiy field off the northwestern shore of Sakhalin, are held by Rosneft, Rosneft–SMNG and until recently ARCO. Following its acquisition by BP, ARCO withdrew from the project, leaving the Russian partners to carry on with exploration work, which they have done at their own expense. However, the lack of a PSA led BP to make an initial decision to withdraw. The company has since reconsidered the situation and in the spring of 2001 reached an agreement to work on the project in a 50/50 partnership with Rosneft and Rosneft–SMNG, extending the agreement they have for Sakhalin-5 to cover Sakhalin-4 as well. The exploration phase is expected to last six years and the total cost of the project is put at $2.6 billion. Most recently, the press has reported that the Tomsk-based subsidiary of Gazprom, Vostokgazprom, may be interested in the Sakhalin-4 project, but in what capacity is unknown.

Sakhalin-5

The Sakhalin-5 East-Schmidtovskiy block has yet to be tendered. However, Rosneft, Rosneft–SMNG and BP have an agreement to form a partnership to bid for the block. Until recently it was expected that the entire block would be tendered as one. The Ministry of Natural Resources has now decided that it wishes the block to be split up into four smaller blocks for tender. It hopes that this will speed up development and encourage the entry of new actors; tendering is due in 2002. Oil industry analysts contend that the individual 25 per cent blocks are too small to justify exploration in deep water with difficult ice conditions. Rather than speed things up, splitting the block may slow them down. However, it seems likely that the blocks will be bid in pairs and the BP–Rosneft–SMNG consortium seems happy to bid for the first two blocks. It remains to be seen who else will. These projects involve offshore exploration, something in which none of the major Russian companies has experience.

Sakhalin-6

The final Sakhalin project is Sakhalin-6, the so-called Progranichnyy block off the southeastern shore of Sakhalin. This block borders onshore fields which have been developed by Petrosakh. Until recently Petrosakh was a joint venture with Nimir Petroleum (Saudi Arabia) involved in modest local production on Sakhalin. However, in September 2000 the Alfa Group bought a 95 per cent share in Petrosakh and it is now a Russian company. Petrosakh has a geological survey licence for the Sakhalin-6 block and has indicated a desire to develop the acreage without a PSA, simply on the basis of commercial risk. In summer 2001 the company conducted a 3D seismic survey from on shore. The Bashkortostani oil company Bashkirneft wishes to join the project, as it is interested in securing additional oil production for its refining activities.

Realising Sakhalin's potential

Three processes can be identified when assessing the development of the Sakhalin projects. First, there was the withdrawal of some of the smaller actors initially involved in the projects. The first to leave was McDermott (US), one of the founders of Sakhalin-2, and more recently Marathon (US) sold its share of Sakhalin-2 to Shell (UK–Netherlands). Second, global mergers in the industry impacted on the Sakhalin projects. The Exxon–Mobil merger was the most significant. Previously Exxon had been involved in two projects, Sakhalin-1 and two blocks of Sakhalin-3, and Mobil had been a partner in Sakhalin-3 Kirinskiy block. Now the new company is involved in three projects and is the most important player off shore of Sakhalin. This is significant because Exxon has had a troubled relationship with the local administration and with the ministries in Moscow, and the company has also been very outspoken in its criticism of the PSA legislation. BP's purchase of Arco is of potential significance and has certainly increased BP's visibility in the *oblast*. Arco was involved in Sakhalin-4, but withdrew as a result of the takeover. This is largely because the terms surrounding Sakahlin-4 required exploration without the guarantee of a PSA, conditions that BP did not wish to accept. BP still awaits the tender of the Sakhalin-5 blocks, but in a change of heart has extended its agreement with Rosneft–SMNG to Sakhalin-4. It is too early to say what effect Chevron's acquisition of Texaco will have on the Sakhalin-3 Kirinskiy block project, but it is interesting that they declined to become involved in Sakhalin-1.

This constant change in the membership of projects and the merger of key members is a source of instability. It not only means a constant turnover of staff on Sakhalin, which is a problem in developing a relationship with the local political elite, but also means a constant reassessment of the projects as corporate strategies change. Now the Sakhalin projects have become the remit of the big major companies – ExxonMobil, Shell, ChevronTexaco and (potentially) BP – which must attest to the nature of the opportunity that they see off shore of Sakhalin.

The third process, running somewhat contradictory to the second, has been the 'Russification' of the projects. The first two projects limited Russian involvement to a 40 per cent share of the Sakhalin-1 project (now reduced to 20 per cent following the sale of 20 per cent to ONGC). Sakhalin-2 still has no Russian involvement and this remains a bone of contention. The original Sakhalin-3 Kirinskiy block was to be developed by a Mobil–Texaco entity known as 'Pegastar'. However, after protracted PSA negotiations it became clear that substantial Russian involvement was a prerequisite for inclusion on the PSA list. Thus Rosneft and SMNG were

brought on board. At that time the Russian companies were having problems financing their share of Sakhalin-1, and it was agreed that they would
be 'carried' through the exploration phase and would only have to
contribute to the costs of any subsequent development phase. The Sakhalin-
3, 4 and 5 projects differ from the first two in that they are first and foremost
exploration projects; commercial reserves have yet to be delimited. Sakhalin-
1 and Sakhalin-2 were based on rough estimates of known reserves from the
earlier exploration activity (the usefulness of which is now being called into
question). Similar 'Russian involvement' terms have also been agreed for the
other Sakhalin-3 project and for Sakhalin-5, should BP win the tender.
Thus, despite the presence of the world's largest multinationals, the Russian
government has forced them to accept and carry Russian partners in order
to gain access to Sakhalin's offshore acreage. Rosneft (and its affiliates) are
now to be involved in all future PSAs in Russia, so, despite what the globalisation literature might say, the national state is able to set the terms when it
comes to access to natural resources.

Globalisation and regional change on Sakhalin: scales and actors

The collapse of the Soviet Union has resulted in a dramatic change in the
scales of decision-making, the actors involved and the issues that shape
regional economic change in Russia. The regionalisation of Russia's political
and economic systems during the 1990s significantly changed the balance of
power between the centre and the regions.[18] Similar conflicts over revenues
and responsibilities also took place within Russia's eighty-nine federal
subjects. Thus governors and presidents often found themselves in conflict
with city mayors and heads of districts, a conflict intensified by President
Yeltsin, who sought to empower local government to distract the governors
from their conflict with the Kremlin. The fact that Sakhalin *oblast* is the
location of the largest foreign investment projects in Russia and that those
projects have the potential to give a major boost to Russian status in northeast Asia significantly increases the complexity surrounding regional
economic change in Sakhalin.

Many of the changes affecting Sakhalin today can be explained within
the broader context of the literature on globalisation. If we adopt the characteristics of globalisation identified by Held *et al.* ('a process (or set of
processes) which embodies a transformation in the spatial organisation of
social relations and transaction – assessed in terms of their extensity, intensity, velocity and impact – generating transcontinental or interregional flows
and networks of activity; interaction and exercise of power')[19] we see that
they can provide insight into the processes now shaping Sakhalin's future.

First, there is ample evidence of the stretching of social, political and
economic activities across political frontiers, regions and continents. Table
8.3 presents the different scales and the host of actors influencing the

Table 8.3   Scales and actors influencing the progress of the Sakhalin projects

Scale	Actors
Sakhalin	• Sakhalin electorate • governor and *oblast* administration • *oblast* Duma • federal agencies on Sakhalin • city and district administrations • private enterprises (including formerly state owned) • state-owned enterprises (principally Rosneft–SMNG) • joint ventures • local offices of the oil project operators (ExxonNeftegaz and Sakhalin Energy) • offices of foreign governments (ABC, Japan Centre) • NGOs (e.g. training organisations, local interest groups)
Russian Far East	• other administrative units in the Russian Far East • the Far Eastern Federal District and presidential representative • inter-regional Association for Economic Co-operation for the Far East and Transbaykal, and the 'Siberian Agreement' • private Russian enterprises (shipyards etc. seeking oil and gas contracts) • state-owned enterprises
Russian Federation	• president and presidential apparatus • federal government and ministries • Federation Council (governors and Duma chairs) • State Duma • state-owned enterprises (e.g. Rosneft) • private sector (e.g. Moscow-based banks, financial industrial groups, private companies) • Moscow-based NGOs (e.g. environmental groups) • transnational corporation headquarters for Russia • Moscow offices of international agencies (World Bank, EBRD, EU, etc.)
Northeast Asia	• neighbouring states (China, North Korea, South Korea, Japan and the United States) • regional administrations from neighbouring states (Japanese prefectures, Chinese provinces, US states) • regional supranational bodies (APEC) • NGOs from neighbouring states • private sector (oil- and gas-related service companies)
Global system	• private sector (oil and gas multinationals, related support operations) • national governments and their agencies • international lending agencies (World Bank, EBRD, etc.) • international NGOs (Greenpeace, Friends of the Earth International, World Wildlife Fund, Political Economy Research Center, Survival, etc.)

progress of the Sakhalin oil and gas projects. Actors are assigned to the scale at which they gain legitimacy; however, they act at a variety of scales. Equally, it is common for actors at different scales to form coalitions to promote particular interests. Thus the governor and administration (in the form of the Shelf Department) have lobbied the federal ministries in Moscow together with the multinational oil companies to bring about improvements in the PSA legislation. In a rather different manner, the local environmental non-governmental organisation (NGO) 'Sakhalin Environmental Watch' has worked with Greenpeace to protest the production of oil off shore. At present, the governor is actively marketing the Sakhalin projects to potential gas buyers in northeast Asia. Needless to say, he does not take kindly to the actions of Greenpeace. As a consequence of the global mergers, decisions affecting Sakhalin are not taken in boardrooms in Houston and London, so much as in Moscow.

Second, there is evidence of the growing magnitude of connectedness; the fact that the Asian financial crisis of 1997 was probably more damaging to Sakhalin's prospects than the Russian financial crisis of 1998 is indicative of the fact that Sakhalin's economy is increasingly distanced from the rest of Russia and more tuned to the rhythms of northeast Asia. Consequently, foreign trade is playing an increasingly important role in Sakhalin's economy, as is foreign investment.

This connectedness will only increase with the progress of the oil and gas projects. The prospects for Sakhalin are now tied to factors influencing energy supply in northeast Asia, such as global supply of LNG, Japan's attitude to further expansion of nuclear power, the Kyoto Protocols and the introduction of imported gas into China. These developments, in turn, underlie the prospects for multilateral co-operation in northeast Asia. Already, access to finance has become a key issue. The Sakhalin-2 project was the recipient of the EBRD's single largest loan in Russia. The project also has finance from government institutions in the US and Japan. Rosneft–SMNG has gone to financial markets, to the Dutch Bank ABN–AMRO, to raise money to finance its participation in the Sakhalin-1 project.

When it comes to the third characteristic, the speeding up of global interactions and processes, there are contradictory tendencies. Sakhalin is now plugged into the global telecommunications system and there are an increasing number of international flights to Sakhalin – from Alaska, Hokkaido, Seoul and most recently China – but links with Moscow have been very problematic. This reflects the fragile status of Russia's domestic airlines following the financial crisis. The Sakhalin administration has reacted by buying a plane for SAT to fly from Moscow to Yuzhno-Sakhalinsk. The financial crisis also dampened foreign passenger demand. For example, Alaskan Airlines no longer flies from the West Coast of the US to the Russian Far East. Thus, getting to Sakhalin is a major challenge. The current status of the ferry from the Russian mainland to Sakhalin is an even more dramatic indication of the isolation of Sakhalin from the rest of Russia. Plans are being developed to build a bridge from northern Sakhalin to the mainland. The ferry service is now sporadic at best. Instead, Sakhalin has increased its reliance on imports from elsewhere in northeast Asia. This is a trend that will continue as the oil and projects increase the purchasing power of Sakhaliners. Thus, distancing from Moscow is leading to an intensification of international linkages.

Fourth, the growing extensity, intensity and velocity of global interactions is said to be associated with their deepening impact, such that effects of distant events can be highly significant elsewhere and even the most local developments may come to have enormous global consequences. Clearly the progress of the Sakhalin oil and gas projects is not going to change the world; however, it can shape – and likely is – external perceptions of the investment environment in Russia. Outside Moscow, Sakhalin is the centre of attention, and the projects are proving a litmus test for the PSA as an entry vehicle for foreign investment in Russia's resource industries. Russia's resource wealth is the mainstay of its current position in the global economy. Thus, in a very real sense, the success of the Sakhalin projects is important to Russia and the health of the Russian economy is important to the global political economy, as evidenced by the shockwaves caused by the Russian financial crisis. Closer to home, the Sakhalin projects are essential to solving the current energy crisis in the Russian Far East, which is proving a major barrier to economic recovery and is destabilizing Primorskiy *kray*.

Finally, Lechner and Boli note that ' [a]s world society integrates, individuals become conscious of being enveloped in global networks, subject to global forces, governed by global rules'.[20] There is ample evidence of this in our Sakhalin case study. The most obvious examples are to be found in the conflict surrounding the environment and the rights of indigenous peoples. Both are causes championed by citizens of Western democracies who support global NGOs such as Survival, Friends of the Earth and Greenpeace. All have been active in the Russian Far East and some on Sakhalin. Where the likes of ExxonMobil, Shell and BP go, these organisations follow. The local political elite has reacted defensively to what they see as the imposition of external values that threaten their future livelihoods.

The international oil companies see it somewhat differently. They are used to dealing with these groups and are concerned about how they might be perceived in the key markets in the West. Bad press from polluting fishing grounds offshore of Sakhalin soon translates into boycotts in Europe and North America. Similarly, a lack of sensitivity to the rights of indigenous people is political dynamite, as Shell discovered in Nigeria. It is not an issue that the governor of Sakhalin seems particularly concerned about. However, the environmental groups and those who represent the indigenous peoples are increasingly aware of global networks and sensibilities and are seeking to use them to pressure the oil companies, and ultimately the governor and his administration.[21] In a very real sense, the existence of global networks and global concerns is empowering local pressure groups. This is an issue that requires further research and something that is likely to increase in significance.

Conclusions

This chapter has reported on a project that is very much 'in progress', both in terms of the theoretical framework that is being developed and the empirical evidence that is being used to support it. It is my hope that this represents the beginning of a project to develop what one might call a 'new economic geography of Sakhalin'. As such, it raises far more questions than it answers. Figure 8.4 presents a framework which tries to pull together the two sections of the chapter and relate them to the contemporary situation on Sakhalin. The horizontal axis represents the dominant centre–region relationship between Moscow and Sakhalin. There is an obvious danger in overstating the influence of global processes; it is still Sakhalin's relationship with Moscow that is the most important factor shaping its future. It is noteworthy that, despite the poor state of the local economy and the failure of Moscow to provide support, there is no talk of independence for Sakhalin. An oil-rich island state with a population of half a million could do very well. The explanation for this continuing solidarity with the mainland is cultural and historical. Sakhalin sees itself as the frontier between Europe and Asia, Europe in Asia. This Europeanness may also help to explain the resistance to the American way of doing things.

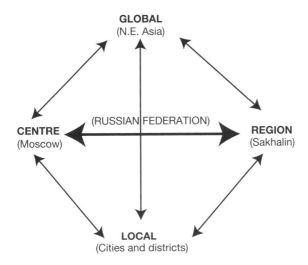

Figure 8.4 Key axes of interaction

The vertical axis demonstrates how global processes cut across the horizontal relationship between centre and region. This global relationship is both a liberating and a constraining influence in Sakhalin's relationship with Moscow: liberating because it provides access to financial resources (such as the Sakhalin Development Fund) independent of Moscow and it also underwrites new economic and political relationships with neighbouring states (and sub-state units). Thus Sakhalin has a degree of political and economic independence from Moscow that is not enjoyed by most of Russia's regions. At the same time, this relative openness and interconnectedness act as a constraint and leave Sakhalin vulnerable to the boom and bust of the international resource markets and the strategies of the global resource companies. If Exxon decided it had had enough of the situation in Russia, it could leave Sakhalin tomorrow. This would have little impact on Exxon's fortunes, but it would seriously damage Sakhalin's near-term economic prospects. In a similar vein, at present the progress of the Sakhalin-2 project is not down to Moscow or Yuzhno-Sakhalinsk, but to decision-makers in Beijing, Seoul and Tokyo. Sakhalin-2's gas reserves will not be developed and the projected LNG will not be constructed unless buyers can be found. The complex and highly dynamic inter-relationship between the global, the national and the regional that now determines the prospects for the future prosperity of Sakhalin is an age away from the time when the latest five-year plan statement was the blueprint for the future. At present Sakhalin is still counting the costs of the old system and is yet to realise the potential of the new system.

Notes

1 This chapter represents a summary of recent work by the author on the economic development of the Russian Far East, and Sakhalin in particular (see Bradshaw 2001a). Much of the information included here has been obtained from interviews and discussions with local officials in Russia and foreign oil-company representatives on Sakhalin and elsewhere. For reasons of confidentiality, those individuals have not been identified. Information on the various projects has also been obtained from various wire services and e-mail newsletters, especially the *Sakhalin Oil and Gas News*, a weekly newsletter produced by the Pacific Russia Information Group (www.rfeoilgas.com).
2 The statistics reported here have been obtained from various editions of the statistical handbook *Regiony Rossii*, published by Goskomstat in Moscow.
3 Vysokov 1996: 68.
4 *Ibid.*: 29.
5 *Ibid.*: 72.
6 *Ibid.*: 78.
7 *Ibid.*: 80.
8 Pacific Russia Information Group 2001: 11.
9 See Akha and Vassilieva 2001.
10 This number comes from an interview with the former deputy minister of energy, Valeriy Garipov, published in *Russkiye Gorkiy*, no. 2, May–June 2001.
11 Bradshaw 1997.
12 Bradshaw *et al.* 2000.

13 Data from the US Department of Commerce Commercial Update on the Sakhalin Region for September 2001.
14 For background on the projects, see Bradshaw 1997, 1998.
15 The scale of this problem was discussed in a presentation by Shell at the 2000 Sakhalin Oil and Gas Conference in London.
16 Bradshaw 2001b.
17 See Paik 2001.
18 See Hanson and Bradshaw 2000; Bradshaw and Treyvish 2000.
19 Held *et al.* 1999: 17.
20 Lechner and Boli 2000.
21 See Wilson 2000.

9 Centre–periphery conflict as a security dilemma

Moscow v. Vladivostok

Dr Mikhail A. Alexseev

Located eight time zones away from the Kremlin, at the junction with China, Korea and Japan, Primorskiy *kray* is one of the focal points of centre–periphery disputes over the internationalisation of local politics, economics and society in post-Soviet Russia. The rise and fall of the principal political actors and institutions in the region since the early 1990s has reflected some of the most intense of these disputes that still continue despite President Vladimir Putin's efforts since mid-2000 to consolidate control over political leaders in Russia's constituent regions and republics. Moscow–Vladivostok relations also reveal major economic and geopolitical tensions between the centre and the Russian Far East.

This chapter examines Moscow–Primorskiy relations as a security dilemma in centre–periphery interactions. According to scholars who have applied the security dilemma theory to domestic politics,[1] conflict arises when the capacity of government institutions to enforce rules and to regulate group and individual behaviour diminishes, giving rise to anarchy and zero-sum perceptions. Wholesale institutional transformation – as in the case of post-Soviet Russia – raises mutual fears and insecurity at the central and peripheral government levels. Centre–periphery disputes then arise because the central government is likely to see increments of political and economic power at the periphery as automatically subtracting from the political and economic power of the central government, and vice versa. Whereas the central government fears an inability to exercise sovereignty, the peripheral leaders fear being abandoned or exploited by the central government. Drawing on a theory of 'fear-producing environments' in a domestic security dilemma,[2] there are three sources of centre–periphery conflict in Primorskiy *kray* and the Russian Far East:

- military decline and increasing threat of unauthorised or accidental use of military capabilities;
- redistribution of resources and concomitant political struggle;
- geographic remoteness and vulnerability (especially when compounded by unfavourable demographic and socio-economic trends).

Military challenges

Home to the Pacific Fleet with its bases along Primorye's coast, army and air force bases along the border with China, the Far Eastern Regional Directorate of the Russian Border Service, and defence industries, Primorskiy *kray* entered the post-Soviet era as a strategic outpost of the Soviet Union. The collapse of the communist government, the end of the Cold War and the normalisation of relations with China (codified in the 1991 Border Demarcation Treaty) exposed this strategic military outpost to internal and external market forces, giving rise to a complex mix of political, economic and environmental challenges.

Since the early 1990s federal debt and wages to the military and defence industry workers – unpaid for months – have imposed massive economic burdens on Primorye. In 1997 workers at the Zvezda nuclear-submarine repair plant in Bolshoy Kamen, north of Vladivostok, and at the Progress helicopter and missile plant at Arsenyev not only staged strikes and demonstrations and blocked roads, but also demanded that Primorye become a Maritime Republic. A senior official from Moscow who came to negotiate with the striking nuclear-submarine workers said the federal government would at best deliver one-third of the funds allocated for the plant. By November 1997 the backlog in outstanding payments for military orders fulfilled by the plant exceeded R63 billion, the equivalent of about 100,000 average monthly wages. Investment from Hyundai was expected to plug this federal budget hole,[3] but the solution was incomplete.

The legacy of the Soviet military deployment resulted in economic inefficiencies and environmental damage. Ammunition depots exploded, military personnel starved, and garbage and hazardous waste were dumped illegally. In one of the explosions in the late 1990s twelve mine-and-torpedo systems detonated at a depot in Gornostay, sending shock waves through the city of Vladivostok and causing power cuts and heat-supply breakdowns. Specialists later concluded that if all fifty-six mine-and-torpedo systems had exploded Vladivostok would be lying in ruins.[4]

Large military bases of the Pacific Fleet and the Far Eastern Military District failed to pay for energy supplies and maintenance provided by local and regional governments and businesses. By September 1998 workers at the 27th Electricity Grid Facility, which supplies Russia's naval bases on the Pacific, had gone fourteen months without pay. And when five workers went on hunger strike a special commission set up by the Pacific Fleet to investigate their demands failed to arrive due to a shortage of fuel.[5] Federal funding for conversion of military industries to peacetime production – critical to Primorye's industrial development and employment – was chronically delayed and by mid-1997 fell 80 per cent short of original promises.[6] In 1996 governor Yevgeniy Nazdratenko had complained that Moscow's defence strategy seriously hampered the development of energy resources in Primorye:

> We have always depended on free electricity transfers amounting to 5 million megawatts. Without this Primorye cannot survive because the [federal] government has not built and will not build new power plants here. Meanwhile, we have access to sites rich in natural resources blocked by military airfields where air defence fighter planes and strategic aircraft are stationed. That's because according to our former political ideology and military doctrine we were always at the first line of defence.[7]

After the end of the Cold War Moscow broke this strategic deal, retaining the military installations while cutting off free electricity and providing few rules for working out solutions or for bargaining. In 1997 the vice-governor, Vladimir Kolesnichenko, said the federal and *kray* government contracts could finance no more than 60 per cent of defence industry projects, even if all the funds were disbursed on time (a big 'if' in Russia). Kolesnichenko then said that 'it should be easier for current [industry] leaders to develop projects more reliant on international investment than government contracts'. The director of Varyag, a major Vladivostok company, complained that frequent changes to federal laws and neglect by bureaucrats made such investment proposals impossible, despite relative economic stability at the time.[8]

Moreover, Primorye has the legacy of what was arguably the world's worst nuclear-submarine explosion, at Chazhma Bay near the secret Shkotovo-22 village in 1985. According to the Russian government report eight years after the accident, radioactive fallout caused intense contamination covering approximately 100,000 square metres. Ten people died in the accident, forty-nine got radiation sickness and 290 were overexposed to radiation.[9] Radioactive waste from the accident was dumped in a temporary burial trench in the fallout trace. The site was left unguarded, and local residents passed at will through the barbed-wire fence erected around it while hunting for mushrooms (an extremely popular pastime in Russia).[10]

Moreover, in the post-Soviet period the Pacific Fleet deteriorated. Valery Butov, a thirty-year veteran of the Soviet nuclear-submarine programme and President Yeltsin's representative in Primorye from 1991 to 1994, told *Vladivostok* in 1997 that about sixty retired nuclear-powered submarines were floating in harbours around the Russian Far East posing a threat from leaking hulls. Butov echoed the reasoning of many Lithuanians and Ukrainians when they campaigned for independence from the Soviet Union in 1989–91: 'Waiting for the Russian government to deal with the situation is foolish. It [radioactive waste] will all go sooner or later into the sea – because Russia doesn't care.'[11] However, deriving economic and security benefits from international co-operation, Russian and Primorskiy governments have recently been co-operating with the US Navy programme, which provides up to $35 million to assist in the decommissioning and re-use of these submarines.

Since his arrival in power President Putin has repeatedly stressed the importance for Russia of having a stronger military; he initiated substantial spending increases in the defence sector in 2000. Yet the scale of socio-economic problems arising from managing the military sector in Primorye, the limitations of the federal budget and implementation problems suggest that Primorskiy leaders are likely to face persistent uncertainty over trends in Russia's military capabilities and the military balance in Northeastern Eurasia. For example, the vice-governor, Stegniy, said:

> At present our military capabilities are such that, according to one esti-mate, we can destroy China thirty-three times. But the future of the military balance is uncertain. In the future, the military balance will worsen for us. China has a lot of money that it can spend on the military. We [Russia] cannot invest at the same rate. Whereas President Putin ordered us to strengthen the armed forces, our Pacific Naval Fleet had no resources to stage a traditional show of naval vessels [on Navy Day].[12]

A photo display at the entrance to the Primorye government building in August 2000 – witnessed by this author – showed Navy Day festivities featuring a lot of young females but no naval vessels. The rusting Kilo-class submarines floating in Ulis Harbour and the decaying electronic intelligence and space communications vessel *Kosmonavt Komarov* aground nearby provided reminders of the challenges facing the post-Soviet military in the Russian Far East.

Three trends were at work by mid-2001 addressing these challenges. On balance, these trends suggest an easing of tensions between economic inter-nationalisation and geopolitical security threats in Primorskiy *kray*. First, Putin's bid to reassert Russia's military power – implicit in the new military and naval doctrines – has resulted in increasing activities, readiness, and centralised command and control of Primorye-based military. On 21 May 2001, for the first time in seven years, warships put to sea as part of celebra-tions of the Pacific Fleet Day.[13] In March 2001 the Pacific Fleet command issued an order to prepare Primorye-based Kilo ('Varshavyanka') class diesel submarines – capable of approaching other submarines undetected – to put to sea in the summer.[14] Despite fundraising problems, the Pacific Fleet's large anti-submarine vessels *Admiral Panteleyev* and *Admiral Vinogradov* sailed to Mumbai and Ho Chi Min City in April 2001 – the first such voyage by the Pacific Fleet in a decade. Proud of the resumption of Russia's naval presence in the Indian and Pacific Oceans, the Pacific Fleet commander, Admiral Mikhail Zakharenko, said: 'They were met with surprise abroad, because nobody could believe Russian ships are still capable of going to sea.' In late April 2001 the Chief Naval Staff of Russia inspected the Pacific Fleet's combat-readiness in a series of combat exercises. The navy's commander-in-chief, Admiral Vladimir Kuroyedov, pronounced the Pacific Fleet 'abreast of all modern requirements'.[15]

To deal with the negative externalities of the military presence, in spring 2001 the Vladivostok city government asked the Federal Security Service to control the storage and removal of highly toxic missile fuel from the city. Rear Admiral Nikolay Sotskov assured the government that 167 tonnes of missile fuel had been poured into a special cistern and transported out of the city; the remaining 91 tonnes would be removed by the end of the quarter.[16]

Second, Primorskiy leaders partially adapted to post-Soviet challenges by opening the local defence industry to economic internationalisation and by reorienting defence industries somewhat towards civilian production. Developments at the Zvezda nuclear-submarine repair facility at Bolshoy Kamen in the late 1990s provide a focal point. To offset the funding shortage resulting from lack of government orders for submarine repair, the local authorities, the Primorskiy government and Russia's federal agencies struck a series of deals to maximise the economic benefits derived from Bolshoy Kamen's special standing in Russia's military industrial complex while allowing Zvezda to solicit international contracts and investment. In 1997 Bolshoy Kamen regained its status as a 'closed administrative entity' (ZATO) after giving it up in 1992; this status grants tax breaks and federal subsidies. This 'secret city's' economy has been sustained since 1999 by a contract to repair ten Chinese diesel submarines – resulting from an agreement to increase economic ties between Russia and China, with inputs from the Primorskiy government.[17] In April 1999 the Babcock and Wilcox division of the US construction and engineering company McDermott was completing a multi-million-dollar project in Bolshoy Kamen to provide pollution-control facilities.[18] Elsewhere, contracts to produce *Moskit* seaborne missiles for the Chinese navy and for Vietnam, as well as orders from Japan for large containers, accounted for a 13 per cent increase in production volume in 1999 against 1998 at the Progress aircraft company in Arsenyev.[19] In August 1999 the Primorskiy government hosted an Indonesian delegation, showcasing local enterprises capable of repairing warships and fishing vessels.[20]

Third, the Russian military continued to develop international contacts and co-operation. In January 2001 a thirty-strong delegation from the Japanese National Defence Agency visited the Pacific Fleet command in Vladivostok to discuss future contacts.[21] Following his visits to Japan while serving as Pacific Fleet commander, Admiral Kuroyedov became the first commander-in-chief of the Russian Navy to pay an official visit to Japan in April 2001. Admiral Kuroyedov proposed a moratorium on submarine reconnaissance, joint assessment of security threats in the Asia-Pacific region and a hotline between the two Navy Staffs. The Japanese invited up to five Russian Navy ships to visit Japan and one Russian ship to take part in a Japanese–Korean rescue exercise.[22] Since 1990 US warships have visited Vladivostok more than twenty times and have taken part in joint exercises practising disaster relief to civilian populations. In June 2001 the commander of US forces in the Pacific, Admiral Dennis Blair, visited a warship and other naval formations in Vladivostok after attending Russian exercises in Khabarovsk. In April 2001 the US inspected the Rybachiy submarine base in accordance with strategic arms-reduction treaties.[23]

The Pacific Fleet also maintained multilateral co-operation through Russia's membership in the Western Pacific Naval Symposium, set up in 1988 to provide a framework for interaction and discussion among its twenty-one members on common maritime interests. In 2001 Russia participated with eleven other countries in multilateral tactical training in Singapore, practising computer-simulated manoeuvres and search-and-rescue operations,[24] and in a twelve-day mine-countermeasure exercise in Indonesia, which featured 1,500 naval personnel and fifteen ships from sixteen navies – including China, Vietnam, Japan, Indonesia and the US.[25]

Nevertheless, the capacity of the Putin government to sustain these positive trends in the Far East remains severely constrained by economic hardship, political uncertainty and geographic vulnerability.

Redistribution of wealth and political power

The collapse of communist institutions, the opening of Primorskiy *kray* to international exchanges and wholesale privatisation of state-run property across Russia necessitated a rapid, if ruthless, consolidation of political and economic power, especially in a border region rich in tradable resources, as is the case with Primorskiy *kray*. The turning point in this consolidation came with the ouster from office of Vladimir Kuznetsov – a young, English-speaking and market-reform-oriented former oceanographer appointed by Yeltsin to run Primorskiy *kray* in 1991. Kuznetsov's policy called for an incremental transition to self-government in Primorye through integration with the Pacific Rim economies and developing free-market institutions in the region. His goal was to raise foreign investment for fast development of free economic and trade zones ('Greater Vladivostok') stretching from the port of Nakhodka down to the North Korean and Chinese border along the Pacific coast.[26]

Threatened by this programme, local industrialists and former Party *apparatchiks* attacked Kuznetsov from a power base in the region's Soviet of People's Deputies, supporting a former mining executive, Yevgeniy Nazdratenko, who forged a winning coalition that displaced Kuznetsov in spring 1993. Nazdratenko presented himself as a stronger supporter of regional economic independence than his political rivals, as someone capable of ensuring Primorye's economic interests against the background of plummeting subsidies from Moscow, skyrocketing prices and privatisation.

Nazdratenko's largest and most important constituency coalesced around an old-boys' network of Primorye's defence industry bosses and new private businessmen, which Nazdratenko referred to as 'a legal union of industrialists'.[27] The official name for this 'legal union' was PAKT, a joint stock company founded in 1992 by 213 executives representing thirty-six leading enterprises in Primorye. PAKT's primary goal was to replace Governor Kuznetsov with someone more sympathetic to the profit motives of the industrialists, especially in the face of the federal privatisation programme urging leaders in the regions to define who got what, when and how. Top officials in Nazdratenko's first administration – A. Pavlov, I. Lebedinets and V. Shkrabov – were all leading executives at PAKT. The new political and economic alliance quickly went into action, with PAKT members acquiring 236,000 shares in privatised enterprises for half the market price at closed auctions manipulated through the administration.[28]

After consolidating his position in power Nazdratenko distanced himself from PAKT, but only to establish a new conglomerate in November 1994, recycling key PAKT players and strategies. Named the Primorye Joint Stock Company (JSC), this financial-industrial group was avowedly set up to 'promote structural reorganisation of the *kray*'s economy, integrate Primorye's economic and financial resources, improve the competitiveness of local products, create rational technological and collaborative relationships, increase export potential, promote defence factory conversion and attract investment'. With the *kray* property committee listed as a founding member with a 10 per cent interest and with the *kray* administration offering special deals to its members, Nazdratenko was clearly increasing his leverage with regional industry.[29] Thus, Nazdratenko built a powerful political base (the 'administrative resource') while striking a workable balance with key economic players – an interdependent relationship that proved resilient throughout the 1990s, ensuring Nazdratenko's election as governor and his political survival through multiple crises. Most notable among these were a report by the pro-Yeltsin Democratic Choice Party commission in 1994 that accused Nazdratenko of instituting a personalised dictatorship, and Yeltsin's bid to remove Nazdratenko from office in 1997.

Having consolidated control over government institutions at the *kray* level, Nazdratenko proceeded to undermine and eventually displace major political opponents within other institutional niches. Within Primorye the most serious opposition to Nazdratenko's rule came from the mayor of Vladivostok, Viktor Cherepkov. As an elected official, Cherepkov was someone whom Nazdratenko could not fire. And, as mayor of Vladivostok, Cherepkov was in charge of about two-thirds of the region's industrial capacity and nearly one-third of its population.[30] The power struggle between the two turned ugly. In February 1994 armed riot police occupied the Vladivostok city government building in order to question the mayor on charges of corruption. Only an outpouring of public support for Cherepkov enabled him to remain in office. Yet a month later Cherepkov and his closest assistants were physically removed from office by OMON, the police special operations forces. Nazdratenko procured Yeltsin's decree suspending Cherepkov so that he could be investigated for taking a R3 million bribe.[31]

Nazdratenko also used police to close down the pro-Cherepkov news-paper *Primorets* (its editorial office moved to Khabarovsk and continued distribution in Primorye through undercover networks). Other newspapers and local TV stations were forced to change editors and to abstain from challenging Nazdratenko's policies.[32] The solid local power base and support in Russia's Federation Council by other elected governors after 1996 enabled Nazdratenko even to have the Federal Security Service (FSB) general Viktor Kondratov – whom Yeltsin charged with Nazdratenko's ouster in the summer of 1997 – reassigned to Moldova. Having established control over local courts, Nazdratenko repeatedly annulled the results of elections to Vladivostok City Duma, in which Cherepkov supporters continued to win the majority of votes. Only after Nazdratenko's departure was a city Duma elected in Vladivostok, in May 2001, on the twentieth attempt and for the first time since 1993.[33]

An important dimension of Nazdratenko's power consolidation that is constantly talked about in Vladivostok – but is little investigated due to its very nature – concerns its relationship with organised crime. In a 1997 report to Boris Yeltsin, General Viktor Kondratov, the president's Primorskiy *kray* representative – who was also the local FSB chief – implicated Nazdratenko's right-hand man and first vice-governor, Konstantin Tolstoshein, in allegedly hiring gangsters to neutralise business rivals. Kondratov said the FSB investigation established that Tolstoshein used 'the leader of an organised crime group, Alexeyenkov', to leverage the sale of the then largest hotel, 'Vladivostok', to Amis & Co. at a price 315 times less than market value. Further, according to the FSB report, '[a]long with illegal financial operations, Tolstoshein uses his connections with criminal groups in order to conduct violent operations toward competitors. ... He organised the abduction of radio reporters Alexey Sadykov and Andrey Zhuravlev'.[34] Media reports also suggested that Nazdratenko engineered a rapid whole-sale management replacement in a local shipping company, Vostoktransflot, in 1999. One of its outcomes was the assassination of lawyer Taisiya Ponomareva, killed by a bomb that exploded under the floorboards beneath her bed a few hours before she was scheduled to leave for Moscow, where she intended to present evidence of criminal law violations in the takeover. Control over shipping and refrigerator vessels – and evading the repayment of a $7 million balance on a Bank of Scotland loan – were at stake in the hostile takeover of Vostoktransflot.[35]

Paradoxically, the endurance of Nazdratenko and the robustness of the 'administrative resource' he created manifested themselves most explicitly after his ouster from office in February 2001. An unusually harsh winter combined with the *kray* government's failure to procure coal and heating oil left an estimated 90,000 people in Primorye without heat and electricity and prompted President Putin to charge his envoy to the Far East Federal District, General Konstantin Pulikovskiy, with Nazdratenko's removal. At the time it appeared that Putin's reform of May 2000 instituting federal districts supervised by presidential envoys had worked precisely as intended, enabling the replacement of a recalcitrant governor. Yet fears that Nazdratenko had enough clout to destabilise the political situation in Primorskiy *kray* prompted Putin to offer the ex-governor a sweetener – a transfer to Moscow as fisheries minister. Charged, among other things, with the assignment of fishing quotas, Nazdratenko thus maintained a hold on power in Primorye's critical economic sector.

The outcome of the May 2001 gubernatorial election showed that Nazdratenko maintained political influence too: his winning candidate, Sergey Darkin, prevailed against both candidates backed by the Kremlin, Gennadiy Apanasenko and Valentin Dubinin. Not only did Darkin still serve as the head of the Primorye Bank – which Nazdratenko set up during his governorship with Darkin's assistance to service the *kray* government accounts – but Nazdratenko's former press secretary, Nataliya Vstovskaya, reportedly worked as one of Darkin's campaign masterminds.[36] While Darkin stated that he would replace all of the old governor's top appointees,[37] Nazdratenko staged a warm reception for Darkin at the presidential administration in Moscow and arranged a meeting with Putin's chief of staff, Aleksandr Voloshin. Nazdratenko was also reported to have mobilised his Primorskiy *kray* network of state employees to help Darkin win the second round on 17 June 2001. In an interview to an online news agency, strana.ru – sponsored by the Kremlin administration – Nazdratenko stated: 'Of the candidates who ran, he was the most optimal, in my view.'[38] Moscow had failed to break the hold on power of the coalition of Nazdratenko's political and economic backers.

The net result of Nazdratenko's removal and the subsequent election was squarely in favour of Nazdratenko's Primorskiy coalition: first, the former governor was given charge of quota distribution critical to Primorye's fishing business; second, the presidential envoy suffered a political defeat by failing to get his choice elected; and, third, the candidate 'most optimal' from Nazdratenko's perspective won. The Primorye case suggests that the interconnection between political power ('the administrative resource') and industrial-financial groupings (PAKT and Primorskiy JSC) is indeed decisive for consolidation of regional power structures.[39] Yet, despite enhancing uniform policy (which in Primorskiy *kray* evolved into bargaining with Moscow over tariffs, resource allocation and subsidies), this type of regional power consolidation is not necessarily conducive to efficient policy and socio-economic development.[40]

Following the arrival of Vladimir Putin, the departure of Nazdratenko and the election of Sergey Darkin, the political landscape in Primorskiy *kray* has undergone changes which suggest that the regional government is unlikely to pursue a foreign and security policy that would come into conflict with the central government. The political incentives for 'paradiplomacy' – if one considers as such Nazdratenko's visit to North Korea on his own initiative in March 1995 to sign agricultural co-operation agreements, and his meetings with the leaders of the neighbouring Heilongjang and Jilin provinces of China, in part to establish local economic ties while stalling the Tumangan free-trade project supported by Moscow[41] – have diminished for at least three major reasons.

First, Moscow has consolidated control over federal government agencies in the regions, especially in the foreign and security policy domain. Moscow's institutional advantage in this area became evident when federal agencies dealing with foreign relations established offices in the regions. The Russian Foreign Ministry expanded its regional offices from three in the late Soviet period to twenty-six in the late 1990s, and planned to open an additional twenty – signalling, if anything, a tighter federal control over international interactions at the regional level.[42] Moreover, the passage of the Law on Co-ordination of Foreign Relations and International Trade of the Subjects of the Russian Federation (No. 4Ф–3, Russian State Duma, 4 January 1999) meant that conclusion of international agreements by the regions would violate the law unless they went through a complex process of securing approval at federal level from all government agencies potentially affected by the agreement. The law also makes it illegal for regional leaders to engage in anything other than trade and economic relations, scientific and technological exchanges, and environmental, humanitarian and cultural projects. With the presidential envoys empowered to secure the resignation of non-compliant governors by initiating lawsuits (the fate Nazdratenko avoided by filing a resignation), violating this law carries significant political risks.

Second, Darkin's election victory meant that a protégé of the Nazdratenko coalition attained power while explicitly foregoing anti-Moscow posturing on foreign and security policy issues, such as border demarcation, the Tyumen River project, Chinese migration or the Kurile Island dispute with Japan. Darkin has few incentives to package techno-cratic, functional interactions abroad in terms of opposition to Moscow as something that demonstrates Primorskiy *kray*'s potential to pursue its own international agenda. Third, Darkin has so far eschewed political grand-standing, being rhetorically challenged and introverted – he is more likely to tweak the implementation of technical provisions of Russia's international treaties than to risk losing political capital by exposing his deficiencies as a public figure. Darkin's economic programme also suggests that he is likely to favour quiet lobbying of the Russian executive agencies rather than 'paradiplomacy', while seeking to increase Primorye's gain from international economic interactions.

Over the long term – depending on Darkin's political standing within Primorye and on the popularity of Putin and his reforms – the Primorskiy government may engage in some form of regional foreign policy distinct from Moscow's in Northeast Asia, depending on whether the regional leaders develop high stakes in a 'contact zone' programme and whether Moscow supports it. Potential for Primorskiy 'paradiplomacy' has been articulated on economic issues on which Moscow is viewed as incapable of having a decisive and beneficial bearing. For example, Yuriy Likhoyda, director-general of the Primorye energy monopoly Dalenergo, argued in June 2001 that his company needed R350 million in July alone to finance coal procurement for autumn and winter heating. Yet local banks, Likhoyda complained, had no such assets and federal loans could only be obtained with Primorye government guarantees. These were limited, however, to R140 million. So Dalenergo began an analysis of the feasibility of buying coal in China, Vietnam and New Zealand – threatening to leave Russia's railway companies without delivery orders.[43] Moscow, however, has little to lose in supporting the 'contact zone' politically while encouraging the new leadership of Primorskiy *kray* to seek (and share) financial resources that are likely to materialise if the new Asia-Pacific integration agenda is implemented.

In mass opinion, however, Primorskiy *kray* and the Russian Far East exhibited a political distance from Moscow typical of the 1990s. The extreme nationalist and grossly misnamed Liberal Democratic Party of Vladimir Zhirinovskiy has enjoyed disproportionately strong support in Primorskiy *kray*, winning approximately twice as many votes as the national average in the Russian Duma elections in 1993, 1995 and 1999. In the 1999 Duma election, despite the arrival of two large centrist blocs (Putin's 'Unity' and Luzhkov's 'Fatherland') cutting into the nationalist and communist electorate, the Communist Party won 4.4 per cent more votes (about 23 per cent, close to Russia's average) than in 1995.[44]

Partly reflecting these preferences, electoral support for Putin has been among the weakest in Primorskiy *kray*. In the March 2000 presidential election Putin won only 40.1 per cent of the vote (in contrast to 52 per cent nationwide), beating the second-placed leader of the communists, Gennadiy Zyuganov, by less than 4 per cent. Elsewhere in the Far East, Putin won close to 50 per cent of the vote in Khabarovsk, 49 per cent in Amur, 47 per cent in Sakhalin, 49 per cent in Kamchatka and 62 per cent in Magadan. Only in Magadan, however, did Putin score above the nationwide average.[45]

Remoteness, demographic vulnerability and socio-economic distress

Primorskiy *kray* is the location of the only armed dispute over interstate borders in the Russian Federation since the Second World War – when Soviet and Chinese armed forces fought over Damanskiy Island on the Ussuri River in March 1969. After this the Soviet government invested heavily in border infrastructure, including an electrified barbed-wire fence along the border.[46] Following Gorbachev's visit to China in 1989 and the signing of the Border Demarcation Treaty in 1991, territorial disputes affecting Primorskiy *kray* were resolved at the Moscow–Beijing level. In a memorandum to this author in May 1999 the Far Eastern Regional Directorate of the Russian Border Service stated: 'The situation on the border with the PRC [People's Republic of China] in recent years has been stable and predictable. It reflects the mutual aspiration of China and Russia to develop the necessary political conditions for a constructive partnership.'[47] And, despite the wide publicity given to governor Nazdratenko's confrontation with the Russian Foreign Ministry about transferring three pieces of Chinese land under the 1991 border treaty, these disputes largely subsided after Nazdratenko's re-election in December 1999. Sergey Darkin has explicitly ignored this issue, in sharp contrast to Nazdratenko, who made opposition to border demarcation a prominent theme in every campaign. This shift has partly to do with the rise to power of Vladimir Putin, whose pronouncements and military campaign in Chechnya made it impossible to accuse Moscow of a lack of support for Russia's territorial integrity.

However, the shadow of territorial disputes with China is likely to be a factor in Primorskiy *kray* politics for the foreseeable future. An article in a local paper, *Dalnevostochnoye Vremya*, during the gubernatorial campaign, and entitled 'Expansion: The China Leadership Encourages the Robbing of Russia', reflects the views of some key regional and federal decision-makers (the chief of the Russian Federal Migration Service for Primorskiy *kray*, Sergey Pushkarev, 'totally agreed with the points the article made'). These views also represent an 'idea pool' on which local politicians would be likely to draw if, for example, they perceived that the Kremlin's patriotic credentials were weakening or if they needed to attract Moscow's attention and resources to deal with security and socio-economic issues arising from cross-border exchanges. At the heart of these views is the conviction that China's leaders entertain territorial claims on Russia and conceal their aggressive intentions:

- According to China's leaders, the 1858 Treaty of Aigun and the 1860 Treaty of Beijing – the basis for present-day border demarcation – were unjust treaties imposed on China by Russia when China was weak.
- To this day, China's leaders have failed to state that they no longer adhere to Mao Zedong's declaration in 1964 claiming 1.5 million hectares of Russian territory for China.
- In Primorskiy *kray* Chinese leaders are guided by China's official strategy entitled 'The Concept of Geographic and Strategic Borders' – implying that migration of Chinese nationals into Primorskiy *kray* would over time result in Primorye's 'Chinification', thus extending China's 'geographic borders. These new 'natural' borders would pave the way for China eventually to establish its strategic (military) control over territories in the Russian Far East.
- Instructions issued by the Central Committee of the Communist Party of China for provincial party leaders state that in recent years [1990s] the Russian government's capacity to control migration weakened significantly, laying down favourable conditions for the establishment of Chinese migrant colonies.[48]

- One of the policy scenarios commissioned by China's leadership envisions Primorskiy *kray* or the entire Russian Far East seceding from Russia, and recommends promoting China's control over these territories by encouraging Chinese nationals to infiltrate local government institutions and businesses.
- Facing overpopulation and high unemployment rates, the Chinese leadership passed a resolution, 'On Measures to Further Stabilise the Problem of Employment and the Distribution of Labour Resources', that encourages export of labour from China's northeastern provinces to the Russian Far East. According to *Dalnevostochnoye Vremya*, this resolution instructs Chinese businesses to seize upon every opportunity for converting seasonal labour contracts to annual contracts to promote the permanent settlement of Chinese citizens in Russia.[49]

A public opinion survey designed by this author and conducted in September 2000 by the Centre for the Study of Public Opinion at the Vladivostok Institute of History, Ethnography and Archaeology of the Russian Academy of Sciences shows that the local public also fears China's territorial claims. The survey included 1,010 respondents selected randomly from six locations within Primorskiy *kray*.[50] Excluding the 'don't knows', almost 82 per cent of those polled say the Chinese see Primorskiy *kray* as historically belonging to China and 74 per cent feel that China will, in the long run, annex Primorskiy *kray* or parts of it. The perception of Chinese takeover also fits into a 'tidal wave' pattern similar to the perception of increasing migration. For example, most respondents believe that military clashes with China over border territories – such as the one at Damanskiy Island in March 1969 – are unlikely at present. In the next 5–10 and 10–20 years, however, they see such military conflicts as more likely than not. The shadow of the future is rather dark for Primorye residents – the more they look ahead, the greater their anticipation of hostile actions by China amidst increasing uncertainty.

Most respondents do not associate the military power balance with the likelihood of China's takeover of Russian territories (statistical correlation is close to zero). Of those who said that Primorskiy *kray* or parts of it would be taken over by China, the minority (19 per cent) thought this would happen through the use of force. Relations between Moscow and Beijing are, in fact, inversely related to threat perception: 25 per cent of respondents in the same group feel that Moscow is simply likely to negotiate Primorye away. This perception is consistent with the message of governor Nazdratenko, who persistently accused Moscow of neglecting Russian interests in the Far East.

From among 57 per cent of respondents in the sample who see Chinese takeover as imminent, 56 per cent believe the main threat comes from seemingly mundane activities of Chinese nationals in Primorye, such as work, trade, tourism and marriages. In a sense this logic can be described as a 'demographic security dilemma'. A local Russian respondent who fears that through these routine activities the ethnic Chinese would settle down, start families, have children and invite friends and relatives from across the border could never be certain whether the real intentions of Chinese migrants in the area were offensive or co-operative. In the shadow of the worst-case scenario, insecurity perceptions can quickly spiral out of control, as bad intentions are more likely to be ascribed than good.

Underlying these concerns about Chinese intentions – among both officials and the public – is a strong sense of demographic vulnerability and socio-economic distress. One scholar in the Russian Far East has quantified demographic pressure from China on the southern part of the Russian Far East (Primorskiy and Khabarovsk *krays*, Amur Region and the Jewish Autonomous District). By his indicators, this pressure amounts to 63,000 Chinese nationals for every Russian, to every kilometre of the Russian–Chinese border in the Far East. Population density pressure amounts to 380,000 Chinese for every Russian, to every kilometre of the border inside a 1 kilometre band along the same border.[51]

Demographic decline has been evident. Since 1992 – and to a greater extent than on average in Russia – Primorskiy *kray* has experienced a demographic crisis. From 1992 to 2001 the *kray* population declined by 151,500 (6.6 per cent), dropping to 2,157,700. Prevalence of deaths over births remained the principal factor behind population decline. In 2000 the number of deaths increased by 6.1 per cent on 1999, offsetting the 5 per cent increase in births (the first increase since 1994). The deaths-to-births ratio amounted to approximately 1.6:1 in 1999 and 2000. A negative population momentum thus emerged in Primorskiy *kray* during the 1990s. The number of 0–4-year-olds amounted to 8.8 per cent and the number of 5–9-year-olds to 8.3 per cent of the Primorskiy population in 1989, but to only 4.2 per cent and 5.7 per cent, respectively, in 2000. At 19.1 per 1,000 people, infant mortality in the region was nearly 17 per cent higher than the Russian average in 1999. The Primorskiy *kray* statistics committee attributed these trends to 'a decline in living standards, the inadequacy of social services and basic medical services, inaccessibility of effective treatment methods to the overwhelming majority of the population, criminalisation of society and increasing crime rates'.[52] These conditions, in turn, created incentives for emigration – mostly to central Russia (or, as the locals put it, 'to the West') – with a net migration loss to the *kray* population amounting to 9,400 in 1996, 11,000 in 1997, 12,000 in 1998 and 11,600 in 1999.[53]

Demographic vulnerability registered strongly in public perceptions. Local Russians significantly overestimate the scale of the Chinese presence in Primorye. When asked in my September 2000 survey what proportion of Primorskiy population was Chinese, 46 per cent of respondents excluding the 'don't knows' said this proportion amounted to 10–20 per cent (the modal response). Looking to the future, most respondents (41 per cent) said the proportion of ethnic Chinese would grow to 20–40 per cent in 5–10 years, while another 20 per cent said it would be 40–60 per cent. Moreover, this survey reveals a strong perception that Chinese migration in Russia's southernmost Pacific province is much more likely to increase than to stay the same or decline in the next twenty years. For example, respondents who estimated that up to 5 per cent of the local population was Chinese were most likely to believe that 10–20 per cent of the local population would be Chinese in 5–10 years. The same holds for those who said this proportion would be 10–20 per cent in 5–10 years and then rise to 20–40 per cent in 10–20 years.

A former presidential representative in Primorye, Vladimir Ignatenko, summarised these fears:

> If we let our economy deteriorate and collapse, then with Chinese migration we may end up with the problem similar to the problem of Israel. We'll be okay, as long as the proportion of Chinese nationals does not exceed one-third of the local population, but if it does, we will be in trouble.[54]

Demographic decline has socio-economic roots. And social conditions in Primorskiy *kray* – whose development was mortgaged to Nazdratenko's bargaining with Moscow – deteriorated faster and more significantly in the 1990s than in central Russian regions, raising questions about the sustainability of Russia's governance in the Far East. Low wages under high inflation – a problem exacerbated by chronic wage arrears and payment of incomplete wages but alleviated by undeclared income from private entrepreneurial activities – has been one of the main factors in the decline in living standards. In 1999 only about 15 per cent of the Primorye population had estimated per capita incomes above R2,000 (approximately $77) per month, whereas 40 per cent had monthly incomes below R1,000 (about $38), an income distribution suggesting that close to half of the population is at risk of slipping into poverty. The Primorye statistics committee estimated that the average disposable income in January 2000 was about 74 per cent of that in December 1997 in real terms. The gross regional product per capita (the share of Russia's gross national product [GNP] generated in Primorskiy *kray*) stood at approximately 80 per cent of the Russian average from 1996 to January 2000, suggesting a lack of financial resources in the *kray* to improve living standards significantly in the short term. Nevertheless, incomes showed some positive trends in 2000 – the number of people making less than R1,000 per month decreased by 27 per cent on 1998, and disposable income increased by 23 per cent. Unemployment (measured as the number of people without jobs who sought assistance from government employment services) was close to 8 per cent in 1996, but steadily declined to 4.7 per cent by the end of 1999. Increases in income, however, continue to be superseded by rising consumer prices – from 1996 to 2000 average wages grew by about 5 times while the consumer price index rose about 40 times.[55]

Testifying to the failure of post-Soviet regional governments to translate the *kray*'s location, resources and business capacity into sustainable financing of the public sphere is Primorye's ranking as 57th of Russia's 89 regions on the United Nations Human Development Index in 1998. Among the Far East regions, this rating was higher than the Jewish Autonomous Region (74th), Sakhalin (71st), Amur (63rd), Kamchatka (62nd) and Magadan (61st). Primorye fell behind in human development to Khabarovsk (33rd) and Sakha-Yakutiya (39th). At $4,837 per year, Primorskiy *kray*'s gross domestic product (GDP) per capita by purchasing power parity amounted to only 75 per cent of the Russian average and was the lowest in the Russian Far East except for the Jewish Autonomous Region. In contrast, GDP per capita in Khabarovsk was $6,552, in Sakha $6,434, in Kamchatka $5,748, in Sakhalin $5,120, in Magadan $4,980 and in Amur $4,929. Primorye's life expectancy, at 65.7 years, was also lower than the Russian average (67 years) and among the lowest in the Far East. Primorye's share of students in the 7–24 years group (69.1 per cent) was the highest in the Far East, however, and only slightly below the Russian average (71.4 per cent), and Primorye had the highest education index (0.894) in the Russian Far East.[56]

For most observers in Russia and for local residents, the plight of the Primorskiy economy is not so much in statistical data as in severe and persistent energy and environmental crises. Local residents rely on multi-stage water filters or use bottled water, even to brush teeth. Hot water was a rarity in Vladivostok for most of the late 1990s and electricity shortages are endemic. Central heating routinely fails, leaving whole neighbourhoods, counties and towns exposed to severe weather, with January temperatures habitually reaching $-20°C$ in wall-piercing winds. The energy crisis came to a head in 2001, when, according to the Russian Ministry for Emergency Situations 90,000 people in Primorskiy *kray* were left without heat in early January. The crisis prompted the allocation of emergency funds by Moscow to provide fuel and electricity.[57] Another energy crisis in the winter of 2001/2 was narrowly averted.

Implications for centre–periphery relations

Developments in Primorskiy *kray* following the resignation of Nazdratenko suggest that the regional political and economic elites that rose to power in the 1990s have the capacity to survive even the most aggressive efforts of the Kremlin envoys to place their own cadre in key government positions. At the same time, Putin's push for state consolidation in Russia diminished the utility of seeking political capital by publicly articulating opposition to Moscow's policies. Darkin replaced the portrait of maverick nineteenth-century governor-general Muravyev-Amurskiy, who was admired by Nazdratenko, with a portrait of Vladimir Putin. Darkin also agreed to appoint Putin's designee, Colonel-General Valery Manilov, as the *kray* representative in the Federation Council.[58] But while it ended high-profile symbolic standoffs, Putin's consolidation strategy also helped the consolidation of entrenched regional elites associated with the defence sector, the fishing industry and natural resource extraction. Moreover, Nazdratenko's promotion to head the State Fisheries Committee provided these elites with a powerful channel through which to exert political influence in Moscow.

Moscow–Primorskiy disputes are therefore likely to centre on functional (economic and legal) issues, rather than on 'high politics' as was the case during Nazdratenko's opposition to privatisation, border demarcation and cross-border Chinese migration. Developments in recent years indicate that economic interests have converged on increasing production in the defence-related industries in Primorye, with Moscow increasing procurement orders, staging military exercises and promoting international military contacts, and with the regional elites gaining experience in securing international contracts for local defence enterprises. The development of international economic interactions involving Primorskiy *kray* remains uncertain, however, as it is unclear whether Moscow would support the newly elected governor's ambitious projects for converting the Primorye coastline into a 'contact zone' with Japan and other Pacific Rim states. Whereas the new governor has reversed the Primorskiy position to support the United Nations Development Programme-sponsored US$30 billion development project for the Tyumen River Delta, Moscow is yet to ratify a much smaller project envisioning a Korean-owned and -operated high-technology park in the Nakhodka free-trade zone.

Economic development in Primorskiy *kray* also hinges on the ability of the central and regional governments – thus far uncertain – to alleviate the region's persistent energy shortages and to improve the ecological situation, especially by reducing water and air pollution. The resolution of these problems will remain a major challenge since the regional elites have shown little interest in promoting transparency, rule of law, political accountability and free media – conditions that discourage interest in the provision and maintenance of public goods. And while the federal government understands the economic challenges facing Primorye, its ability to design solutions and co-operate with regional leaders remains weak. Moscow has a long record of failing to deliver on its economic development programmes for the Russian Far East. The programme for economic development of the Russian Far East and the Transbaykal region up to 2005 remained largely on paper after being developed in the mid-1990s. In October 2001 a new federal programme was being designed at the Ministry of Trade and Economic Development, directed by Putin's close associate German Gref. At the same time, Putin's special envoy to the Russian Far East continued to associate federal assistance with redistribution of political power by putting Darkin's election rival Gennadiy Apanasenko in charge of a working group 'to check the performance of the president's decrees and orders, the course of the realisation of federal programmes and utilisation of budget funds and federal property in Primorye'.[59] Political uncertainty is therefore likely to undermine the capacity of the federal and regional authorities to resolve socio-economic problems in concert, even though Moscow acquired additional economic leverage over Primorye by increasing the federal tax revenue share from 50 to 58 per cent in 2000.

While these problems persist, a worsening demographic crisis will continue increasingly to impede Primorye's economic development. Given these conditions, recent changes in Primorye's government and in institutions regulating centre–regional relations are unlikely to have a significant impact. To the extent that these challenges demand increasingly urgent and costly responses, this study suggests that Primorskiy–Moscow conflict will increasingly be waged, not between the regional and the federal government agencies, but within the executive branch of the Russian federal government, as the Primorskiy leaders learn to exploit divergent interests between and within federal government agencies. Thus, while the absence of symbolic political standoffs between Vladivostok and Moscow and the Kremlin's emphasis on central power consolidation diminish the 'fear-producing environment' in centre–periphery relations, some of the fundamental political and economic rivalries remain in place. These rivalries are likely to have a negative impact on Primorskiy development, since it requires simultaneously a major commitment of resources from Moscow, liberalisation of the *kray* politics, political stability and attractive conditions for integration into the Pacific Rim economic area.

Notes

1 Posen 1993; Van Evera 1995; Snyder and Jervis 1999.
2 Walter and Snyder 1999: 4–8.
3 *Kray* Administration Press Department, 'Bolshoy Kamen: za Grekhi Pravitelstva Otduvayetsya Gubernator', *Vladivostok*, 7 August 1997, electronic edition (http://vl.vladnews.ru); RIA Novosti, 'South Korean Corporation Hyundai Is to Place Orders for Building and Repairing Civilian Vessels with Zvezda Military Plant', *Hotline*, issue 23, 10 November 1997 (http://www.ria-novosti.com/products/hotline).
4 RIA Novosti, 'Torpedo Depot Explodes in Primorye Territory', *Hotline*, issue 21, 7 November 1997; Valeriy Bakshin, 'Na Gornostaye 7 Noyabrya Vzorvalsya Minno-torpednyy Sklad', *Vladivostok*, 11 November 1997.
5 Tatyana Motorina, 'Dovedennye do Otchayaniya Energetiki Golovnoy Bazy Tikhookeanskogo Flota Nachali Bessrochnuyu Golodovku', *Vladivostok,* 10 September 1998.
6 'Business Briefs', *Vladivostok* (English edition), no. 151, 1997.
7 *Vladivostok,* 27 February 1996: 5.
8 Nick Waldhams, 'Defence Directors Feel the Squeeze', *Vladivostok* (English edition), no. 150, 1997.
9 Yablokov *et al.* 1993: 2, para. 3, 4.
10 Joshua Handler, 'Testimony for the US Senate Permanent Subcommittee on Investigations on Threat Posed by the Proliferation of Weapons of Mass Destruction', 13 March 1996, Washington, DC, at http://www.greenpeace.org/home/gopher/campaigns/military.

11 Heidi Brown, 'Critic Warns of Pending Nuclear Sub Disaster', *Vladivostok* (English edition), no. 152, 1997.

12 Interview with the author, Vladivostok, 15 August 2000.

13 *Kommersant*, 22 May 2001: 9, on Lexis-Nexis.

14 *Pacific Fleet Diesel Subs Prepare to Put to Sea*, Russia TV, Moscow, in Russian 0800 GMT, 19 March 2001, on Lexis-Nexis. The report, however, also suggests that major recruitment and funding problems persist as the crew complement of the 'Varshavyanka' sub whose captain was interviewed was seventeen instead of the required sixty-seven.

15 Marina Shatilova, *Russian Pacific Fleet Meets All Combat Requirements*, ITAR–TASS news agency, 26 April 2001, on Lexis-Nexis.

16 'Vladivostok City Administration Forced to Obtain Information About Pacific Fleet's Missile Fuel Over the Head of Fleet Command', *Yezhednevnyye Novosti* (Vladivostok), 21 March 2001: 2, on Lexis-Nexis.

17 *Shipyard in Russia's Far East to Repair Chinese Submarines*, Interfax, 9 March 1999, on Lexis-Nexis.

18 Sergei Vyatkin, *Pollution Control Equipment Market*, Global News Wire, Industry Sector Analysis, 23 April 1999, on Lexis-Nexis.

19 Yevgenia Lents, *Primorye Territory Witnesses Boom in Defence Industry*, ITAR–TASS news agency, 10 February 2000, on Lexis-Nexis.

20 *Indonesia Delegation Has Got to Know the Military-Industrial Complex of Primorskiy Kray*, RIA OREANDA, 3 August 1999, on Lexis-Nexis.

21 *Japanese Defence Delegation Visits Russian Naval Base*, Agence France Presse, 24 January 2001, on Lexis-Nexis.

22 Ivan Zakharchenko, *Russia Navy Chief Rounds Off Japanese Visit*, ITAR–TASS news agency, 22 April 2001; *Russian Pacific Fleet Ships to Visit Japan*, Interfax, May 3, 2001; both on Lexis-Nexis.

23 *Head of US Pacific Fleet Visits Russian Naval Base in Vladivostok*, Agence France Presse, 20 June 2001; *US Military Inspects Russian Nuclear Submarine Base*, Agence France Presse, 13 April 2001; both on Lexis-Nexis.

24 *Japan Participates in Computer-Simulated Naval Exercise in Singapore*, Kyodo News Service, Tokyo, in English, 0938 GMT, 9 May 2001, on Lexis-Nexis; *RSN Hosts Western Pacific Naval Symposium*, Channel News Asia, 9 May 2001. Other participating countries were Australia, Canada, Chile, France, Indonesia, India, Malaysia, New Zealand, South Korea, Thailand and Singapore.

25 '16 Navies in Mine-Disposal Exercise', *Straits Times* (Singapore), 13 June 2001: H2, on Lexis-Nexis.

26 Troyakova 1995: 450–1.

27 *Utro Rossii* (Vladivostok), 2 June 1993: 2.

28 For 'Primorskiy Watergate', see *Izvestiya* (Moscow), 1 December 1993: 5.

29 Kirkow 1998: 926–7; S. Izzhogov, 'Komu I Zachem Nuzhna Primorskaya FPG?', *Zolotoy Rog* (Vladivostok), 14 December 1994:3.

30 Author's interview with Oleg Zhunusov, the *Izvestiya* correspondent in Vladivostok, 22 August 2000.

31 Troyakova 1995: 124.

32 Author's interview with Oleg Zhunusov, 22 August 2000.

33 Oleg Zhunusov, 'Nazdratenko-Backed Candidate Leads after First Round, Kremlin Routed', East–West Institute, *Russian Regional Report*, vol. 6, no. 20, 30 May 2001.

34 *St Petersburg Times*, 28 December 1999, on Lexis-Nexis.

35 *Moscow Times*, 12 February 2000; *Sunday Herald* (Scotland), 18 February 2001; both on Lexis-Nexis.

36 Author's interview with Oleg Zhunusov, 28 May 2001.

37 *Izvestiya*, 2 June 2001: 3.

38 Anatoly Medetskiy, 'Darkin Winner in Election', *Vladivostok Daily*, 15 June 2001, at http://vd.vladnews.ru. The same article also reported on allegations against Darkin of connections with organised criminal groups – another dimension that explained why, from Nazdratenko's standpoint, he was 'an optimal candidate'. One allegation rested on the fact that Darkin's wife, Larisa Belobrova, is the widow of Igor Karpov (nicknamed 'Carp') – 'a businessman and reportedly prominent figure in Vladivostok's organised crime ring' assassinated in 1998. The other allegation concerned Darkin's own association with Sergey Baulo, involved in Darkin's Roliz company. In 1995 Baulo drowned while scuba diving under what *Vladivostok Daily* (15 June 2001) described as 'questionable circumstances'.

39 Perovic 2000: 23.

40 For alternative cases, see Stoner-Weiss (1997).

41 Even these instances – which Nazdratenko presented in the local press as evidence of his battle with Moscow to preserve Russian territories and influence in the Far East – may not qualify as 'paradiplomacy'. Nazdratenko's talks in North Korea focused on economic issues and they were conducted in the presence of the Russian ambassador to Pyongyang ('Russian Far East Invites North Koreans to Grow Rice', ITAR–TASS news agency, 23 March 1995). Nazdratenko's contacts with Chinese provincial leaders were consistent with the letter of Russia–China bilateral treaties that called for enhancement of province-to-province economic co-operation.

42 In a telling example, Russia's Foreign Ministry held a special meeting on 30 January 2001, attended by President Putin and a group of governors, at which the Russian president 'criticised the ministry for not doing a better job in coordinating foreign policy'. Responding to the criticism, the foreign minister, Igor Ivanov, warned the governors that they should not pursue foreign relations without prior approval from Moscow. Moreover, the foreign minister criticised the governors for friendly ties with the president of Belarus, Alexander Lukashenko, stressing that 'the national interests of Russia and Belarus are not identical', and thus suggesting that decision-making centralisation supersedes the stated goal of Commonwealth of Independent States (CIS) integration (see East–West Institute, *Russian Regional Report*, vol. 6, no. 4, 31 January 2001). This clearly stated preference underscores Moscow's acute perception that international co-operation – even with a closely related state that is part of a Union State with Russia – poses a threat to domestic governance.

43 Nikolay Kutenkikh, 'Ttagatsya s Tyagoy', *Vladivostok* (Russian edition), 19 June 2001, at http://vl.vladnews.ru.

44 Michael McFaul, Nikolay Petrov and Andrey Ryabov (eds), *Byuleten 4: Itogi Vyborov*, Moscow: Moscow Carnegie Centre, Table P3, at http://pubs.carnegie.ru/elections/Bulletins/default.asp?n=bulletin0400.asp.

45 *Putin Proves Particularly Popular in 'Ethnic Republics' But Less So in Far East, Siberia*, IPR Strategic Business Information Database, 30 March 2000, on Lexis-Nexis.

46 Photographs from the author's visit to the Grodekovo border crossing and papers on Russia–China cross-border interactions in Primorskiy *kray* are available on the author's 'Russia in Asia' website, at http://www-rohan.sdsu.edu/dept/polsciwb/Alexseev/index.htm#top.

47 TORU 1999: 1.

48 Kirkow 1998.

49 All of the points in this bulleted list are made in Sergey Muravyev, 'Ekspansiya: Rukovodstvo KNR Pooshchriayet Razgrableniye Rossii,' *Dalnevostochnoye Vremya* 13 May 2001: 4.

50 The sample was stratified by location (border v. non-border), population change and population density, rural–urban population split and economic indicators (average wage purchasing power and trade with China). The areas include the cities of Vladivostok and Artem, and the counties of Ussuriysk (including the city of Ussuriysk), Dalnerechensk, Khasan and Lazo. Voting districts served as primary sampling units (*psu*s). In cities the *psu*s were selected randomly (by drawing lots) and in rural areas, where voting districts vary significantly in size, by random selection proportionate to estimated population size (a method which ensures random representation of small and large *psu*s without skewing the sample towards either one or the other unit type). The number of dwellings in each *psu* was then counted and classified by type, and proportions of residents in each *psu* by dwelling type were estimated. Interviewers then selected the dwellings and the respondents randomly by drawing lots. This procedure improves on ROMIR and VTsIOM sampling methods, which are based on various types of quota sampling where interviewers are allowed to choose respondents themselves.
51 Baklanov 1999.
52 Goskomstat Rossii 2000a: 1–2.
53 Goskomstat Rossii 2000b: 24.
54 Interview with the author, 2 June 1999.
55 Goskomstat Rossii 200b: 29, 38, 39, 47, 54.
56 United Nations 1998: 77–8.
57 *Current Digest of the Post-Soviet Press*, 3 January 2001, vol. 52, no. 49: 12.
58 *Current Digest of the Post-Soviet Press*, 26 September 2001, on Lexis-Nexis.
59 *Economic Press Review*, RIA OREANDA, 22 September 2001, on Lexis-Nexis.

10 The 'power vertical' and horizontal networking

Competing strategies of domestic and international integration for Nizhniy Novgorod *oblast*

Dr Andrey S. Makarychev

Introduction

From the very beginning of Putin's presidency, integration became the most widely used concept for Russia's regional development. It is hard to question the need for domestic institutional integration, which is rightly considered the precondition for Russia's survival in the twenty-first century. What is still debatable are specific models of integration and their relevance to the challenges of globalisation.

By the end of the 1990s it became clear that, due to the emergence of new political, economic and public actors, Russian political space had become much more complex than ever before. New patterns of institutional and non-institutional interaction were coming into being, with new corporate actors emerging on the basis of new labour ethics. These new trends were very much consonant with the worldwide crisis of hierarchical models and the mushrooming of networking models of management, which in Russia have their own specific characteristics.

Regional survival in an increasingly complex and demanding environment consisting of a variety of actors depends on how the regions are positioned in the frameworks of both horizontal co-operation and vertical subordination. Traditionally, the regions in Russia were perceived as administrative units looking for their place in the 'administrative staircase' of political power. Vertically, the regions are parts of what could be called an 'administrative market' composed of political institutions, each with its niche in a newly reconstructed 'vertical of power'. Yet this is just one part of the story, since the regions increasingly find themselves interacting with other structures and institutions which in a strict sense are not a part of this 'administrative market' and are not attached to a specific territory to the same extent as the regions. Horizontally, the regions have yet to discover the potential of coalition building with what James Rosenau called other 'sovereignty-free actors'. Social interaction with other members of the regional milieu, interchange of resources and information, co-ordination of political and social practices, and the combination of different economic experiences have become increasingly important.[1]

This chapter examines the vertical/horizontal mechanisms of the regional political process in Nizhniy Novgorod *oblast*. It seeks to analyse and characterise the relationship between state-directed vertical integration and globalisation-driven horizontal integration. Two questions are of primary importance in this analysis:

1   Does vertical integration undermine or underpin horizontal dynamics?
2   What does this tell us about globalisation and its impact on Nizhniy Novgorod *oblast*, and therefore the rest of the federation?

Studying the case of Nizhniy Novgorod *oblast* as a regional actor in a wider international context is worthwhile for different reasons. First, this region was a closed area until 1990 due to heavy militarisation of its industry in Soviet times. The whole decade of the 1990s was a period of gradual adjustment by the regional elites and institutions to the international environment. Nizhniy Novgorod *oblast* started to reclaim its historical reputation as the commercial 'pocket of Russia'.

Second, during the 1990s the region experienced different patterns of governance. The first one, explicitly liberal and innovative, was associated with its first post-Soviet governor Boris Nemtsov, while the second one, much more conservative and traditional, was under the governorship of Ivan Sklyarov. Under Boris Nemtsov Nizhniy Novgorod *oblast* became a laboratory of economic reform, working closely with the World Bank, the International Finance Corporation, the British Know How Fund, the US Peace Corps, the International Executive Service Corps, the Citizens' Democracy Corps, the Eurasia Foundation and numerous Western non-governmental organisations (NGOs) on privatisation and economic reforms. The transition from a closed region to one of the regional pioneers of market reforms has given us a good opportunity to trace the evolution of Nizhniy Novgorod *oblast* from the viewpoint of both domestic and foreign policies.

Third, from 1997 a number of politicians from Nizhniy Novgorod were promoted to the federal government. Sergey Kiriyenko (prime minister in 1998) and Boris Nemtsov (leader of the Union of Right Wing Forces party, which finished fourth in the 1999 parliamentary election) are the two most prominent.

Fourth, in May 2000 Nizhniy Novgorod was selected by the president, Vladimir Putin, as the centre of the newly created Volga Federal District. This made Nizhniy Novgorod *oblast*'s political credentials distinctive from those of the neighbouring regions. As the 'capital' of the Volga Federal District, Nizhniy Novgorod had a new chance to become one of the locomotives of Russia's transition. New models of governance are being developed here, and new anti-crisis solutions are being sought.

Nizhniy Novgorod *oblast* has always had far-reaching international ambitions (historically, Nizhniy Novgorod Fair was an important international trade point; nowadays the *oblast*'s government has launched a project to turn the region into a leading Eastern European cultural centre). This case study shows that it is impossible to achieve international goals and reach world standards by relying on purely administrative measures. Globalisation basically concerns networking between equal partners, horizontally associated by mutual interests. The globalisation agenda encompasses interconnectedness, intensification of political, economic and cultural links, growth of mutual dependencies, and an integrated global economy. Nizhniy Novgorod *oblast* provides a good example of the changing roles of regional governmental and non-governmental institutions under the pressures of globalisation.

The networking strategies of Nizhniy Novgorod *oblast* actors

There are five types of key regional actors in Nizhniy Novgorod *oblast* that widely apply networking strategies. First, there are industrial and business institutions. To foster domestic co-operative links between small and medium-sized enterprises a number of associations were established, such as 'Partnerstvo' (Partnership), 'Delovaya Perspektiva' (Business Perspective) and others. For the business community, creating technological and production chains is an important asset. For example, NORSI oil company, one of the most successful enterprises in Nizhniy Novgorod, builds its strategy on closely co-operating with oil-reprocessing factories located in Kstovo and Dzerzhinsk and the Sibur-Neftekhim corporation.[2] Insurance companies (both local and Moscow based) are also developing business networks in Nizhniy Novgorod, using a variety of means like e-trade and Internet advertising.

International networking strategies are also widely applied to integrate Nizhniy Novgorod business actors more fully into the world markets. NBD Bank, one of the largest in Nizhniy Novgorod *oblast*, is taking part in a number of co-operative projects, which include overseas partners such as the World Bank and the European Bank for Reconstruction and Development (EBRD). Nizhniy Novgorod Commodities and Currency Exchange has initiated the 'Investment in Russia' project, with a special focus on Volga Federal District territories.

The second group consists of educational and scholarly institutions. Among those actors developing the conceptual framework for networking strategies and implementing them in practice are the Centre for Social and Economic Expertise, Nizhniy Novgorod Research Foundation, Nizhniy Novgorod Regional Fund for Personnel Training and other non-governmental public policy research institutions.

The university community in Nizhniy Novgorod is one of a few 'islands of globalisation'. It was the Institute for Applied Physics, Russian Academy of Science, that started 'Sandy', the first electronic network in Nizhniy Novgorod. Intel Corporation has developed its educational programmes in information technologies in Nizhniy Novgorod State University. The Higher School of Economics has launched a pilot project in human resources management and business education. The head of the Yukos company has started a major educational project, 'Generation', to compete with the Soros Foundation and its regional branches.

The third group of networking actors comprises NGOs working in the public policy domain. Environmentalists (e.g. the 'Dront' centre), human rights associations and gender organisations are among the most influential public actors in Nizhniy Novgorod. The International Forum 'Great Rivers', which is periodically convened in Nizhniy Novgorod, frames discussions around a wide range of problems of national interest – from the environment to Caspian Sea oil extraction.

Information actors are the fourth group. TUS Information Centre is committed to the mission of restructuring the region's communications space on the basis of new information and managerial technologies. The Nizhniy Novgorod branch of the Moscow-based Sterling Group is the region's leader in inculcating state-of-the-art technologies of corporate decision-making, personnel retraining and strategic planning.[3] Internet business (including web design, e-commerce and communication technologies) is mushrooming in the region. The strategic goal of these actors is to make information work for the sake of commercial and managerial efficiency.

The fifth group includes ethnic, religious and cultural actors that tend to develop their outward strategies regardless of administrative and territorial borders. Cultural exchanges are by definition about networking; they develop beyond state and administrative borders.

These five groups differ from each other a great deal – for example, the first group is composed of self-oriented actors, while all other groups have a strong public-interest background. Each of them possesses a different type of capital, as shown in Table 10.1.[4] Thus networking strategies are not exclusively based on market, profit-seeking principles, and include important social dimensions (information sharing, education, use of intellectual capital, joint values and shared ethics, interlacing of responsibility, etc.). Networking relations are primarily about mutual agreements, including informal ones, and trust. In comparison to market operators, networking actors can and do refuse to apply strategies that would undermine the interests of their partners. These differences are summarised in Table 10.2

Establishing networking relations is a time-consuming process, which makes participation in the network more effective than withdrawal. In this sense, networking successfully combines two different principles – competition and co-operation. Its effectiveness might be explained in terms of facilitating access to key resources and knowledge, lowering the risks and speeding up innovations. By and large, networking leads to growing integrity within specific social and economic segments, be it in the business community or in the world of NGOs. Most likely, in the future networking will

Table 10.1   Capital of networking actors

Networking actors	Type of capital
Industrial and business institutions	Financial and physical capital (economic assets, funds, material property)
Educational and scholarly institutions	Human capital (trained skills, know-how, expertise)
Public policy NGOs	Social capital (socialisation, relationship)
Information actors	Intellectual capital (data possession and distribution, interpretation of key events)
Ethnic and religious actors	Cultural capital (cultural knowledge that ultimately redounds to the owner's advantage)

flourish in those sectors which defy both market selfishness and administrative regulation.[5]

What matters is that these are basically networking actors that foster a liberal agenda and institutional pluralism in Nizhniy Novgorod. Many of them are in the vanguard of the region's global integration, since their practices and experiences seem to correlate with the 'global networking' concepts being developed and widely implemented in the West in the last few decades.[6] Foreign investments predominantly go to those sectors which are based on networking principles and are relatively free of excessive administrative regulations. This was one of the basic messages of the US treasury secretary, Paul O'Neil, who visited Nizhniy Novgorod in August 2001.[7]

Of course, in order to avoid oversimplification we should not treat absolutely all actors in the categories above as strong promoters of a globalisation agenda in the region. For example, in the media and university communities of Nizhniy Novgorod we can easily find nationalistic and protectionist attitudes.[8] A significant part of the regional business elite is overtly critical of joining the World Trade Organisation (WTO) because of its fear of losing in competition with strong international contenders. For

Table 10.2   Market v. networking strategies

Market strategies	Networking strategies
The main objective is material gain	The main objective is establishing long-term co-operative communications with multiple partners
The objects of exchange are well fixed in legal terms	What is exchanged are experiences and values
Sanctions against deviant actors are based on litigation mechanisms	Sanctions are a part of social relations and are based on moral and ethical standards

example, the anticipated entry of Russia into the WTO will eventually force insurance companies to increase their capital assets, which will automatically push many small regional companies out of the market.

Yet, despite these reservations and fears, the very nature of non-governmental actors' operations makes them a part of global networking. They are pioneers of what could be called community-based development initiatives (including education, project support, technical assistance and institution building), which promote an open-society agenda and democratic institution building in the region.[9]

Lobbying, grassroots activity, public relations, litigation, mass communication and contributing to political campaigning constitute the core of networking strategies. To the extent that networking actors influence government officials, they make them more accountable and responsive.[10] The networking actors are in most cases the leaders of public opinion, making specific demands of government representatives on behalf of identifiable interests in society. They are modifiers of members' behaviour and opinion, and vehicles by which interest groups can realise their political, economic and social goals, both inward- and outward-oriented.[11]

Most of the networking actors are more efficient and resourceful than their administrative counterparts. For example, private TV channels in Nizhniy Novgorod are more popular than the state-owned ones. Business managers are generally perceived as more trustworthy than local politicians.[12]

It is very indicative that the public activity of networking actors is not always applauded in Nizhniy Novgorod political life, and frequently receives negative administrative feedback. Indeed, horizontal networking might become a matter of security concern for regional officials. For example, in summer 2001 the Nizhniy Novgorod administration issued a warning statement identifying those 'non-traditional' religious sects that were considered to be detrimental to the region's stability, with Ron Hubbard's Scientology Church at the top.[13]

A host of regulations were imposed by regional public authorities in response to the perception that the networking sector was violating the public good.[14] Nizhniy Novgorod Human Rights Society was heavily criticised for its peace initiative in Chechnya, while 'Dront' ecological centre received negative media coverage for allegedly making money out of ecological concerns and impeding some industrial projects in the region.[15] Nizhniy Novgorod Association of Soldiers' Mothers failed to gain City of Nizhniy Novgorod Duma support to conduct a referendum aimed at introducing non-military service as an alternative to current conscription regulations.

All this leads us to take a closer look at a different segment of the region's political and economic milieu, namely the 'administrative market'. These channels include a variety of official institutions, each having its well-defined place in the hierarchy of state power.

Administrative strategies and their actors

Federal administrative institutions

The federal centre understands that regions have an important impact on federal policy issues. The main challenge is to find appropriate strategies and institutions to foster co-operative relationships between the centre and the regions.

The Volga Federal District, established in May 2000, is a major institutional element of this administrative market. On the one hand, the federal district is an instrument for conducting coherent federal policies at subnational level. In an attempt to supervise regional economic developments, Sergey Kiriyenko, presidential envoy in the Volga Federal District, has suggested that, where subjects of the federation have become insolvent or are mismanaged, crisis managers and mechanisms comparable to bankruptcy will have to be applied.[16]

On the other hand, Kiriyenko has been widely using the advantages of this new institution to lobby for the interests of Nizhniy Novgorod both domestically and internationally. For instance, attending Salzburg Economic Forum in 2001, Kiriyenko advertised the investment opportunities in Nizhniy Novgorod.[17]

In the sphere of international relations one of the most important formal institutions is the local branch of the Ministry of Foreign Affairs in Nizhniy Novgorod, which was established in 1992 and is in charge of visa support and issuing passports for foreign travel. It also assists the tourist industry and travel companies, as well as business institutions wishing to check information concerning their international partners.[18]

Regional administrative institutions

During the last decade (1991–2001) Nizhniy Novgorod has experienced three different types of regional governance (summarised in Table 10.3). The governorship of Boris Nemtsov (1991–7) was considered one of the most liberal in Russia. However, it was based on the predominance of administrative instruments and measures in political consensus building and economic reforms. Nemtsov's leadership contained strong authoritarian inclinations, since his strategy was one of subordination of the most loyal non-state institutions to the regional authorities, and marginalisation of those which were treated as unco-operative. Politically, Nemtsov's leadership was a 'one-man show', which by and large corresponded to the 'winner takes all' model of regional political regimes developed by Vladimir Gelman.[19]

The governorship of Ivan Sklyarov (1997–2001) was a period of political and economic stagnation. Sklyarov, a follower of Nemtsov who won the election after Nemtsov's resignation, lacked a clear understanding of the region's mission and interests. In comparison to Nemtsov, his successor

Table 10.3   Regional governance 1991–2001

	Boris Nemtsov	Ivan Sklyarov	Gennadiy Khodyrev
Type of political regime	'Winner takes all'	'Struggle by the rules'	'Struggle by the rules'
Political agenda	Democratic and pluralist (right wing)	Conservative (centrist)	Left-oriented (pro-communist)
Relations with the federal centre	Excellent	Unstable and controversial	Enforced compromise
Economic orientation	Liberal reforms	Stagnation	Socially oriented economic platform
Relations with non-state actors (media, NGOs, etc.)	Very selective, based on corporate loyalty and administrative interest	Generally tense and ambiguous, with multiple ups and downs	Unclear (still nascent)
Major political resources	Publicity- and news-making	Political apparatus (regional *nomenklatura*)	Protest voting and Communist Party affiliation
Major political successes	Opening the region to the world, turning Nizhniy Novgorod *oblast* into one of the most important political regions in Russia	Starting to build relations with major domestic investors, forming a regional government	Freezing membership in the Communist Party
Major political defeats	Accusations of corruption, unfinished reforms	Inability to mitigate clashes of interests, failure to secure a regional budget	Slow team building, low transparency in decision-making procedures
Major rivals in the region	Communists and nationalists	The mayor of Nizhniy Novgorod city	Liberal groupings, presidential representative in the Volga Federal District (potential)
International credentials	Good reputation in international financial and political circles	Mediocre, tending to decrease by the end of its term in office	Almost non-existent

stuck to a conservative agenda, and to an even greater degree preferred to rely heavily on the support of the regional *nomenklatura*.

Gennadiy Khodyrev, a communist who defeated Sklyarov in the 2001 election, is still searching for his regional political identity. He has to oscillate between loyalty to the federal centre and his left-wing credentials. As a 'goodwill gesture' addressed to the Moscow Kremlin he declared his decision temporarily to freeze his membership of the Communist Party. The first personnel nominations of Khodyrev's administration revealed a great deal of uncertainty and a number of controversies: the first secretary of the regional Communist Party Committee, Vladimir Kiriyenko, received the job of governor's chief of staff, while all key ministers dealing with economics and finance were taken from Moscow – surprisingly, a new practice for

Nizhniy Novgorod *oblast*, which has always been proud of the qualities of its own cadres. What makes Khodyrev's job even harder is the growing economic weight of major financial and industrial groups in the region. Without their consent no decision can be taken in industrial and business policies, which might demonstrate the shrinking capabilities of the institution of governor in the long term.

However, all three political regimes have much in common. All of them were based on overtly administrative strategies for achieving their political goals and underestimated the importance of heeding the needs and interests of non-state actors. All three governors were rather suspicious of the capacity for autonomous action of financial and information agencies, and basically neglected their potential. These protectionist instincts were particularly visible when it came to Moscow-based companies wishing to extend their business operation to Nizhniy Novgorod: past and current experience is that multiple red-tape impediments are being erected to exclude out-of-region competitors.[20]

One of the greatest problems of the region's administrative market is that its institutions seem to be rather vulnerable to electoral constraints. In Sergey Obozov's words, the governor is the sole guarantor of institutional stability within the region.[21] The resignation of Obozov's right-wing government in the aftermath of the victory of the communist candidate Gennadiy Khodyrev in the July 2001 gubernatorial election was proof of the fragility of the political and administrative market in the region. In August–September 2001 Khodyrev – with the consent of the regional legislature – drastically diminished the powers of the regional government by eliminating the post of regional prime minister (the government is now run directly by the governor).

Of course, this is not to say that administrative strategies are doomed in principle. Administrative tools might, indeed, be rather effective in solving a number of issues. For example, many in Nizhniy Novgorod now argue that the whole concept of offshore zones needs to be drastically revised, despite the fact that the Sarov zone was instrumental in launching a number of re-conversion projects. Yet the authorities in Nizhniy Novgorod *oblast* believe that the offshore zone in Sarov takes money away from the regional budget and is a sort of financial 'black hole' which brings substantial losses to regional finances.[22] Of course, there are legal and political tools that should first be applied to make the enterprises pay taxes to the regional budget.

Some sub-national administrative institutions are rather effective in going global. The Bor county administration – which is a part of Nizhniy Novgorod *oblast* – is widely known for its well-thought-out strategy of attracting foreign investors (including Glaverbel, Gallina Blanca and other European companies). The Bor administration has pledged to reimburse its foreign partners for any losses that are incurred due to bureaucratic procedures and unexpected changes in legislation.[23]

Industrial actors

The relationship between industrial actors and the administrative institutions is very complex and controversial. On the one hand, almost all the new owners of major Nizhniy Novgorod industrial enterprises have stayed aloof from regional politics. Oleg Deripaska, one of the most influential Russian tycoons and the owner of the GAZ car-building factory, refused to run for the governorship in 2001 despite the insistence of some in the regional elite. Later Deripaska pointedly refused to give his approval to the government of Nizhniy Novgorod *oblast*, thus demonstrating his unwillingness to become involved in political and administrative issues.

Yet, on the other hand, industrial actors are in one way or another closely associated with regional and federal administrative institutions. Regional authorities are, of course, very interested in retaining control of major plants and factories for financial, social and political reasons: they pay taxes to the regional budget; control large segments of the constituency; and the authorities are keen to keep a balance in the regional labour market and avoid large-scale unemployment. Even if the regional administration is not formally among the stakeholders in an industrial enterprise, it has a variety of tools to exert its influence over industrial policies. Of course, the regional 'party of power' is not a consolidated political institution, and contradictions between its factions over economic and financial issues are widely exploited by other regional and out-of-region actors.

Major financial and industrial groups (FIGs) are eager to keep 'special relations' with certain factions of the federal policy-making elite. For example, Oleg Deripaska is known to have good relations with influential people in the Moscow Kremlin – Anatoliy Chubays was instrumental in forcing the Ukrainian president, Leonid Kuchma, to allow Deripaska's companies to take over the Nikolayev Aluminium Works. Moreover, Deripaska badly needs state protection from multiple international lawsuits charging him with money laundering and illicit business operations.[24]

The very structure of Russian legislation makes the federal authorities indispensable for tackling a plethora of practical issues related to the everyday activities of industrial actors. For example, the federal centre's consent was needed to restructure the debts of GAZ[25] and establish the GAZ–Fiat joint venture.

For their part, under President Putin the federal authorities have developed their own strategies towards regional industrial actors. One of them is the creation of a number of all-Russian business associations, which are eventually supposed to become the backbone of Putin's 'new social contract' and the cornerstone of federal industrial policies. Another strategy is to encourage individual firms to merge into larger industrial corporations of transregional reach. According to Kiriyenko, four sectors were given high priority for Nizhniy Novgorod *oblast* and the Volga Federal District in general: the petrochemical industry, car building, aviation and transport.[26]

In Nizhniy Novgorod the pioneers of industrial enlargement were the radio-electronic enterprises, which in summer 2001 formed three corporations – Radar, Radiopribor and ATC.[27] Each is supposed to get preferential treatment from the federal government (their debts will be restructured and federal contracts will be secured). Another recent example of a new trans-regional vertically integrated company is Volga Hydro-energy Cascade, also created in summer 2001.

The fact is that the appearance of new business agglomerations lessens the political and administrative resources of the regional 'party of power'. As the economist Yakov Pappe suggests, the possibilities of administrative bargaining are decreasing because the spectrum of issues to be solved exclusively by the regional administration is shrinking. Should this trend persist, in the future FIGs will treat the regional administration as merely one of their counterparts to deal with. In this case, FIGs as coalitions of partner business organisations will play a major role in Putin's institutional reforms.[28]

Bridging the gap between administrative and networking strategies

The main message of the previous section was that administrative strategies have their clear functional and institutional limitations. Many efforts of the networking actors fail to achieve their full potential because of multiple administrative institutions each erecting their red-tape barriers. That is why for the sake of market efficiency they have to be coupled with non-administrative networking instruments.

Regional administrative institutions have started developing a wide range of relations with autonomous and semi-independent actors. This is increasingly true in the financial sector. Some commercial banks were among creditors of the Nizhniy Novgorod administration (NBD Bank, 'Garantia' and others).[29] The Regional Fund for Supporting Small and Medium Businesses, affiliated to the *oblast*'s Department of Developing Entrepreneurship, is a guarantor of the programme to finance socially important projects initiated by local private companies.[30] One of the first moves of Gennadiy Khodyrev in his capacity as new Nizhniy Novgorod *oblast* governor was to sign a protocol with the Gazprom corporation in order to reschedule the regional budget's debts to this mighty gas monopoly.[31]

The close interconnection of administrative and non-administrative tools is well illustrated by the project of establishing a Free Customs Zone (FCZ) 'Russia's Pocket' in Nizhniy Novgorod *oblast*. This project surfaced in summer 2001, when the government of Nizhniy Novgorod *oblast* drafted a concept and solicited the federal centre's support in issues of taxation and passing appropriate legislation.[32] The federal centre's attitude to this idea was indifferent, and it is unlikely to get off the ground. This shows that purely administrative channels are not sufficient for economic autonomy projects. What is necessary is to find appropriate business partners who have vested interests in upgrading local communication and transport infrastructure, environment, urban architecture, tourist facilities and other components of a business-friendly climate in the region.

There are other instances of potentially fruitful linkages between administrative (vertical) and non-administrative (horizontal) strategies. As soon as Nizhniy Novgorod became the main city of the Volga Federal District, the regional authorities came up with the idea of 'exploiting the resource of the capital city'. The point is, however, that Sergey Obozov, the first head of the Nizhniy Novgorod *oblast* government, treated this resource in predominantly administrative ways: with its new political role as the 'capital' of the district, Nizhniy Novgorod attracts more attention from the president, and more ministers come here on official visits.[33] Meanwhile, there are competing – yet not mutually exclusive – concepts of development for Nizhniy Novgorod: turning it from the administrative 'district capital' into the 'business capital', with a market-friendly climate, entrepreneurial culture and business-sensitive policy-making.

Russian investors – major financial industrial groups like Sibal, Interros, Severstal, LUKoil, Kaskol, United Car-Building Plants – have in fact become major networking partners of the Nizhniy Novgorod *oblast* administration.[34] Their advent to the Nizhniy Novgorod market was a consequence of their inability to operate abroad successfully – for many reasons, including the protectionist policies of some Western countries and the slow adaptation of Russian FIGs to the demands of the international markets. Each of these FIGs has purchased major industrial enterprises like GAZ, the Pavlovo Bus plant, 'Krasnoye Sormovo' shipyards and other industrially important plants. Relations within FIGs are usually characterised by coalition building and 'soft' co-ordination of interests between numerous business operators. For example, in the petrochemical industry a new holding is being formed with a far-reaching strategy of competing with leading international producers. As a precondition for entering the world markets, the holding is oriented to keeping high standards in accounting, consulting and securing shareholders' rights.[35]

Inevitably, the creation of such corporations will make the regional authorities rethink their old-fashioned strategies of industrial development. There is no longer much, if any, room for Soviet-style orders to industrial actors – they are motivated by making money and expanding their markets. If the business climate in the region is insufficiently friendly, major investors might leave the Nizhniy Novgorod *oblast* as fast as they have appeared. In response to the changing procedural framework, the administration has introduced the practice of signing co-operation agreements with major investors (Sibur-Neftekhim and others), which is testimony to the emerging comprehension of horizontal co-operation strategies in the region.

To boost investment potential the government must co-operate on the horizontal plane with a number of autonomous partners, including NGOs such as Transformation Technologies, the Institute of Commodities Market and Management, the Expert Institute, the Institute of Urban and Regional Development and the Institute of Direct Investments. According to Obozov, the role of the regional administrative structures is to accumulate resources in the private sector for launching major cost-sharing projects co-sponsored by foreign and domestic investors. This fruitful approach is one of the results of the strategy of foreign financial institutions of encouraging regional administrations to raise matching funds for collaborative projects.[36]

Yet it is not only administrative institutions which have to co-operate with non-state economic actors. These actors need positive administrative feedback as well. For example, insurance companies operating in Nizhniy Novgorod *oblast* are certain that lack of interest in their business on the part of local and municipal authorities is one of the major deficiencies in the insurance market in the region.[37]

The concept of mixing horizontal and vertical strategies is applicable to the political domain as well. Politically, the region might secure its interests (both nationwide and internationally) via parliamentary institutions: both chambers – the State Duma and the Federation Council – have strong regional backgrounds. Yet those representing the region in the federal parliament are members of different political parties and public movements, and in this sense are participants of various political networks rather than of administrative hierarchies.

The humanitarian sphere, too, necessitates constant interaction between administrative bodies and non-administrative actors (media, think tanks, voluntary and professional associations, etc.). For example, Nizhniy Novgorod Law Institute of the Interior Ministry became a partner of the US Emerald Group in an anti-corruption project that involves – by the very nature of the problem tackled – public authorities. Similarly, the Nizhniy Novgorod Human Rights Association, created in August 2001 by a number of local NGOs (the Committee of Soldiers' Mothers, 'Dront' ecological centre, the Society Against Torture and others), is looking for nomination of its activists to the Volga Federal District Human Rights Commission, which from the outset has been made up basically by administrators.[38]

District building and the changing strategies of transregional actors

The district-building process is a mix of administrative (vertical) and networking (horizontal) strategies. Domestically, administrative cadres in the Volga Federal District are predominantly recruited – due to Kiriyenko's efforts – through open competition, which allows us to discuss the new principles of political management technologies being tested in the district, which are based on using communication and information resources. It is no coincidence that the bulk of candidates for public-service offices in the Volga Federal District come from business.[39]

This is an understandable trend because small and medium-sized businesses are searching for a niche somewhere between the administrative market and networking strategies. Nizhniy Novgorod is the consolidation centre of the Volga Federal District branch of the All-Russian Union of Entrepreneurial Associations. This nascent institution is clearly supported by the presidential administration, eager to find new communication channels for state–business dialogue. On the other hand, its function is the co-ordination of sectoral and territorial interests between multiple business organisations.[40] To foster investments and credits it will have to establish a network of connections with international institutions as well.

Big business, too, is leaning towards the administrative decision-makers. For example, LUKoil's purchase of the NORSI oil-processing plant in Nizhniy Novgorod *oblast* was negotiated from early 2001 under the auspices of Sergey Kiriyenko, as part of the creation of new large industrial holdings from existing small ones in the Volga Federal District.[41]

Networking principles are also projected onto those spheres lying beyond Russia's borders. Sergey Kiriyenko, for example, noted that the territorial area of responsibility of Russia's leaders, both national and sub-national, is defined not by administrative borders but by cultural factors – he refers to the 'area within which people think and speak Russian'.[42] Kiriyenko is known for his commitment to supporting the networking of non-governmental organisations, fostering horizontal integration of local communities in culture, arts, ecology, social partnership, youth policy, sports and gender groups.

The interdependence of administrative and networking strategies can be illustrated by the changing roles of many actors of transregional reach, for example the Volga Customs Board, one of the key institutions in charge of the Volga Federal District's foreign economic contacts. On the one hand, like all district-level institutions, the Board is an instrument for achieving greater centralisation and unification of customs operations. On the other hand, it has to find a means of co-operating with individual exporters and importers, customs brokers and other actors outside the administrative market.

Nizhniy Novgorod *oblast* is a part of the 'Greater Volga' Association of Inter-regional Economic Co-operation. Though Association members are regional administrations, organisationally it is based on networking principles. For example, Nizhniy Novgorod *oblast* has had the idea of establishing a Volga Board on Foreign Trade to co-ordinate and monitor foreign economic relations of the regions in the Association.[43] This can only be achieved by respecting the mutual interests and equality of all parties involved.

The same applies to extending to Nizhniy Novgorod *oblast* the trans-European transport corridor running from Berlin through Minsk to Moscow and further east. Closely related is the federal programme 'Roads of the Twenty-first Century', in which Nizhniy Novgorod *oblast* – due to its location at the crossroads of North–South and East–West transport axes – plays one of the key roles. Basically, these projects are based on administrative structures, namely the public authorities in charge of investing in upgrading the transport infrastructure, including airports, highways and river ports.[44] It is the responsibility of the regional authorities to find adequate solutions to the critical problems that might undermine the project – for example restructuring the huge debts of Gorkiy Railroad or finding the most appropriate areas of industrial co-operation with the failing economies of Belarus (within the framework of the trans-European transport corridor) and Central Asia (a North–South transport project is still under consideration).

The truth is, however, that administrative strategies sometimes lack transparency and competitiveness. For example, there were alarming signs that the Moscow–Nizhniy Novgorod highway was mismanaged by Nizhniy Novgorod authorities, threatening the implementation of the international transport corridor project.[45] Yet the most important thing is that there is plenty of room for non-state actors (investors, providers of retail services, travel agencies, communication companies, etc.) to contribute to the success of each of the projects. Such infrastructure projects in the Volga Federal District, apart from mobilising administrative resources, clearly require regular horizontal interaction with a wide range of actors relatively independent of the regional governments, like car producers, catering services and the media.[46] Hence, the basic challenge for project implementation is co-ordination – non-administrative, interest driven – between multiple actors each having a stake in its success.

The results of applying international strategies

It is still debatable whether Nizhniy Novgorod *oblast* has managed to raise its international credentials. Learning to live in the world of networking relations (including using communication technologies, recruiting a skilled labour force, and business education) is a difficult challenge for the region's political and economic actors. Building balanced co-operative relations is a true departure from Soviet-style decision-making and has brought a certain disorientation to the decision-makers. The first reaction of Nikolay Pugin, former general director of the GAZ car-building factory, to the entry of Severstal into the market in Nizhniy Novgorod *oblast* was extremely negative.[47] Pugin wrongly predicted that this new powerful economic actor would undermine stability. There was a period of relative uncertainty for GAZ, with its purchase by another wealthy newcomer – the Sibal group. GAZ also went through a review of its relations with its major foreign partner Fiat, and started negotiations with Ford and Volkswagen.[48]

A number of problems are still unsolved in the area of international engagement of Nizhniy Novgorod *oblast* actors: first, there is a critical deficit of skilled managers in the region; second, customs regulations are outdated and obsolete; third, foreign investors are not comfortable with the economically mighty monopolies like Gazprom and United Energy Systems, which might raise energy tariffs and thus damage existing projects; fourth, many enterprises are unwilling to apply international accounting standards, mainly because they are afraid to lose the informal financial mechanisms they are used to; and, fifth, some public authorities are still not ready for long-term international co-operation. The Swiss-based foundation Swisscontact, for example, had to withdraw from funding a business incubator in the city of Dzerzhinsk because the municipal authorities were unable to find an appropriate office in time, a task stipulated in the initial agreement.[49] Another notorious example is the much-debated conflict between the Nizhniy Novgorod *oblast* authorities and international investors who defended their right to continue erecting a hotel in Nizhniy Novgorod city centre, despite objections from local religious and nationalist groups, who found an ancient cemetery under the building's foundation.

A very important factor shaping the region's strategy of internationalisation is that many enterprises lack obvious customers in the West. That is why the success in establishing and developing networking relations so far has been very limited. Pavlovo Bus Plant has succeeded in co-operating only with partners from Ukraine and Vietnam, which were interested in buying its vehicles and providing spare parts for them.[50] This and other cases demonstrate the need for better international marketing strategies.

Conclusion

Nizhniy Novgorod *oblast* is a regional actor that benefits from both vertical and horizontal types of communication. The difference between the two is summarised in Table 10.4. Nizhniy Novgorod *oblast*, like all Russian regional institutions, shares a sort of 'double identity' – it functions in two spheres (the administrative and networking ones) simultaneously. This may lead us to believe that the future model of federalism in Russia could be described by the formula 'administrative strategies + networking'. Three basic obstacles, however, might slow down its implementation.

First, the case of Nizhniy Novgorod *oblast*, which went through three different types of political leadership during one decade, suggests that the road to global integration should not be paved exclusively by administrative structures. Of course it is important that the regional administration signs investment agreements, takes loans, introduces tax relief for foreign business wishing to operate in the region and looks for co-operation with foreign counterparts.[51] Yet 'red-tape globalisation' inevitably faces severe constraints in resources, scope and effectiveness. The region's 'administrative market' works extremely ineffectively in vital spheres like strategic planning, legislative support of business, energy supply, labour relations, fighting corruption and many others.

Second, each time state and non-state actors have to interact multiple conflicts arise – those of communication, decision-making and joint

Table 10.4   Types of communication

Vertical communication	Horizontal communication
Administrative market of state institutions	Networking between equal actors, including non-state ones
Patronage politics	Interest-group politics
'Hard hierarchy' based on administrative connections and personal loyalties	'Soft hierarchies' based on resource potential (chiefly economic and informational)
Existence of a single centre of strategic decision-making	No single decision-making centre exists; the rules are plurality and diffusion of authority, rivalry between competing poles of gravitation
Subordination of political relations	Co-ordination of political relations
Strict and highly formalised rules of officialdom	Flexible and adaptable frameworks of relations based on emerging agendas (often informal ones)
Strict borders of institutional influences	No strict borders; all influences are of transregional and transnational reach
Bureaucratic rivalries of different institutions each eager to augment their influence at the expense of others (zero-sum game)	Self-restraint is an indispensable condition for the effective functioning of the system
Inward-oriented relationship aimed at mustering domestic resources	Outward-oriented relationship fostering internationalisation and globalisation

management of public issues. Administrative structures are very reluctant to share their powers with non-governmental actors.

Third, non-state (networking) actors frequently lack the necessary resources to implement their agendas fully and have to go cap in hand to administrative decision-makers.

In sum, plugging into the global world has to start with domestic changes within the regional milieu. Living in the global world presupposes a greater weight of horizontal, networking relationships in all spheres of regional life – in politics, the economy and social processes. Administrative efforts should complement the non-administrative strategies, but not be a substitute for them. The more influential and resourceful are NGOs, the media, private enterprises and professional communities, the faster and more effectively the integration into the global infrastructure ought to proceed. As this happens, the administrative institutions should react to these changes, acknowledging the new roles for networking strategies as a part of the region's global agenda.

Nizhniy Novgorod *oblast*'s experience in this regard is very telling. Despite the communist 'revenge' of 2001, regional society is based on institutional pluralism and competition among different interest groups, which paves the way for new openings in non-governmental networking. The toughest challenge for the political elite is to adjust speedily and effectively to the new structural environment, both inside the region and internationally.

Notes

1 Lawson 1999.
2 *MK v Nizhnem Novgorode*, 30 August–9 September 2001: 12.
3 *Monitor*, no. 14, 16–22 April 2001: 10.
4 see Light 2001: 1–2.
5 Sterlin and Ardishvili 1991: 70–80.
6 Zacher and Sutton 1996.
7 *Delo*, 10–17 August 2001: 3.
8 These attitudes were in evidence at the Nizhniy Novgorod 29th Academic Symposium and 4th Fair of Ideas, 'Chelovechestvo v 21 Veke: Indikatory Razvitiya'.
9 Shuman 1994: 2.
10 Mundo 1992: 11.
11 Kvak 1976: 11.
12 *MK v Nizhnem Novgorode*, 30 August–6 September 2001: 12.
13 *Portal NN* website, 7 June 2001, at http://www.Nizhniy.ru.
14 Andel and Devos 1979: 23.
15 *Delo*, 24–31 August 2001: 16.
16 The Volga Federal District website, at http://www.pfo.ru/main/news.phtml?id=1399.
17 National News Service website, at http://www.nns.ru/interv/int3950.html.
18 *Monitor* weekly website, at http://www.monitor.nnov.ru/2000/number43/art16.phtml.
19 Gelman 2000b: 45–8.
20 *Birzha*, no. 32, 30 August 2001: 10.
21 Nizhniy Novgorod News Service, 7 July 2001, at http://www.infonet.nnov.ru/nsn/arch/print.phtml?mess_id=62445.
22 *Zakon. Finansy. Nalogi* weekly website, at http://www.zfn.Nizhniy.ru/?n=10&article=3.
23 *Monitor* weekly website, at http://www.monitor.nnov.ru/2001/number27/art13.phtml.
24 *Novaya Gazeta*, no. 25, 14–20 August 2001: 3.
25 *Zakon. Finansy. Nalogi*, no. 45, 9 November 2000: 15.
26 *Strana* website, at http://volga.strana.ru/print/985290985.html.
27 *Strana* website, at http://volga.strana.ru/print/994859204.html.
28 Centre for Political Technologies website, at http://www.politcom.ru/c_b.html.
29 *Gubernia*, no. 35, 24–30 August 2001: 2.
30 *Gorod i Gorozhane*, no. 35, 28 August 2001: 4.
31 *Kurs*, no. 33, August 2001: 3.
32 Nizhniy Novgorod News Service, at http://www.infonet.nnov.ru/nsn/arch/print.phtml?mess_id=59891.
33 *Birzha* weekly website, at http://www.birzhaplus.sandy.ru/birzha/4.htm.
34 http://www.hotcom.ru/main/?id=10449.
35 *Versia Digest*, Nizhniy Novgorod edition, 7–13 May 2001: 5.
36 'Investment Opportunities of Russia' website, at http://www.ivr.ru/conference/06_09_00/material_1.shtml.
37 *Birzha Plus Finansy*, no. 30, 16 August 2001: 4.
38 *Delo*, no. 31, 17–24 August 2001: 2.
39 Aksionova, Yelena, 'Nuzhnyye Lyudi s Ideyami', *Birzha*, no. 28, 2 August 2001: 2.
40 *Pikantnyye Novosti*, no. 32, August 2001: 12.
41 *MK v Nizhnem Novgorode*, 30 August–6 September 2001: 14.
42 Sergey Kiriyenko, 'My ne Yavlyayemsya Samostoyatelnymi Igrokami', *Nezavisimaya Gazeta*, 25 October 2000: 8.

43 *Zakon. Finansy. Nalogi*, no. 9, 6 March 2001: 3.
44 *Strana* website, at http://volga.strana.ru/print/99302695.html.
45 *MK v Nizhnem Novgorode*, 19–26 April 2001: 14.
46 *Obozrevatel* website, at http://www.nasledie.ru/oboz/N07_00/07_02.HTM.
47 *Portal NN* website, at http://www.Nizhniy.ru, 15 February 2001.
48 *Ibid.*, 2 March 2001.
49 *Birzha* weekly website, at http://www.birzhaplus.sandy.ru/birzha/2.htm.
50 *Zakon. Finansy. Nalogi* weekly website, at http://www.zfn.Nizhniy.ru/archive/010626/?15.
51 Nizhniy Novgorod *oblast* keeps regular contact with twenty-two countries. It is quite remarkable that such countries as Great Britain, Germany, Switzerland, France, Denmark, Hungary, Japan, Taiwan and Namibia are basically motivated by developing cultural and educational projects; Finland is active mostly in spheres of agriculture and transportation, while the United States is more interested in political and security-related projects. Italy, Poland, the Czech Republic, New Zealand, Malaysia, Singapore, India, China, South Korea and Iran place more emphasis on industrial co-operation.

11 Regionalisation of Russian foreign and security policy

The case of St Petersburg

Dr Stanislav L. Tkachenko

Introduction

St Petersburg has always been a 'special case' – it was the capital of Russia when Russia was a participant in the 'European concert' and St Petersburg was one of the diplomatic capitals of Europe. Against the background of Russian history, whether one starts counting from Dmitriy Donskoy or Ivan III, the period when St Petersburg served as a capital is pretty short – slightly over two centuries. But it was precisely at that time when a political and economic basis was given to Russia's claim to be called a European state. Since the time of Tsar Alexey Mikhaylovich Russia had been involved in a wide network of communication with Europe. St Petersburg inherited from Novgorod traditions of North European culture, democratic politics and trade. St Petersburg also imported from Novgorod the traditional rivalry of northwestern Russia with Moscow.[1] In Soviet times

> This Lenin's town had a firm and clearly defined position in the Soviet ideology as well as a distinct hierarchy of influence and power. It was firmly linked with various statist concerns, above all defence, and was part and parcel of an anti-western stance.[2]

Nowadays the leaders of Russia stress that Russia is a European country. Consequently, while the European direction remains most important St Petersburg will occupy a special place as a symbol of Russia's affinity to Europe. In fact, built in an area with extremely unfavourable conditions, it can be seen as one big monument to Russia's desire to be called a European country, part of European civilisation. On the other hand, if the European direction loses its importance St Petersburg's role will decline and it will simply become the world's greatest northern city, with its own place in the country's socio-economic life and with some influence on the Baltic Sea region, but nothing more. This would be a tragedy both for the city and for Europe, because for Europe Russia starts with St Petersburg.

Legal status

The basic document defining the political structure of the city is the Charter of St Petersburg passed by the Legislative Assembly in early 1998 after several years of intensive discussions between the Legislative Assembly and the city's administration. The charter was also the subject of persistent struggle at the federal level. Representatives of federal authorities located in St Petersburg argued against it, or at least for significant changes. According to the presidential plenipotentiary representative in St Petersburg, a number of charter provisions contradicted the federal constitution. Some believed that the charter was too restrictive on the governor in favour of the Legislative Assembly. However, the charter was adopted, and in summer 2000 the Charter Court was established (chairman Nikolay Kropachev, the Dean of the Faculty of Law of St Petersburg State University), with the main task of interpreting its provisions and harmonising with it other legislation passed by the St Petersburg authorities.

For the first time in Russian history the Constitution of 1993 extended federalist principles to the sphere of international relations and created real opportunities for the regions to enhance their activity at the international level.[3] A 'Treaty on limitation of powers between federal authorities of the Russian Federation and the city of federal status St Petersburg' was signed on 13 June 1996. The city administration, headed by Anatoliy Sobchak, worked out this treaty, but it was signed by the newly elected governor, Vladimir Yakovlev. This document has much in common with the analogous agreements signed by President Boris Yeltsin and the heads of other Russian regions. Among the objectives mentioned in the preamble we find 'preserving the territorial integrity of the Russian Federation, the unity of its economic space'. Article 2, dealing with areas of shared competence between Moscow and St Petersburg, refers also to the 'functioning of enterprises of the military complex ..., except production of armaments and military equipment, conversion of these enterprises and participation in the selling of their production'.

Transport – that is, 'issues of the development of St Petersburg transport complex as an international transport centre of federal significance, including sea, river, railway, automobile and air transport' – is referred to as an area of common interest in the same article. There is growing discussion about the role of transport and transit in the city's economy. According to a former deputy chairman of the Legislative Assembly, Sergey Mironov, who was recently appointed to the Federation Council and represents the 'federal centre' in relations with St Petersburg, 'St Petersburg should not become a transit centre for someone else's goods'.[4]

It is important to note that, long before President Putin launched policies aimed at harmonising legislation in the regions with federal law, Article 6 of the treaty contained a provision stating that 'laws and other legal standard acts of St Petersburg cannot be applied if they contradict federal legislation'.

Article 16 covers the limitation of powers in international activities between St Petersburg and the federal centre. It mentions in particular that

> St Petersburg has a right to establish international and external economic links on its own initiative or on the request of federal authorities of the Russian Federation ..., has a right to conclude respective treaties (agreements) with subjects of foreign federal states, administrative units of foreign states, and ministries and departments of foreign states.

But it ends with an eloquent proviso that 'federal authorities of the Russian Federation in accordance with federal legislation co-ordinate the international and external economic links of St Petersburg'.

The rights which St Petersburg obtained after signing this treaty are fully realised only in the economic sphere. Indeed, scores of regions, cities, states and departments in quite different countries have become economic partners to St Petersburg. The principle of seeking partners only at the sub-national level is very strictly followed, with the single exception of Belarus. The objective there was to demonstrate special relations between Russia and Belarus and the success of the integration process. If St Petersburg and many other Russian regions thereby violated treaties on limitation of powers, they did so with Moscow's consent.

Foreign policy and security actors

The political system of St Petersburg, as well as that of many other Russian regions, is still in the process of construction. The situation in the city is unique, in that the political model being created is oriented, with some reservations, towards Western-style democratic values.[5] Most Russian regions are less democratic and more authoritarian. These authoritarian tendencies predominate both in regions with developed market institutions (Moscow, Vladivostok, Novgorod) and in regions whose leaders are actively opposed to any market reforms (Tatarstan, Bashkortostan).

It should also be noted that the level of education and culture in the city is significantly higher than in Russia in general. About one-third of the region's population have diplomas of higher education. During Soviet rule St Petersburg (Leningrad) was able to maintain its role as an international centre of culture, art and science. Despite communist repression against the intelligentsia, a significant part of the local population kept alive the democratic traditions of previous centuries. That is why St Petersburg led the democratic movement among Soviet and Russian regions at the end of the 1980s.

The Legislative Assembly of St Petersburg is a permanent legislative body, with fifty members elected by direct secret vote. The Assembly has a four-year term and this cannot be shortened. Members of the Assembly receive a salary from the local budget and may not be involved in any other activity except academic or teaching posts. This legal framework is unique in the Russian political system.

The responsibilities of the assembly's members are significant, and its powers are really used. Through the Chamber of Control and Audit the assembly receives full information concerning St Petersburg's budget and how the St Petersburg government spends it. In practice, there are no limitations on legislative initiatives at the local level. The only exception is the power of the assembly to influence the appointment of members of the city government. So we may conclude that, in contrast to the majority of Russian regions, where local Dumas and legislative assemblies were transformed into departments of the institutions of local executive power, the principle of division of powers is respected.

But in reality the power of the Legislative Assembly is significantly less than that of the institutions of executive power. The governor of St Petersburg is elected every four years by direct secret ballot of all citizens of the city. In the structure headed by the governor, the Committee of Foreign Relations plays a very important role. This may partly be explained by the fact that before his departure to Moscow Vladimir Putin was chairman of the committee. As the number-two man in the administration of Anatoliy Sobchak, Putin simultaneously occupied the positions of chairman of the committee and first vice-mayor of St Petersburg. That led to significant growth in the power of the committee. After the elections of May 1996 the title of the head of executive power in St Petersburg changed – to governor instead of mayor. Anatoliy Sobchak was the last mayor of St Petersburg, and Vladimir Yakovlev the first governor; both performed the same duties. Gennadiy Tkachev, who replaced Vladimir Putin as the chairman of the committee, also became vice-governor, but not first vice-governor as had his predecessor. Currently the committee and its head occupy a less important place in the political life of St Petersburg than they did before 1996, when Sobchak lost power to Yakovlev. But the committee is still among the largest structures of the St Petersburg government, both in staff and in areas of activities.

In the 1990s the presidential plenipotentiary representative played a minor role in the political life of St Petersburg. In fact Dr Sergey Tsyplyayev held this position throughout the 1990s. The ambiguity of his position was related to the fact that his power was very limited in the city, and his influence in the presidential administration in Moscow was also small. However, Tsyplyayev actively participated in discussions on international politics, and on many occasions was the only politician in the city who made immediate comments on international events in conferences, TV programmes and in local newspapers. It is unclear to what extent he co-ordinated his statements with the presidential administration, but in many of his public presentations and interviews he spoke about the need to prioritise the development of relations between the Russian Federation and the European Union (EU), and he was one of the few Russian politicians who openly discussed the importance of positive and growing relations between Russia and the Baltic states.

In May 2000 the reform of federal institutions started, and St Petersburg was proclaimed the capital of the Northwestern Federal District. One of Putin's closest friends, General Viktor Cherkesov, became his plenipotentiary representative. There is much evidence of his influence in the Kremlin, and in the presidential administration in particular. There is the impressive transfer of money from the federal budget to St Petersburg in 2000, mostly for infrastructure projects and the celebration of the 300th anniversary of the city in 2003. In 1997 Moscow celebrated its 850th anniversary as a holiday for the whole nation, and in 2003 St Petersburg would like to go further, transforming its celebration into an important international event. But during his first year in office Viktor Cherkesov tried to avoid any comments on issues related to Russian foreign policy, even about Kaliningrad, which is part of his federal district. His interest in foreign countries is typical of the St Petersburg political elite of the 1990s – foreign investments and big geo-economic initiatives like the North–South transport corridor, designed to connect the EU and India, in which St Petersburg should be one of the most important connection points.

In the 2000 gubernatorial election Yakovlev won with an even greater majority than in 1996, but the federal district and its presidential plenipotentiary created another power centre in the region. In fact, governor and plenipotentiary compete in exerting influence on regional elites. They also compete for a monopoly on representation of St Petersburg in its contacts with the federal centre. Formerly the governor's primacy was indisputable, but now the situation has changed profoundly. Besides regular bilateral meetings with Russia's president, plenipotentiaries are members of the Security Council, which is the key formulator of Russia's foreign and domestic policies. This ranks them much higher in Russia's power hierarchy.

The party system in St Petersburg largely reflects the system in Russia, though the influence of democratic parties and groups is stronger than average. One of the biggest challenges for the Union of Right Forces is the generation gap. Many of the older generation of political activists are political dissidents of the Soviet era, who cannot find common ground with the young leaders whose political careers started in post-Soviet Russia. The Yabloko group still has an active faction in the Legislative Assembly as well as 300–400 active party members. But an attempt to control the Legislative Assembly and establish itself as the leading political party in the city failed. Its declining influence can probably be explained by its relationship with Governor Yakovlev. Yabloko supported him in the gubernatorial elections in 1996, and this was enough to guarantee the defeat of Sobchak. But in just two years relations between Yabloko and Yakovlev deteriorated and the party then headed political opposition to him. Members of Yabloko are very active in the local and federal media on foreign policy problems. Vladimir

Lukin, one of the founders and current leaders of the party visits St Petersburg often, delivering lectures and interviews on Russian foreign policy. One of the key elements of his foreign policy thinking is the strategic importance of the EU for the future of Russian democracy and the key role of St Petersburg in establishing and keeping good relations with major European partners.

During the late 1990s liberal political groups lost their influence in St Petersburg. One reason for this was the citizens' growing disappointment with reforms. Another was the weakness of the private sector. Much more active processes are underway in the centrist sector of political life. The Unity movement, created by the Kremlin in 1999 for parliamentary elections in December, enjoyed excellent results both in Russia and in St Petersburg. For a majority of voters the movement is closely associated with Putin. Its only well-known leader, Boris Gryzlov, moved to Moscow and the post of Interior Minister from St Petersburg, where he was a businessman with significant contacts with Western partners. Unity proclaimed support for the reform programme of German Gref – a liberal economist from St Petersburg, now the Russian Federation's minister of economic policy and trade. Gref's programme is oriented towards further continuation of economic reforms and deeper integration of the Russian economy into the international economy on democratic principles. But the real problem for Unity's leadership is that, despite their pro-market thinking, a majority of its members lean more to the left and perceive the real power of the party in its proximity to the Kremlin.

An important new political movement is the 'Will of St Petersburg'. This movement has the democratic intelligentsia of St Petersburg as its electoral base. Its leaders are studying the experience of the city's Baltic neighbours, and see them and EU countries as the most important political and economic partners for St Petersburg and western Russia. There was speculation in St Petersburg and Moscow that if Unity did not survive the inter-election period (1999–2003) the 'Will of Saint Petersburg' and 'Will of Moscow' groups would create the basis for a new pro-Putin party for the next parliamentary elections.

Leftist political forces have been weak in St Petersburg since the early 1990s, despite the fact that the Communist Party has more members there (about 6,000) than any other political party or movement. The majority are old people, and it is important to underline that this party is very unpopular with the younger generation. Foreign policy issues are not popular for leaders of the local organisation and usually reflect the anti-American, anti-NATO rhetoric of party leaders in Moscow. The issue of the Russian-speaking minorities in Latvia and Estonia is the most popular foreign policy theme for local communists.

According to popular opinion, St Petersburg politics is weakened by the outflow of leading local politicians to Moscow.[6] It is true that there are few prominent politicians among the local political elite.[7] In political discussions on the regional and local levels foreign policy issues are seldom raised and the quality of foreign policy analysis is usually very low, frequently consisting merely of slogans. After an explosion of interest in the early 1990s in the possibility of a sovereign existence for St Petersburg, outside other Russian regions but integrated into a common European space, the political elite of St Petersburg have abandoned this topic as outdated and impossible to implement. Other foreign policy discussions need deep knowledge, which the local political elite lacks.

The socio-economic situation

The status of St Petersburg was finally defined as one of eighty-nine regions in the 1993 Constitution of the Russian Federation. Moscow has the same status, as a city of federal importance. Being encircled by Moscow Region and Leningrad Region, respectively, the two cities are very closely connected to the political life and economic resources of their neighbours. In the case of St Petersburg, Leningrad Region is its biggest competitor in attempts to attract foreign investment and tourists. The region and the city each have two representatives on the Federation Council. But there is a significant difference between the two in economic potential and political influence.

The level of employment in the city is very high, with single-digit unemployment and a strong demand for specialists in many sectors of industry and services (especially high-tech areas in private companies or joint ventures). But beside this there is growing tension among low-paid workers and pensioners. As one of the most developed regional markets in Russia, St Petersburg combines a limited number of very wealthy people, a growing middle class and a still significant number of people who are just able to survive in a city with high prices for food and services. The general socio-economic situation in St Petersburg is difficult, and changes for the better are very slow.

Retail prices in St Petersburg are among the highest in the country. Even with a large international port on its own territory, the prices of imported goods in St Petersburg are higher than in many other regions, where goods and food products come from the northwest region. St Petersburg has the second-highest prices for services and apartment rents. This may be explained by the high concentration of capital and inflow of foreign investments, as well as relatively high standards for part of the city's population. But at the same time there is quite a significant differentiation of incomes in St Petersburg, and there are no local programmes of assistance to elderly people, such as were implemented in Moscow and several other regions. This results in additional social tension.

Despite that, the rating of investment reliability in St Petersburg is rising and it is now in the 'b-zone' of major rating agencies (this means that the economy is stable but investments are still rather risky). Usually St Petersburg is given the same credit rating as Russia in general due to the rule that any region may not have a credit rating higher than the country. Its previous drop coincided with the August 1998 financial-economic crisis. But even in the course of this crisis St Petersburg's economy suffered visibly less than other regions' – regular payments on internal and foreign loans practically did not stop. In 1999 the growth of gross regional product was 5.6 per cent, and in 2000 about 10 per cent.[8] In combination with the city's deficit-free budget in 1998–2000, this creates favourable conditions for foreign investors and local businesses.

As an economic partner, St Petersburg has experience of mutually beneficial co-operation with foreign businesses, who are attracted by the city's foodstuffs and non-food market ($3–4 billion per year), the developed infrastructure, the high level of education and experience with foreign partners. St Petersburg's company Pyatyorochka has become Russia's largest supermarket chain and one of St Petersburg's most successful retail companies.[9] It is a very good example of using Western know-how to develop new forms of business in Russia, where St Petersburg plays an important and effective role. In 2000 the administration began publishing an annual *St Petersburg Developers' Handbook* for Russians and foreigners planning to invest in construction in the city.[10] At the same time a special permanent exhibition of investment projects was opened in the centre of the city – on Nevskiy Prospect.

According to Russia's Ministry of Foreign Affairs, there are two small regional constellations in Russia which have significant and stable levels of activity in foreign economic relations. One group, with multiple and successful joint ventures, is small and consists of Moscow, Moscow Region and St Petersburg. The second group includes regions which are very dependent on foreign trade (export of oil and gas) – Yamalo-Nenets Autonomous District and Tyumen Region, and border regions like Murmansk and Karelia.[11] St Petersburg is a subsidising region, paying several times more funds to the federal budget than it receives from it. Thus city authorities have greater independence in dealing with some economic questions – like, for example, privileged taxation for large foreign investors. According to official data, the taxation regime in St Petersburg is among the most friendly in Russia for both Russian producers and foreign direct investment.

St Petersburg is a leader in territorial strategic planning.[12] In 1997 its administration initiated preparation of the *Strategic Plan for St Petersburg*,[13] which European experts evaluated as one of the best on the continent. The plan is based on liberal values and fixes important characteristics of the city's future: multifunctionality, development as a transport hub, becoming an interface centre for the Baltic region and northwest Russia.[14] The plan includes the following targets:

- Improve the quality of the environment, provide high-quality drinking water and reduce air pollution; meet international ecological standards in all these areas.

- Assist city enterprises in obtaining federal and international contacts and in promoting competitive products on Russian and world markets.
- Switch to St Petersburg not less than 20 million additional tonnes of cargo from Russia's total foreign trade volume; develop related industries; utilise the city's research potential; reinforce St Petersburg's role as a national centre of innovation and high technology.
- Transform St Petersburg into a centre of higher education for all regions of Russia, the Commonwealth of Independent States (CIS) and a number of developing countries, and into the major international centre for the study of Russian language and culture.
- Implement a programme to make St Petersburg one of the world's cultural centres; plan world-class international-level events; attract visitors to the city; transform cultural events into a tourism product.
- Integrate St Petersburg into the world information network; develop modern communications and information systems in education, industry and administration.[15]

When the plan was adopted by an alliance of political institutions in St Petersburg, the immediate reaction of many sceptics was that the document was not very radical. As the journalist Elena Zdravomyslova suggested, much more attention would be paid to the document if its authors included the idea of a city-state beyond the direct control of Russia's federal government, or membership of the EU.[16] The suggestion was presented with irony, but it is rather a common one – a European option for St Petersburg. Another idea quite popular in the city is to strengthen the Baltic Rim beyond Moscow's control and to participate in Baltic politics as an equal and independent subject. The city participates very actively in several international organisations (including, for example, the Baltic Sea States Subregional Co-operation – BSSSC) and organises several meetings for foreign investors each year to promote the city's interests, frequently in competition with neighbouring regions. It is too early to say that these ideas of semi-independent city politics are popular in St Petersburg. But a search for a regional and city identity may easily change this. The fact that St Petersburg followed other major Baltic Rim cities (Gdynia, Gdansk, Vilnius, Riga, Tallinn) in preparing a strategic plan reflects the city's intention to be in line with regional trends.[17]

St Petersburg is among national leaders in terms of joint ventures (650; fourth place in Russia) and representative offices of foreign companies (276, second in the country).[18] This demonstrates both the interest of foreign capital in the region and the relatively comfortable atmosphere for foreign investors. A good example of successful co-operation between the St Petersburg administration and foreign investors is the first industrial zone in the city established and managed by private, mostly foreign, investors. The Northwestern TechnoPark is a joint venture between Finnish holding NW TechnoPark and an alliance of Russian companies headed by St Petersburg's bank Inkasbank.[19] The idea of the project is to develop the infrastructure for inviting five or six foreign companies to move their production to St Petersburg. The first foreign investor – the Finnish steel construction company NordProfil – has already started building a modern factory. After the success of this project regional authorities are now discussing opportunities to create several additional private industrial zones in different parts of St Petersburg.

A brief overview of the development of several Internet-based projects illustrates the special traits of St Petersburg's economy. Many of Russia's Internet-based projects originate in Saint Petersburg. The head of the PayCash project, Mr Dostov, explained why: 'There are a lot of smart people in Petersburg, but lack of money. That is why people should be more inventive. It is much more difficult to earn money in Petersburg in traditional business compared to Moscow.'[20] But all successful ideas move to Moscow sooner or later – only there is it possible to find venture capital for their development into nationwide projects.

One more distinctive trait of St Petersburg is its image as the criminal capital of Russia. According to the media, organised crime controls the city[21] and local police are unable to restore order on the streets, especially when dealing with contract killings. Indeed, statistics demonstrate that the number of criminal incidents, contract killings and some other ratings are terribly high. The level of corruption in regional authorities is illustrated by the estimate that 'in St Petersburg twice as much public money is disappearing compared to the national average'.[22]

Another topic of constant speculation in local media is the close relationship between organised criminal groups and the administration of St Petersburg. For many years this was just speculation. A significant change occurred in July 2001, when the vice-governor, Valery Malyshev, was charged 'in connection with a criminal case over receiving a particularly large bribe'.[23] Yakovlev's closest ally, Malyshev had been viewed as the governor's likely successor when his term expired in 2004, or if Yakovlev were appointed to a position in Moscow. Malyshev was reappointed one of the city's thirteen vice-governors in October 2000, and was the chair of the Sports, Transport and Communications Committee. He also held these posts before being elected to the State Duma on the 'Fatherland–All Russia' party list in December 1999, but he resigned his seat to take the St Petersburg position. This episode may be just one example of the fight against corruption in Russia, but another and more popular explanation in St Petersburg was that it marked the beginning of a campaign by the presidential administration and the plenipotentiary against Governor Yakovlev.

Despite speculation about the alliance between the political elite and organised crime, the role of the city in Russia's political life grew slowly during the 1990s – 'St Petersburg [was] gradually gaining the status of unofficial political capital'.[24] This is certainly an exaggeration of the attention that the present president of Russia devotes to his native city. However, a certain political demand exists in St Petersburg and it is possible that Putin will experiment there with a number of unorthodox actions (bilateral and multilateral summits, initiatives on improvement of relations with Western countries).

The St Petersburg Economic Forum has become an important event in Russian external political life. Its unofficial name, *CIS economic Davos*, indicates the organisers' pride. Indeed, for a couple of days each year St Petersburg turns into the economic capital of the post-Soviet area, where federal and regional government bodies, CIS countries, international financial institutions and intergovernmental organisations meet.[25] This forum gives the city a chance to attract the attention of key figures to its economy, adding to the city's reputation and paying considerable dividends to the city's economy in the form of investment in intergovernmental projects.

Regional awareness

The political elite and officials of St Petersburg readily use the city's 'capital' image in their day-to-day activities, especially in international contacts. However, such policies can turn out to be an obstacle to the formation of a strong regional identity. We can discuss 'St Petersburg patriotism', but feelings of that kind could hardly be associated with the surrounding region or northwest Russia as a whole. At the same time, 'St Petersburg patriotism' contains a significant 'anti-Moscow' element. The city's influence is also noticeable in other sectors of Russia's life. Decades ago St Petersburg's style of pronunciation was accepted as the standard for broadcasting agencies, and the city's TV served as an example of openness at the beginning of the 1990s, all of which contributed to a St Petersburg-specific regional identity. Nevertheless, the city's cosmopolitanism prevents 'St Petersburg patriotism' from becoming a significant phenomenon in city life. This is probably a significant problem for real federalisation in the future. The region has its history and wishes to reinvent it in postmodern international relations, where the key partners are European democracies.

Yet even as the 'northern capital' of Russia it should not use the idea of *north* in its search for identity. *North* has very uncivilised and unfriendly connotations in Russia. For local politicians and the intelligentsia it is impossible to name the city the northwestern capital – simply because it is possible to have several other capitals of the type (northeastern, eastern and so on). Thus the only type of quasi-capital status which the city is ready to utilise in its search for identity is *the European capital* of Russia.

St Petersburg in its international environment

External political factors

At the beginning of the 1990s attention was given to possible territorial claims by Finland regarding Karelia, and by Estonia to Leningrad *oblast*.

But Russia's firm refusal to discuss such problems at an intergovernmental level finally led Estonia to disavow officially any territorial claims to Russia. St Petersburg representatives always comprised the core of the Russian delegation. They have also dominated the working groups discussing particular issues of Russia–Estonia bilateral relations.

Karelia has not been an issue of the utmost importance in relations between Russia and Finland. The activities of Finnish associations inclined to revise the results of the Second World War, including the new Russian–Finnish border, were carefully observed from St Petersburg, but the negative attitude of the Finns was noted. Nevertheless, Karelia will remain topical. The issue appears when press and politicians start discussing the territorial claims of Japan to the Kurile Islands and different scenarios for the EU (i.e. Germany) taking Kaliningrad under its control. There is an obvious conclusion: if Russia defers to Japan or Germany, the problem of Karelia will immediately emerge on the political stage.

Foreign economic relations

According to Zbigniew Brzezinski, St Petersburg and Moscow are 'the primary beneficiaries of Western financial inflows'.[26] A number of foreign banks opened offices and subsidiaries during the 1990s.[27] St Petersburg's economy has its own interests in the external market, which differ from those of most neighbouring regions. Pskov and Novgorod *oblasts*, lacking sufficient natural resources and for this reason having a developed industrial base, are the exceptions. Given the relatively small size of the city and the absence of natural resources, St Petersburg has to count on drawing investments into its industry, creating business structures, exploiting its qualified and cheap labour force. In this way the interests of St Petersburg and other regions adjacent to the Baltic states coincide almost fully. This identity of interests leads to more intensive competition for investment and trade routes.

Its border location is well observed in the whole of St Petersburg's external policy. The city regularly hosts meetings of international organisations (UN, the Council of Europe, the Organisation for Security and Co-operation in Europe [OSCE], the Council of the Baltic Sea States [CBSS], the Union of Baltic Cities, etc.). Such popularity might possibly be explained by its architectural beauty, but there is a point that should not be missed: the city government actively supports these events and takes part in them. Not by chance was it said by the famous Russian businessman Artem Tarasov that 'St Petersburg is the most attractive city in Russia for the foreign businessman'.[28]

Attracting foreign investments into Russia is viewed almost as the main way out of a crisis. As the first deputy foreign minister, Alexander Avdeyev, stated, '[a]ttraction of foreign capital lies among current government priorities'.[29] Since the late 1990s St Petersburg has become one of the Russian leaders in this sphere – foreign investment into the city's economy is growing, and consists mainly of capital investment. However, converting the city into a kind of 'contact centre', as envisaged by the strategic plan, prevents it from developing as a military base.[30] This primarily concerns the navy, which traditionally considers the city its 'private domain'.

One problem for St Petersburg is the growth in foreign investment elsewhere – it attracted 2.7 per cent in January–March 2001, compared to Moscow's 11.8 per cent and Sverdlovsk Region's 3.7 per cent (see Table 11.1).[31] The Ministry of Foreign Affairs kept the city and region in mind – '[the] interests of the northwestern regions were taken into account in the Northern Dimension of the EU'.[32] This concerned economic interests only. As the foreign minister, Igor Ivanov, stated, the most important paper regulating Russian policy on the EU – the Strategy of Development of Relations Between Russia and European Union for the Mid-Term Perspective (Years 2000–2010) – was an example of 'the Ministry of Foreign Affairs' economic activities'.[33] This is not true, but it is viewed as a dogma for the regional policy implemented by Russian diplomatic circles. Another idea of Russia's government, which was probably designed especially for Kaliningrad but potentially may have a great impact on the economic situation in St Petersburg, is the suggestion to the EU that the Phare programme for applicant countries of Central and Eastern Europe could also apply to northwest Russia.[34] Russia has suggested that the EU should extend to the Russia–Baltic states border the same programmes as are used on the EU's Finnish border with Russia.[35] This would allow the use of INTERREG projects and financing from the European Investment Bank in the region.[36]

The importance of the St Petersburg sea port grew tremendously during the 1990s. Soviet foreign trade in a western direction was traditionally served by the Baltic republics' and Ukraine's ports. For Russia the use of Ukrainian

Table 11.1   Regional foreign investment in 2000

Region	Share in total foreign investment into Russia, %
Moscow	40.3
St Petersburg	13.3
Krasnodar *kray*	6.9
Chelyabinsk *oblast*	6.7
Sverdlovsk *oblast*	4.5
Orenburg *oblast*	2.8
Sakhalin *oblast*	2.1
Moscow *oblast*	2
Samara *oblast*	1.9
Republic of Sakha (Yakutiya)	1.9
Other regions	17.6

Source: Goskomstat

and Baltic ports is economically profitable because of their well-developed infrastructure, relative inexpensiveness and – most important – the lack of suitable infrastructure in the western part of Russia. Until the economic crisis of 1998 there was no political will to create alternative port facilities in Russia, despite the desire of some Russian politicians to exploit the problems of transit as pressure on the Baltic states. New factors were born of the crisis: rising prices for the transit of Russian goods through foreign ports; and more attention for the problems of the border regions in the northwestern part of Russia. These resulted in a growing belief in the importance of state and private investments in developing transit trade and modernising port facilities as a strong boost to the economy of this region. Port and road building are less profitable for the country's budget and private companies than the use of the Baltic states' ports, but non-economic reasons currently prevail, impelling the government to apply significant investments to modernising St Petersburg's port and constructing new ports in Primorsk, Ust-Luga and Batareynaya bay.

The transit of oil is becoming a significant factor in the economic and political life of St Petersburg. Extraction of oil in the Russian northwest started relatively recently, but an important future oil and gas field – Timano-Pechora – is not very far from St Petersburg. Its explored sector alone is estimated to hold 1.2 billion tonnes of crude oil. It is expected to produce more than 30 million tonnes of oil a year, about 10 per cent of Russian capability.[37] As yet, though, there are not enough facilities in the Russian northwest. The only large oil-refinery plant, owned by Surgutneftegaz of the Kirishinefteorgsintez joint enterprise ('KiNef'), is not coping with the volume of oil extracted. This leads to export of oil produced in the region and increases the role of the oil terminals of the St Petersburg sea port as transit points. The St Petersburg Oil Terminal Company, which in 1995 provided transfer of less than 1 million tonnes of oil, has raised this volume to 3.5 million tonnes and is planning to extend it to 5 million tonnes.[38] This is still small, but it helps create a new economic situation in the Baltic region, with Russian ports as major players in the quickly growing market for transit of goods in the Baltic Sea.

For a number of St Petersburg's largest enterprises the preservation (or reconstruction) of their economic ties with countries whose relations with the EU are far from cordial is much more significant. One of the city's economic giants, Izhorskiye Zavody, has little chance of entering European markets with its products in the foreseeable future – it makes equipment for nuclear power plants. After ten years of inactivity, at the end of the 1990s Izhorskiye Zavody started to manufacture again, not for the country's plants, but for Iran and China.[39] The visit by the Iranian president, Khatami, to St Petersburg in March 2001 confirmed the significance of Iran as a promising region for the city's industry.

In the middle of the 1990s large-scale programmes of the investment foundation USA–Russia (TUSRIF) and the European Bank for

Reconstruction and Development (EBRD) started in St Petersburg. The aim of these programmes was the development of small business in accordance with US and European experience. Since the mid-1990s small businesses in the city have been granted $9 million in the form of credits from TUSRIF and $48 million from the EBRD. The vice-president of TUSRIF, I. Karasev, has noted that the experience has been successful and the repayment of credits very high. But it is necessary to mention that small businesses make up only 15 per cent of gross regional product, three or four times less than in most European countries. This will be a major obstacle to future stable development. The city's leading industrial enterprises are highly dependent on the world market and on bilateral relations (especially with China and India). Small and medium-sized enterprises may provide stability, but there are few examples of policy on the federal or regional level which is oriented towards the growth of this sector of the economy.

'Independent' foreign and security policy

An independent foreign policy for the city is hardly ever discussed in business circles or by the media. But it is no chimera. According to A. Bessudnov, '[t]he decision-making mechanisms [in St Petersburg] are hidden from the electorate, citizens don't know a lot of influential people. There are no structures in the city which can produce outstanding leaders'.[40] But despite that, political parties, their leaders and the media in the end create a St Petersburg view on major events and processes in the international arena.

The Foreign Ministry of Russia thinks that 'the remote regions bordering developed countries and countries with fast growth are the most vulnerable in terms of disintegration process'.[41] As St Petersburg fits this criterion, we can suppose that the ministry keeps an eye on the situation within the city and around it. The question of whether the federal authorities estimate the risk of separatism as a real one is rather urgent.

In fact, all prosperous firms in St Petersburg work for export or serve the export-oriented spheres. Markets in the CIS and other Russian regions are becoming less attractive to key industrial companies and financial institutions. International activity by regions is possible only in the economic sphere, but the risks run by regions as a result of the development of economic contacts with their neighbours are more widespread. According to A. Avdeyev, 'Cross-border cooperation should be regarded warily. We have to build it so as to avoid the economic, demographic, cultural and religious expansion of neighbouring countries onto Russian territory'.[42]

An important element in foreign policy is visits by foreign delegations to St Petersburg and by official delegations from St Petersburg to foreign countries. Official foreign delegations are usually invited to St Petersburg, and sometimes that is the only city in Russia they visit.[43] The city sponsors 'St Petersburg Days' in major world cities – among them in 2000–1 were Helsinki, New York, Vienna, Hamburg, London and Lugano. Since 1998 St

Petersburg has started to open offices in such cities as Hamburg and London. These 'embassies' perform several important functions, including assisting local enterprises in creating links with foreign companies.[44]

Consequences

St Petersburg, simultaneously a subject of the Russian Federation and the capital of the Northwestern Federal District, occupies a visible place in global economic and political processes. As one of the most stable regions of Russia politically and economically, it 'ennobles' the image of Russia, in contrast to news from Chechnya and evidence of economic disaster in Primorye. The federal government is keen to use this image.

President Putin's next step after the introduction of seven federal districts will probably be the consolidation of some Russian regions. St Petersburg and Leningrad Region are the most obvious candidates for the process. This idea has been discussed on the regional as well as on the federal level for many years.[45] It is important to note that the reform of taxation, started in 2001, demonstrated the distinction between Leningrad Region, 'always subsidised' by the federal budget, and St Petersburg, 'always donating' to the same budget.[46]

Yet an important new factor in northwestern Russia in respect of the unification of these two regions is the growing economic power of Leningrad Region. Such well-known companies as Ford, Philip Morris and Kraft moved their production for the growing Russian market as well as export to Europe and the CIS into the region. Due to its good location on the borders of the Russian Federation and its well-developed transport system, the Leningrad Region has a fast growing economy. The annual industrial growth in the region in 2000 was tremendous – about 127 per cent. In the first half of 2001 industrial growth was lower (112 per cent) but still among the highest in Russia. There is clear competition between St Petersburg and Leningrad Region to attract Russian and foreign investment, and during the late 1990s Leningrad Region was very successful (oil refinery, aluminium, sea port construction in Ust-Luga and Primorsk, huge transport projects). Even tourist infrastructure, which in practice did not exist a few years ago, is now rapidly developing and tourism itself is a promising sector of Leningrad Region's economy.

It is quite clear that the unification of St Petersburg and Leningrad Region into the proposed Nevskiy *kray* is a reasonable decision given the growing role of transit in the regional economy, booming industry and socio-economic interdependence. It will be an alliance of equal regions, very dependent on each other, especially given the proximity of the EU and its dominant role in their economy.

From the economic point of view St Petersburg will hardly be able to compete with Moscow in the near future:

Generally speaking, Petersburg is a province. And the majority of people living in the city likes [*sic*] it for that. Moscow gives totally different opportunities, money and rate of decision-making. From the business point of view, there are no advantages of Petersburg over Moscow, just cheapness and a good system of education.[47]

But in the political life of Russia in the 1990s the role of St Petersburg was extremely important. It is in this city that democratic forces established their political power on the regional level, first in the legislative body (Lensovet), and then in the regional government. At the beginning of the new century St Petersburg demonstrates other trends – towards stability of the regional elite and the depoliticisation of executive powers, and towards the growing role of the legislature compared to the executive power of regional leaders (presidents, governors and so on).

The CIS factor

For several years there has been a suggestion to relocate to St Petersburg all major institutions of the CIS, not just the Inter-Parliamentary Assembly.[48] This would make the city the capital of the CIS, or the emerging Euro–Asian Economic Community. But in this, as in arguments about transferring federal institutions from Moscow (the Federal Assembly, the Russian Academy of Sciences, the Ministry of Culture, the Central Bank), intentions predominate that have nothing in common with objective analysis. An example is the idea of the speaker of the State Duma, Gennady Seleznev, that moving the Federal Assembly to St Petersburg would be a powerful tool in the fight against corruption: 'Divorce of executive and legislative powers is also one form of the fight with corruption.'[49] There are less expensive ways to fight corruption than to move the Parliament to another city, even if the city is very important.

It is possible that for former Soviet republics St Petersburg is preferable to Moscow as the capital of the CIS. The image of Moscow as capital of the Soviet Empire is probably preventing reintegration in the post-Soviet area. It is absolutely crucial to the prestige of Russia to have on its territory the headquarters of CIS institutions as well as other integrative bodies of post-Soviet states (the Union of Russia and Belarus, the Customs Union, the Euro–Asian Economic Community). Apart from Moscow, St Petersburg faces no competition in the Russian Federation in its attempts to invite all these institutions.

Despite all this, the economic interests of local companies in the CIS are insignificant. St Petersburg companies are investing in Belarus (the Baltica brewery) and developing co-operation with leading Belarus industrial enterprises. Some Ukrainian regions are trying to recreate economic links with St Petersburg which existed in Soviet times. For example, in February 2001 a delegation of the Republic of Crimea visited St Petersburg, discussing prospects for Russian investment in agriculture and resorts there.

Europe/world

The 'CIS factor' for St Petersburg is mostly political. Relations between the city and partner countries and regions in Europe and elsewhere are mostly economic. However, in relations with the three Baltic states, politics and economics are extremely closely connected. In the bilateral EU–Russia dialogue issues of 'high politics' still dominate. As the Russian ambassador to the EU, Vasiliy Likhachev, put it:

> The more deep and developed relations between the EU and Russia, the more real and concrete are opportunities for behaviour as interconnected poles of today's world order. ... It is exactly in the role of "legislators" of political fashion that the EU and Russia need each other.[50]

But experience shows that the more 'high-flown' Russian views on relations with foreign partners on the international arena are, the less concrete are the results reached. That is why the regional factor is defining St Petersburg's foreign policy.

The city is much more concerned with developing relations with the EU than any other Russian region, except perhaps Kaliningrad. But St Petersburg will be interested in co-operation with the EU only if it involves real and concrete projects and is aided by appropriate legislation on the federal level. Until now neither federal government nor local legislators[51] have been following the region's interests. In Russia's Mid-term Development Strategy for relations with the EU in 2000–10 there are ten priorities, but only one (number 8) touches, in very general terms, the problem of transborder co-operation. And according to the official text the 'essence' of this co-operation should consist of problems of 'security, ecology, struggle with organised crime and others'.[52] Under 'others', St Petersburg should probably understand opportunities for developing economic, cultural and political links with European partners.

Possible NATO enlargement to include the Baltic states might be a serious test of such relations. The reaction of Russia to this prospect could hardly have anything to do with the increasing military danger to St Petersburg and the whole northwestern region. However, significant psychological losses, as well as the deterioration of the Russian image as a great power, force Moscow to prepare for a decisive confrontation. Russian foreign policy in the very near future will be built on a Moscow–St Petersburg basis, and therefore St Petersburg is now preparing the future path, which involves firming up relations with NATO and the Baltic states. It is the St Petersburg part of Russian foreign policy that will make future Russian steps more moderate. It is also likely that if relations do worsen, the first signals aimed at rebuilding Russia–NATO relations, even on a new, less propitious basis, will also come from St Petersburg.

Notes

1 Aleksander Ivanov, 'Veche Zamolchalo. Osnovaniye Peterburga Naneslo Uron Statusu Novgoroda', *Ekspert Severo-Zapad*, no. 20, 27 November 2000: 16.
2 Joenniemi 1996.
3 Orlov 2000b: 45.
4 Besik Pipiya, 'Spravedlivost Cherez Kompyuter', *Nezavisimaya Gazeta*, 16 March 2001.
5 McAuley 1997: 221.
6 A. Bessudnov, 'Posle Yakovleva. Otkuda Peterburgtsam Zhdat "Gubernatora 2004"', *Ekspert Severo-Zapad*, no. 8, 15 May 2000: 26.
7 Vladimir Kostrov, 'Pravyye Golodayut. V Pitere im ne Khvatayet Politichaskikh Kadrov', *Izvestiya*, 31 January 2001: 1.
8 Vladimir Yakovlev, 'Ekonomika Sankt-Peterburga', *Ekonomika, Politika, Investitsii*, no. 1(7), 2001: 10, 11.
9 Thomas Rymer, 'Pyatyorochka Sets its Sights on the Capital', *St Petersburg Times*, 13 July 2001: 7.
10 City Council of St Petersburg 2001: 6–7.
11 Orlov 2000b: 48.
12 'Vsemirnyy Bank Rassmatrivayet Vozmozhnosti Predostavleniya Peterburgu Vtorogo Zayma', www.strana.ru, 7 December 2000.
13 City Council of St Petersburg 1998.
14 B. Zhikharevich, 'Replika iz-za Shirmy. Chto Skrivayet "Strategicheskiy Plan Sankt-Peterburga"', *Ekspert Severo-Zapad*, no. 17, 9 October 2000: 28.
15 City Council of St Petersburg 1998: 103.
16 Elena Zdravomyslova, 'Helsinki Dlya Nas Vazhneye Chem Moskva', *Chas Pik*, 17 December 1997.
17 Zhikharevich 2000: 55.
18 Orlov 2000b: 48.
19 Elena Krom, 'Finskoye "okno" dlya investorov', *Expert Severo-Zapad*, no. 10(39), 4 June 2001: 6.
20 A. Bessudnov, 'Regionalnoye Litso Globalnoy Ekonomiki', *Ekspert Severo-Zapad*, no. 17, 9 October 2000: 14.
21 'Kriminalnaya Stolitsa', *De Groene Amsterdammer* (Russian edition), January 2001: 22.
22 Besik Pipiya, 'Peterburg Ustal', *Nezavisimaya Gazeta*, 11 May 2000.
23 Masha Kaminskaya and Vladimir Kovalev, 'Vice Governor Faces Bribery Accusations', *St Petersburg Times*, 13 July 2001: 1–2.
24 A. Bessudnov, 'Posle Yakovleva...', *Expert Severo-Zapad*, no. 8, 15 May 2000: 26.
25 '"Peterburgskiy Davos": Pyataya Vstrecha na Neve', *Ekonomika, Politika, Investitsii*, no. 1(7), 2001: 5.
26 Brzezinski 2000: 6.
27 'Tomas Klestil Otkryl v Peterburge Filial Avstriyskogo Banka', strana.ru/state/foreign/2001/06/24/993380144.html.
28 Besik Pipiya, 'Peterburg Ustal', *Nezavisimaya Gazeta*, 11May 2000.
29 Avdeev 2000b: 92.
30 B. Zhikhrevich, 'Replika iz-za Shirmy. Chto Skryvayet "Strategicheskiy Plan Sankt-Peterburga"', *Expert Severo-Zapad*, no. 17, 9 October 2000: 28.
31 Yulia Butrina, 'Investory ne Toropyatsya', *Kommersant-daily*, 9 July 2001: 6.
32 Ivanov 2000: 25.
33 *Ibid.*: 26.
34 Joenniemi 2001: 151.
35 Fairlie 2000: 97.
36 Baltic Sea region INTERREG III 2000: 41–8.

37 V. Chernitsyn, 'Tranzitnaya Zona', *Expert Severo-Zapad*, no. 12, 24 July 2000: 8.
38 A. B. Kabanov, 'Rost Exporta Nefteproduktov Cherez Yevropeyskiye Vorota Rossii', *Expert Severo-Zapad*, no. 12, 24 July 2000: 14.
39 E. Ageyev and S. Pravosudov, 'V Petersburg Perenesut Vse?', *Nezavisimaya Gazeta*, 10 March 2000.
40 A. Bessudnov, 'Posle Yakovleva. Otkuda Peterburgtsam Zhdat "Gubernatora 2004" ', *Ekspert Severo-Zapad*, no. 8, 15 May 2000: 26.
41 Orlov 2000b: 48.
42 Avdeev 2000b: 96.
43 'Ministr Vneshney Torgovy Finlandii Pribyl s Vizitom v Sankt-Peterburg', www.strana.ru, 13 November 2000.
44 Interview with Dr Grigoriy Rozhkov, representative in London of the Non-Commercial Association 'St Petersburg–London 2003', St Petersburg City Administration.
45 A. Bessudnov, 'Sem Bogatyrey', *Ekspert Severo-Zapad*, no. 9, 29 May 2000: 10.
46 A. Klepikov, 'Reforma "v Polzu Bednykh" ', *Expert Severo-Zapad*, no. 17, 9 October 2000: 8.
47 A. Bessudnov, 'Regionalnoye Litso Globalnoy Ekonomiki', *Ekspert Severo-Zapad*, no. 17, 9 October 2000: 14.
48 'Mezhparlamentskaya Assambleya SNG', *Ekonomika, Politika, Investitsii*, no. 1(7), 2001: 7.
49 Besik Pipiya, 'Peterburg – Vozmozhnaya Stolitsa SNG', *Nezavisimaya Gazeta*, 7 March 2000.
50 Likhachev 2000: 40.
51 For example, the Northern Dimension Programme of the European Union has never been discussed at sessions of the Legislative Assembly of St Petersburg (telephone interview with Vatanyar Yagya, a member of the Legislative Assembly).
52 Likhachev 2000: 48.

12 Kaliningrad

A pilot region?

Dr Steven J. Main

Kaliningrad *oblast* is unique, not in its economic or political relationship with the centre, but in its strategic value to Moscow as Russia's most westerly point facing Europe. A quick look at the map shows that Kaliningrad is further west than Warsaw, and yet for many in Russia itself, let alone elsewhere in Europe, Kaliningrad is little talked about and badly understood. Although small in terms of size and production compared with many of the other subjects of the Federation, it is of great value as a window on Europe, with a vital ice-free port on one of the most important trading seas in Europe, the Baltic Sea.

Kaliningrad could also represent a model for the future development of the relationship between Russia and Europe: President Putin has described it as a 'pilot region' in Russia's dealings with the European Union (EU), and this view is partially reciprocated by the EU. Thus the region's significance far outweighs its size or domestic economic indices. Its relationship with Moscow has been a relatively stable one over the years, apart from an apparent hiccup in autumn 1998.[1] The governor, former Baltic Fleet commander Admiral V. G. Yegorov, appears to enjoy a fair degree of popularity within the *oblast* and in the Kremlin, and is unlikely to step far out of line.

History

While there are a number of very good Russian histories, in English very few scholars have devoted much attention to the area known as Kaliningrad. To Germans, it is Königsberg/East Prussia; to Lithuanians, Karaliaucius – so complicated has its recent history been.[2] Kaliningrad has been a witness and a victim of the effects of war and conquest in the region, and of enforced deportations and resettlements carried out even in the twentieth century.

As part of East Prussia, Königsberg was a prosperous part of Hitler's Third Reich. It had long been part of German history: the Order of Teutonic Knights had made Königsberg their seat in 1457; Frederick III had himself crowned there in 1701; Immanuel Kant was born in Königsberg. The whole concept of 'Prussianness' was born and nurtured in the region.

More menacingly, in June 1941 it was used as a staging ground for one of the main axes of attack against the Union of Soviet Socialist Republics (USSR) and remained an important naval base for the duration of the war. The final assault against East Prussia, launched by the Red Army in April–May 1945, witnessed intense fighting, and the operation cost thousands of lives on both sides. Even today, the local leadership recalls the sacrifice of the men who took the city:

> It is obvious that Kaliningrad is a military trophy of the Soviet Union. Our region is a small piece of compensation for the millions of lives given in World War Two. … Fifty-five years ago, Soviet soldiers entered this land. And today, there are still survivors of the East Prussian operation living in our *oblast*. … Simply, we must understand that all of us are protectors of our Fatherland.[3]

As early as December 1941, Stalin felt confident enough of eventual victory to open discussions with British foreign minister, Anthony Eden, concerning post-war frontiers. In effect, he proposed the dismemberment of East Prussia between Lithuania (technically, at the time of the German invasion, part of the USSR) and Poland.[4] The proposal resurfaced at the Tehran Conference (December 1943). Having won a decisive victory at the Battle of Kursk – which effectively wrested the strategic initiative from the Germans on the Eastern Front – the Soviet delegation could now ensure its demands were treated with respect. By January 1944 the British War Cabinet agreed that it had no 'decisive objections' to the Russian 'absorption' of Königsberg. Despite an earlier promise to the Poles, the Yalta (February 1945) and Potsdam Conferences (July–August 1945) sealed its fate.[5]

The USSR had never claimed that these lands had been held or inhabited by Slav peoples, not least because Poles and Lithuanians also had very strong claims on the territory. This was a small part of Germany won at high cost, which with Allied agreement became part of the USSR's war booty. Königsberg had long been a coveted prize; indeed, had been a war aim of the Tsarist government in the First World War, boasting the best port facilities in the area: pre-1914, 75 per cent of the goods exported from Königsberg were Russian in origin.[6]

By decree of the Praesidium of the USSR's Supreme Soviet, the region was transferred to the administrative control of the Russian Soviet Federative Socialist Republic (RSFSR; Russia), not the Lithuanian Soviet Socialist Republic (SSR), on 7 April 1946.[7] A few months later, after the death of the USSR president, Mikhail Kalinin, the city and the *oblast* were renamed in his honour.

However, to ensure the 'sovietisation' of the region two things had to happen: the Germans had to leave, and other Soviet nationalities had to be brought in. Given Soviet authorities' past experience, deporting the Germans was not a problem: over 102,000 Germans were forced out; the final trainload left on 21 October 1948. The last 193 Germans, mainly highly qualified specialists, left the area by the end of 1951.[8]

Thousands of Russians and non-Russians from different parts of the USSR poured into Kaliningrad, or were sent there in order to ease the burden on the USSR's war-devastated western regions. On average, from 1946 to 1951 36,600 annually settled there; the number then fell sharply, to 5,000 per year. But by then the twin processes of deportation and importation had more or less been completed. Kaliningrad had not only been 'de-Germanised' but also 'sovietised'. This produced its own problems, not least the immediate drain on scarce resources (the region was still recovering from the famine of 1946), as well as a feeling, which even after three generations is still prevalent among the population, that they do not belong there. They are, at best, third-generation 'immigrants'. Most young people lack an emotional attachment to the region, despite the fact that it has been an 'integral part' of Russia for over fifty years.

Given its strategic position, it was not long before the region became a closed area to foreigners and many Soviet citizens. As the USSR's most forward region facing the West – and the use of East Prussia as one of the main axes of attack in June 1941 was not forgotten either by Soviet military planners or the political leadership – it became one of the most secretive, highly militarised areas of the USSR, becoming 'home' to the Baltic Fleet and, at one point in the 1990s, containing some 200,000 military personnel.

This very brief overview points to a number of issues which are relevant today. First, a number of states have potentially awkward claims to the territory, in terms of history and shared culture. Germany has the strongest claim, but both Poland and Lithuania also have important links to the region: in the early Middle Ages the Order of Livonia was in charge of the area and the first printed work in Lithuanian was published there; in the fifteenth century it was occupied by the Polish crown; only in the seventeenth century did it become part of the kingdom of Prussia.[9] Thus, these lands have been fought over and ruled by all the major powers in the region. Emotional, historical and cultural attachment to them should neither be overlooked nor underestimated. Chancellor Schröder, meeting President Putin, referred to Kaliningrad as Königsberg, and there are still many Lithuanians, not necessarily nationalists, who refer to Kaliningrad as 'Lithuania Minor' and who believe that Kaliningrad is an inalienable part of Lithuania's statehood, deeply interwoven into their culture and history.

Second, as the USSR/Russia's most westerly point, security interests have always been uppermost. Attention was focused on ensuring that the military was in a high state of combat readiness. Not only did the border become hermetically sealed, even against 'fraternal' Poland and 'socialist' Lithuania, but the region also earned itself the sobriquet of 'garrison state'.[10]

Third, when the *oblast* was part of a large Union and could rely on a share of a Union federal budget it could cope with the additional burden of a significant military presence, but given the shrinking Russian budget and initial increase in the military presence in the 1990s, as well as the outdated nature of the local economy, the defence burden became excessive. Not enough was invested in the region's social infrastructure, and the local economy has found it difficult to absorb yet another influx of Russian migrants after 1991. Kaliningrad is one of the very few cities in Russia where the population has increased since 1989.

Fourth, if the region is to move forward it has to take into proper account all its historical roots, in particular its German past. This is something which Kaliningraders themselves have little difficulty with – witness the number of 'nostalgic tourists' visiting the region, 60 per cent of whom are German.[11] It is more of a problem for the Russians in Moscow. Having been denied knowledge of the region's history, Kaliningraders are now very keen not only to discuss openly the less pleasant side of their historical record – such as the deportation of the Germans – but also to re-emphasise their overall 'Europeanness', while not denying or denigrating their Russian identity. Their history has been closely tied in with that of the ethnic Baltic populations, but Russians predominate in this particular community.

The socio-economic profile

Kaliningrad *oblast* is 15,100 square kilometres in size, with a population (as of 1 January 2000) of 948,500; 78.5 per cent were ethnic Russian in 1989. Population density is 62.8 per square kilometre, one of the highest in Russia. Those fit to work comprise 60.9 per cent of the population, those too young to work 19.6 per cent and those too old 19.5 per cent. Reflecting its complicated history, the *oblast* has representatives of ninety-seven different nationalities, including Belarussians, Ukrainians, Lithuanians, Poles and Armenians.[12]

The vast majority live in the region's capital, Kaliningrad (423,700). The other towns are considerably smaller: Sovetsk 43,900; Chernyakhovsk 43,000; Baltiysk 31,500 (also the Baltic Fleet's home port) and Gusev 28,000.[13] The *oblast* has thirteen administrative subregions, including twenty-two towns and five smaller settlements.[14] Its Baltic coastline is just under 184 kilometres. To the north and the east it shares a 280 kilometre border with Lithuania, and to the south a 232 kilometre border with Poland. Contrary to popular belief, it does not share a border with Belarus (they are around 80 kilometres apart). Had this been the case, Russia would not have had to secure transit rights through Lithuania.

Highlighting its relative geographical isolation from the rest of the Federation is the fact that the nearest *oblast* centre to Kaliningrad is Pskov, some 800 kilometres away. From Kaliningrad to the nearest point on the Polish border is 70 kilometres, to Lithuania only 35 kilometres. These are important statistics when examining Russian concerns over NATO expansion and the region's links with its neighbours.

The regional economy is industrial-agrarian. According to official figures, in 1998 the industrial sector accounted for 30.5 per cent of the gross regional product; agriculture only 6.7 per cent. Goskomstat also recorded the *oblast*'s share in Russia's overall gross national product (GNP) as 0.4 per cent; industrial and agricultural production 0.4 per cent each.[15] Food (including fishing), energy, machine-building and timber play the dominant role. Even so, the number of officially registered unemployed grew from 26,200 in 1992 to 79,000 in 1998 (14.7 per cent).[16] The real rate, though, may be considerably higher, especially in the countryside, where it may have reached 40 per cent in certain areas, given the fall in agricultural production between 1991 and 1998.[17]

The region has reserves of brown coal and amber. Commercial oil extraction started in 1975, reaching an annual peak of 1.5 million tonnes in 1986.[18] As the *oblast* lacks a refinery, all oil has to be exported – to Lithuania – for refining. The region's oil reserves have been estimated at 130 million tonnes, 50 million on land and the rest off shore. Commercial gas extraction began in 1983 and a pipeline runs from Kaliningrad to Vilnius. In 1994 Kaliningrad exported 300 million cubic metres of gas.[19] Kaliningrad also has an estimated 400 million tonnes of peat.[20] Despite all these energy resources, though, its annual production of 400 million kilowatts of electricity is not enough to meet its own requirements, so it still has to import electricity from the Ignalina nuclear power plant in Lithuania.[21] It goes without saying that this gives Lithuania an important card in its relations with Russia.

Kaliningrad has a well-developed transport infrastructure, at least in comparison with many other regions of the Russian Federation. There are regular international rail services,[22] and its road network places it on a par with the other Baltic countries and in a much stronger position than the other regions of northwestern Russia.[23] There are regular international bus connections[24] and an airport.

However, arguably its single most important transport asset is its ice-free port, although its share of freight traffic in the Baltic Sea has declined (the port complex is working at around 30 per cent capacity).[25] In 2001 freight was shipped to the Caribbean, Germany and US ports. With proper investment – an ongoing call from many within the region – the port system could play an important role in rejuvenating the local economy, help Russia regain lost trade and create new business.

Kaliningraders now have the opportunity to interact with all their neighbours. And yet geographical proximity to major European cities actually serves to underline that Kaliningrad is still far from Europe. Since 1991 Poland and the Baltic states have visibly progressed. Unless radical changes happen in Kaliningrad too, as their neighbours' living standards continue to improve – as a result, for instance, of joining the EU – Kaliningrad's perception of isolation could lead to a growing demand for greater control over its own affairs. This danger seems to have been in the mind of Governor-Admiral Yegorov in February 2001:

If the federal centre does not develop a clear programme, or a concept for the development of Kaliningrad *oblast*, there will be an outburst of separatism, based on economics – everyone all around us lives better than we, this means that we must separate from Russia.[26]

Although Yegorov is against any loosening of the bond between Kaliningrad and Moscow, he is very aware of the danger of a continuing lack of investment by the federal centre. The Baltic Republican Party actively campaigns for Kaliningrad to become a subject of international law.[27] While it is unlikely for the time being that separatists will win the wider political struggle, Moscow had better clearly map out the way ahead for Kaliningrad as an 'integral part' of the Federation.

Governor-Admiral V. G. Yegorov

On 19 November 2000 the Baltic Fleet commander, Admiral V. G. Yegorov, was overwhelmingly elected governor, winning just slightly under 57 per cent of votes cast.[28] His opponent, the incumbent governor Leonid Gorbenko, was generally accepted to have presided over a local administration which had become hopelessly corrupt.[29]

His election confirmed a trend in Russian politics since Putin came to power – strengthening the senior political leadership by men from the 'power ministries' (Ministry of Defence, Interior Ministry, Tax Police, Security Services, etc). In the country's influential State Council, which consists of around a hundred members, there are twenty-one generals and one marshal. Outside the senior political apparatus, many 'graduates' of these structures manage commercial enterprises, banks and public organisations.[30] Against this background, Yegorov's election as governor was not surprising. Putin is keen to move 'men in uniform' into positions of power in the regions in order to reform the relationship between the centre and the regions further in favour of the centre, arguing that such a process will be to the overall betterment of the Federation.

A person like Yegorov, especially in a region like Kaliningrad, would certainly appeal to Putin. First, Yegorov knows the importance of working within a clearly defined hierarchy. This does not imply that he is simply there to carry out the Kremlin's instructions. His victory was as much due to his personal standing within the *oblast* and care of the Fleet[31] as to the tacit backing of Putin or the large military-related electorate.[32] Second, given his exemplary career, Yegorov has not been involved in any of the political or economic wrangling that was such a prominent feature of the previous administration. He has not been involved in the 'dirt' of Russian politics. Finally, Yegorov realises the best interests of the region lie in the political unity of the Federation.

Yegorov's election campaign was a mixture of 'bread and butter' local concerns – such as growing poverty within the region (officially, 39 per cent live below the poverty line) and the increasing social crisis (15,000 officially registered drug users, 3,500 with AIDS, over 10,000 in prison) – and the larger picture: the necessity of maintaining the territorial integrity of Russia and the 'model' nature of the *oblast* in relation to Russia's future.[33] His programme, drafted by a group of 'experts', contained something to appeal to as many potential supporters as possible.[34] The electorate's age profile should be borne in mind. According to one locally based researcher the over-50s make up 35 per cent of the electoral register, but thanks to their turnout (usually about 75–80 per cent) comprise 50 per cent of those who vote.[35] Given that the 'military' electorate in Kaliningrad numbers 200,000 of around 725,000,[36] it is clear that Yegorov would have wide appeal:[37]

> The only force that has not completely discredited itself in the eyes of society is the men in uniform. That is why the choice of the Baltic Fleet Commander Yegorov is a wise one.[38]

Moscow–St Petersburg–Kaliningrad

Having secured a solid mandate and enjoying Putin's support, Yegorov's political base was firm. However, within his first year Moscow seemed determined to play a much greater role in the region's affairs. The federal centre, directly and through the apparatus of the Northwestern Federal District (based in St Petersburg and headed by V. Cherkesov, Putin's presidential plenipotentiary), took a number of steps to exert greater control over Yegorov's regional economic and political apparatus. A deputy presidential plenipotentiary representative was appointed specifically for the region, attached to Cherkesov's office, and Moscow announced that the 2002 regional budget would be controlled directly by the state chancery and not locally by the *oblast* Duma.

This increase in federal control had been on the cards for some time. In October 2000, for instance, S. Ivanov, then secretary to the Security Council, asserted that

> The strategic position of Kaliningrad *oblast* in the system of maintaining security and the political and economic interests of Russia in the western direction has assumed an exceptionally important significance.[39]

In February 2001 Ivanov once again stressed that, despite rumours that Russia was on the verge of doing a deal with Germany to grant economic privileges in the region in return for dropping part of the debt between the two countries, not only would Russia not grant any special privileges to any country attempting to work within the Federation, but 'Kaliningrad *oblast* was, is and will be a component part of Russia':[40]

For Moscow Kaliningrad is not only an economic, but also a military, 'outpost' of Russia in the western direction. That is why ... the significance of the Kaliningrad military group in maintaining the defence of the western *oblasts* of the country 'is difficult to overestimate'.[41]

During his official visit to the *oblast* early in March 2001, the foreign minister, I. Ivanov, not only reasserted Moscow's determination to hold onto the region, but also said that the region itself should be careful not to challenge the country's 'vertical of power':

> For us, Kaliningrad *oblast* is an integral part of the Russian Federation and its internal market, our leading outpost on the country's western borders. Already today the region is gradually becoming a unique laboratory for working out new, improved forms of co-operation with foreign countries, including the EU. ... At the same time, it is necessary with all our efforts to suppress careless attempts – and, unfortunately, they do exist – at conducting the affairs of Kaliningrad by avoiding the federal centre. We cannot allow, in questions of developing the region's foreign ties, anyone to succeed in breaking the Russian power vertical, dividing and setting us against one another.[42]

The 'power vertical' had been recreated with the appointment of presidential plenipotentiary representatives and federal districts. Others may have had their doubts as to what the position actually meant, but the Northwestern Federal District plenipotentiary, Cherkesov, had no doubt about Putin's priorities:

> The problem of strengthening Russian statehood was viewed as one of the most important. In recent years, the state had become ineffective.[43]

A month later Cherkesov stated that, 'objectively speaking', plenipotentiaries were created in order to stop the decentralisation of the Russian state and were not simply concerned with easing its administration.[44] By April 2001 Cherkesov reported to Putin that, at least in his federal district,

> The collapse in the system of state power, in the unity of the country in Russia had been halted. In the North-Western Federal District, the regional laws, virtually all of them, had been brought into line with the Constitution and laws of the Russian Federation.[45]

It would be interesting to speculate about the relationship between Putin, Cherkesov and Yegorov and compare it with other such relationships. Unfortunately, present information does not allow an in-depth examination. However, judging by the official list of Yegorov's meetings (published on Kaliningrad *oblast*'s official website) from December 2000 to July 2001, it would appear that Cherkesov and Yegorov met on no more than four occasions, the last on the eve of the important Security Council session on 26 July.[46] Given the region's stated importance to Russia, this seems a bit on the slim side. And yet Kaliningrad had attracted a great deal of attention over the same period:

> From the beginning of the year [2001], we have been visited by the Minister of Transport S. Frank, the Minister of Foreign Affairs I. Ivanov, the Minister for Economic Development and Trade G. Gref, the presidential plenipotentiary to the North-Western Federal District V. Cherkesov, S. Ivanov – when he was still Secretary to the Security Council. With their own eyes, at least forty deputies from the State Duma have seen the situation in the region ... and ... the Federal Assembly. ... Not all that long ago, we were visited by the Minister for Press, TV and Mass Communication M. Lesin, the Minister for Communications and Information L. Reyman and the adviser to the President S. Yastrzhembskiy.[47]

The explanation was that its geo-strategic importance was likely to increase as a consequence of potential NATO expansion and Lithuania and Poland joining the EU. Their membership will impose significant new negative factors on Kaliningrad's development, not least in the visa regime between Kaliningrad, Poland and Lithuania, making it more difficult (and more expensive) for Russians in Kaliningrad to travel to and from Russia. It might also increase the cost of goods in transit to and from the *oblast*.[48]

Of course, part of the solution to Kaliningrad's myriad economic and social problems may lie in Brussels, but Kaliningrad will have to rely on Moscow providing the bulk of the money to develop its economy, surrounded by increasingly better-off states, while its goods become too expensive to produce or to sell locally.

Increasing impoverishment will have obvious political consequences for Kaliningrad and Moscow. However, Moscow needs Kaliningrad, because of the ice-free port and its excellent potential transport routes to the Baltic region and Western Europe. Most importantly, its abandonment would be a recipe for social and political disaster and a clear signal that Putin's Russia was no different from its Soviet predecessor.

Hence the government's decision to hold a two-hour session on 22 March 2001 to discuss the many problems facing the region and to begin drafting a federal programme for the development of the *oblast* to 2010. As Yegorov was keen to point out, only one other region in Russia has recently been accorded such an 'honour', namely the Kurile Islands (given their strategic importance to Russia, surely this is not a coincidence?) Yegorov listed the main aims behind the programme:

Steady development, comparable with the level of development of neighbouring states, bringing closer our life to the quality of life of our neighbours.[49]

Yegorov had spent the previous few days in Moscow, no doubt going round the government ministries and departments. Optimistic that his time in Moscow had not been spent in vain, he told the government newspaper:

> Our region is an integral part of the Russian Federation. In this lies the key to examining both our present and our future. ... At all levels, there is a clear understanding that the region becomes its own type of laboratory for working out new forms of co-operation in all areas between Russia and the EU and plays a particular role in maintaining the national interests of our country in the Baltic region and in Europe as a whole.[50]

His emphasis on the possibilities of future co-operation between Russia and the EU reflected official thinking. For instance, at a session of the Security Council on 15 February 2001, the secretary to the Security Council, S. Ivanov, called on the region 'to become Russia's pilot region for mutually advantageous co-operation between Russia and the EU in the twenty-first century'.[51] Ivanov reiterated that Kaliningrad *oblast* should not be left to become 'a besieged fortress', but developed to become 'a natural part of the European space with free movement of people, goods and services'.[52] The foreign minister, I. Ivanov, also spoke about the region developing 'higher forms of co-operation with foreign countries, including the EU'.[53]

When all is said and done, 'in principle, Kaliningrad is an area of responsibility for Russia'.[54] This is a view shared by many Kaliningraders themselves. Sociological surveys in the *oblast* show a clear preference to remain part of the Federation; one concluded that 'the overwhelming majority of the region's inhabitants reacted with alarm to any news about the possible separation of the region from Russia' and only '11 per cent of the city's population thought it necessary that laws in Kaliningrad *oblast* should be formulated in accordance with EU legislation'.[55] In a slightly later survey, of those polled only 8 per cent wanted independence from Russia; 35 per cent wanted 'special status' but to remain within the Russian Federation; a further 26 per cent wanted the region to have greater economic control, but no change in its political status; and only 9 per cent thought that no change was required at all.[56] Obviously bad news for S. Pasko's Baltic Republican Party and very little for the centre to fear in terms of a possible separatist threat. And yet there is a clear signal that the majority of those polled were not happy with the current situation and asked for change.

Thus the federal centre had to be careful to demonstrate that it was being proactive in its search for solutions to present and future concerns. The federal programme for the socio-economic development of the region to

2010 was produced by the Ministry of Economic Development and Trade, headed by G. Gref, along with the region's vice-governor, V. Pirogov, experts from the Institute of Economics of the Transition Period (headed by S. Prikhod'ko) and the Centre for Strategic Plans (headed by V. Mau).[57]

Gref's ministry reasoned that Kaliningrad *oblast* faced three main problems. 'First, infrastructure – 80 per cent of the region's energy resources come by transit through neighbouring states. After Lithuania's inclusion in the European energy system, supplying Kaliningrad with energy could be difficult'.The Ministry's solution? Complete the new power station, TETs-2, as quickly as possible and instruct the private company Gazprom to supply more gas, with the building of another pipeline to the region.[58]

'Second ... the area of competitiveness', i.e. the under-utilisation of certain assets, like the region's port system, allied with instances of economically wasteful overproduction, e.g. of amber. The ministry's solution is to create a single port authority for the entire region, thereby reducing duplication of effort, and to cut back the production of amber.[59] But, given the extensive criminalisation of the amber industry, even if successful such a policy will not mean a large sum of 'new' money flowing into the regional coffers. Criminalisation has to be tackled first, before economics can take over.

The third block of economic problems is in the area of customs and tax. Earlier tax breaks had been clawed back by the tax authorities at the beginning of 2001, leading to a massive hike in the prices of a number of goods. Special Economic Zone status was eventually restored by the central authority, but only after pleading by the regional governor – although in one newspaper report Cherkesov claims the credit for changing Putin's mind on the issue.[60] Gref's proposal is to turn the region into 'a zone of export production', in which it will be profitable to produce and export goods. If such a strategy succeeds, he postulates that it will encourage investors to come to the region and this in turn will help develop the service and manufacturing sectors of the local economy. Then, as the analysis concludes, EU enlargement will turn out to be 'a good thing' for Russia.[61]

The programme was described as being '*konkretnaya*' (practical), as opposed to '*tezisnaya*' (theoretical). Thus, it envisaged allocating R100 billion to develop 132 'objects of state property' and a further R13 billion for various commercial projects. These are vast sums of money and, if put into effect, the impact on the region would be enormous. However, a degree of cynicism is in order: the federal centre underfunded Kaliningrad's regional budget to the tune of R326 million in 2000, and of 100 special federal projects due to receive funding in 2001 from the federal budget, by July only three had actually received anything.[62]

In order to consolidate the idea that the region is an integral part of Russia, in April 2001, by presidential instruction, a meeting took place in Kaliningrad involving the press and communications ministers, M. Lesin and L. Reyman, the presidential adviser S. Yastrzhembskiy, Governor

Yegorov and his regional media chiefs. It was largely concerned with two main issues: reincorporating the region into Russia's 'information space' and portraying the region in a more positive light than had been the case to date:

> [I]n the shortest possible time, a working group will be created which will work out a strategy and tactics for integrating Kaliningrad *oblast* in the general information space of Russia, underlined by ... the necessity of the region to meet the European processes fully armed.[63]

Remarking that the most commonly used term in relation to the region was 'outpost', Yastrzhembskiy pointed out that this had too much of a military ring to it and emphasised the need to change this image:

> Attention towards Kaliningrad *oblast* is enormous, both from Russia and from the West. That is why it is important for the *oblast* to have an attractive image in all aspects of its activity so that, on the one hand, it gains political dividends and, on the other, creates a good investment climate for self-development.[64]

The federal centre had realised that one way to combat the region's 'psychological isolation' was to ensure that, through the mass media, the region is kept regularly and 'reliably' informed about developments in 'big Russia'. This could be done very cheaply and effectively – by supplying more centrally produced Russian newspapers and magazines, by ensuring that Russian TV and radio broadcasts are easily received by the *oblast* and that TV weather reports feature Kaliningrad on the map (which had not been the case). Reducing the feeling of remoteness from the mainstream of developments in Russian society will help prevent the growth of political separatism – if Moscow does not care about us, why should we care about Moscow?

There is a hint that Moscow feels that Kaliningrad *oblast* could soon, if it had not already, become the target of an 'information war' between the West and Russia, the West keen to increase dissent in Kaliningrad in an attempt to upset the balance of power between the centre and this important region. There was a whiff of this in January 2001 when *The Times* published an article alleging secret talks between Germany and Russia concerning a debt-for-equity deal involving Kaliningrad *oblast*.[65] The report was heavily condemned both by the German Embassy in Russia and by the Russian Ministry of Foreign Affairs.[66]

These moves may also imply that the region should not become too attracted by NATO/EU expansion in the region, that an ideological war will be waged to try to raise the region's 'resistance' to the dangers, particularly from NATO (hence the phrase 'fully armed'). Remembering I. Ivanov's pointed remark about Kaliningrad not disrupting Russia's power vertical, the centre may be hiding a threat behind its words: Kaliningrad must not cut deals with foreign countries without Moscow's blessing.

Yastrzhembskiy was correct in pointing out that, in overall terms, Kaliningrad's image is far from a positive one. 'Information war' or not, articles written on the region tend to portray it in anything but a positive light, usually focusing on its social problems or general state of neglect (Chris Patten, EU commissioner, publicly called the region a 'hell-hole').[67] This is an important point: the more positive the region's image at home and abroad, the more likely it is to attract foreign investment (in 1999 official statistics show that Kaliningrad Region attracted a mere $65 million in foreign investment).[68]

Following the Security Council session of 26 July 2001, the relationship between the centre and Kaliningrad underwent a fundamental change. The decision to create a deputy plenipotentiary specifically for Kaliningrad, but attached to and appointed by Cherkesov, changes the balance in the triangular relationship, Kaliningrad–St Petersburg–Moscow.[69] Earlier, the press had speculated that the Security Council would do no more than debate Gref's development programme for the region. However, one paper reminded its readership that for the first time in the history of the Security Council the problems of one region were to be examined at the highest level: only one other region had received this accolade before, namely Chechnya. The media speculated that three possible solutions to its problems had been discussed before the session:

> First variant – to introduce direct presidential rule ... second variant, to create the eighth federal district, appoint an extraordinary governor-general in the role of presidential plenipotentiary ... third variant – to strengthen the position of the governor.

According to this source, the last variant was not taken too seriously, as Yegorov was seen in the Kremlin as a 'fairly weak politician and economic manager'.[70] At the session Putin called for a rethinking of the region's possibilities:

> It is time to rethink the concept of the region's development in the light of the new European realities and the new potential of the Russian economy. ... Kaliningrad region may serve as a testing ground for interaction between Russia and Europe.[71]

It would appear that Putin restricted his remarks to the region's economic future rather than its political status. However, appointing a deputy plenipotentiary could undermine the effectiveness of the governor. Yegorov admitted that it was not his idea: 'It was a commonly worked out decision, examined on the eve of the session by the presidential administration ... Viktor Cherkesov, and myself.'[72] However, in an interview immediately after the session he had stated: 'I myself suggested to Vladimir Putin to put into practice the variant of introducing the post of deputy representative to

Cherkesov in Kaliningrad'.[73] In discussing the powers of the new post, Yegorov stated:

> I think that there will be no particular complications in the distribution of functions between the head of the administration and the deputy presidential plenipotentiary representative. Strictly speaking, we had such a situation in the *oblast* earlier, when the representative of the president, Aleksandr Orlov, worked here. The present deputy presidential plenipotentiary representative will have approximately these same powers.[74]

Yet despite his protestations that he still enjoys the centre's trust, the decision to create such a post – the first of its kind in the Federation – must be a clear sign that not only is the centre not satisfied with the governor's performance, but it thinks that it does not have sufficient control over the federal structures in the region. Given the changes over the next few years in this part of the world, the Kremlin is strengthening its hold. The election of another 'man in uniform' was obviously not enough; the lack of rapport between governor and plenipotentiary has also had an impact on the Kremlin's thinking about Kaliningrad. Yegorov may be correct in his argument that this step was more a belated reaction to the activities of the previous governor than any reflection on him or his team, but it does not alter the fact that the centre has now a very strong hold over Kaliningrad's political machine and its regional economy.

The geo-strategic importance of the *oblast*

There are a number of reasons – historical, geographic, economic, military – which explain why the centre is determined to keep a tight hold on the region's affairs. Whilst Moscow has until now not paid enough attention to solving Kaliningrad's problems, it is determined that Russia should maintain its presence in the Baltic. Moscow needs Kaliningrad; without it, Russia's presence would be severely diminished, decreasing Moscow's standing in one of the world's most important trading regions (in 1997 10 per cent of the world's shipping trade passed through its 250 ports).[75] Kaliningrad's share of the traffic has declined in recent years; nevertheless, with proper investment and a more competitive pricing policy, it could have an important role in the further economic revitalisation of Russia, locally and nationally.[76]

Of course, Kaliningrad's economic development can only be assured if the central power has the wherewithal to defend the region; hence the importance attached to the Baltic Fleet. Interviewed when he was still Baltic Fleet commander, Yegorov pointed out its importance in protecting Russia's economic interests:

> Defenceless at sea, according to P. A. Stolypin,[77] is as hazardous as defenceless on land. ... [T]his logic is traditional for all countries which

have access to the sea and boils down to a battle for trade routes and fields of raw materials on the continental shelf. Moreover, a state's ability to use these resources in its own national interests is also traditionally determined by sea power. ... [T]hroughout these three centuries, the Baltic Fleet has been the main factor of stability in the Western maritime direction. Russia's vital interests in the Baltic Sea have currently not diminished, but just the opposite, have expanded.[78]

According to one analyst, the rail network makes Kaliningrad unique in one other vital respect:

The *oblast* has one important economic and strategic advantage, unique in the entire Baltic Maritime Zone: it is the only place where the port's infrastructure meets all the standard European railway gauges. The military-strategic significance of this is much more important than the economic, in as much as it increases the possibilities for Russia to protect the Russian Fleet in the Baltic.[79]

The tie-in between the region's economic and military infrastructure should not be underestimated and is not accidental. However, bordering Lithuania and Poland, with relatively easy access to German and Scandinavian markets, Kaliningrad can use its location to its own advantage, while benefiting the Russian economy. Former foreign minister Kozyrev stated in 1993, in the Council of Baltic Sea States:

There is no need to explain the exceptional significance of Kaliningrad *oblast* in being an important link in Russia's military-strategic and economic interests in the Baltic region. Especially now, when every metre of Baltic shoreline, for us, is literally worth its weight in gold.[80]

The Baltic Fleet, the Russian Navy's oldest, is celebrating its 300th anniversary. As Baltic Fleet commanders point out, Russia/USSR has shed much blood to gain and maintain an ice-free port to join St Petersburg and Kronstadt, where Russia has always had a military presence. The Baltic Fleet is an obvious manifestation of Russia's military power, but one that was not created overnight, or in response to the political upheaval of the early 1990s.

Peter the Great said, 'Without mastery of the Baltic Sea, Russia will not be a great European power'.[81] As Admiral Gromov, then naval commander-in-chief, put it:

[T]he appearance of a regular Russian military fleet was brought about by a historic mission – to gain entry to the community of European nations. Having secured Russia's entry to the Baltic Sea and having created a military fleet, Peter the First made us a great European power.

Since then, Russia has not been a guest in a wider Europe, but an equal partner.[82]

The long history of the Baltic Fleet was outlined in a 1994 article by Yegorov, its then commander:

> The Baltic Fleet is [the navy's] oldest component, tracing its origins to January 29, 1702, when Tsar Peter the First ordered the construction of six 18-cannon vessels on the Syas river. In the Northern War with Sweden, the newly-built fleet scored brilliant victories at the battles of Hanko Head (1714), Esel (1719) and Greengam (1720). … [T]he Russian–Swedish War of 1788–1790 saw the successful rebuff by the Baltic Fleet of attempts to seize Kronstadt and St Petersburg and its triumph in the battle of Gotland, Rokjensalm, Revel, Krasnogorsk and Vyborg. … In World War One, the Baltic Fleet inflicted major losses on the German Fleet, preventing its breakthrough to the Gulfs of Finland and Riga and provided the seaborne defence of the Aland Islands and Petrograd. … [I]n the course of the [Second World] War Baltic seamen participated in two defensive and seven offensive operations, their submarines were active all across the sea basin. Wartime losses amounted to 267 vessels and 1,619 planes but … the fleet preserved its fighting capacity.[83]

In short, Russia has earned its Baltic Sea coastline and the Baltic Fleet guarantees Russia's presence in the region. Admiral Gromov was very explicit on the role of the Fleet:

> It is difficult to overestimate the significance of the Baltic Fleet in the defence of the national interests of Russia in the Baltic Sea – an objective and historically justified necessity, confirmed by almost 300 years of history, one of the indispensable conditions [guaranteeing] the security of the country, its economic development and international authority. The deployment of the Fleet's main forces to Kaliningrad *oblast* ensures Russia's status as a Baltic power and its ability to defend its interests at sea.[84]

This link between Russia's presence and the military power maintaining it is made clear time and time again. Then Security Council secretary, Ivan Rybkin, on a visit to the region in May 1997, noted:

> The Russian military presence in Kaliningrad *oblast* has two aspects: it is important both as a symbol of Russian sovereignty on this territory and as a sign of Russia's firm intention to preserve its position in the Baltic Sea. In light of NATO enlargement, Kaliningrad *oblast* is one of the key elements in ensuring the security of Russia and its ally-state, Belarus.[85]

The then commander of Northwestern Group of Forces, L. S. Mayorov, expanded on the *oblast*'s military importance to the defence of the Federation:

> The role of the region and the military here – and I am not scared by accusations of excessive exaggeration – is very great. Look, if earlier in the direction of Moscow there was the Western Group of Forces, the Northern Group of Forces and the Belarussian Military District, now from Smolensk, the capital is within easy reach. That is why, from a military point of view, the military force here is vital.[86]

As a direct result of the collapse of the USSR and the refound independence of Latvia, Lithuania and Estonia, Kaliningrad's importance increased significantly, not least from the military point of view. But Russia's military force there cannot be interpreted as a response to its physical separation from 'Mother Russia'. Although the size of the force fluctuated wildly throughout the 1990s (as a result of withdrawal from Eastern Europe and Yeltsin's 1997 force reductions), giving the other regional states real cause for concern at times, this was only a temporary phenomenon.

This position is likely to change very soon, as Russia copes with further EU and NATO expansion in the Baltic area. As yet, Russia has little problem with the idea of EU expansion; however, the same cannot be said about NATO, especially in the Baltic. Russia's military presence has been dearly bought (the storming of the city of Königsberg, an operation that lasted only two weeks, cost the lives of 100,000 Soviet soldiers)[87] and many in the West have yet to realise the impact of this on Russian attitudes. As NATO has increased its military presence in the area – for instance, with Poland's accession in April 1999 – Russians are increasingly concerned that NATO's growing influence comes at the expense of Russia's. In one of his last published interviews as Fleet commander, Yegorov discussed the 'strengthening of NATO's position in the strategically important for Russia Baltic Sea coastline and … Kaliningrad *oblast* – Russia's vital bulwark in the western region'.[88]

Navy commander-in-chief Admiral V. Kuroyedov has also expressed his deep misgivings about further NATO expansion:

> Russia must view as *a direct threat to its national security* [any] increase in the military presence of states bordering our territorial waters, even more so *the possible use of territory of former Soviet republics by the armed forces of third countries or military blocs.*[89]

There is no room here for any misunderstanding: if NATO expands to Lithuania, Latvia or Estonia, Russia will take steps to enhance its military presence in the region. Its proposal to cut further the number of military personnel in Kaliningrad – announced in February 2001[90] – will be frozen; it may also improve their equipment. However, it is unlikely that the Russian authorities would re-deploy tactical nuclear weapons to the region, as 'there is nothing to be gained by keeping them at the border'.[91]

Despite the new warmth in the NATO–Russia relationship, Russia has made it clear that her own defence remains a priority, and therefore any enlargement will trigger a review of Russia's defences. That there will be some military reassessment when any former USSR republics join NATO cannot be in doubt. At a Baltic Fleet exercise in July 2001 the chief of the General Staff, General Kvashnin, noted that '[u]nder conditions of NATO expansion in the East, the structure and composition of the [military] grouping in Kaliningrad *oblast* would depend on the position of the NATO countries'.[92] Less than a week later the chairman of the Duma's international affairs committee, D. Rogozin, said at a meeting in Kaliningrad that Russia's military presence in the region may be increased as a result of NATO action in the area.[93] The Baltic Fleet Commander, Vice-Admiral Valuyev, also pointed out the direct connection between NATO membership for the Baltic states and Russia's military presence:

> The naval grouping created in our region in conjunction with neighbouring districts, according to the assessment of specialists from the General Staff is self-sufficient in every respect. In the future, everything will depend on the situation taking shape in the region in connection with the entry of the Baltic countries in NATO. Their [military] potential will be increased – correspondingly, so must ours. These will be natural steps which, under these circumstances, any state would adopt to defend the security of its citizens, rights and freedoms.[94]

That Russia will review its security in the light of further NATO expansion should come as no great surprise. Russia has been a Baltic power for centuries and will not be intimidated out of the region. The circumstances in which it acquired the territory now known as Kaliningrad may not have been ideal, but it is populated overwhelmingly by Russians and is very much seen in Moscow as part of the Federation. The territory may not rate much in terms of economic wealth, but its main asset is its geographical position: investment could develop it into a transport-freight conduit between eastern and western Europe. But even if this does not happen, Kaliningrad is vital to Russia in that it both allows Russia to be a power in a very important part of the world and gives Moscow, literally, some degree of physical protection should the political and military situation deteriorate. Although it may not quite be Russia's unsinkable aircraft carrier, nevertheless it affords Moscow a useful platform to survey and respond to events in the region.

The relationship between Moscow and Kaliningrad has developed along a number of interesting avenues, particularly recently. The nature of the future relationship is not quite clear. Will the *oblast* be used as a model for a new open relationship between the EU and Russia or will NATO's further expansion compel Moscow to turn Kaliningrad back into a fortress? The answer may lie just as much in Brussels as in Moscow or Kaliningrad. The *oblast*'s fate rarely lies in its own hands and, as long as it remains an integral part of the Russian Federation, it is unlikely that this situation will change.

Notes

1 The then governor, L. Gorbenko, declared a 'state of emergency' in the light of the August 1998 rouble crisis. As a 'state of emergency', within the terms of the Constitution, can only be declared by the president of the Russian Federation (at that time Yeltsin), this put Gorbenko on a direct collision course with Yeltsin. The matter was eventually resolved within twenty-four hours, following Gorbenko's admission that he had not declared a 'state of emergency', but simply an 'emergency situation'. For more on this, see *State of Emergency Declared in Kaliningrad Region*, Interfax–BNS, Kaliningrad, 8 September 1998; P. Akopov, 'V Kaliningrade – chrezvychaynaya situatsia', *Nezavisimaya Gazeta*, 9 September 1998; S. Uvarov, 'Kaliningradskaya *Oblast* Zhivet v Rezhime Chrezvychaynoy Situatsii', *Komsomol'skaya Pravda*, 23 September 1998; A. Chesnakov, 'Mify i Pravda o Kaliningradskom Separatizme', *Nezavisimaya Gazeta,* 30 September 1998.
2 For a 'taster' of how complex the history of this area is, consult R. A. Smith 1992.
3 *Kaliningradskaya Pravda*, 22 February 2001.
4 For a detailed and balanced treatment of this whole question, see Sharp 1977–8: 156–62.
5 Grenville 1974: 234.
6 Sharp 1977–8: 162.
7 Gorodilov 1998: 43.
8 *Ibid.*: 46.
9 Gubin and Strokin 1991: 23–5; Fedorov *et al.* 1997: 19–32.
10 See Petersen and Petersen 1993: 59–62.
11 Lubocka-Hoffmann and Szymgin 2000: 103.
12 Official website of the Kaliningrad regional administration, at http://www.gov.kaliningrad.ru/rintro.php3.
13 Goskomstat Rossii 2000c: 599 (*Regiony Rossii*).
14 Gorkin 1998: 225.
15 Goskomstat Rossii 2000c: 599 (*Regiony Rossii*).
16 *Ibid*, 600.
17 Bilchak and Zakharov 1998: 120, 123.
18 *Ibid.*: 116.
19 Alayev *et al.* 2001: 65.
20 *Ibid.*
21 *Ibid.*
22 Foreign Relations Department of the City Hall of Kaliningrad 2000: 21.
23 Anon. 2000: 24.
24 Foreign Relations Department of the City Hall of Kaliningrad 2000: 22.
25 Khlopetskiy 2000: 100.
26 A. Vorontsov, 'Admirala NATO ne Pugaet', *Chas*, no. 45, 22 February 2000.
27 *Ibid.*
28 'Navy Commander Elected Kaliningrad Regional Governor', *BBC Summary of World Broadcasts*, 20 November 2000.
29 Gorbenko's vice-governor, Mikhail Karetniy, has been the object of a number of criminal investigations by the local authorities since 1998. An international arrest

warrant was due to be issued, in connection with allegations of inappropriate use of state property and money laundering, when Karetniy was in charge of the region's Development Fund (V. Zhukov and A. Igorev, 'Kaliningradskiy Chinovnik Otmyl $15 Million', *Kommersant*, 18 January 2001).

30 P. Akopov, 'General'naya Liniya', *Izvestiya*, 8 February 2001.

31 In 2000 the Baltic Fleet was awarded the title of Best Fleet of the Russian Navy, on the basis that it won 7 out of 13 annual prizes for combat readiness (*Baltiyskiy Flot Nazvan Lushchim v VMF Rossii po Itogam Boyevoy Podgotovki*, at http://www.strana.ru/print/974379369.html); apparently, a common remark heard in the navy's officer's club when Yegorov was Fleet commander was: 'I will serve as long as Yegorov commands the Fleet. When he goes, I'll sign out', *Krasnaya Zvezda*, 19 September 2000.

32 V. Zhukov and I. Petrov, 'Zapadnyy Forpost Ukrepyat Admiral-gubernatorom', *Kommersant*, 3 August 2000, which estimates that the 'military' electorate in the region, i.e. not only those serving, working in the naval dockyards and the like, but those with any connection to the armed forces, like the workers in the defence plants and their families, numbers approximately 200,000 men and women.

33 'Stenogramma Vystupleniya Kandidata na Post Gubernatora Kaliningradskoy Oblasti Admirala V Yegorova', *Vybory v Rossii*, 21 September 2000, at http://www.egorov.kaliningrad.ru/press/210900_1.php.3.

34 *Kaliningradskaya Pravda*, 26 October 2000.

35 Abramov 1998: 36.

36 V. Zhukov and I. Petrov, 'Zapadnyy Forpost Ukrepyat Admiral-gubernatorom', *Kommersant,*, 3 August 2000.

37 I. Yegorov, *Gorozhan Razbudilo Solntse i Parad Orkestrov*, at http://www.strana/ru/print/974624726.html.

38 I. Bulavinov, 'Generaly Idut Mirnym Putem', *Kommersant*, 8 August 2000.

39 Interfax/BNS, 31 October 2000.

40 TV interview, RTR, 12 December 2001, cited in the programme 'Podrobnosti'.

41 Yu Golotyuk, 'Baltiyskiy Transit', *Sankt-Peterburgskiye Vedomosti*, 16 February 2001.

42 Interview with the foreign minister I. S. Ivanov, *Kaliningradskaya Pravda*, 7 March 2001.

43 V. Cherkesov, 'Ya Verny Gosudarstvu Gosudarstvennoye', *Rossiyskaya Gazeta*, 23 September 2000.

44 V. Cherkesov, '20,000 Narusheniy', *Izvestiya*, 20 October 2000.

45 B. Pepiya, 'Viktor Cherkesov Reshayet Vsye', *Nezavisimaya Gazeta*, 11 April 2001.

46 'Khronika', at http://gov.kaliningrad.ru/ocronics.php3.

47 'Otvety Gubernatora Kaliningradskoy Oblasti na Voprosy Gazety Dostoinstva', at http://gov.kaliningrad.ru/intervus.php3?uid=3. See also 'Khronika', at http://gov.kaliningrad.ru/ocronics.php3.

48 For a much more comprehensive and detailed analysis of the impact of Kaliningrad on future EU enlargement, see Fairlie and Sergounin 2000.

49 'Otvety Gubernatora Kaliningradskoy Oblasti na Voprosy Gazety Dostoinstva', at http://gov.kaliningrad.ru/intervus.php3?uid=3.

50 V. Yegorov, 'Kaliningrad Nikuda ne Ukhodit', *Rossiyskaya Gazeta*, 22 March 2001.

51 *Soobshcheniye No. 6*, Security Council, 15 February 2001, at http://194.226.83.2/news/2001/02/ps.htm.

52 Kaliningrad, 25 March 2001, *Interfax Severo-Zapad*.

53 I. Ivanov, 'Intervyu Ministra Inostrannykh Del ...', *Diplomaticheskiy Vestnik*, no. 4, 2001: 71–3; here 72.

54 G. Koval'skaya, 'Osobaya Zona. Avangard Vmesto Forposta', *Itogi*, 31 March 2001: 12–18; on 16.
55 'Pyat' Mifov o Yantarnom *Kraye*', *Rossiyskaya Gazeta*, 7 July 2001.
56 K. Ugodnikov, 'Russkiy Peyzazh v Tsentre Yevropy', *Rossiyskaya Gazeta*, 26 July 2001.
57 Press conference of V. Yegorov, at http://gov.kaliningrad.ru.intervws. php3?uid=6.
58 G. Osipov and I. Khrennikov, 'Zona ne Svobodnaya, no Eksportnaya. Mery po Razvitiyu Kaliningradskoy Oblasti Odobreny Pravitelstvom', *Segodnya*, 23 March 2001.
59 *Ibid.*
60 B. Pepiya, 'Viktor Cherkesov Reshayet Vsye', *Nezavisimaya Gazeta*, 11 April 2001.
61 G. Osipov and I. Khrennikov, 'Zona ne Svobodnaya, no Eksportnaya. Mery po Razvitiyu Kaliningradskoy Oblasti Odobreny Pravitelstvom', *Segodnya*, 23 March 2001.
62 V. Yegorov, 'Komu Vygodno v Yantare Delat "Chernye Dyry"?', *Rossiyskaya Gazeta*, 28 July 2001.
63 'Novyy Oblik Rossiyskogo Anklava', *Krasnaya Zvezda*, 19 April 2001.
64 *Ibid.*
65 R. Boyes, 'Germany Goes Back to Roots of Prussia', *The Times*, 23 January 2001.
66 'German Ambassador Denies Negotiations with Putin on Kaliningrad', ITAR–TASS news agency, 23 January 2001; 'Kaliningrad Byl i Ostanetsya Rossiyskim', *Krasnaya Zvezda*, 24 January 2001.
67 C. Patten, 'Russia's Hell-hole Enclave', *Guardian*, 7 April 2001.
68 'Ekonomicheskiy Potentsial Kaliningradskoy Oblasti i Perspektivy Yeye Razvitiya', at http://www.gov.kaliningrad.ru/eintro.php3.
69 V. Zhukov, 'V Kaliningradskoy Oblasti Gryadut Tyazhelyye Vremena', *Kommersant-b*, 31 July 2001.
70 Andrusenko and Solovyev 2001: 1.
71 'Putin Says Exclave Could Become Part of Europe', *Interfax*, 26 July 2001.
72 V. Yegorov, 'Tsentr Mne Doveryayet', *Izvestiya*, 31 July 2001.
73 V. Zhukov, 'V Kaliningradskoy Oblasti Gryadut Tyazhelyye Vremena', *Kommersant-b*, 31 July 2001.
74 V. Yegorov, 'Tsentr Mne Doveryayet', *Izvestiya*, 31 July 2001.
75 Rodionov 1997: 364.
76 For more on this particular topic, see Khlopetskiy 2000: 110–15.
77 Russian prime minister at the turn of the twentieth century, known, amongst other things, for his summary treatment of internal 'terrorists': the hangman's noose eventually became known as 'Stolypin's necktie'.
78 V. G. Yegorov, *'The Baltic Fleet and Russia's Future'*, FBIS–SOV–96–211, 19 October 1996.
79 E. Sorokin, 'Polzuchaya Anneksiya Kaliningradskogo Anklava', *Nezavisimoye Voyennoye Obozreniye*, no. 8, 1–6 March 1997.
80 A. Kozyrev, 'Vystupleniye v Kaliningrade', *Diplomaticheskiy Vestnik*, no. 7–8, April 1993: 32–4; here 32.
81 Quoted in V. G. Yegorov, 'V Usloviyakh Geopoliticheskikh Peremen', *Armeyskiy Sbornik*, no. 7, 1996: 8–11; here 10.
82 Admiral F.N. Gromov, 'Znacheniye Kaliningradskogo Osobovo Rayona dlya Oboronosposobnosti Rossiyskoy Federatsii', *Voyennaya Mysl'*, no. 4, 1995: 11.
83 Admiral V. G. Yegorov, 'Baltic Fleet: From Peter the Great's Decree to Our Days', *Military News Bulletin*, no. 12, December 1994: 11–13; here 11.
84 *Ibid.*

85 V. Gromak, 'Kaliningrad – eto Baltiyskaya Rossiya', *Krasnaya Zvezda*, 10 June 1997.
86 L. S. Mayorov, 'Baltiyskiy Flot ne Budet Byvshim', *Morskoy Sbornik*, no. 1, 1998: 10–11; quote from 10.
87 Daryalov 1995.
88 Admiral V. G. Yegorov, 'Vzaimootnosheniya Baltiyskogo Flota s Gosudarstvami Baltii', *Morskoy Sbornik*, no. 11, 2000: 11–15; quote from 12.
89 Admiral V. Kuroyedov, 'Bezopasnost Baltiki – Realno Dostizhimaya Tsel', *Strazh Baltiki*, 27 December 2000; my emphasis.
90 'Troop Numbers to be Cut in Kaliningrad Region by 2003 – Governor', ITAR–TASS news agency, 14 February 2001.
91 Colonel-General (Retd) E. Maslin, former chief of the 12th Directorate, Russia Federation Ministry of Defence, quoted in V. Litovkin, 'Kaliningradskiy Anklav – Krepost ili Torgovyy Gorod', *Obshchaya Gazeta*, at http://www.grani.ru/enclave/articles/koenigsberg/.
92 'Komandno-shtabnyye Ucheniya Baltiyskogo Flota Zavershatsya v Voskresenye', 7 July 2001, at http://strana.ru/state/2001/07/07/994528916.html.
93 'Russia Military Presence in Kaliningrad May Increase, Depends on NATO – MP', *BNS*, 13 July 2001.
94 Admiral V. Valuyev, 'I Segodnya Baltflot Svoikh Pozitsiy ne Sdayet', *Kaliningradskaya Pravda*, 28 July 2001.

13 Moscow

Centre and periphery

Oleg Alexandrov

Moscow occupies a special place on the political map of the Russian Federation. It is not only the capital and the political centre of the Federation, but also Russia's most developed and prosperous region, with considerable authority delegated to it by the federal centre in exchange for its loyalty to Boris Yeltsin. The dual status of the region was a starting point both for the creation of a city management system independent of the federal centre and for the adoption of such a model for political and economic resource management, which allowed Moscow to maximise its huge investment potential.

The fact that Moscow combines the functions of both an all-Russian political centre and an independent subject of foreign economic and international relations could not but lead to conflicts between the federal centre and the city. Thus, the foreign economic policy of the capital's leadership, interested in establishing economic contacts with foreign countries, regions and international organisations, was for a long time in sharp contrast with the foreign policy of the federal centre, which lacked the economic component.[1]

The second source of conflicts is linked to the economic policy of the Moscow authorities. Having entrusted the steering wheel of Moscow to Mayor Luzhkov's team, the federal centre still kept a jealous eye on its singular model of reforms and financial well-being. For a decade the federal centre lodged claims against the city's regional authorities because of the special privatisation model and Luzhkov's political ambitions, as well as expressing doubts over the division of federal and regional jurisdictions in respect of administrative and territorial units and city property. The conflict between Yuriy Luzhkov and Anatoliy Chubays over the dismissal of the head of the Moscow power supply company Mosenergo, Alexander Remezov, was another confirmation of the fact that the federal centre has never accepted its lack of control over the huge inflow of foreign and domestic investment to Moscow that makes it the principal donor to Russia's budget.[2]

The main reasoning used by Luzhkov's adversaries is that Moscow's economic prosperity is largely based on its using its status as Russia's capital. Indeed, in 1998 Moscow's official ante-crisis budget was $9 billion, or one-third of Russia's budget for 1999. However, according to rating agencies its actual capacity was 30–40 per cent higher. The main source of income for the city budget is tax revenue from the biggest tax-payers in the country – gas and oil companies (LUKoil, Gazprom, etc.) – because their head offices are located in Moscow. In 1997 Gazprom's tax payments alone ($1.2 billion) accounted for 15 per cent of the city's income.[3] On the other hand, it should also be remembered that the Moscow authorities have spent substantial sums on maintaining the part of Moscow's property portfolio which belongs to the federal centre.

During President Yeltsin's rule interaction between federal and Moscow authorities differed slightly from the classical centre–periphery model which could be observed in relationships between the centre and other constituent entities of the Federation. The difference was not only that the Moscow authorities succeeded in creating channels of efficient interaction with representatives of the federal centre, but also that some of its representatives, such as the prime minister, Yevgeniy Primakov, the secretary of the Security Council, Oleg Lobov, the presidential affairs manager, Pavel Borodin, and the director of the Federal Border Service, Andrey Nikolayev, belonged at different times to the Moscow mayor's 'inner circle'.

During the 1998 crisis Luzhkov hoped that Boris Yeltsin would appoint him prime minister, which would have greatly increased his chances at the coming 2000 presidential election. When he failed to secure the appointment, Luzhkov established close contacts both with leaders of anti-Yeltsin opposition in the Kremlin (mainly politicians of centrist and moderately leftist convictions) and leaders of national republics, critically minded as regards the federal centre.

In the opinion of many experts, Luzhkov's main mistake was the premature start to his presidential campaign, based on the expectation of Yeltsin's prompt withdrawal from the political stage. It soon became clear that putting his emphasis on centrist views was misconceived in a context of strongly polarised opinions. As it also turned out, Luzhkov was not able to become leader of the regional opposition to the centre, as he could not create a clear platform acceptable to leaders of republics, to politicians who joined him and to the Moscow bureaucracy. Both the leaders of republics representing centrifugal forces and the Congress of Russian Communities, which left Alexander Lebed to join Yuriy Luzhkov and represented centripetal forces, had tried to join the Fatherland movement headed by Luzhkov.

The federal centre accepted the challenge laid down by the Moscow mayor and organised a powerful propaganda campaign against him, mainly financed by oligarchs close to the Kremlin, who saw a threat to their money in Luzhkov's presidential ambitions. At the December 1999 election for mayor of Moscow Luzhkov had to compete with former prime minister of the Russian Federation Sergey Kiriyenko and presidential affairs manager Pavel Borodin. Although Luzhkov was re-elected without much difficulty, he was left without the strength to run for the highest post.

Tensions between the federal centre and Moscow were further aggravated when Vladimir Putin came to power. This was linked to peculiarities of the 1999–2000 pre-election struggle, when the Moscow mayor was the most dangerous competitor of the president-to-be. The gravity of the discord between President Putin and the capital's mayor is evidenced by the fact that by September 2001 they had still failed to reach a compromise. The Kremlin interpreted its attack against Luzhkov as an attempt to put an end to Moscow 'freemen' and bring the region's legislation in line with federal legisation. In turn, the mayor was trying to save face and disengage from the conflict with minimal damage.

Losses sustained by Luzhkov in his struggle with the Kremlin during 2000–1 substantially altered the power balance between the city and the federal centre, threatening to transform Moscow from a political and financial centre competing with the federal power into a periphery actor.[4] An important factor which could have brought about considerable changes in the power struggle was the re-election of the Moscow City Duma on 16 December 2001, which could have turned this legislative assembly known for its loyalty to Luzhkov into real opposition to him. To prevent this scenario, Moscow city authorities initiated the union of the pro-Luzhkov Fatherland party with the pro-Kremlin Unity movement. Fatherland and Unity agreed to nominate joint candidates to the City Duma and formed a joint General Council. As Fatherland and Unity joined forces Luzhkov lost control over an independent political base on which he could rely in the case of a crisis.

A serious blow to Luzhkov's position was dealt by the verdict of the Russian Federation Supreme Court on 30 March 2001, which declared Moscow's existing power division as contradicting the Constitution of the Russian Federation and ruled that self-government should be introduced at the local level, thus eliminating the authoritarian institution of district *upravas* (councils), which reported to the Moscow city head directly. This would create 125 new municipal constituents in Moscow with their own charters and budgets, and deprive the Moscow mayor of the important administrative resource necessary for his possible re-election for a third term in 2003. The same court decision forced Yuriy Luzhkov, who had held both the post of regional head and that of head of local government for a long time, to choose between these two positions.

Realising these threats, on 13 July 2001 Luzhkov and the Moscow City Duma, under his control, adopted a new Charter of Moscow, which along with establishing a local self-government system included a number of restrictions providing for the gradual introduction of local self-government by 2004; meanwhile, the Moscow government preserves its financial and controlling functions.[5] The chairman of the Moscow City Duma, Vladimir Platonov, and the heads of district *upravas* opposed this plan. Platonov made an attempt to prove the legitimacy of the existing power system in the city, and the mayor's representative in the Moscow City Duma, Anatoliy

Petrov, warned against the resurrection of district separatism as a result of delegating authority to future heads of local self-government.[6]

Another attempt to buy time was the mayor's statement on Moscow's uniqueness and the necessity to pass a law which would take into account the 'federal status' of Moscow and St Petersburg. Good news for Luzhkov was the amendment to the 16 October 1999 law on elections, which legalised the right of governors to be re-elected for a third and fourth term. Under the amendment Yuriy Luzhkov, who was elected for his second term in December 1999, can be elected for a third term only.

The third front of attack on Luzhkov's position concerned limiting his right to discuss the nominee to head the municipal militia, which posed a threat of new disclosures about Moscow government officials, who had already been accused of serious corruption.[7] For a long time Yuriy Luzhkov opposed the dismissal of the loyal head of GUVD (the city department of internal affairs) Nikolay Kulikov and the appointment of Viktor Shvidkin to the post. As a result the city mayor had to reach a compromise with the centre and agree to the appointment of a more or less neutral candidate, Vladimir Pronin. This meant that the powerful regional division of the Ministry of Internal Affairs (MVD), which used to be under Luzhkov's wing, now comes under the direct control of federal structures.

A further threat hanging over the city and Luzhkov is the tax reform initiated by the federal centre, which has already caused the Moscow authorities to lose a large part of their taxation base. Besides, Moscow was stripped of the well-established municipal pension system, there were cuts in district employment centres and municipal authorities had their hands tied on migration issues. The threat of further losses forced the Moscow leadership to mobilise internal resources and repay the capital's external debt, which had accumulated after the August 1998 crash.

The city's information resources were also attacked by the centre. But while the mayor managed to keep the TVC channel reflecting the viewpoint of the city, with the change of the NTV channel ownership he lost an important information resource, which was fundamentally loyal to Luzhkov. Nowadays, the official viewpoint of the Moscow authorities is reflected by the *Tverskaya, 13* newspaper, the TVC channel and partly by the *Moskoviya* channel. The influential *Moskovskiy Komsomolets* and *Vechernaya Moskva* newspapers are on the whole friendly to the mayor.

Finally, the creation of seven federal districts certainly altered the mechanisms of interaction between Moscow and the Kremlin. Luzhkov, who at one point spoke in favour of larger regions, was not too enthusiastic about Putin's initiative. It was not until 2 September 2000, in his Moscow Day speech, that Yuriy Luzhkov declared that Moscow was going to help President Putin to 'strengthen the unity of the country and its solidity, strengthen the vertical line of power'.[8]

A basically neutral relationship with the head of the Central Federal District, Georgiy Poltavchenko, is fraught with possible complications along two lines. The head of the Central Federal District opposes the system of registration for people arriving in Moscow, which is at odds with the Constitution of the Russian Federation, although he understands the problems which led to the preservation of the system. The issue of economic development of the district seems much more important, as Moscow can play the key part in its solution. At present, Moscow invests virtually nothing into other regions of the Central Federal District, while it actively invests in other regions of Russia and its own development. This could lead to a conflict with Poltavchenko, who is interested in levelling economic imbalances in the district.

The above points of conflict between the city and the federal centre characterise the relationship between Moscow the federal centre and Moscow the city as quite tense and tending to become aggravated. However, the Moscow authorities have opportunities to solve the difficulties. In reality, Moscow stands to lose a number of investors in the event of a lengthy conflict over municipal and federal property in Moscow or of increased political instability in the city. Demonstrating his will to make peace with the centre, Yuriy Luzhkov has already compromised, which was impossible for him before, when he agreed to hand over important economic levers to federal districts, including the Central Federal District. Georgiy Boos, a Fatherland MP close to Luzhkov, spoke in favour of strengthening the vertical line of power through a consolidated budget for each district, as well as giving the heads of federal districts the right to control financial transfers to regions. By doing so Luzhkov was supposedly trying to win over Georgiy Poltavchenko and improve his relationship with President Putin.[9]

The reform of federal relationships initiated by Vladimir Putin in the first year of his presidency had a great impact on the capital's authorities. As a result of the reform of the Federation Council the Moscow mayor lost a great part of his influence over the law-making process, which he exerted through this organisation. The creation of the State Council only partly compensated for Luzhkov's losses in the Federation Council reform, because leaders are appointed to the Presidium of the State Council on a rotating basis.

On the whole, after President Putin came to power there was an evident change in the rules of the game between Moscow and the federal authorities. While under President Yeltsin relations between the centre and regional leaders, including Moscow, were based on the formula of loyalty and political support on the part of regions in exchange for legislative concessions on the part of the centre, Putin is enforcing the formula of selective concessions to some regional leaders as part of a general course towards unification of the legislation of constituent entities of the Federation. The cause of the city authorities' dissatisfaction was the realisation that Moscow was no longer a region to which the centre was ready to make any concessions. It is noteworthy that the tension in the relationship between Moscow and the centre was caused more by political than by legal disagreement. Undoubtedly, the current president's administration considers Luzhkov as its main political opponent at the 2004 presidential election.

This means that as a result of continuous pressure from the federal centre Moscow will have to become accustomed to a somewhat lower political status and demonstrate whether the authoritative city model of power can be transformed, and whether Moscow's economy is able to function success-fully without administrative levers consolidating the relationship between power and business. Until recently there was a symbiosis of power and busi-ness in Moscow under the leading role of the mayor, who controlled the activities of the financial and industrial groups in the capital. As a rule, these companies were allowed access to the Moscow market in exchange for participation in some of the Moscow government's investment projects.

At the same time, it is evident that the federal centre's powerful attack against the position of the Moscow authorities has achieved rather modest results, which could be wiped out altogether if the reform of federal institu-tions is too slow, the experiment with federal districts fails, the political situation in the country is destabilised, etc. Under these circumstances external factors can substantially influence the domestic situation in Moscow and Russia.

External factors influencing Moscow's domestic and foreign policies

Although Moscow is basically self-sufficient due to its large population, its privileged position among Russian regions and the existence of a gigantic internal market, it has experienced the impact of two generic processes – globalisation and localisation. In a World Bank report, localisation is defined as a process of increase in the role of cities, provinces and other sub-national entities which concentrate mechanisms of economic and political influence over the state in their hands.[10] The report also pays attention to increased political activity by local communities and autonomous groups in a situation where trade, transport and communications barriers disappear, which prompts them to look for their niche in the changing world. Globalisation, in turn, is often defined as a qualitative jump brought about by achievements in information and computer technologies, which have altered the course of political, social and economic processes and given developed countries an opportunity for sustainable development.

The influence of globalisation on the city's external links and internal development has a dual nature. On the one hand, the advance of the global economy poses a threat of crisis to states, including Russia, and promotes flexible and economically developed regions, which are not so tied down by social liabilities as national states and are able to adapt better and faster to the transnational nature of the modern economy.[11] In this regard Moscow has an exceptionally favourable potential both to develop external ties with foreign counterparts at different levels and to assert itself in the system of international and transregional relationships.

On the other hand, the development and comprehensive use of communication technologies in politics and business require from the ambitious capital authorities, not so much the preservation of social and political stability and reliable management of the metropolis, but operative and transparent decisions, skilful information policy, the setting up of long-term business facilities for growth and the attraction of investment. According to Expert Institute scholars,

> The current relatively favourable situation in Moscow is due to the fact that in the early 1990s it was practically the only convenient economic facility in the country. Its infrastructure allowed business to expand with fewer problems than in other cities, thus attracting money flows from the whole country.[12]

At the same time, the authoritarian and centralised model of governance used in Moscow, insufficient transparency of decision-making, lack of a clear model of interaction between the authorities, the business community and public organisations are obvious obstacles to the maximum utilisation of Moscow's foreign economic and investment potential.

The growing involvement of Moscow in the network of global ties carries certain benefits and risks. The rapid development of Moscow in the past decade, the transition of the major part of its economy into the post-industrial age has led to a noticeable improvement in the living standards of Muscovites, while increasing the gap between that and the living standards and culture of the Russian provinces. The capital is already failing to fulfil the role of locomotive for the country's industrial economy, as it has become the biggest Russian seller and buyer of intellectual products and manager of financial flows. The gap between living standards in Moscow and in the provinces could lead to alienation between the capital and poorer regions; thus Moscow has to take upon itself a certain burden of social obligations in respect of subsidised regions.

While globalisation and localisation can be considered external factors of influence, the process of regionalisation, in which Moscow has taken an active part and accumulated substantial power and authority in domestic and foreign spheres at the expense of the federal centre, is a Russian phenomenon. Unlike foreign countries, where regionalism has become a means of socio-cultural adaptation to the internationalisation of the world economy and a competitive factor in the 'borderless economy', in Russia regionalism developed in the framework of growing national self-realisation and was a reaction to the decentralisation of the country. Nevertheless, in the decade or so since the start of reforms Russian regions have partly adopted the practices of foreign regions and are also maintaining and developing foreign economic links with European and Asian regions and provinces.

Considering the essential features of localisation, globalisation and regionalisation, it is of interest to observe the influence of these processes on the development and transformation of the foreign, trans- and inter-regional ties of the Moscow region. There is no doubt that the opening of outer borders had a positive impact on the development of the city's economic potential, and familiarity with global trends of integration and transborder regional and municipal co-operation pushed the region towards develop-ment of multilevel and multidirectional collaboration with foreign partners. The importance of international co-operation for the Moscow authorities is evidenced by such city- and country-wide projects as the future-oriented construction of the Moscow City complex, designed to project the capital as one of Europe's financial centres, and the construction of Europe Square, to symbolise the growing sympathy between the European Union (EU) and Russia.[13]

In the sphere of external links the Moscow leadership has succeeded in attracting the investment of major foreign and domestic capital. The highest level of foreign investment was reached in 1997, when $7 billion was invested in Moscow's economy. After the 1998 crisis Moscow experienced a decline in investment activity. In 1999 and 2000 up to $3–4 billion was invested in Moscow annually. According to the State Statistics Committee (Goskomstat) of Russia, in the first quarter of 2001 the Central Federal District received $1,212 million in foreign investment, $53,414,000 invested in the Moscow *oblast* and $1,095 million in Moscow city.[14] These figures show that Moscow dominates economically in the Central Federal District.

On the whole Moscow is the most attractive Russian region for foreign investors: in the first quarter of 2001 alone 40.3 per cent of all foreign investments into Russia went to Moscow. Moscow's foreign trade volume in 2000 was $17.3 billion: $8.1 billion export and $9.2 billion import. Moscow also succeeded in improving its credit rating in the foreign market after the threat of default in 1998. The international rating agencies Standard & Poor and Moody's awarded category B to Moscow and St Petersburg, which allows the capital's government to borrow money in the international market.[15]

The intensity of Moscow's external links almost equals that of the federal centre. By virtue of its status, Moscow builds its relationship with foreign partners at three levels: regional, city and as the capital of the Russian Federation. In the last of these competences the city authorities receive high-ranking guests who come to pay official and unofficial visits to the head of state. At a city level, in the first nine months of 2001 alone the city authori-ties held meetings with heads of executive power of Sofia, Brussels, London, Minsk, Beijing, Seoul, Astana, Zagreb, Kharkov, Prague, Tel-Aviv, Dushanbe, Tashkent and Berlin. These meetings are not merely ceremonial. For instance, a memorandum was signed with Berlin officials dealing with restoration of large-block buildings constructed in Moscow in the 1960s as well as waste recycling.[16] During the same period at the regional level

Moscow authorities visited or received delegations from Bavaria, the Dnepropetrovsk and Lugansk Regions of Ukraine, and Moldova.

Moscow maintains successful links with international organisations and non-government foundations. Thus, a meeting with the regional representative of the United Nations High Commissioner for Refugees, John McCullin, was devoted to issues of migrants' legal status.[17] At a meeting with George Soros on 30 May 2001 the mayor spoke of his wish to continue co-operation with the Soros Foundation. The capital's leadership also has links with Metropolis and the International Assembly of Commonwealth of Independent Sates (CIS) capitals and large cities. A popular form of inter-municipal and inter-regional co-operation is the celebration of Moscow Days in different world cities to demonstrate the Russian capital's economic, scientific and cultural achievements. This form of co-operation is actively used by Moscow's foreign partners as well. Thus, Bavaria Days were held in Moscow from 18–29 July 2001; Bavaria is a major supplier of agricultural products to Moscow and the main trade partner of Moscow along with Berlin. Helsinki Days were held from 1–3 September 2001 and Tashkent Days are scheduled for 2002.

While these are quite show-offish events, the second form of co-operation with cities and regions is opening Houses of Moscow in them, i.e. representation offices which provide information on the economy, tourism, goods and services of the Moscow Region. The Moscow mayor's office has signed an agreement in Sofia on property exchange with the Bulgarian capital. The agreement provides for construction and handing over to Moscow of the former Russian embassy building and the embassy school. In response Moscow will give to Sofia the building of the Bulgarian cultural centre on Leningradskiy Prospekt and a building on Bolshaya Dmitrovka, where it is planned to open a store selling Bulgarian goods.[18]

There is an evident growth in information technologies and the number of Internet users in Moscow and Russia as a whole, showing the impact of global processes on the city's internal development.[19] The strategy of advancement towards an information-based society adopted by the Moscow government in August 2001 demonstrates that the city authorities understand global tendencies. In 2002 the Moscow authorities will start to implement the Last Mile project, which will computerise many spheres of life for Muscovites. The aim is to use fibre-optic cables, which can transmit huge volumes of information at a great speed, to create systems 'which would connect information sources with each of three million Moscow apartments'. Such a network can simultaneously provide apartments with telephone communications and deliver radio and TV programmes, as well as affordable Internet and e-mail. The new system will also co-ordinate the work of municipal services and simplify payment for public utilities. The project is to be carried out within five to six years and will cost the city budget $600 million.

This, in short, is how globalisation processes influence the external links and domestic policy of the region. In its turn, the process of localisation in

Russia also increases the influence of the country's major metropolises, Moscow and St Petersburg, on Russia's foreign and domestic policy. While throughout its previous history Moscow had expanded by taking over areas of the Moscow *oblast*, of which it was the capital, since the city separated from the Moscow *oblast* and became a self-dependent constituent entity of the Federation in 1991, it has developed strictly within the city borders. At present Moscow is a metropolis with a very high density of population and investment, and its influence over Russia's foreign and domestic policy is based on use of its financial, informational and cultural potential. The system of population registration and migration deterrence inherited from the Soviet era highlights Moscow as an autonomous community with a singular mentality and lifestyle.

The impact of localisation is also reflected in the fact that the city and its political, financial and industrial elite attempt to increase their zones of political and economic expansion in line with the growth of the capital's economic prosperity. While Moscow's political expansion as expressed in Luzhkov's presidential plans failed, Moscow's economic growth is succeeding and forming centripetal mechanisms of co-operation. Nowadays Moscow is the largest domestic investor in Russia's regions.

The Moscow Banking Union has become an important partner of the Moscow government in restructuring and modernising basic branches of the city's industry. An agreement on co-operation was signed 'designed to declare and establish areas of common strategic interests and common goals'.[20] Areas of common strategic interests are 'the financial market and banking sector of the Moscow region, creation of a favourable investment climate and normal conditions for small and medium-sized businesses in the capital'. Under the agreement the parties intend to promote a more transparent and open financial market, develop the investment market infrastructure, and promote activities of credit organisations and other business structures.

In light of the possible restoration of Moscow's lost position there arise the issues of the future of the Moscow Region, its influence on the transformation of Russia's regional space, the acceptability of the Moscow model for the development of medium-sized and smaller cities and regions of Russia. Moscow's potential to become a powerful integration centre for Russia and the CIS is of special importance, as it could implement a single-centre integration model by creating a reliable and multilevel system of interaction between regions and concentrating financial flows on itself, thus hindering the development of other types of integration.

Moscow-style integration: threat of opportunity?

The type of territorial integration of Russia's regions is not important only from the point of view of the prospects for regionalism in Russia, but even more so as regards the regions' integration into the world economy. Will there be some levelling of the regions' legal space under the dominant role of the federal centre or will the regions split into groups depending on European and Asian centres of gravitation? Will donor regions be able to develop strong integration links with other regions? Is the experience of such large regions as Moscow and St Petersburg useful to them in principle? In the 1990s attempts made by regions to form effective inter-regional associations based on geographic proximity failed. The institution of federal districts, formed on a similar territorial principle, is showing contradictory results. Considering that Moscow has accumulated considerable expertise by strengthening links between regions, it is of interest to assess the pros and cons of this integration model based on horizontal links with Moscow as the lead region.

Perhaps one of the most important changes in the regions since Putin came to power is the centre's decision to terminate power-sharing agreements between the federal centre and forty-six regions that had signed them, including Moscow city, which signed the same agreement with the federal centre on 16 June 1998. Elimination of the agreement system somewhat improved the equality of regions in respect to the law and the Russian Constitution. In the preceding few years Moscow had established economic, social and cultural ties with practically all regions of the Russian Federation, and had signed agreements on socio-economic and cultural co-operation with many of them. Considering that the provinces have always perceived Moscow as the political, economic, scientific, industrial and spiritual centre of the state, it is time to ask whether Moscow can offer the regions its own concept of an integration model with a new centre, whether the regions will benefit from it and whether this course of development corresponds to the interests of power and business in Moscow.

There are many examples of how, by implementing a large number of investment projects in the regions, Moscow ties together and mends the disintegrated chains of inter-regional and international co-operation, not always oriented at Moscow as the end-user. It is sufficient to mention the support given by Moscow authorities to the construction of a railway in Karelia, the placing of industrial orders with the backward Kurgan *oblast* and Kabardino-Balkar Republic, investments in the development of the Crimean infrastructure and renovation of the Dushanbe communications network. City authorities are always finding new targets for investment of Moscow capital, which in itself goes beyond supplying Moscow with the goods and services necessary for its functioning. However, it seems that the far-reaching economic projects of Moscow city in many cases reflect the political ambitions of the Moscow mayor rather than the integration drive of the Moscow city authorities.

Currently, approximately one-third of projects implemented with Moscow's investment support are all-Russian or international. Much coverage was given to the construction project for the Kerch Bridge, which is to link the Crimea (Ukraine) with Krasnodar *kray* (Russia). The project has already gained the support of the Ukrainian president, Leonid Kuchma, and President Putin.[21] Also noteworthy is the construction of houses, hospitals and schools for servicemen of Russia's Black Sea Fleet and their families financed by Moscow, as well as major Moscow investments in developing a resort area in Kuban.

On the other hand, the capital makes active use of its potential as the country's largest economic centre to develop its own market. Trading houses and shops of Mordovia, Vologda, Altay, Nizhniy Novgorod and Yaroslavl are thriving in Moscow. Moscow is building commercial property to open trading houses of Tatarstan, Saratov, Udmurtia, Sverdlovsk and Irkutsk Regions, and it has held the first inter-regional exhibition, 'Export Potential of Central Russia'.

At the request of the Moscow government its construction complex is developing mutually beneficial contract-based relationships with the regions of Russia and CIS countries. For example, joint ventures for the extraction of natural stone blocks and their delivery to OAO Moscow stone-processing combined works were organised in the Republic of Karelia and Krasnodar *kray* within the framework of inter-regional co-operation. The capital's enterprises and organisations receive metal-rolling products and other goods from Tula, Yekaterinburg and Vologda Regions, non-metal materials from Voronezh and Smolensk Regions, cement from Bryansk, Ryazan and Lipetsk Regions and the Republic of Mordovia, and glass from Nizhniy Novgorod Region. The principal aim of contract-based relationships with the regions is to create a regime of mutual preference in economic development, above all in the real sector of the economy.

Moscow *oblast* plays a pivotal role in the city's integration potential, as road, air and railway routes passing through the territory of the *oblast* connect the city with other regions and the outside world. The city authorities are on friendly terms with the governor of the Moscow *oblast*, Boris Gromov. At the gubernatorial elections in January 2000 the Kremlin and Moscow City Hall supported different candidates. While the Kremlin actively backed the State Duma speaker, Gennadiy Seleznev, the Moscow authorities gave support to Gromov, who then became a member of the political department of the Fatherland movement. It is interesting that not only the centrist Luzhkov but also the democratically minded Yavlinskiy and Kiriyenko supported General Boris Gromov.

Despite the fact that Moscow city has for a decade been an independent region and a constituent entity of the Federation, the leadership of the *oblast* continues to regard Moscow as the administrative centre of the Moscow *oblast*. Meanwhile, a number of problems complicate their relationship. Thus, Moscow *oblast* authorities call into question the city's property rights in the airports Sheremetevo II (with an annual turnover of $2.6 billion) and Vnukovo. The fact that almost 300 small, medium-sized and large enterprises working in the *oblast* pay their taxes in the city but look for social support for their workers and their families in the Moscow *oblast* irritates the *oblast* leadership. Ecological issues in the relationship of the city and the *oblast* are also acute, since Moscow continues to pollute the territory of the *oblast* with the city's garbage.

An obvious difficulty for the regions' integration under the auspices of Moscow is the difference in the level of development between the capital and Russian regions. While Moscow companies are investing in the development of Russian computer and information technologies, as well as modern agricultural complexes, the majority of regions depend on sales of raw materials to a greater or lesser extent. At present, realistically, integration between Moscow and the regions can be based either on using the capital's great industrial potential to create new technological chains, or on the capital's investments in the most efficient branches of regional science and industry. In view of the above, it may be supposed that the strong tendency towards integration of Russian political and economic space in the efforts of the Moscow Region carries both a number of opportunities and a number of threats to the position of regional leaders.

Threats of integration under the auspices of Moscow concern fear of the expansion of Moscow capital and the rise of Moscow, a fear of becoming dependent on the Moscow ruling elite. Undoubtedly, the respect enjoyed by the Moscow authorities poses a threat to the political ambitions of regional leaders. From the opposite point of view, Moscow is a gigantic unexploited sales market for regional products, which account for up to 34.9 per cent of Russian import annually, a stable source of investment into regional economies; and it is also the best place to promote regional products to international markets.

Another obvious obstacle to deeper integration under the leadership of Moscow is the policy of federal districts; it is linked to a struggle for redistribution of regional budget revenues between the federal centre, federal districts and local self-government bodies. These difficulties, taking account of the problems in the relationship between the city and the federal centre, substantially diminish the chance of Moscow being a long-term leader in any integration projects, without excluding it altogether.

A situation whereby Moscow would agree to become the integration centre of the Central Federal District without leaving its boundaries, though good for the head of the district as well as its constituent regions, seems unrealistic. The map of Moscow's economic interests covers the area from Murmansk *oblast* and the Republic of Karelia in the north to Krasnodar *kray* in the south, and from Belarus in the west to Novosibirsk *oblast* and Altay *kray* in the east, while many regions in this area, e.g. the Republic of Kalmykia, are overseen by Moscow authorities.

Meanwhile, an important test of Moscow's unifying potential was the December 1999 election to the State Duma. The 1999 parliamentary election showed, above all, the lack of unity in the ranks of regional leaders, which prevented them from using their resource advantage to fill the majority of seats in the lower house of the Parliament. The election also dispelled the myth that regions would support Luzhkov as a single candidate of the regional governors.

Still, Moscow is likely to keep its leading status among Russia's regions. The only potential rival to the Moscow Region is the Russian Northwest, headed by St Petersburg, which has improved its geo-economic situation; but the poor condition of transport routes, underdeveloped transport and municipal infrastructure, as well as insufficient capacity in the regional market due to the small population, will not allow it to become a real competitor to the Russian capital for a long time to come. The situation might be somewhat improved by the St Petersburg team which entered the corridors of state power with President Putin, but its influence is limited by the small amount of foreign investment into St Petersburg's economy, inter-state tension between Russia and the Baltic states, and the system of interaction between the city and national business, which is underdeveloped in comparison to Moscow. Besides, the Kremlin team is not well disposed to the St Petersburg governor, Vladimir Yakovlev, who is often accused of criminalizing the northern capital and of collusion between law-enforcement units and criminal groups.

As a result, in spite of some difficulties in its relationship with the federal centre Moscow has extensive potential to shape Russia's political space and create regional integration unions. It is quite possible that the views of the capital's elite on important issues of Russian and international politics will continue to be respected. The proof that Moscow will not give up this role is the resounding statement made by the mayor on behalf of Russian busi-nessmen that the country's economy was not ready to join the World Trade Organisation (WTO): 'No one is against Russia's joining the WTO, but at the moment the country is not ready to make this step'. According to Luzhkov, who spoke at the Third All-Russia Congress of Manufacturers, the entry of Russia into the WTO, then scheduled for 2002, could have dangerous consequences for the country's economy, and would have an extremely negative impact on domestic market development.[22]

Moscow as the mirror of all-Russian social and demographic shifts

Moscow is not only generally held to be the leader of Russian regions, but also exhibits many negative tendencies and problems characteristic of Russian society as a whole, such as the authoritarian system of power, the worsening demographic situation, growing income-based differentiation of social groups, inter-ethnic conflicts, etc. For instance, despite its experience in international contacts, and the participation of democracy-minded parties and public organisations in the city's political life, as well as considerable weight and influence of mass media, Moscow remains a city with an authori-tarian management system, a high level of corruption among officials and practically every sphere of economic activity penetrated by criminals.[23]

It may be surprising, but the authoritarian system of power in Moscow is more beneficial than harmful to the dialogue with heads of executive bodies of other Russian regions, since it more or less corresponds to similar power systems in most Russian regions. Moreover, compared with unstable democratic establishments at the federal level, regional authoritarianism is often more reliable in the view of foreign investors, as it creates a stable and predictable environment.

The complex demographic situation remains a most acute current problem for Moscow and Russia. Like Russia, Moscow has faced increased migration, with peaks in the early 1990s (the so-called 'brain drain', when a great many qualified specialists and active population left for prosperous Western countries) and the second half of the 1990s (an inflow of immigrants from poorer Russian regions, the CIS and other countries). Both in the country and the capital there is a decline in the population due to natural causes, brought about by the low number of births and the high mortality rate, including infant mortality. In the period from January to May 2001 30,626 people were born in Moscow and 55,898 people died, a decline due to natural causes of 25,272. Taking account of the positive balance of migration at this time, which amounted to 17,428 people, the number of permanent residents in Moscow declined by 7,800, and in 2001 was 8,538,000.[24] In the previous ten years the number of permanent residents has diminished by more than 430,000. Since 1989 there has been a negative natural increase, and the mortality rate is twice as high as the birth rate.[25] These depressing statistics plead for the necessity of inward migration.

As in Russia as a whole, there is an increase in the number of disabled people in Moscow, but the main evidence of unfavourable demographic tendencies is lower life expectancy. Having reached 71.4 years by the mid-1980s, it started to fall and in 1995 was 64.9 years; for men it fell from 66.6 to 58.2 years, and for women from 75.4 to 72 years.

Moscow is rapidly getting older. According to demographers, by 2010 the number of elderly people will reach one-third of the total Moscow population, and by 2050 the older generation of Muscovites will consist of twice as many people as the younger generation.[26] Meanwhile, judging by the employment structure and by leisure facilities, which are aimed exclusively at young people, Moscow is not reacting in any way to this unfolding process.

An important social indicator is the living standard of Muscovites. Moscow is a city of contrasts as regards income differentiation between the wealthy and the poor parts of the population. So 20 per cent of the poorest people in Moscow account for only 3.2 per cent of individual income (Russian average: 5.3 per cent), and 20 per cent of the wealthiest people account for 62 per cent of income (Russian average: 46 per cent). In other words, the poor in Moscow are comparatively poorer and the wealthy are comparatively wealthier.[27] For several years Moscow has managed to keep unemployment at the level of 0.68 per cent of the economically active population. This is largely a result of the development of small and medium-sized businesses, which employ about 2 million people. Including families, about two-thirds of Muscovites depend on small enterprises. This figure gives Moscow an advantage compared to other Russian cities, where the percentage of people employed by small businesses is extremely low.

Meanwhile, the multi-ethnic composition of the population, which took shape throughout years of migration and demographic revolutions, is a unique factor and also a source of conflict. With about 140 ethnic groups, Moscow is one of the most multi-ethnic metropolises of the world. The political and economic shocks of the last decade have distinctly changed the look of the capital and led to an uncontrolled inflow of population. According to various sources, in the last decade Moscow received approximately 1.5 million legal and illegal immigrants, mostly from the CIS, countries of the Far East and Southeast Asia. A massive inflow of migrants has led to serious complications in the economic sphere, as different branches of the city's economy fell under the control of criminal groups formed on ethnic lines.

The events of recent years have tended to aggravate inter-ethnic relations in Moscow. Muscovites feel wary of migrants from the south who have arrived in Moscow since the mid-1990s. While appreciating the positive role of migrants from the south in trade and the economy, Muscovites emphasise their negative role in the maintenance of law and order (1996 – 74.8 per cent of criminals convicted; 1998 – 77.9 per cent). Sociological data show not only that some Russians feel antipathy towards migrants, but also that representatives of other ethnic groups are sceptical about migration from Russian republics and CIS countries to Moscow. Thus, the main result of the last decade is the aggravation of inter-ethnic relations against the background of an increased inflow of population to Moscow.

The multi-ethnic Moscow population is complemented by religious diversity, a unique experiment in the interaction of different cultures, important to the whole of Russia. The capital is home to representatives of all major world religions and denominations: the Russian Orthodox Church, Islam, Catholicism, Protestantism, Judaism, Buddhism. There are over a hundred different ethnic organisations in the capital (cultural, public and religious community-based centres), with the Jewish, Azerbaijani and Tatar communities considered the most active. Educational establishments with an ethno-cultural component are being reopened in Moscow, including schools with a Russian national component, 'where children study the language, history, literature, traditions of the Russian Orthodox culture in depth'.[28] The Moscow authorities demonstrate a rather liberal approach towards these existing confessions.

On the whole, persistent negative trends in the development of Moscow and the regions are indicative of a common disease of Russian regionalism, which is more preoccupied with issues of stability and preservation of power than development. At the same time, regions, including Moscow, are increasingly feeling the influence of large capital flows to regions with a favourable investment climate and little social cost (or even leaving the country), which makes it more difficult to correct social distortions. The demographic situation in the city is much more favourable than in other Russian regions, but it is tending to deteriorate for lack of a municipal policy aimed at its improvement. The Moscow economy is still criminalised to a great extent and corruption flourishes among metropolitan officials, which testifies to a substantial distortion in the city's internal policy and the greater influence of large capital of obscure origin over the city authorities, who are thus losing their independence.

Conclusion

The decade after the disintegration of the Soviet Union were years when Moscow established itself in the dual role of national capital and major autonomous regional centre of Russia, as well as years when the city tried to find its place in global and regional processes. Having chosen an independent model of development, Moscow managed to build its own system of interaction of power, business and society, resting on an authoritarian government style within the boundaries of formally active democratic establishments, and on the large-scale introduction of market mechanisms, which allowed the city to become the country's leading economic and financial centre, as well as to use the capital's enormous intellectual, scientific and technical potential.

The experience of Moscow as Russia's political and economic centre and as part of the periphery in respect of federal power establishments located in Moscow is of great interest. On the one hand, its status as capital facilitated the development of links with other Russian regions and the region's integration into the world economy. Moscow authorities made extensive use of proximity to the federal centre to increase the region's powers in foreign and domestic policy. On the other hand, the centre was always jealous of Moscow's economic success and tried to make the city authorities completely loyal to the president. The cost of the political and economic rise of Moscow was the attempts made by the federal centre to limit the city's influence over the development of regionalism, and to control financial and investment flows channelled to leading branches of the city's economy.

When Vladimir Putin came to power the pressure on the region increased noticeably. The official reasoning was that it was necessary to bring Moscow legislation in line with federal legislation, but few doubted that in truth this had to do with power politics, which explained the desire of the president's entourage to smother the centre of regional resistance to the federal authorities' policies and gain control over a portion of the financial flows passing through the region.

Diversification of Moscow's external links, elaboration of its own domestic and foreign policy, and the increased authority of Moscow among Russian regions took place under the influence of globalisation, localisation and regionalisation processes. Following the logic of *globalisation*, the city discovered great opportunities for international, inter-regional and inter-municipal co-operation. Active development of information technologies by city authorities can also be attributed to the impact of the globalisation process. Among Russian regions Moscow showed the highest degree of awareness of the globalisation process unfolding in the world; many representatives of the ruling elite, political and public organisations are champions of globalisation ideas. The role of *localisation* is seen in the increased role of the city, its administrative and financial elite in addressing issues of national importance. Election technologies created and tested in Moscow have spread throughout the Russian provinces. Under *regionalisation*, the region assimilated new managerial functions delegated to it by the federal centre.

Moscow has made successful use of its economic potential to develop integration processes in Russian and post-Soviet space, but has encountered the suspicion of the federal centre, which had never been comfortable with strengthening the Moscow Region for political reasons, and the unpreparedness of some regions to upgrade their agricultural and industrial economies. Nevertheless, the city and its business elite have succeeded in creating a number of technological chains through bilateral and multilateral agreements, thus integrating a substantial proportion of economically active regions and cities. The obvious complexity and, at the same time, the advantage of Moscow integration projects lies in the fact that they go beyond the existing and newly formed administrative boundaries, in the form of inter-regional associations and federal districts.

In spite of its uniqueness, in many ways Moscow is the mirror of all-Russian social and demographic tendencies. Problems of inter-ethnic relations, the negative social and demographic situation reflected in growing income differentiation, declining life expectancy and living standards, the prevalence of mortality over the birth rate, including high infant mortality, are still of great urgency both to Russia and Moscow. The penetration of criminals into all spheres of economic activity and the high level of corruption among federal and city officials are characteristic of both Moscow and Russia as a whole.

To summarise these factors, Moscow not only stimulates regional and integration processes, but is largely influenced by indigenous features of Russian regionalism. Nevertheless, the progress achieved in multilevel integration of the city makes it possible to say that Moscow has largely succeeded in overcoming the centre–periphery dilemma and creating a vertical and horizontal system of links with regions and institutions of the federal centre.

Notes

1 See, for example, the table portraying the interplay between the geopolitics of the federal centre and geo-economics of regions in Makarychev 2000b: 29.

2 'Mayor Vows To Fight for Remezov', *Moscow Times*, 13 September 2001.
3 Jensen 1999.
4 'Luzhkov in Putin's Russia: Cutting the Mayor Down to Size', *EWI Russian Regional Report*, no. 19, 2001.
5 *Novyy Ustav Moskvy Vstupil v Silu*, Strana.ru website, at http://strana.ru/state/2001/08/09/997346283.html.
6 Anatoliy Petrov, 'Samostoyatelnost – Znachit Otvetstvennost', *Pokrovka*, no. 12, 2001.
7 Sergey Topol, 'Tayny Moskovskogo Dvora', *Kommersant-Dengi*, no. 51, 2000.
8 *Luzhkov Poobeshchal Vsyacheski Pomogat Putinu Ukreplyat Vertikal Vlasti*, Polit.ru website, at http://www.polit.ru/documents/307397.html.
9 'Poltavchenko Aligns with Duma Deputies against Governors', *EWI Russian Regional Report*, no. 10, 2001.
10 *World Bank Sees 'Localization' As Major New Trend In Twenty First Century*, at http://www.worldbank.org/html/extdr/extme/032.htm.
11 Ohmae 1995.
12 *Rossiya, Kotoruyu Pora Uvidet*, at http://www.exin.ru/test/doc7.html.
13 'Glava Pravitelstva Moskvy "Navodit Mosty" s Bryusselem', *Moskva: mer i biznes*, no. 7, 2001.
14 *Delovaya Moskva Segodnya*, no. 21, 2001.
15 'Moscow Looks to Borrow Millions', *Moscow Times*, 14 September 2001.
16 *Moskva: mer i biznes*, no. 4, 2001.
17 'Mer Vozobnovil Druzhbu s OON', *Rossiyskiye Politicheskiye Portrety*, no. 33, 2001, at http://www.businesspress.ru/newspaper/default.asp?mld=33&numld=1556.
18 'Moskva i Sofiya Namereny Razvivat Delovoye Sotrudnichestvo', *Moskva: mer i biznes*, no. 5, 2001.
19 Russia has recently reached fifteenth place in the number of Internet users. The city alone has the largest Internet community among the Russian regions.
20 'Dogovor o Vzaimodeystvii Podpisali Pravitelstvo Moskvy i Moskovskiy Bankovskiy Soyuz', *Moskva: mer i biznes*, no. 6, 2001.
21 'Most "Ukraina-Rossiya": Idet Razrabotka Proyektnykh Dokumentov', *Moskva: mer i biznes*, no. 6, 2001.
22 *Moskva: mer i biznes*, no. 9–10, 2001.
23 Jensen 1999.
24 *Statisticheskaya Informatsiya*, Mosgorkomstat website, at http://www.mosstat.ru/st_an.htm.
25 *AIF – Moskva*, no. 1, 2001.
26 Yekaterina Bychkova, 'Stolitsa ne Gotova k Bumu Pozhilykh', *AIF–Moskva* website, at http://www.aif.ru/moskva/376/m02_01.php.
27 Nikolay Vladimirov, 'Mify o Bogatoy i Sytoy Moskve', *Nezavisimaya Gazeta* website, at http://ng.ru/politics/1999–12–17/3_moscow.html.
28 Shcherbakova 2000a.

Part IV

Conclusions

14 Russian federal stability and the dynamics of the twenty-first century

Anne Aldis and Professor Graeme P. Herd

The extent and quality of Russian federal stability cannot be captured easily within a single comparative study of centre–periphery relations, Putin's federal policy initiatives or the pressures of external actors and processes. In Russia, it appears that the sum is always more or less than its parts, and therefore analysis can only identify potential frameworks and provide prisms which invariably distort and cloak a more complex reality. Nevertheless, the range of analysis presented in this volume can provide insights into the evolving nature of Russian federal stability.

The theme that links the chapters – strength through weakness – provides a paradoxical leitmotif to capture the nature of Russia. Aristotle defined the essence of Greek tragedy as strength through suffering – a process that affected the audience as well as the characters in the classical tragedy. In a sense there is a similar motif that runs through Russian historical development. Russian leaders – from Ivan the Terrible, Peter the Great, Catherine the Great through to Stalin, Gorbachev and Yeltsin – have been hoist by hubristic failings of personal ambition or paranoia, the relentless and unforgiving demands and opportunities of geography, or more recently by rapid globalisation and mis-modernisation. Russia and its peoples have experienced appalling losses and endured terrible sufferings in a struggle against enormous odds. The outcome of such struggles has always been mixed: some sectoral interests have been strengthened as others are weakened, local success have not translated to the pan-Russian stage, and the idea of 'Great Russia' has proved to be the enemy of Russia itself. One example suffices: Komi Republic, rich in resources but poor in revenues. According to Nikolay Moiseyev, head of the Yabloko regional branch:

> In fact, everything that is of any value is being stolen: oil, timber, coal. Indeed, it is not clear on what terms and at what price. You can wake up in the morning and find out that a titanium deposit is no longer yours but has been handed over to one international company or other; simply handed over without it bringing any revenue to the republic's budget. Everything here was long ago split between visiting tycoons and the local elite.[1]

In short, modernisation within the Russian arena has unfolded as a zero-sum game. The body politic appears to be in constant conflict or metaphorical civil war, and the state exercises power as it were with one hand tied behind its back, hamstrung by self-imposed limitations.

Russia is a state full of paradoxes and a paradoxical state. It has both highly globalised centres, institutions and processes, mostly located within Moscow, and at the same time weak, marginalised – even ghettoised – regions, particularly those in the far north and the Russian Far East. If we turn to the economy, the nature of strength through weakness is at once apparent. As the Russian premier, Kasyanov, noted in an address to the Duma:

> Hothouse conditions – in the form of low charges for energy and transport, low pay rates, high customs barriers, and protectionist measures in state policy – cannot be sustained for ever. And assertions that our industry is uncompetitive in principle do not stand up – the examples of a range of successful enterprises which have renewed their funding and introduced modern management methods convincingly prove the opposite. But if things go on like that – I mean these hothouse conditions, and failure to recognise the need for urgent modernisation – then we may find ourselves falling hopelessly behind even our nearest neighbours.[2]

The Russian economy projects strength through massive and exploitable hydrocarbon reserves, precious metal deposits and a potentially vibrant industrial base, and yet an overdependence on such reserves creates structural weaknesses within the economy as energy prices fluctuate. For example, delivery of budget-funded policy initiatives for 2001/2 was dependent on global oil prices of $18 per barrel, with the distinct possibility that prices could fall below this benchmark by the end of the financial year. The systemic shock of the August 1998 crash led to a financial and banking collapse within the Federation, but at the same time the devaluation strengthened Russian enterprises, allowed for labour productivity gains as production capacity and thus enterprise effectiveness increased, and improved the relative position of trade surplus against capital flight. It helped re-monetarise the Russian economy, diminishing the need for barter transactions, and living standards in 2001 at least were able to return in real terms to the levels last experienced in 1991. The systemic weaknesses evident within the Russian economy in 1998 directly contributed to a swift recovery in 1999, 2000 and 2001.

In terms of foreign policy, Russia is at once weak if compared to the West. Here the impact of the Western modernisation revolution of the 1990s is the key factor, but relative to its near neighbours Russia remains the overriding Eurasian power. The Russian Federation inherited the economic burden of Soviet-era debt (at around US$165 billion), with large-scale repayments (30 per cent of gross domestic product [GDP]) due in 2003, a year in which the associated problems of lower growth and a declining infrastructure combine to produce the '2003 problem'. The acceptance of all of the Soviet-era debt imposed a post-imperial economic burden on Russia, allowing the West a lever of influence over Russia's spending. At the same time, it provided Russia with control over Soviet-era diplomatic infrastructure, military bases and strategic assets. Thus, although Russia was weakened relative to the West, it was greatly strengthened in comparison with the former republics that constituted its neighbours.

In terms of internal security and stability, the dynamic of strength through weakness can also be seen to operate. Within the Federation it is clear that similar paradoxes abound; the exercise of power, the ability to influence, control over structures, the nature of personalities, and the location and policies of regions all constitute both strengths and weaknesses. The centre can be strong relative to the periphery or vice versa; power distribution between centre and regions has yet to be channelled to allow for strong centre, strong regions. Traditionally Russia's power elite has been perceived to gain its strength at the expense of an impoverished, subjugated and weakly integrated society. Russia's bureaucracy and political groups similarly gain their coherence and power to pursue their interests at the expense of a thriving democratic political culture and emergent civil society. As Putin himself has observed:

> In recent times we have finally become convinced that crime retreats only where all bodies of state power function effectively on the basis of the law, where law and order triumph. This is why, in strengthening the law-enforcement departments and their vertical structure in the regions, we are simultaneously improving the judicial system and legislation. It is only in their entirety that all these reforms can yield the necessary result expected by society, and a weakness in any of these links deforms the state and society.[3]

How, then, does Russia resolve this paradox? The paradox of strength through weakness would normally be resolved by the idea of flexibility or elasticity – but while this may be a characteristic of individual Russians, it is not a concept that springs to mind in dealings with Russian officialdom or institutional structures. Yet the capacity of the seemingly inflexible 'system' to accommodate and to adapt to changes in the political climate internally and internationally while retaining its essential characteristics has been amply demonstrated over the last century. The Russian government institutions of 2002 bear a marked resemblance to those of the late nineteenth century.[4] Communist-era bureaucrats and political activists were past masters at the art of reflecting the slogans and projects of their leaders while pursuing their own careers. Thus, while flexibility may not be a feature of the structural diagrams, in practice it does exist within the Russian federal system. Were this not the case, the strains to which the Russian Federation has been exposed recently would have caused it to shatter with the storming of the Duma in October 1993, the First Chechen War in December 1994, or the August 1998 financial meltdown. Flexibility within the system has instead facilitated a soft-landing withdrawal from empire and tentative reintegration into the world economy.

Persistent regional variety

Clearly any evaluation of the policies of the Russian leadership must rest on an appreciation of its goals and an assessment of costs and benefits incurred in achieving those goals, and such an analysis must occur within a realistic comprehension of the constraints, opportunities and alternatives open to that leadership. Martin Nicholson's chapter (Chapter 1) provides the context within which to place an evaluation of Yeltsin's effectiveness. Yeltsin was determined to hold the balance of power both at the centre and between centre and periphery within the framework of a traditional Tsarist and soviet top-down vertical administration. He understood that the suppression of nationalist tendencies generally backfired and added fuel to smouldering resentments, only realising the very threat he sought to diminish. As a consequence the centre was accommodating with all but the most recalcitrant of constituent parts, preferring mutually agreed bilateral ties – turning a blind eye where necessary to promote stability or gain political support – to ambiguities between the Russian Constitution and Federal Treaty. In the late 1990s, given the 'political inflation' within the Federation (indicative of the lack of accountability of the political elite within an unconsolidated system), the ad hoc nature of the power relations between centre and periphery proved a source of federal strength rather than weakness. This led, as Christer Pursiainen notes (Chapter 5), at the extreme edges of such a strategy, to the phenomena of regional foreign policy initiatives and 'regionology' as a new branch of research. At the centre the president assumed the role of arbiter of interests between fractious military-security power ministries, financial-industrial groups and agricultural lobbies. The conflicts and compromises of the Yeltsin era raised key questions about the management of power for his successor.

Would Putin project 'Yeltsinism without Yeltsin'? In other words, would a system led by Putin and dominated by the 'Putinistas' adopt and further develop the weaknesses of the Yeltsin system without the personality strengths (and weaknesses) of the man himself? Would Putin maintain 'equal distance' between interest groups while facilitating further insider privatisation and making more explicit the link between wealth and power within the Federation? Would a Putin presidency continue to exacerbate regional resentments and instability through the gradual regionalisation of federal power by the periphery and sectoral interest groups at the expense of the power, moral legitimacy and legal-constitutional primacy of the centre?

The newly empowered regional governors might, for example, push for greater decentralisation of power (at least to the level of regional governor), while shadowy groups in the security services could attempt to foster a neo-authoritarian presidency on the lines of Pinochet's. Or would Putin be his own man, and mobilise popular support behind a programme of change?

This latter scenario is indeed what has appeared to unfold. Following his inauguration as president on 7 May 2000, Putin began to advance a series of policy initiatives that were to radically transform Yeltsinite conceptions of federal politics. Putin indicated the end, if not the means, which would serve as his policy objectives. Two key tenets were constant in Putin's programme: the centre (or vertical axis) was to be strengthened; and regional powers were to be restricted. As Mark Smith has shown (Chapter 2), Putin has reinforced centripetal tendencies within the Federation. He has created the seven federal districts, removed governors from the Federation Council and reasserted the principle of a single unified legal space in Russia in which local laws and statutes are secondary to the constitution of the state. However, to what extent are the structural changes introduced by Putin concrete and substantive? Are alliances between oligarchs and regional elites undermining the power of federal governors, while the peculation of civil servants and businessmen and the erosion of real civil liberties continue apace? Partial answers to these questions are to be found in our case studies.

Moreover, even if we accept that Putin's reforms are substantive and are having appreciable and practical effect, to what extent do other dynamics impact on centre–periphery relations? The rising importance of transborder security issues is directed not so much by Moscow's ability to formulate and implement centralised policy, but by the new impact of economic interdependence and the relationship with neighbouring foreign states on the territory of the border regions. This in turn has led, as Derek Averre indicates (Chapter 4), not to a unitary centre–periphery policy, or the continuation of the series of bilateral agreements between centre and periphery favoured by Yeltsin, but rather to the elaboration of a series of subregional policies within the Federation. The centre appears to have adopted a range of policy instruments to deal with the different security issues in northwest Russia, on its Slavic borders and in the Far East.

The interplay between domestic and international factors more generally within the Federation has also shaped the centre's ability to articulate meaningful and substantive change. At the local level, however, as the chapter by Alexander Sergounin (Chapter 6) clearly shows, domestic factors have a predominant impact on the majority of regions – the exceptions of Sakhalin and Kaliningrad apart. One example of this phenomenon can be seen in Volgograd Region. Here the influx of refugees from Central Asian areas affected by the situation in Afghanistan has dramatically increased, while the border service appears unprepared to cope with patrolling the all but open 200 kilometre sector of the border with Kazakhstan. As one report noted:

Although federal security agencies are doing everything within their power to keep the border defence system from collapsing, regional officials still are not paying enough attention to this problem. The situation will not change for the better unless federal officials participate in solving the problem of the 'Volgograd breach' on the Russian–Kazakhstan border.[5]

Sakhalin (see Chapter 8), though on the extreme periphery of the Federation, provides a microcosm of the key problems facing the Russian Far East in particular and Russia in general in achieving Putin's declared purpose of real economic growth in a globalised context. Sakhalin exhibits simultaneously both extreme particularism and localist tendencies, and integration with the global economy and global networks. Eleven time zones away to the west, Kaliningrad has the potential, as yet unrealised, to fulfil a similar function – as a 'pilot project' of Russian co-operative capacity with the European Union (EU) and a transport-freight conduit anchoring Russia into the global economy. Here, as Steven Main observes (Chapter 12), geo-economic potential may find itself hamstrung by the strategic-military value placed by the centre on this Russian exclave. Whereas stability in Sakhalin is vulnerable to the withdrawal of state interest and international development of its energy potential, in Kaliningrad stability is largely determined by the centre's ability, or inability, to co-ordinate and implement a consistent policy towards the West.

Primorskiy *kray* (see Chapter 9) also demonstrates the extent to which the power of central policy-making is both limited and vital. It is not so much the ability of Putin's federal architecture to transform relations between centre and periphery, but rather systemic factors within the Federation, the geo-strategic importance of Vladivostok as a border region, and transborder imperatives and dynamics which determine stability in this region. Here, the indicators of systemic degradation – the decline of the military, high levels of internal migration to the European core coupled with a declining population and the rise of socio-economic stresses and cleavages – are most evident. As a result, the key issues that will dominate centre–periphery relations in this region will be functional: economic revitalisation and legal uniformity.

Nizhniy Novgorod Region and the two cities of federal importance, Moscow and St Petersburg (see Chapters 10, 11 and 13), promote a range of perspectives on the key questions which shape our understanding of stability in Putin's Russia. These case studies illustrate how regions – at least those with economic muscle and access to the levers of power at federal and international levels – are integrating into both 'hard hierarchy', patronage-based vertical relations with the centre and networking, 'soft hierarchy', pluralistic, adaptable horizontal types of communication at the transregional and transnational level. The horizontal networking activity fosters the growth of the middle classes, and such bottom-up activity supports the emergence of a civil society within Russia.

Moscow appears as state capital, federal centre and, paradoxically, periphery – marked by the growth of a powerful city management system independent of the federal centre. Oleg Alexandrov (Chapter 13) underlines the influence of systemic factors such as globalisation, localisation and regionalisation processes upon the ability of this magnetic pole to fulfil its multiple and at times schizophrenic functions, while at the same time reflecting and exacerbating internal migration patterns and the drive to depopulate the periphery. St Petersburg, by contrast, as former capital and imperial centre, now suffers from relative decline in national-identity terms, and yet is poised to benefit from any strategic realignment westwards as Russia's 'European capital' with a high international profile. Its access to the policy-making elite in Moscow may well give it an influence on Putin's foreign policy, leading to greater co-operation with the West and further integration with the global economy.

Internal stability and trends for the future

The interplay of internal and external dynamics, systemic factors, state policies and the personalities of the elite all impact on stability in Putin's Russia. The critical determining factor, in the Soviet era and now in the 'post-post-Cold War' era following 11 September 2001 will be Russia's strategic alignment with the West. Such a reorientation may provide a further international impetus and normative framework within which internal reform processes within Russia will be shaped and driven.

Throughout the 1990s most analysts were surprised at the extent to which the Russian Federation was unable – albeit burdened by an unenviable legacy – to move more rapidly towards embracing market democracy based on the rule of law and international norms and standards. The failure of the state to consolidate its democratisation project was perceived to be the central failing of the Yeltsin years. Russia's slow democratic transition challenged the logic of liberal institutionalism, the apparently persuasive rhetoric of 'democratic peace' theory, and not only raised the question of Russia's relationship with the wider world, but itself provided ammunition for alternative global modernity paradigms to be suggested.

Neither Fukuyama's 'end of history' nor Huntington's 'clash of civilisations' paradigm has sufficient explanatory power to account for the full range of dynamics that drive and characterise the international system and Russia's internal development, however. By the mid- to late 1990s globalisation was increasingly promoted as a process that offered to account for integratory pressures and fragmentation processes ('fragmegration') unleashed by ever-closer global interconnectedness. A growing awareness of the role of non-state actors, such as international business and environmental movements, was evident within the Russian centre and in the regions.

Anti-globalist movements appeared in Russia, though not as violent as in the international arena, where they formed the radical edge of a transnational undercurrent of unease at the perceived destructiveness of globalisation.

The events of 11 September 2001 were seized upon as the catalyst for the creation of an international coalition to promote justice and to wage war against the networks, groupings and states that sponsored 'global terror'. In an effort to legitimise this enterprise, political elites in the US and the UK have unwittingly fused the paradigms of Fukuyama and Huntington together within the context of globalisation discourse. President Bush explicitly addressed the issue in terms of mounting a defence of the values of 'freedom-loving peoples' in democratic states. The world was to be divided between 'Civilisation', underpinned by global justice and a new moral order, and its antithesis – violence, terror and 'evil'. Those who were not 'for' Western liberalism, embracing market democracy and the universal benefits for peace and stability it promised, were 'against us'. In Bush's words, there was to be no 'neutral ground' – either states join the coalition of the 'good' market-democratic civilisation or they are, by default or design, 'sleeping with the enemy', part of an 'evil' force that supports global terror. This 'other' must be defeated and consigned to the ubiquitous 'dustbin of history'.[6]

Faced with this choice, Putin did not hesitate; he crossed the symbolic Rubicon and aligned himself with the forces of 'Good Civilisation'. Indeed, he argued that he was there well before them in the struggle with international terrorism.[7] With the crisis of 11 September, several new opportunities for rapprochement were in evidence; intelligence sharing and other forms of collaboration were speedily announced. A new strategic framework appeared to be in the process of construction.

The Politika Foundation president, Vyacheslav Nikonov, observed that Russia was contributing more to the USA's efforts against international terrorism than any of the NATO allies, except the UK, despite the threats this posed to Russian internal security. Indeed, a paradox emerged in that the longer the war on terrorism continued, the more time was available to institutionalise a NATO–Russia relationship based on joint action in collective security-type operations, but the more dependent NATO became on Russian support, and the more US presence in CIS states might antagonise the Russian military-security elite. Indeed, for some within the Russian elite September 11 strengthened rather than weakened the logic of their opposition to NATO enlargement. Aleksey Arbatov, vice-chairman of the Duma Defence and Security Committee, stated in October 2001: 'If NATO expands, despite Russia's objections and without taking into account its interests, this will hamper our interaction in the fight against international terrorism'.[8]

Yet, despite Putin's announced co-operation with the West in the 'war against global terror', many Russian analysts disputed positive assessments of Russia's transformed attitude towards NATO enlargement in particular and the West in general. September 11, in their view, provided a temporary coincidence of interest, but co-operation was in fact limited and the 'watershed' was simply akin to *détente* in the Soviet period, in that it was easily reversible. It provided a justification for the 'anti-terrorist operation' in Chechnya and gained Western support for Russian entry into the World Trade Organisation (WTO). The war in Afghanistan and the war against global terrorism were a fragile basis for building an enduring strategic relationship. There was also the danger of Putin being perceived as a Gorbachev figure; and the Gorbachev syndrome of being feted abroad but hated at home ultimately precipitated the collapse of the Soviet Union.

However, both of these analyses fail to accept the geo-strategic realities and constraints facing Russia. Prior to September 11 Putin had explored the multi-polar alternatives to the domination of the international system by the US. His trips to North Korea, Cuba and China had convinced him that these states did not provide viable models of development or templates of modernisation for the Russian Federation. Russian attempts to use the US plans for National Missile Defence to drive a wedge between European NATO members and the US also proved fruitless.

A traditional Russian geopolitical assessment of Russia's position within the international system would analyse the implications of trends in global systemic factors and state dynamics that impacted on Russia's ability to sustain its power in the twenty-first century. Even as he took up the reins of presidential power, on 30 December 1999 in his statement 'Russia on the edge of the millennium' Putin identified economic weakness as the main problem for Russia, as it inhibited Russia's power to act both domestically and internationally. Putin's stark warnings that Russia was in danger of falling from second-world to developing-state status caught the attention of analysts when placed in a comparative context. Putin argued that by 2015 Russian GDP might equal that of Guandong province in China, allowing economists to note that China's total GDP in 2001 equalled that of Japan, and if current Chinese GDP growth continues (7.4 per cent in 2001) will equal the USA's by 2010. Even with 8 per cent GDP growth year on year for the next fifteen years, Putin noted, Russia would only equal the GDP per capita income of Portugal in the year 2001 ($12,200).[9] These comparisons only served to highlight the extent to which Russia had been marginalised from the global economy in the 1990s and to underscore the fact that Russia no longer had the economic power base to project a Great Power military-security-based foreign policy.

This all suggests that prior to 11 September 2001 Putin had carried out a pragmatic and strategic re-evaluation of Russia's future role within the international system. He realised that only strategic realignment with the West would provide Russia with the stability it needed to develop. As US secretary of state Colin Powell noted at a hearing of the Foreign Relations Committee on 25 October, '[i]t is clear that President Putin understands that Russia's future primarily lies to the West. That's the source of technology, it's the source of capital, it's the source of debt relief, it's the source of security'.[10] Putin now has to carry the rest of the Federation with him.

Thus, though the question of whether there is a fundamental transformation or realignment of the strategic framework of the international state system is hotly contested, this study of centre–periphery relations within the Russian Federation through the 1990s and into the new century provides insights into Russia's potential for strategic reorientation. It has highlighted the fact that Russia is a real federation of diverse regions and interest groups that has to be actively managed, and not a monolith identical in all its manifestations. It also underscores the key role in federal politics played by the president. Putin's ability to persuade or impose policy on regional governors and recalcitrant regions, particularly over regional foreign policy formation, is a vital factor in the perception of Russia as a great power, and hence Russia's ability to remain an important international player. The capacity of the military to maintain its coherence in the face of regionalisation, the rising strategic importance of transborder regions, localised depopulation and the impact of globalisation all play a role in shaping Russia's response to the question of 'strategic realignment' as well as Russia's own future. Understanding the nature of state power in Russia is of critical importance, as that power is what determines Russia's ability to interact in a coherent and consistent manner with other states. Our study has shown how regional policy also impacts on Russian internal stability, particularly the cohesiveness of federal policy-making, and the ability of the centre to implement policy rather than simply proclaim it. Internal stability is essential for developing Russia's relationship with the global international system and hence will play a large part in characterising that system itself.

President Putin has indicated a willingness to institute strategic realignment with the West, and in order to do so he needs solid and coherent internal political support. Moreover, having only been president since 2000, and given the legacy of Yeltsinite decentralisation he inherited, reform of Yeltsin's Russia can only take place once he has secured his supporters to positions of power, consolidated their presence and undermined alternative extra-parliamentary opposition groupings within the power elite. For these reasons a final paradox is likely to emerge. Putin has made it clear that he will adopt a 'liberal' foreign policy that realigns Russia with the West to promote Russia's long-term strategic interests. In order to buttress this transformation in foreign affairs, Putin will continue to promote a more authoritarian domestic policy. However, such a domestic policy will safeguard his support within Russia in the short and medium term only to the extent that he still manages to preserve and protect core Russian state interests abroad. Strategic realignment will be defined and delimited by a clearer understanding of these state interests; Russia under Putin will gain a more coherent identity upon which to generate them.

The analysis offered by this book suggests that this effort, driven by the centre, will be characterised by expanded centralised control, conformity and unanimity. However, from Kaliningrad to Sakhalin, St Petersburg to Nizhniy Novgorod, Putin's Russia will continue to be characterised by divergent agendas, the differential impacts of modernisation and globalisation processes, and the growth of transnational security threats. Putin has changed the superficial aspects of Russian regional architecture, but the blueprint and structural constraints remain fundamentally unaltered. Russia will continue to exhibit strength through weakness and be governed through a series of accommodations, paradoxes and balancing acts. Chief among these will be Putin's ability to reposition Russia between the extremes of Soviet-era unitary state building and the anarchy of decentralisation that characterised the Yeltsin years. The real strength of Putin's Russia, his synthesis of the approaches, political cultures and apparatus of the two preceding political systems, will be in the acknowledgement of Russian weakness: strength through adversity; strength in diversity.

Notes

1 Ren TV, Moscow, 17 November 2001.
2 Russia TV, Moscow, 30 November 2001.
3 Russia TV, Moscow, 10 November 2001.
4 For an entertaining analysis of this, see 'Continuity and Conflict in Russian Government', in Kennaway 2000: 19–45.
5 Andrey Serenko, 'The Volgograd Breach in the Russian Defence', *Nezavisimaya Gazeta*, 10 November 2001: 4.
6 Herd and Weber 2001.
7 See Plater-Zyberk and Aldis 2001 for Russia's reaction and initial policy considerations.
8 *NATO Enlargement Daily Brief*, 5 October 2001.
9 'The World in 2002', *Economist*, 2001: 76, Portugal.
10 *NATO Enlargement Daily Brief*, 25 October 2001.

Appendix
Russia's regional structure[1]

Central Federal District
Capital Moscow
Presidential representative   Georgy Poltavchenko
Belgorod Region, Bryansk Region, Vladimir Region, Voronezh Region, Ivanovo Region, Kaluga Region, Kostroma Region, Kursk Region, Lipetsk Region, Moscow Region, Orel Region, Ryazan Region, Smolensk Region, Tambov Region, Tver Region, Tula Region and Yaroslavl Region

Territory 650,700 sq. km
Population 36.7 million
       78.9 per cent are urban residents
       58.9 per cent are of working age
Employed: 17.4 million
       Industry: 21 per cent
       Agriculture: 11 per cent
       Non-production sphere: 32 per cent

Northwestern Federal District
Capital St Petersburg
Presidential representative   Viktor Cherkesov
Republic of Karelia, Republic of Komi, Archangel Region, Vologda Region, Kaliningrad Region, Leningrad Region, Murmansk Region, Novgorod Region, Pskov Region, St Petersburg and the Nenets Autonomous Area

Territory 1,677,900 sq. km
Population 14.4 million
       81.1 per cent are urban residents
       62 per cent are of working age
Employed: 6.5 million
       Industry: 23 per cent
       Agriculture: 6 per cent
       Non-production sphere: 33 per cent

Southern Federal District (initially the North Caucasus Federal District)
Capital Rostov-on-Don
Presidential representative   Viktor Kazantsev
Republic of Adygeya (Adygeya), Republic of Dagestan, Republic of Ingushetia, Kabarda-Balkar Republic, Republic of Kalmykia, Karachay-Cherkess Republic, Republic of North Osetia-Alania, the Chechen Republic, Krasnodar Territory, Stavropol Territory, Astrakhan Region, Volgograd Region and Rostov Region

Territory 589,200 sq. km
Population 21.5 million
          57.4 per cent are urban residents
          57.8 per cent are of working age
Employed: 8.2 million
          Industry: 18 per cent
          Agriculture: 22 per cent
          Non-production sphere: 30 per cent

Volga Federal District
Capital Nizhniy Novgorod
Presidential representative   Sergey Kiriyenko
Republic of Bashkortostan, Republic of Mari El, Republic of Mordovia, Republic of Tatarstan (Tatarstan), the Udmurt Republic, the Chuvash Republic, Kirov Region, Nizhniy Novgorod Region, Orenburg Region, Penza Region, Perm Region, Samara Region, Saratov Region, Ulyanovsk Region and the Komi-Permyak Autonomous Area (*okrug*)

Territory 1,038,000 sq. km
Population 31.8 million
          70.7 per cent are urban residents
          59.6 per cent are of working age
 Employed: 14.2 million
          Industry: 25 per cent
          Agriculture: 16 per cent
          Non-production sphere: 30 per cent

Urals Federal District
Capital Yekaterinburg
Presidential representative   Petr Latyshev
Kurgan Region, Sverdlovsk Region, Tyumen Region, Chelyabinsk Region, Khanty-Mansi Autonomous Area and the Yamal-Nenets Autonomous Area
Territory 1,788,900 sq. km
Population 12.6 million
          80 per cent are urban residents
          62 per cent are of working age

Employed: 5.8 million
>Industry: 26 per cent
>Agriculture: 9 per cent
>Non-production sphere: 30 per cent

Siberian Federal District
Capital Novosibirsk
Presidential representative   Leonid Drachevskiy
Republic of Altay, Republic of Buryatia, Republic of Tyva, Republic of Khakassia, Altay Territory, Krasnoyarsk Territory, Irkutsk Region, Kemerovo Region, Novosibirsk Region, Omsk Region, Tomsk Region, Chita Region, Aga Buryat Autonomous Area, the Taymyr (Dolgan-Nenets) Autonomous Area, the Ust-Orda Buryat Autonomous Area and the Evenki Autonomous Area

Territory 5,114,800 sq. km
Population 20.7 million
>70.4 per cent are urban residents
>61.5 per cent are of working age
Employed: 8.7 million
>Industry: 22 per cent
>Agriculture: 14 per cent
>Non-production sphere: 32 per cent

Far Eastern Federal District
Capital Khabarovsk
Presidential representative   Konstantin Pulikovskiy
Republic of Sakha (Yakutia), Primorskiy (Maritime) Territory, Khabarovsk Territory, Amur Region, Kamchatka Region, Magadan Region, Sakhalin Region, the Jewish Autonomous Region, the Koryak Autonomous Area and the Chukotka Autonomous Area

Territory 6,215,900 sq. km
Population 7.1 million
>75.9 per cent are urban residents
>64.8 per cent are of working age
Employed: 3.2 million
>Industry: 20 per cent
>Agriculture: 8 per cent
>Non-production sphere: 35 per cent

Note

1 Goskomstat (http://www.gks.ru/eng/bd.asp). Population figures as at end 2000; employment figures as of 1999. For biographical data on the seven presidential representatives see Vadim Pechenev (2001) *Vladimir Putin – Russia's Last Chance?*, Moscow: Infra-M, pp. 110–15.

Bibliography

ABRAMOV, V. N. (1998) *Formirovaniye Partiynoy Sistemy Rossiyskoy Federatsii*, Kaliningrad: Partiyno-politicheskaya Sfera Kaliningradskoy Oblasti.

AFANASYEV, Yuriy (1994) 'Russian Reform Is Dead', *Foreign Affairs*, vol. 73, no. 2, March–April: 21–6.

AKHA, T. and Vassilieva, A. (2001) 'Sakhalin Citizens' Views of Offshore Oil and Gas Development', *ERINA REPORT*, no. 41: 37–43.

ALAYEV, Ye B., Gracheva, T. S. and Kachalova, Ye Sh (2001) *Entsiklopediya SNG Vypusk. Regiony Rossii*, Moscow: Finansy i Strakhovaniye.

ALEXSEEV, Mikhail A. (2001) 'Decentralization Versus State Collapse: Explaining Russia's Endurance', *Journal of Peace Research*, vol. 38, no. 1: 101–6.

ALEXSEEV, Mikhail A. and Vagin, Vladimir (1999) 'Russian Regions in Expanding Europe: The Pskov Connection', *Europe–Asia Studies*, vol. 51, no. 1: 43–64.

ALLISON, Roy and Bluth, Christoph (eds) (1998) *Security Dilemmas in Russia and Eurasia*, London: RIIA.

AMATO, G. and Batt, J. (1999) *The Long-Term Implications of EU Enlargement: The Nature of the New Border* (Final Report of the Reflection Group), Florence: Robert Schuman Centre for Advanced Studies, European University Institute.

ANDEL, Jay and Devos, Richard (1979) 'The Government Versus the Entrepreneur', *Policy Review*, fall.

ANDRUSENKO, L. Solovyev, V. (2001) 'V Kaliningrade budet vvedeno "myagkoye" prezidentskoye upravleniye', *Nezavismaya Gazeta*, 27 July: 1.

ANON. (2000) *Kto yest kto v Kaliningrade*, Kaliningrad: Atlas Press.

ANTONOV, Anatolii (2000) 'It Would Be Not Bad at All to Have Three Wives: Can Legalized Polygamy Prevent a Demographic Catastrophe', *Anthropology & Archaeology of Eurasia*, vol. 38, no. 4, spring: 79–85.

ARBATOV, Alexei (1998) 'Military Reform in Russia', *International Security*, Spring: 83–134.

ARBATOV, Alexei, Chayes, Abraham, Chayes, Antonia Handler and Olson, Lara (eds) (1997) *Managing Conflict in the Former Soviet Union,* Cambridge: MIT Press.

ARON, Leon (2000) *Boris Yeltsin: A Revolutionary Life*, London: HarperCollins.

AVDEEV, A. (2000a) 'International Economic Relations of the Russian Regions', *International Affairs* (Moscow), vol. 46, no. 3: 168.

—— (2000b) 'Mezhdunarodnyye i Vneshne-Ekonomicheskiye Svyazi Rossiyskih Regionov', *Mezhdunarodnaya Zhizn*, no. 4.

—— (2000c) 'Russian-Lithuanian Relations: An Overview', *International Affairs* (Moscow), vol. 46, no. 6: 75–80.

AVERRE, D. L. (2001) *Security Perceptions Among Local Elites and Prospects for Cooperation on Russia's Northwestern Borders*, ETH Zurich Centre for Security Studies and Conflict Research, Regionalisation of Russian Foreign and Security Policy project working paper, June.

AZRAEL, Jeremy and Pain, Emil A. (eds) (1998) *Conflict and Consensus in Ethno-Political and Center–Periphery Relations in Russia*, Conference Proceedings, Santa Monica, CA: RAND Center for Russian and Eurasian Studies.

BAEV, Pavel (1994) 'Russian Military Thinking and the Near Abroad', *Jane's Intelligence Review*, December: 531–3.

—— (1996) *The Russian Army in a Time of Troubles*, London: Sage.

—— (1999/2000) 'Why Are the Russian "Power Structures" Falling Apart so Slowly?', *Perspectives*, vol. 13, special issue, winter: 91–104.

—— (2000) *Will Russia Go for a Military Victory in Chechnya?*, PONARS Memo 107, Harvard University, February.

—— (2001a) 'Russia's Policies in the Southern Caucasus and the Caspian area', *European Security*, vol. 10, no. 2.

—— (2001b) 'The Russian Armed Forces: Failed Reform Attempts and Creeping Regionalization', *The Journal of Communist Studies and Transition Politics*, vol. 17, no. 1, March: 23–42.

—— (2001c) 'The Russian Army and Chechnya: Victory Instead of Reform?', in Stephen J. Cimbala (ed.) (2001) *The Russian Military into the Twenty-First Century*, London: Frank Cass: 75–93.

BAKLANOV, P. Ya (1999) *Geograficheskiye, Sotsial'no-ekonomicheskiye i Geopoliticheskiye Faktory Migratsii Kitayskogo Naseleniya v Rayony Rossiyskogo Dal'nego Vostoka*, paper presented at the Roundtable, 'Prospects for the Far East Region: The Chinese Factor', Institute of History, Archeology, and Ethnography of the Far Eastern Branch, Russian Academy of Sciences, Vladivostok, 28 June.

BAYLIS, John and Smith, Steve (eds) (1997) *The Globalization of World Politics. An Introduction to International Relations*, Oxford: Oxford University Press.

BERENDSEN, V., Forsberg, T., Heikka, H., Jakobson, L., Jänis, I., Lintonen, R., Ojanen, H. and Pursiainen, C. (1999) *'The Third Force' – Yuri Luzhkov and the Fatherland*, Russia Beyond 2000, 3, Helsinki: The Finnish Institute of International Affairs.

BERG, E. (2000) *Writing Post-Soviet Estonia onto the World Map*, COPRI working paper no. 32/2000, Copenhagen: Copenhagen Peace Research Institute.

BILCHAK, V. S. and Zakharov, V. F. (1998) *Regionalnaya ekonomika*, Kaliningrad: Yantarny skaz.

BORT, E. (2000) *Illegal Migration and Cross-Border Crime: Challenges at the Eastern Frontier of the European Union*, EUI Working Paper (RSC no. 2000/9), San Domenico: Robert Schuman Centre for Advanced Studies.

BRADSHAW, M. J. (1997) 'Sakhalin: Right Place at the Right Time', *Russian and Euro-Asian Bulletin*, vol. 6, no. 9: 1–7.

—— (1998) 'Going Global: The Political Economy of Oil and Gas Development Offshore of Sakhalin', *Cambridge Review of International Affairs*, vol. 12, no. 1: 147–76.

—— (ed.) (2001a) *The Russian Far East and Pacific-Asia: Unfulfilled Potential*, Richmond: Curzon Press.

—— (2001b) ' Is Sakhalin Worth the Wait?', *Pacific Oil and Gas Report*, vol. 3, no. 4: 1, 11–12.

BRADSHAW, M. J. and Treyvish, A. (2000) 'Russia's Regions in the Triple Transition', in P. Hanson and M. J. Bradshaw (eds) *Regional Economic Change in Russia*, Cheltenham: Edward Elgar: 17–42.

BRADSHAW, M. J., Kirkow, P. and Chernikov, A. (2000) 'Sakhalin and Irkutsk', in P. Hanson and M. J. Bradshaw (eds) *Regional Economic Change in Russia*, Cheltenham: Edward Elgar: 184–224.

BRECHER, Jeremy, Childs, John Brown and Cutler, Jill (eds) (1993) *Global Visions: Beyond the New World Order*, Montreal: Black Rose Books.

BROWN, Archie (ed.) (2001) *Contemporary Russian Politics: A Reader*, Oxford: Oxford University Press.

BROWN, Archie and Shevtsova, Liliya (eds) (2001) *Gorbachev, Yeltsin and Putin*, Washington, DC: Carnegie Endowment for International Peace.

BROWN, Michael E. (ed.) (1993) *Ethnic Conflict in International Politics*, Princeton: Princeton University Press.

BRZEZINSKI, Zbignew (2000) 'Living with Russia', *The National Interest*, no. 61, fall.

BUSZA, Eva (1999) *Chechnya: The Military's Golden Opportunity to Emerge as an Important Political Player in Russia*, PONARS Memo 98, Harvard University, December.

BUZAN, Barry, Waever, Ole and de Wilde, Jaap (1998) *Security: A New Framework for Analysis*, London: Boulder.

BYLOV, Gleb V. (1998) *The Wealth of Russian Regions*, Discussion C3/1998, Turku School of Economics and Business Administration, Business Research and Development Centre, Institute for East–West Trade.

CENTRE FOR EUROPEAN POLICY STUDIES (2000) *A Stability Pact for the Caucasus*, Working Document No. 145, May.

CERNY, P. (2000) 'The New Security Dilemma: Divisibility, Defection and Disorder in the Global Era', *Review of International Studies*, vol. 26, no. 4.

CIMBALA, Stephen J. (ed.) (2001) *The Russian Military into the Twenty-First Century*, London: Frank Cass.

CITY COUNCIL OF ST PETERSBURG (1998) *The Strategic Plan for St Petersburg*, approved by the General Council, 1 December 1997, St Petersburg.

—— (2001) *The St Petersburg Developers' Handbook*, 1st edition, St Petersburg.

CLEM, Ralph S. and Craumer, Peter (2000) 'Spatial Patterns of Political Choice in the Post-Yeltsin Era: The Geography of Russia's 2000 Presidential Election', *Post-Soviet Geography and Economics*, vol. 41, no. 7: 465–82.

COTTEY, A. (2000) 'Europe's New Subregionalism', *Journal of Strategic Studies*, vol. 23, no. 2.

COTTEY, A. and Averre, D. (eds) (2002) *Securing Europe's East: New Security Challenges in Postcommunist Europe*, Manchester: Manchester University Press.

CROFT, S. and Terriff, T. (eds) (2000) *Critical Reflections on Security and Change*, London: Frank Cass.

CRONBERG, T. (2000) *The Making of Euregions: the Case of Euregio Karelia*, paper for COST A10 workshop 'The Borders of Defence Restructuring', Joensuu, Finland, 14–15, September.

CRUTCHER, Michael (ed.) (2000) *The Russian Armed Forces at the Dawn of the Millennium*, Carlisle Barracks: US Army War College.

DARYALOV, A. (1995) *Kenigsberg: Chetyre Dnya Shturma*, Kaliningrad.

DAVANZO, Julia (ed.) (1996) *Russia's Demographic 'Crisis'*, Santa Monica, CA: RAND, CF–124.

DAVANZO, Julia and Grammich, Clifford (2001) *Dire Demographics: Population Trends in the Russian Federation*, Santa Monica, CA: RAND, MR–1273.

DEBARDELEBEN, Joan (1997) 'The Development of Federalism in Russia', in Peter J. Stavrakis, Joan Debardeleben and Larry Black (eds) *Beyond the Monolith: The Emergence of Regionalism in Post-Soviet Russia*, Washington, DC: Woodrow Wilson Center Press: 35–66.

DERYABIN, Yu S. (2000) *'Severnoye Izmereniye' Politiki Yevropeyskogo Soyuza i Interesy Rossii*, Russian Academy of Sciences Institute of Europe report no. 68, Moscow: Ekslibris-press.

DESCH, Michael C. (1993) 'Why the Soviet Military Supported Gorbachev and Why the Russian Military Might Only Support Yeltsin for a Price', *The Journal of Strategic Studies*, December: 455–89.

EASTWEST INSTITUTE, *Russian Regional Report, passim.*

EVANGELISTA, Matthew (2000) *Russia's Path to a new Regional Policy*, Harvard University PONARS Memo 157, October.

FAIRLIE, Lyndelle (2000) 'Will the EU Use the Northern Dimension to Solve its Kaliningrad Dilemma?', in Tuomas Fosberg (ed.) *Northern Dimensions 2000: The Yearbook of Finnish Foreign Policy*, Helsinki: Finnish Institute of International Affairs: 85–101.

FAIRLIE, Lyndelle and Sergounin, A. (2000) *Are Borders Barriers? EU Enlargement and the Russian Region of Kaliningrad*, Helsinki: Finnish Institute of International Affairs.

FALK, R. (1993) 'The Making of Global Citizenship', in Jeremy Brecher, John Brown Childs and Jill Cutler (eds) *Global Visions: Beyond the New World Order*, Montreal: Black Rose Books: 39–50.

FEDOROV, G. M., Zverev, Yu M., Korneyevets, V. S. (1997) *Rossiyskiy Eksklav na Baltike*, Kaliningrad: Kaliningrad State University.

FIELD, Mark (1995) 'The Health Crisis in the Former Soviet Union: A Report from the "Post-War" Zone', *Social Sciences & Medicine*, vol. 41, no. 11: 1,469–78.

FIELD, Mark and Twigg, Judyth L. (eds) (2000) *Russia's Torn Safety Nets: Health and Social Welfare During the Transition*, New York: St Martin's Press.

FOREIGN RELATIONS DEPARTMENT OF THE CITY HALL OF KALININGRAD (2000) *Kaliningrad dlya Rossiyan i Inostrantsev*, Kaliningrad: Raduga.

FOSBERG, Tuomas (ed.) (2000) *Northern Dimensions 2000: The Yearbook of Finnish Foreign Policy*, Helsinki: Finnish Institute of International Affairs.

FOYE, Stephen (1993) 'Russia's Fragmented Army Drawn into the Political Fray', *RFE/RL Research Report*, 9 April: 1–7.

GADDY, Clifford G. and Ickes, Barry W. (1998) 'Russia's Virtual Economy', *Foreign Affairs*, vol. 77, no. 5, September/October: 53–67.

GALEOTTI, Mark (1998) 'Russia's Nuclear Attack on Its Conventional Forces', *Jane's Intelligence Review*, December: 3–4.

—— (1999) 'Kalashnikov Confederalism', *Jane's Intelligence Review*, September: 8–9.

GARNETT, Sherman W. (ed.) (2000) *Rapprochement or Rivalry? Russia–China Relations in a Changing Asia*, Washington, DC: Carnegie Endowment for International Peace.

GEIR, Flikke (ed.) (1998) *The Barents Region Revisited*, Oslo: NUPI.

GELMAN, Vladimir (1999) 'Regime Transition, Uncertainty and Prospects for Democratisation: The Politics of Russia's Regions in a Comparative Perspective', *Europe–Asia Studies*, vol. 51, no. 6: 939–56.

—— (2000a) *Dictatorship of Law: Neither Dictatorship, nor Rule of Law?*, Harvard University PONARS Memo 146, October.

—— (2000b) 'Transformatsiya i Rezhimy. Neopredelennost i yego Posledstviya', *Rossiya Regionov: Transformatsiya Politicheskikh Rezhimov*, Moscow: Ves Mir.

GENTLEMAN, Amelia (2000) 'Wanted: More Russian Babies to Rescue a Fast Dying Nation', *Observer*, 31 December: 19.

GERMAN, Tracey (ed.) (1999) *Moscow, the Regions and Russia's Foreign Policy*, Conflict Studies Research Centre, Camberley, UK, June, paper E103.

GLINSKI-VASSILIEV, Dmitri (2001) *Islam in Russian Society and Politics: Survival and Expansion*, Programme on New Approaches to Russian Security, Policy Memo Series, Davis Centre, University of Harvard.

GOBLE, Paul (2001a) 'A Demographic Threat to Russian Security', *RFE/RL NEWSLINE*, vol. 5, no. 33, Part 1, 16 February.

—— (2001b) 'An End to Russia's Ethnic Federalism?', *RFE/RL NEWSLINE*, vol. 5, no. 165, Part 1, 30 August.

GODZIMIRSKI, Jakub M. (ed.) (2000) *New and Old Actors in Russian Foreign Policy, Conference Proceedings*, Oslo: Norwegian Institute of International Affairs.

GOERTER-GROENVIK, W. T. (1998) 'History, Identity and the Barents Euro-Arctic Region: The Case of Arkhangelsk', in Flikke Geir (ed.) *The Barents Region Revisited*, Oslo: NUPI: 95–109.

GOLDMANN, Kjell (1989) 'The Line in Water: International and Domestic Politics', *Cooperation and Conflict*, vol. 24, no. 3/4: 103–16.

GORKIN, A.P. (ed.) (1998) *Geografiya Rossii. Entsiklopedicheskiy Slovar*, Moscow: Nauchnoye Izdatelstvo.

GORODILOV, A. A. (1998) *Rossiya v Tsentre Yevropy*, Kaliningrad: Zapad Rossii.

GOSKOMSTAT ROSSII (2000a) *O Demograficheskikh Izmeneniyakh v Primorskom Kraye v 2000 Godu*, Document No. 10–26/103, Vladivostok.

—— (2000b) *Primorskiy Kray v 1999 Godu (Statisticheskiy Yezhegodnik)*, Vladivostok.

—— (2000c) *Regiony Rossii*, Moscow; other issues of this annual publication may also be of interest.

GRABBE, H. (2000) *The Sharp Edges of Europe: Security Implications of Extending EU Border Policies Eastwards*, Western European Union Institute for Security Studies, occasional paper no. 13, March, Paris.

GRANBERG, Alexandr (2000a) 'Frontier Regions in the National Strategy for Development: Russian View', unpublished manuscript.

—— (ed.) (2000b) *Regional'noye Razvitiye: Opyt Rossii i Evropeyskogo Soyuza*, Moscow: Ekonomika.

GRENVILLE, J. A. S. (1974) *The Major International Treaties, 1914–1973. A History and Guide With Texts*, London: Methuen.

GREZHEYSHCHAK, S. E. (2000) 'Regional'noye Liderstvo v Sovremennom Politicheskom Protsesse Rossii', *Vestnik Moskovskogo Universiteta*, series 12, Politicheskiye nauki, no. 1/2000: 21–35.

GUBIN, A. B. and Strokin, V. N. (1991) *Ocherki Istorii Koenigsberga*, Kaliningrad: Kaliningradskoye knizhnoye izdatelstvo.

HAHN, Jeffrey W. (1997) 'Regional Elections and Political Stability in Russia', *Post-Soviet Geography and Economics*, vol. 38, no. 5: 252–3.

HANSON, P. and Bradshaw, M. J. (eds) (2000) *Regional Economic Change in Russia*, Cheltenham: Edward Elgar.

HANSON, Stephen E. (2000) *Can Putin Rebuild the Russian State?*, Harvard University PONARS Memo 148, November.

—— (2001) 'Can Putin Rebuild the Russian State?', *Security Dialogue*, vol. 32 no. 2, June: 263–6.

HEDENSKOG, Jakob (2000) 'The Foreign Relations of Russia's Western Regions', in Ingmar Oldberg and Jakob Hedenskog *In Dire Straits: Russia's Western Regions Between Moscow and the West*, Stockholm: FOA (Defence Research Establishment): 55–77.

HEININEN, Lasse and Kakonen, Jyrki (eds) (1998) *The New North of Europe: Perspectives on the Northern Dimension*, Tampere: Tampere Peace Research Institute.

HELD, D., McGrew, A., Goldbatt, D. and Perraton, J. (1999) *Global Transformations: Politics, Economics and Culture*, Cambridge: Polity Press.

HELENIAK, Timothy (1999) 'Out-Migration and Depopulation of the Russian North during the 1990s', *Post-Soviet Geography and Economics*, vol. 40, no. 3: 155–205.

HERD, Graeme P. (1998) *Russian Federal Instability and Baltic-Nordic Security*, paper delivered at the Baltic-Nordic Conference Vilnius, Lithuania, 24–27 September.

—— (1999) 'Russia: Systemic Transformation or Federal Collapse?', *Journal of Peace Research*, vol. 36, no. 3: 259–69.

—— (ed.) (2000) *European Security & Post-Soviet Space: Integration or Isolation?*, Conflict Studies Research Centre, Camberley, UK, December, paper no. G87.

—— (2001) 'Russia and the Politics of 'Putinism', *Journal of Peace Research*, vol. 38, no. 1: 107–12.

HERD, Graeme P. and Weber, Martin (2001) 'Forging World Order Paradigms: "Good Civilization" Versus "Global Terror"', *Security Dialogue*, vol. 32, no. 4, December: 119–221.

HERMANN-PILLATH, C. (2000) *The Relation Between Federal Government and Regions in the Russian Federation*, INTAS project report, May.

HERSPRING, Dale and Kipp, Jacob (2001) 'Understanding the Elusive Mr Putin', *Problems of Post-Communism*, vol. 48, no.5, September/October: 3–18.

HOMER-DIXON, Thomas F. (1991) 'On the Threshold: Environmental Changes as Causes of Acute Conflict', *International Security*, vol. 16, no. 2, fall: 76–116.

HONNELAND, G. and Blakkisrud, H. (eds) (2001) *Centre–Periphery Relations in Russia: The Case of the Northwestern Regions*, Vermont: Ashgate.

HUNTINGTON, Samuel (1969) *Political Order in Changing Societies*, New Haven, CT: Yale University Press.

HUSKEY, Eugene (1999) *Presidential Power in Russia*, Armonk NY: M. E. Sharpe.

—— (2001a) 'Political Leadership and the Center–Periphery Struggle: Putin's Administrative Reforms', in Archie Brown and Liliya Shevtsova (eds) *Gorbachev, Yeltsin and Putin*, Washington, DC: Carnegie Endowment for International Peace: 113–42.

—— (2001b) 'Overcoming the Yeltsin Legacy: Vladimir Putin and Russian Political Reform', in Archie Brown (ed.) *Contemporary Russian Politics: A Reader*, Oxford: Oxford University Press: 95.

HYDE, Matthew (2001) 'Putin's Federal Reforms and their Implications for Presidential Power in Russia,' *Europe–Asia Studies*, vol.53, no.5, July: 719–43.

IVANOV, I. D. (2000) 'Rossiyskaya Diplomatiya V Usloviyakh Otkrytoy Rynochnoy Ekonomiki', *Mezhdunarodnaya Zhizn* no. 8–9.

JANE'S (2001) *Putin's Russia: Scenarios for 2005*, London: Jane's Publications Special Report.

JENSEN, Donald N. (1999) *The Boss: How Yuriy Luzhkov Runs Moscow*, Conflict Studies Research Centre, Camberley, UK, December, paper no. E105.

JOENNIEMI, Pertti (1996) *Finland, Europe and St Petersburg in Search for a Role and Identity*, tomus XIIII, Helsinki: Studia Slavica Finlandensia Institute for Russian and East European Studies): 101–8;.

—— (1998) 'The Karelian Question: On the Transformation of a Border Dispute', *Cooperation and Conflict*, vol. 33, no. 2, June: 183–206.

—— (2000) *Kaliningrad: A Pilot Region in the Russia/EU Relations?*, paper presented at a research seminar on the Northern Dimension, Helsinki, August.

—— (2001) 'Kaliningrad: A Pilot Region in Russia/EU Relations?' in Hanna Ojanen (ed.) (2001) *The Northern Dimension: Fuel for the EU?*, Helsinki and Berlin: Programme on the Northern Dimension of the CFSP, no. 12: 151.

JOENNIEMI, Pertti and Sergounin, A. (2000) 'Russia, Regionalism and The EU's Northern Dimension', in Graeme P. Herd (ed.) *European Security & Post-Soviet Space: Integration or Isolation?*, Conflict Studies Research Centre, Camberley, UK, December, paper no. G87.

JOENNIEMI, Pertti, Dewar, S. and Fairlie, L. D. (2000) *The Kaliningrad Puzzle – A Russian Region Within the European Union*, Baltic Institute of Sweden/Aland Islands Research Institute.

KAHN, Jeff (2001) 'What is the New Russian Federalism?', in Archie Brown (ed.) *Contemporary Russian Politics: A Reader*, Oxford: Oxford University Press: 374–84.

KATZENSTEIN, Peter J. (1996) 'Regionalism in Comparative Perspective', *Cooperation and Conflict*, vol. 31, no. 2: 123–59.

KENNAWAY, Alexander (2000) *Collected Writings*, Conflict Studies Research Centre, Camberley, UK, paper M20.

KEOHANE, Robert O. and Nye, Joseph S. (1991) 'Transgovernmental relations and international organizations', in Richard Little and Steve Smith (eds) *Perspectives on World Politics*, 2nd edition, London and New York: Routledge: 229–41 (originally published in 1974).

KERR, David (1996) 'Opening and Closing the Sino-Russian Border: Trade, Regional Development and Political Interest in North-east Asia', *Europe–Asia Studies*, vol. 6: 931–57.

KHLOPETSKIY, A. (2000) *Kaliningrad kak 'Zona Svobody': Vzglyad Iznutri*, Kaliningrad: Yantarnyy skaz.

KIRKOW, Peter (1998) *Russia's Provinces: Authoritarian Transformation Versus Local Autonomy?*, New York: St Martin's Press.

KOBRINSKAYA, Irina (2000) 'The Foreign Policy Decision-Making Process in Russia', in Jakub M. Godzimirski (ed.) *New and Old Actors in Russian Foreign*

Policy, Conference Proceedings, Norwegian Institute of International Affairs: 43–60.

KOLSTO, P. (2000) *Political Construction Sites: Nation-Building in Russia and the Post-Soviet States*, Boulder, CO: Westview Press.

KONTOROVICH, Vladimir (2000) 'Can Russia Resettle the Far East?', *Post-Communist Economies*, vol. 12, no. 3: 365–84.

KOVALEV, Sergei (2000) 'Putin's War', *New York Review of Books*, 10 February.

KUPCHAN, Charles A. (ed.) (1995) *Nationalism and Nationalities in the New Europe*, Ithaca, NY: Cornell University Press.

KUZMIN, E. (1999) 'Russia: The Centre, the Regions, and the Outside World', *International Affairs*, no. 1: 105–22.

KVAK, Robert (1976) *Interest Groups in Norwegian Politics*, Oslo: Universitetsforlaget.

LAPIDUS, Gail W. (ed.) (1995) *The New Russia: Troubled Transformation*, Boulder, CO: Westview Press.

—— (2001) 'State Building and State Breakdown in Russia', in Archie Brown (ed.) *Contemporary Russian Politics: A Reader*, Oxford: Oxford University Press: 348–54.

LAPPO, G. M. (ed.) (1983) *Sovetskiy Soyuz: Obshchiy Obzor, Rossiyskaya Federatsiya*, Moscow: Mysl.

LAWSON, Clive (1999) 'Towards a Competence Theory of the Region', *Cambridge Journal of Economics*, no. 23: 159–61.

LECHNER, F. J. and Boli, J. (2000) *The Globalization Reader*, Oxford: Blackwells.

LIEVEN, Anatol (1998) *Chechnya: Tombstone of Russian Power*, New Haven, CT: YUP.

LIGHT, Ivan (2001) *Social Capital's Unique Accessibility*, paper presented at EURA Conference on Area-based Initiatives in Contemporary Urban Policy, at www.by-og-byg.dk/eura/workshops/papers/workshop6/light.htm.

LIKHACHEV, V. (2000) 'Russia and the European Union: A Long-Term View', *International Affairs* (Moscow), vol. 46, no. 2: 40–9.

LITTLE, Richard and Smith, Steve (eds) (1991) *Perspectives on World Politics*, 2nd edition, London and New York: Routledge.

LIU, Yuanli, Rao, Keqin and Fei, John (1998) 'Economic Transition and Health Transition: Comparing China and Russia', *Health Policy* vol. 44: 103–22.

LUARD, Evan (1990) *The Globalization of Politics: The Changing Focus of Political Action in the Modern World*, London: Macmillan.

LUBOCKA-HOFFMANN, Maria and Szymgin, Boguslaw (2000) *Conservator's Programme of the Old Town's Complexes: Rebuilding in Economic Transformation Condition*, Elblag.

McAULEY, Mary (1997) *Russia's Politics of Uncertainty*, Cambridge: Cambridge University Press.

MAKARYCHEV, Andrei (2000a) 'Foreign Policies of Sub-national Units – the Case of the Russian Regions', in Jakub M. Godzimirski (ed.) *New and Old Actors in Russian Foreign Policy, Conference Proceedings*, Norwegian Institute of International Affairs: 121–52.

—— (2000b) *Islands of Globalization: Regional Russia and the Outside World*, ETH Zurich Centre for Security Studies and Conflict Research, Regionalisation of Russian Foreign and Security Policy project working paper no. 2, August.

—— (ed.) (2000c) *Russian Regions as International Actors*, Nizhniy Novgorod: Nizhniy Novgorod Linguistic University.

MAKARYCHEV, Andrei and Bradshaw, Michael J. (2001) *Globalization: the International Relations of Russia's Regions*, at www.geog.arizona.edu/web/rrwg/global-text.html.

MAKARYCHEV, Andrei, Sergounin, Alexander, Valuev, Vasily N. (2000) *Foreign and Security Policy Issues in Volga Federal District: Analytical Monitoring*, September, at www.iatp.nnov.ru/amakarychev/September.html.

MATVIYENKO, Valentina (1996), The Centre and the Regions in Foreign Policy', *International Affairs* (Moscow), no. 4: 88–97.

MINISTRY OF FOREIGN RELATIONS OF THE REPUBLIC OF KARELIA (1998) *Republic of Karelia 2000*, Petrozavodsk.

MOELLER, F. (2000) *Toward a Post-Security Community in Northeastern Europe – Policy Initiatives of the Clinton Administration toward the Baltic Sea Region*, paper presented at the 18th General IPRA conference, Tampere, August.

MOMMEN, A. (2000) 'Zayavka V Putina na Vlast: Konets Federalizma?', *Polis*, no. 5/2000: 70–80.

MONAR, J. (2000) *Justice and Home Affairs in a Wider Europe: The Dynamics of Inclusion and Exclusion*, ESRC 'One Europe or Several?' Research Programme, Working Paper 07/00.

MORGENTHAU, Hans (1967) *Politics Among Nations*, 4th edition, New York: Alfred A. Knopf.

MOROZOV, V. (2001) *The Baltic States in Russian Foreign Policy Discourse*, Copenhagen: COPRI working paper no. 8.

MOROZOVA, T. G. (ed.) (2000) *Regionalnaya Ekonomika*, Moscow, Yuniti.

MOSHES, A. (1999) *The Baltic Sea Dimension in the Relations Between Russia and Europe*, FOA (Swedish Defence Research Establishment) Report, February.

—— (2001) 'Russian–Ukrainian Relations: Current State and Prospects', *Svobodnaya Mysl*, no. 8.

MOUKHARIAMOV, Nail Midkhatovich (1997) 'The Tatarstan Model: A Situational Dynamic', in Peter J. Stavrakis, Joan Debardeleben and Larry Black (eds) *Beyond the Monolith: The Emergence of Regionalism in Post-Soviet Russia*, Washington, DC: Woodrow Wilson Center Press.

MUNDO, Philip (1992) *Interest Groups: Cases and Characteristics*, Chicago, IL: Nelson-Hall Publishers.

NATO (2000) *Russian Demography: Apocalypse Tomorrow*, NATO Unclassified, DPA (2000) 1505.

NICHIPORUK, Brian (2000) *The Security Dynamics of Demographic Factors*, Santa Monica, CA: RAND, MR–1088.

NICHOLSON, Martin (1999) *Towards a Russia of the Regions*, Adelphi Paper no. 330, London: International Institute for Strategic Studies/OUP.

NOVICHKOV, N., Snegovskiy, V., Sokolov, A. and Shvarev, V. (1995) *Rossiyskiye Vooruzhennye Sily v Chechenskom Konflikte*, Moscow: Infoglob.

ODOM, William E. (1992) 'Soviet Politics and After: Old and New Concepts', *World Politics*, vol. 45, no. 1, October: 66–98

—— (1998) *The Collapse of the Soviet Military*, New Haven, CT: YUP.

OHMAE, Kenichi (1995) *The Evolving Global Economy*, Boston, MA: Harvard Business Review Book.

OJANEN, Hanna (ed.) (2001) *The Northern Dimension: Fuel for the EU?*, Helsinki and Berlin: Programme on the Northern Dimension of the CFSP, no. 12.

OLDBERG, Ingmar (2000) 'Russia's Western Border Regions and Moscow', in Ingmar Oldberg and Jakob Hedenskog *In Dire Straits: Russia's Western Regions Between Moscow and the West*, Stockholm: FOA (Defence Research Establishment): 11–54.

OLDBERG, Ingmar and Hedenskog, Jakob (2000) *In Dire Straits: Russia's Western Regions Between Moscow and the West*, Stockholm: FOA (Defence Research Establishment).

ORLOV, V. (2000a) 'Foreign Policy and Russia's Regions, *International Affairs* (Moscow), vol. 46, no. 6: 81–92.

——— (2000b) 'Vneshnyaya Politika i Rossiyskiye Regiony', *Mezdunarodnaya Zhizn*, no. 10/2000: 43–55.

PACIFIC RUSSIA INFORMATION GROUP (2001) *The Oil and Gas Industry of Sakhalin Island: Annual Review – Spring 2001*, Anchorage: Pacific Russia Information Group LLC.

PAIK, K. W. (2001) ' Energy Developments in Northeast Asia: A Role for Russia?', in M. J. Bradshaw (ed.) *The Russian Far East and Pacific-Asia: Unfulfilled Potential*, Richmond: Curzon Press: 166–181.

PAIN, E. (2000) 'Ethnic Conflicts and Border Disputes on Russia's Southern Boundaries', in A. Zagorskiy (ed.) *Bezopasnost Rossii: XXI vek*, Moscow: Prava cheloveka.

——— (2001) 'The Second Chechen War and its Consequences', in Nikolai Petrov (ed.) *Regiony Rossii v 1999 g*, Moscow: Carnegie Center: 280–94.

PASHINTSEVA, N. I., Voronina, I. V., Kazachenko, L. A. (1998) *The Demographic Yearbook of Russia, Statistical Handbook*, Moscow: Goskomstat Rossii.

PATOMÄKI, Heikki (ed.) (2000) *Politics of Civil Society: A Global Perspective on Democratisation*, NIGD Working Papers 2/2000: Helsinki and Nottingham.

PAVLYATENKO, V. (2000) 'Russia's Security in the Asia Pacific Region: Danger of Isolation', in A. Zagorskiy (ed.) *Bezopasnost Rossii: XXI vek*, Moscow: Prava cheloveka.

PEROVIC, Jeronim (2000) *Internationalization of Russian Regions and the Consequences for Russian Foreign and Security Policy*, Working Paper No. 1, Russian Study Group, Centre for Security Studies and Conflict Research, Zurich, Switzerland, April.

PETERSEN, P. A. (1996) 'Russia's Volga Region: Bridgehead for Islamic Revolution or Source for an Indigenous Alternative Political Paradigm?', *European Security*, no. 1: 113–40.

PETERSEN, P. A. and Petersen S. C. (1993) 'The Kaliningrad Garrison State', *Jane's Intelligence Review*, February: 59–62.

PETROV, Nikolai (1999a) *Aleksandr Lebed in Krasnoyarsk Kray*, Moscow: Carnegie Center.

——— (1999b) *Regiony Rossii v 1998 g*, Moscow: Carnegie Center.

——— (2000) *Broken Pendulum: Recentralization Under Putin*, November 2000, Harvard University PONARS Memo 159, October 2000.

——— (ed.) (2001a) *Regiony Rossii v 1999 g*, Moscow: Carnegie Center.

——— (2001b) 'Seven Faces of Putin's Russia', *Security Dialogue*, vol. 32, no. 4, December.

PLATER-ZYBERK, Henry and Aldis, Anne (2001) *Russia's Reaction to the American Tragedy*, Conflict Studies Research Centre, Camberley, UK, September, Occasional Brief 84.

PORTYAKOV, Vladimir (1996) 'Kitaytzy Idut? Migratzionnaya Situatziya na Dalnem Vostoke Rossii', *Mezhdunarodnaya Zhizn* (Moscow), no. 2: 80–4.

POSEN, Barry (1993) 'The Security Dilemma and Ethnic Conflict', *Survival*, spring: 27–47; reprinted in Michael E. Brown (ed.) *Ethnic Conflict in International Politics*, Princeton: Princeton University Press.

PURSIAINEN, Christer (2000) 'Trends and Structures in Russian State/Society Relations', in Heikki Patomäki (ed.) *Politics of Civil Society: A Global Perspective on Democratisation*, NIGD Working Papers 2/2000: Helsinki and Nottingham: 19–28.

PUTIN, Vladimir (2000) *First Person: An Astonishingly Frank Self Portrait by Russia's President*, London: Hutchinson.

PYNNÖNIEMI, Katri (2000) 'The Construction of the Transport Networks in the European North: From Vertical to Horizontal Order of Regionalisation', in Helena Rytövuri-Apunen (ed.) *Russian–European Interfaces in the Northern Dimension of the EU*, Studia Politica Tamperensis No. 8, University of Tampere, Department of Political Science and International Relations: 117–57.

REDDAWAY, Peter and Glinski, Dmitri (2001) *The Tragedy of Russia's Reforms*, Washington, DC: USIP.

REUT, O. (2000) *The Baltic and Barents Regions in Changing Europe: New Priorities for Security*, Centre for European Security Studies, EFP working paper no. 2, Groningen, June.

RODIONOV, I.N. (1997) *Voyennaya entsiklopediya*, vol. 1, Moscow: Voyenizdat.

ROE, P. (1999) 'The Intrastate Security Dilemma: Ethnic Conflict as "Tragedy"', *Journal of Peace Research*, vol. 36, no. 2: 183–202.

ROSE, Richard (2000) 'How Much Does Social Capital Add to Individual Health? A Survey Study of Russians', *Social Science & Medicine*, no. 51: 1,421–35.

ROZENFELD, Boris A. (1996) 'The Crisis of Russian Health Care and Attempts at Reform', in Julia DaVanzo (ed.) *Russia's Demographic 'Crisis'*, Santa Monica, CA: RAND, CF–124.

ROZMAN, G. (2000) 'Turning Fortresses into Free Trade Zones', in Sherman W. Garnett (ed.) (2000) *Rapprochement or Rivalry? Russia–China Relations in a Changing Asia*, Washington, DC: Carnegie Endowment for International Peace: 199.

RYTÖVURI-APUNEN, Helena (ed.) (2000) *Russian–European Interfaces in the Northern Dimension of the EU*, Studia Politica Tamperensis No. 8, University of Tampere, Department of Political Science and International Relations.

SAKHALIN OBKOMSTAT (various years) *Doklad o Sotsialno-ekonomicheskom Polozhenii Sakhalinskoy Oblasti*, Yuzhno-Sakhalinsk.

SAKWA, Richard (1996) *Russian Politics and Society*, 2nd edition, London: Routledge.

SERGOUNIN, Alexander (2000a) 'Regionen contra Zentrum. Ihr Einfluss auf die Russische Aussenpolitik', *Internationale Politik*, no. 5, 55th year, May: 29–36.

——— (2000b) *Russia and the European Union: The Northern Dimension*, Harvard University PONARS Memo 138, April.

——— (2001) *External Determinants of Russia's Regionalization*, ETH Zurich Centre for Security Studies and Conflict Research, Regionalisation of Russian Foreign and Security Policy project working paper no. 3, February.

——— and Rykhtik, Mikhail (2000) 'Regulations on International Activities of the Russian Regions', in Andrei Makarychev (ed.) (2000c) *Russian Regions as International Actors*, Nizhniy Novgorod: Nizhniy Novgorod Linguistic University: 35–60.

SHARP, Tony (1977/8) 'The Russian Annexation of the Koenigsberg Area, 1941–1945', *Survey*, vol. 23, autumn: 156–62.

SHCHERBAKOVA, Yu A. (2000a) 'Problemy Etnicheskikh Menshinstv v Usloviyakh Megapolisa: Opyt Moskvy', in Yu A. Schcherbakova (ed.) *Rossiya i yeye Sosedi*, Moscow: INION RAN: 58–71.

——— (ed.) (2000b) *Rossiya i yeye Sosedi*, Moscow: INION RAN.

SHEVTSOVA, Liliya (2000) *Yeltsin's Russia: Myths and Reality*, Moscow: Carnegie Center.

SHKOLNIKOV, Vladimir and Mesle, France (1996) 'The Russian Epidemiological Crisis as Mirrored by Mortality Trends', in Julia DaVanzo (ed.) *Russia's Demographic 'Crisis'*, Santa Monica, CA: RAND, CF–124.

SHLAPENTOKH, Vladimir (1995) 'Russia: Privatization and Illegalization of Social and Political Life', *Washington Quarterly*, vol. 19, no.1: 65–85.

SHUMAN, Michael (1994) *Towards a Global Village: International Community Development Initiatives*, London and Boulder, CO: Pluto Press.

SIMONSEN, Sven Gunnar (2000) 'Putin's Leadership Style: Ethnocentric Patriotism', *Security Dialogue*, vol. 31, no. 3: 377–80.

SMITH, Mark (2001): *Russia and Islam*, Conflict Studies Research Centre, Camberley, UK, August, paper no. F73.

SMITH, Raymond A. (1992) 'The Status of the Kaliningrad Oblast Under International Law', *Lituanus: Baltic Studies Quarterly Journal of Arts and Science*, vol. 38, no. 1: 7–52.

SNYDER, Jack and JERVIS, Robert (1999) 'Civil War and the Security Dilemma' in Barbara F. Walter and Jack Snyder (eds) *Civil Wars, Insecurity, and Intervention*, New York: Columbia University Press: 15–37.

SOLNICK, Steven L. (2000a) 'Is the Center Too Weak or Too Strong in the Russian Federation?' in Valerie Sperling (ed.) (2000) *Building the Russian State: Institutional Crisis and the Quest for Democratic Governance*, Boulder CO: Westview Press.

——— (2000b) *The New Federal Structure: More Centralized or More of the Same?*, Harvard University PONARS Memo 161, October.

SPERLING, Valerie (ed.) (2000) *Building the Russian State: Institutional Crisis and the Quest for Democratic Governance*, Boulder CO: Westview Press.

STAVRAKIS, Peter J., Debardeleben, Joan, Black, Larry (eds) (1997) *Beyond the Monolith: The Emergence of Regionalism in Post-Soviet Russia*, Washington, DC: Woodrow Wilson Center Press.

STERLIN, Andrey and Ardishvili, Alexander (1991) 'Predprinimatelskiye Seti – Novaya Forma Organizatsii Mezhfirmennogo Vzaimodeystviya', *Mirovaya Ekonomika i Mezhdunarodnyye Otnosheniya*, no. 4.

STONER-WEISS, Kathryn (1997) *Local Heroes: The Political Economy of Russian Regional Governance*, Princeton, NJ: Princeton University Press.

—— (1988) 'Central Weakness and Provincial Autonomy: The Process of Devolution in Russia', in *Program on New Approaches to Russian Security Policy Discussion*, Conference Briefing Book, Cambridge, MA: Harvard University: 21–7.

SUNY, Ronald Grigor (1993) *The Revenge of the Past: Nationalism, Revolution and the Collapse of the Soviet Union*, Stanford, CT: Stanford University Press.

SZPORLUK, Roman (ed.) (1994) *National Identity and Ethnicity in Russia and the New States of Eurasia*, Armonk, NY: M. E. Sharpe.

TEAGUE, Elizabeth (1994) 'Centre–Periphery Relations in the Russian Federation', in Roman Szporluk (ed.) *National Identity and Ethnicity in Russia and the New States of Eurasia*, Armonk, NY: M. E. Sharpe: 21–57.

TENTH CONFERENCE OF RUSSIAN FOREIGN MINISTRY (1999) 'Russian Regions and the Council of Europe', *International Affairs* (Moscow) vol. 45, no. 5: 101–21.

THOMAS, Timothy L. (1995a) 'Fault Lines and Factions in the Russian Army', *Orbis*, fall: 531–41.

—— (1995b) 'The Russian Armed Forces Confront Chechnya: Military Activities 11–31 December 1994', *Journal of Slavic Military Studies*, June: 257–90.

TISHKOV, Valery (1997) *Ethnicity, Nationalism and Conflict in and After the Soviet Union*, London: Sage.

—— (2001) 'War and Peace in the North Caucasus', *Svobodnaya Mysl*, no. 1.

TITARENKO, M. and Mikheyev, V. (2001) 'The Asia-Pacific Region and Russia', *International Affairs* (Moscow), no. 3.

TORU (Pacific Regional Directorate of the Border Service of the Russian Federation) Press Service (1999) *Spravka o Migratsii Grazhdan Kitaya v Rossiyu I Tret'i Strany Cherez yeye Territoriyu v 1998–99 gg.*, Vladivostok.

TRENIN, Dmitri (2001) *The End of Eurasia: Russia on the Border Between Geopolitics and Globalization*, Moscow: Carnegie Endowment for International Peace.

TROYAKOVA, Tamara (1995) 'Regional Policy in the Russian Far East and the Rise of Localism in Primorye', *Journal of East Asian Affairs*, vol. 9, no. 2, summer/fall: 428–61.

TUCHMAN MATHEWS, Jessica (1989) 'Redefining Security', *Foreign Affairs*, vol. 68, no. 2, spring.

ULRICH, Marybeth (2000) 'Russia's Failed Democratic National Security State and the Wars in Chechnya', in Michael Crutcher (ed.) *The Russian Armed Forces at the Dawn of the Millennium*, Carlisle Barracks: US Army War College: 5–22.

UNITED NATIONS (1998) *Human Development Report 1998. Russian Federation*, Moscow: United Nations Development Programme.

VAN EVERA, Stephen (1995) 'Nationalism and the Causes of War', in Charles A. Kupchan (ed.) *Nationalism and Nationalities in the New Europe*, Ithaca, NY: Cornell University Press.

VASSIN, Sergei (1996) 'The Determinants and Implications of an Aging Population in Russia', in Julia DaVanzo (ed.) *Russia's Demographic 'Crisis'*, Santa Monica, CA: RAND, CF–124.

VISHNEVSKY, Anatoliy (1996) 'Family, Fertility, and Demographic Dynamics in Russia: Analysis and Forecast', in Julie DaVanzo (ed.), *Russia's Demographic 'Crisis'*, Santa Monica, CA: RAND, CF–124, 1996, at http://www.rand.org/publications/CF/CF124/CF124.chap1.html.

VOROBYEV, V. (2001) 'From Shanghai to Shanghai: Creation of the Shanghai Cooperation Organisation', *Problemy Dalnego Vostoka*, no. 4.

VYSOKOV, M. (1996) *A Brief History of Sakhalin and the Kurils*, Yuzhno-Sakhalinsk: Sakhalin Book Publishing House and LIK Ltd.

WALKER, Edward W. (1995) 'Nationalism, Regionalism and Federalism: Center–Periphery Relations in Post-Communist Russia', in Gail W. Lapidus (ed.) *The New Russia: Troubled Transformation*, Boulder, CO: Westview Press: 79–113.

WALLACE, W. (1999) 'Europe after the Cold War: Interstate Order or Post-Sovereign Regional System?', *Review of International Studies*, vol. 25, special issue, December.

WALTER, Barbara F. and Snyder, Jack (eds) (1999) *Civil Wars, Insecurity, and Intervention*, New York: Columbia University Press.

WALTZ, Kenneth N. (1979) *Theory of International Politics*, Reading, MA: Addison Wesley.

WARHOLA, James (1999) 'Is the Russian Federation Becoming More Democratic? Moscow–Regional Relations and the Development of the Post-Soviet Russian State', *Democratization*, vol. 6, no. 2, summer: 42–69.

WILLETTS, Peter (1997) 'Transnational Actors and International Organizations in Global Politics', in John Baylis and Steve Smith (eds) *The Globalization of World Politics. An Introduction to International Relations*, Oxford: Oxford University Press: 287–310.

WILSON, E. (2000) *North-Eastern Sakhalin: Local Communities and the Oil Industry*, Russian Regional Research Group Working Paper 21, University of Birmingham, School of Geography and Environmental Sciences, and Centre for Russian and East European Studies, and University of Leicester, Department of Geography.

YABLOKOV, A. V., Karasev, V.K., Rumyantsev, V.M., Kokeyev, M.Ye., Petrov, O.I., Lystsov, V.N., Yemelyanenkov, A.F., Rubtsov, P.M., (1993) *Facts and Problems Related to the Dumping of Radioactive Waste in the Seas Surrounding the Territory of the Russian Federation*, Materials from a government report on the dumping of radioactive waste, commissioned by the President of the Russian Federation, 24 October 1992, Decree no. 613, Moscow: Administration of the President of the Russian Federation; English edition Alberquerque: Small World Publishers, 1993.

YELTSIN, Boris Nikolayevich (1990) *Ispoved na Zadannuyu Temu*, Moscow: Sovetsko-Britanskaya Tvorcheskaya Assotsiatsiya 'Ogonek' – 'Variant'.

—— (1994) *Zapiski Prezidenta*, Moscow: Ogonek.

YOUNG, John F. (1997) 'At the Bottom of the Heap: Local Self-government and Regional Politics in the Russian Federation', in Peter J. Stavrakis, Joan Debardeleben and Larry Black (eds) *Beyond the Monolith: The Emergence of Regionalism in Post-Soviet Russia*, Washington, DC: Woodrow Wilson Center Press: 81–102.

ZACHER, Mark and Sutton, Brent (1996) *Governing Global Networks: International Regimes for Transportation and Communications*, Cambridge Studies in International Relations no. 44, Cambridge University Press.

ZAGORSKIY, A. (ed.) (2000) *Bezopasnost Rossii: XXI vek*, Moscow: Prava cheloveka.

ZAKHAROV, Sergei and Ivanova, Elena (1996) 'Fertility Decline and Recent Changes in Russia: On the Threshold of the Second Demographic Transition', in

Julia DaVanzo (ed.) *Russia's Demographic 'Crisis'*, Santa Monica, CA: RAND, CF–124.

ZHIKHAREVICH, Boris (ed.) (2000) *Osobennosti strategicheskogo planirovaniya razvitiya gorodov v postsovetskih stranakh*, St Petersburg: Leontieff Centre.

ZUBAREVICH, Natalya, Petrov, Nikolai and Titkov, Alexei (2001) 'Federal Districts – 2000', in Nikolai Petrov (ed.) *Regiony Rossii v 1999 g*, Moscow: Carnegie Center.

ZUBOV, A. B. (2000) 'Unitarizm ili Federalizm: K Voprosu o Buduschey Organizatsii Gosudarstvennogo Prostranstva Rossii', *Polis* no. 5: 32–54.

Websites referenced in this book

Additional Russian sites can be found using the search facility at www.yandex.ru.

Argumenty I Fakty newspaper	www.aif.ru
Business Press	www.businesspress.ru
CIA Factbook	www.cia.gov/nic/pubs
Conflict Studies Research Centre	www.csrc.ac.uk
Finance Ministry	www.minfin.ru
Goskomstat (Russian State Committee for Statistics)	www.gks.ru
Harvard University Program on New Approaches to Russian Security (PONARS)	www.fas.harvard.edu/ponars/memos.html
Kaliningrad governor	www.egorov.kaliningrad.ru
Kaliningrad regional administration	www.gov.kaliningrad.ru
Nezavisimaya Gazeta newspaper	www.ng.ru
Moscow city: Mosgorkomstat	www.mosstat.ru/st_an.htm
National Public Opinion Research Centre (VTsIOM) polls	www.polit.ru/vciom
RAND Research Reports	www.rand.org/publications
Russian Expert Institute	www.exin.ru
Russian government	www.strana.ru
Russian News Agency	www.grani.ru
Russian Political Analysis	www.polit.ru
Russian President	www.president.kremlin.ru
US Census Bureau statistics for Russia	www.census.gov/cgi-bin
World Bank	www.worldbank.org

Index